CONSTRUCTING NINETEENTH-CENTURY RELIGION

LITERATURE, RELIGION, AND
POSTSECULAR STUDIES
Lori Branch, Series Editor

CONSTRUCTING NINETEENTH-CENTURY RELIGION

Literary, Historical, and Religious Studies in Dialogue

Edited by Joshua King and Winter Jade Werner

THE OHIO STATE UNIVERSITY PRESS
COLUMBUS

Copyright © 2019 by The Ohio State University.
All rights reserved.

Library of Congress Cataloging-in-Publication Data
Names: King, Joshua, 1979– editor. | Werner, Winter Jade, editor.
Title: Constructing nineteenth-century religion : literary, historical, and religious studies in dialogue / edited by Joshua King and Winter Jade Werner.
Other titles: Literature, religion, and postsecular studies.
Description: Columbus : The Ohio State University Press, [2019] | Series: Literature, religion, and postsecular studies | Includes bibliographical references and index.
Identifiers: LCCN 2018053049 | ISBN 9780814213971 (cloth ; alk. paper) | ISBN 0814213979 (cloth ; alk. paper)
Subjects: LCSH: Religion and literature—Great Britain—19th Century—History. | Religion in literature. | English literature—19th century—History and criticism.
Classification: LCC PR468.R44 C66 2019 | DDC 820.9/382—dc23
LC record available at https://lccn.loc.gov/2018053049

Cover design by Christian Fuenfhausen
Text design by Juliet Williams
Type set in Adobe Minion Pro

∞ The paper used in this publication meets the minimum requirements of the American National Standard for Information Sciences—Permanence of Paper for Printed Library Materials. ANSI Z39.48-1992.

CONTENTS

List of Illustrations vii

Acknowledgments ix

INTRODUCTION
    JOSHUA KING AND WINTER JADE WERNER 1

PART I   REFORMING RELIGION AND THE SECULAR

CHAPTER 1   Religion and the Secular State: Loisy's Use of "Religion" Prior to His Excommunication
    JEFFREY L. MORROW 25

CHAPTER 2   A Commonwealth of Affection: Modern Hinduism and the Cultural History of the Study of Religion
    J. BARTON SCOTT 46

CHAPTER 3   "God's Insurrection": Politics and Faith in the Revolutionary Sermons of Joseph Rayner Stephens
    MIKE SANDERS 65

CHAPTER 4   George Jacob Holyoake, Secularism, and Constructing "Religion" as an Anachronistic Repressor
    DAVID NASH 81

CHAPTER 5   Karl Marx and the Invention of the Secular
    DOMINIC ERDOZAIN 99

PART II RELIGION AND THE MATERIALITIES AND PRACTICES OF READING

CHAPTER 6   From Treasures to Trash, or, the Real History of "Family Bibles"
MARY WILSON CARPENTER   115

CHAPTER 7   Rereading Queen Victoria's Religion
MICHAEL LEDGER-LOMAS   139

CHAPTER 8   Jewish Women's Writing as a New Category of Affect
RICHA DWOR   155

CHAPTER 9   Hybridous Monsters: Constructing "Religion" and "the Novel" in the Early Nineteenth Century
MIRIAM ELIZABETH BURSTEIN   171

CHAPTER 10 Material Religion: C. H. Spurgeon and the "Battle of the Styles" in Victorian Church Architecture
DOMINIC JANES   190

CHAPTER 11 Wilde's Uses of Religion
MARK KNIGHT   206

PART III RELIGION AND POETICS IN POSTSECULAR LITERARY STUDIES

CHAPTER 12 Reading Psalms in Nineteenth-Century England: The Contact Zone of Jewish–Christian Scriptural Relations
CYNTHIA SCHEINBERG   225

CHAPTER 13 Postsecular English Studies and Romantic Cults of Authorship
CHARLES LAPORTE   246

CHAPTER 14 Theologies of Inspiration: William Blake and Gerard Manley Hopkins
MICHAEL D. HURLEY   262

CHAPTER 15 William Blake, the Secularization of Religious Categories, and the History of Imagination
PETER OTTO   281

List of Contributors   303

Index   307

ILLUSTRATIONS

FIGURE 6.1	[Title Page] *The Illustrated Family Bible with Explanatory, Critical and Devotional Commentary* [1876]	119
FIGURE 6.2	*The Self-Interpreting Bible* [1814]	121
FIGURE 6.3	[Floor plan of the Ark] *The Holy Bible . . . Complete Commentary . . . Apocrypha . . . and the New Testament* [1816]	124
FIGURE 6.4	"The Sacrifice of Jepthah's Daughter"	132
FIGURE 6.5	[Ruth and Naomi] *The Illustrated Family Bible with Explanatory, Critical and Devotional Commentary* [1876]	133
FIGURE 6.6	"Queen Esther"	134
FIGURE 10.1	"Catch 'Em Alive O" (Charles Haddon Spurgeon)	195
FIGURE 10.2	E. Johnson, "The Earliest Photograph of the Interior of the Metropolitan Tabernacle: Taken in 1861"	196
FIGURE 13.1	Furnivall's diagram of Browning's "O Lyric Love"	255
FIGURE 15.1	William Blake, *There Is No Natural Religion*	289
FIGURE 15.2	William Blake, "Job's Evil Dreams"	292
FIGURE 15.3	William Blake, *For the Sexes: The Gates of Paradise*	295

ACKNOWLEDGMENTS

CONVERSATION AND COLLABORATION are the lifeblood of all scholarship, but this collection bears special testimony to the fact. Construction on *Constructing Nineteenth-Century Religion* began long before a word was written, through conversations that took place among ourselves and our contributors about the need for interdisciplinary scholarship on nineteenth-century religion that would interrogate its own assumptions about the very category "religion" and consider how these assumptions are shaped by the histories of, and boundaries between, our disciplines. Nourished through in-person meetings at the Armstrong Browning Library at Baylor University in 2016, these conversations matured into collaboration on a sustained, interdisciplinary investigation. Over the last few years, we have been privileged to engage in a lively conversation with fifteen of the most talented and generous scholars of nineteenth-century literature, history, religion, and theology. From the first drafts of chapters through the final edits, this dialogue has productively disrupted familiar boundaries, between disciplines and between editorial roles. Contributors not only responded to our editorial feedback but also used Google Drive to share and critique one another's work within and between the parts into which they were grouped. We believe the resulting collection is—to borrow from Keats—far "more interwoven and complete" than are most, its chapters reflectively speaking to one another across the volume.

If *Constructing Nineteenth-Century Religion* most obviously reflects these scholarly dialogues, it has equally benefited from other conversations and contributions. This collection would be less coherent, and we would have retained less of our sanity in finishing it, without the wise counsel of several previous and current editors at The Ohio State University Press: Lindsay Martin, Kristen Elias Rowley, and Ana M. Jimenez-Moreno. Outside reviewers for Ohio State helped us identify and fill crucial lulls in the conversation within and between chapters. At a crucial juncture, Mark Sandy (Durham University) and Dino Felluga (Purdue University) offered shrewd insight and inspired patient resolve during their visiting fellowships at Baylor's Armstrong Browning Library. Previous and current directors (Rita Patteson, Jennifer Borderud) and staff members at that library have vitally supported this project, from its inception to its completion. Joshua King would especially like to thank his previous research assistants, Elizabeth Travers Parker and Holly Spofford, both of whom are talented English PhD students at Baylor, and Jade Werner would like to acknowledge baby Adeline, who was born in the earliest stages of this book and who has been a constant companion throughout its progress. Essential funding for this project was provided by the Baylor University Research Committee and the Vice Provost for Research, as well as by Wheaton College in Massachusetts. Our deepest gratitude goes to our families, who have renewed—and, at times, graciously tolerated—us at every step.

INTRODUCTION

~

JOSHUA KING AND WINTER JADE WERNER

I. RELIGION—TRANSPARENT AND OBVIOUS?

Religion—the word circulates constantly through popular and scholarly discourse, whether in categories of media coverage, such as the "On Religion" archive of stories hosted online by the *New York Times,* surveys of "The U.S. Religious Landscape" by groups such as the Pew Research Center, or university courses, journals, and book series generated by "the religious turn," a marked uptick of interest in religion in the humanities and social sciences since the mid-1990s (Branch, "Postsecular Studies" 91). As many have remarked, especially since 9/11 "religion" seems an unavoidable "fact" in the modern world from which some had predicted it would fade—it is, to use a hackneyed phrase, "in the air." In consequence, the meaning of religion can seem to be obvious and understood by everyone: when applying the term to institutions, practices, beliefs, literature, and people, we might feel that we are merely recognizing something innate about them rather than actively constructing a representation of them.

Yet, like class, gender, and race, religion is only *apparently* an intuitive and simple abstraction.[1] As Michael McKeon, borrowing from Marx's *Grundrisse,*

---

1. As Stanley Fish famously predicted in the *Chronicle of Higher Education,* "religion" will "succeed high theory and the triumvirate of race, gender, and class as the center of intellectual energy in the academy" (C1). On the whole, as noted below, Fish's prediction about the rise of scholarly interest in religion has proven broadly true. One might pause, however, before

said of categories such as the novel, a "simple abstraction" is never simple, but rather "a deceptively monolithic category that encloses a complex historical process" (20).[2] This collection emerges from the conviction that every apparently obvious articulation or application of religion in fact engages in a complex and relatively modern historical process (or, sometimes, processes). For example, Marx, alluded to just now, was entangled in such a process when representing religion: his critique of "religion" as an ideological smokescreen for unjust economic conditions itself consistently relied on a sense of conscience formed by Judeo-Christian theological criteria (see Erdozain's chapter in part I of this volume). Focusing on nineteenth-century literature and culture, primarily of Britain but also of Europe and the Indian subcontinent, this collection affirms and attempts to supply the need for interdisciplinary dialogue about the ways in which religion has been—and is being—constructed, experienced, and deployed. The participle in our title—*Constructing*—acknowledges that any articulation of nineteenth-century religion is never just a work of the past, a relic we study objectively from a distance: our own scholarly inquiries also actively construct religion, engaging in a dynamic activity by which our disciplinary assumptions, and indeed personal and lived investments, necessarily shape what we find in a "religious" novel, poem, sermon, artwork, event, or activity. For these reasons, *Constructing Nineteenth-Century Religion* brings together an interdisciplinary team of scholars from literature, history, and religious studies who interrogate the variety of ways religion was constructed as a category and region of experience in nineteenth-century literature and culture, even as they also reflect critically on how scholarship invokes and uses religion as a category now.

This language of "construction" and categorization could imply an overly conceptual, removed approach to the study of nineteenth-century religious culture and literature—as if the point were obsessively to expose and re-examine the lenses through which we and previous commentators have seen things labeled "religious," demystifying the subject as "just" a set of constructions and implying our own objective distance from it. Yet, taken together, these chapters refuse such an approach, characterized by a number of scholars in the last decade as a hermeneutics of suspicion, an "invisible norm" in humanistic inquiry that seeks to distance the scholar from the ethical demands of texts

---

endorsing his implication that this interest will or should displace attention to race, gender, and class. As many chapters in this collection demonstrate, these subjects are inseparably involved in any thorough investigation of religion in nineteenth-century literature and culture.

2. Joshua King would like to thank Dino Felluga for suggesting this connection. See Felluga's concise and helpful entry on Marx's term *simple abstraction* in *Critical Theory: The Key Concepts* (281).

and his or her own informing beliefs (Warner 20), under the assumption that acquiring critical intelligence means "moving from attachment to detachment and indeed to disenchantment" (Felski 30). For instance, Mark Knight, in the second part of this collection, suggests the Protestant lineage of this apparently secular drive for critical demystification, while nonetheless identifying as a Protestant and encouraging scholars to acknowledge their own positions as agents in the world who make choices about their actions, including their responses to theological claims and narratives. Charles LaPorte, in the third part, contends that modern literary criticism has emerged out of an effort to refute its persistent theological undertones. Rather than disavowing this unexpected resemblance to attitudes of their Victorian forebears, LaPorte proposes, current literary scholars might admit their participation in an ongoing dialectic between skepticism and reverence—and concede the testimony this offers to the devotion, inspiration, and even love that animates their analysis of texts.

In pursuing our collective inquiry into constructions of nineteenth-century religion, the editors and fifteen essayists in this collection build upon recent developments in interdisciplinary scholarship that have begun to make themselves felt in nineteenth-century literary studies. Despite reports about the acceleration of secularization and decline of traditional mainline religious denominations in the West (Baylor, "American Piety"; Pew, *U.S. Religious Landscape*), the term *religion* has perhaps never been so widely and unreflectively circulated in the global media and cultural commentary. "Secular" modernity seems addicted to using "religion" as a means of understanding—and justifying—itself (Asad, *Formations* 200), a tendency evident in contemporary narratives that commend Western interventionalism in the name of a war between "tolerant" democratic secular societies and radical "religious" fundamentalism (Asad, "Freedom of Speech" 282, 297). For much of the twentieth century, scholarship on nineteenth-century literature and culture traded heavily in its own forms of unreflective discourse about "religion," and it produced narratives that tacitly assumed as a background the battle between "traditional" religion and "modern" secularism, with the advance of secularization often coordinated with liberal "progress" and assumed as the inevitable tendency of intellectual and cultural development.

For several decades, such narratives of secularization have been experiencing their own form of decline in scholarship on nineteenth-century literature. This is not only in reaction to the fact that "religion" has failed to die and has instead increased its presence and following in the modern world. It is also because literary scholars have entered into fruitful and interdisciplinary dialogue with historians, anthropologists, sociologists, political philosophers, theologians, and scholars of religious studies, whose work has been at the vanguard in exploring the genealogies of modern understandings of religion. As a result, "religion" is no longer taken by scholars of nineteenth-century literature and culture as an obvious or natural category of past or present experience.³ The modern category of "religion" now appears a particularly Western construction, one generated and reinvented in mutually constitutive dialogue with "the secular" and forms of secularism.

This "turn to religion" has yielded compelling critical conversations, which have identified the ways that "secularism" in fact was generated from "within religious thought"; examined how "gender and national identities have been mediated by religious ones"; and "moved beyond the reduction of religion to the 'opiate of the masses' [to recover] histories of religious progressivism" (Branch, "Postsecular Studies" 92). Our collection extends such reconfigurations of "religion" and "the secular" to nineteenth-century studies, with particular attention to placing scholarship on Romantic and Victorian literary culture within the interdisciplinary context of what some are now calling "postsecular" studies—a field of inquiry that has found a hospitable and prominent forum in this series on Literature, Religion, and Postsecular Studies. Since *postsecular* is a term with many and hotly contested meanings, we should clarify that in using it we do not affirm any of the following: denial of the secular or secularization; championship of the religious repressed or naive confidence in widespread religious resurgence (see Nash's warning against such conclusions in part I); or naturalization of the Western secular/religious binary. Rather than taking "post" in "postsecular" in a temporal or progressive sense, we see it signifying a new attitude toward secularism and the secular. As Lori Branch observes, "in passing through and moving beyond an unreflective or 'presumptive' secularism—a passage never fully complete and so perpetually in the future—postsecular studies opens up new understandings of religion and secularism as they have been mutually constituted and as they configure themselves in culture" ("Postsecular Studies" 94).

To this end, the chapters in *Constructing Nineteenth-Century Religion* newly analyze the diverse ways in which religion was commodified, debated, and practiced in a wide range of nineteenth-century texts and contexts. While focusing primarily on nineteenth-century Britain, the collection also contributes to the increasingly transnational and transcultural outlook of postsecular studies, drawing illuminating connections between Britain and the United States, continental Europe, and colonial India. Nine chapters are by scholars of

---

3. For concise summaries of the modern construction of "religion," see chapters by Morrow and Scott in this volume. Colin Jager offers a useful review of the ways in which nineteenth-century scholars, especially Romanticists, have begun to think more critically about the genealogy and ongoing construction of "religion" (*Unquiet Things* 5–6, 248–49 n15–17).

literature, and six are by scholars of religion and history. While the collection thereby prioritizes literary studies, it does so in a deliberately interdisciplinary fashion. The tendency of historians and scholars of religious studies to emphasize institutional, denominational, and disciplinary factors in the formation of religion is counterbalanced by literary scholars' tendency to prioritize individual religious expression, genre formation, and the singularity of articulations of faith and doubt in literary works. Motivating this collection in large part is its scholarly commitment to evaluating the "institutional" and "individual" alongside each other. Taken alone, neither tendency adequately expresses the ways that religion was lived, practiced, renegotiated, and made meaningful in the nineteenth century.

Rather, these tendencies must be seen as complementing, even requiring, each other. Thus, each part of the collection—"Reforming Religion and the Secular," "Religion and the Materialities and Practices of Reading," and "Religion and Poetics in Postsecular Literary Studies"—puts chapters by literary scholars in conversation with those by scholars of religion and history. These conversations found precedent in real conversations, both in-person and virtual, among contributors. As detailed in the section "Interdisciplinary Dialogues" (below), contributors have offered written reflections on the unique collaborative process that went into the making of the volume. Their experiences ultimately affirm a key commitment of this collection: the importance, indeed indispensability, of meaningful dialogue in the interdisciplinary study of nineteenth-century religion.

II. SCOPE

With a few crucial exceptions, most of the chapters in this collection attend to Christian religious traditions as practiced and negotiated within nineteenth-century Britain. This is in part a consequence of the decision to concentrate on nineteenth-century British literature and culture: most Britons in that period identified with some form of Christianity, as did most of the scholars, religious leaders, creative authors, and other cultural figures treated in this collection. Even so, many of the chapters in this volume demonstrate how forms of British and continental Christianity were constituted and shaped by encounters with other faiths, both for those who identified as Christians and for those who articulated distinct religious traditions in dialogue with Christianity. When defining "religion" and "world religions," European scholars of biblical criticism and comparative religion tended to represent Judaism and East Asian religions in ways that privileged and redefined Christianity, often in ways that served the colonial interests of imperial states (see Morrow, part I of this volume). Yet prominent Indian intellectuals in the Brahmo Samaj, a Hindu reformist society that achieved international recognition, engaged in their own form of comparative religion, creatively rearticulating Christianity and Hinduism to political and cosmopolitan ends (Scott, part I). While Anglo-American publishers of immensely popular family Bibles responded to a diversifying religious market by packaging the Authorized Version for Jewish families (Carpenter, part II), Anglo-Jewish women writers combined literary and midrashic forms to articulate a distinctly Jewish form of affect in apparently secular literary forms (Dwor, part II). If scholars have long recognized the debt of Romantic lyric theory to Higher Criticism of the Psalms, less often acknowledged is the degree to which both these and subsequent nineteenth-century poetics were complexly and tensely driven by contemporary Anglo-Jewish relations (Scheinberg, part III). This collection, then, complicates supposedly firm boundaries between Christianity and other faith traditions in nineteenth-century scholarship, politics, print culture, poetics, and the lived experiences of religious leaders, writers, and readers. Perhaps just as importantly, it challenges representations of Christianity itself as a monolithic or immutable phenomenon, whether in the nineteenth century or in any other period.

Nearly every chapter in this volume contributes to this interrogation of the dynamic evolutions and permutations of Christian ideas, identifications, and practices across the nineteenth century, but a few examples are illustrative. Turning to Queen Victoria's personal habits of reading, Michael Ledger-Lomas (part II) shows how the Supreme Governor of the Church of England largely eschewed the often-fierce denominational and party lines of her day, joining a growing number of her subjects in creating motley creeds of their own by drawing upon a range of literature, religious and secular. Guided more by inherited assumptions than by evidence, scholars have until recently mirrored Victorian clergy and elites in underestimating or underplaying the creative Christian theological commitments of the British working classes (Brown 18–30). Yet Mike Sanders (part I) argues for renewed attention to the generative role of specific theologies in radical working-class culture, showing how Joseph Rayner Stephens, a renegade Methodist preacher popular among Chartists, envisioned a political economy diametrically opposed to the widespread form of "Christian political economy" documented by Boyd Hilton in the Victorian middle and upper classes (Hilton 57–88).

This collection implicates scholarship, both of the nineteenth century and of the present, in the transformations of Christianity discussed above. As many scholars have observed, modern conceptions of "religion"—formulated theoretically in the seventeenth and eighteenth centuries and widespread in scholarship of the eighteenth and nineteenth—portray it as essentially a matter of private belief and inward experience (see Morrow's chapter, in part I, for a fuller discussion of this trend). Influenced decisively by the Protestant Reformation and later trends in societies dominated by forms of Protestantism, this perception of religion has been labeled broadly "protestant" by scholars of religion such as Winnifred Fallers Sullivan (Scott, part I). Yet such attention to the "protestantism" of modern "religion" can obscure its different inflections—with a greater emphasis upon communal ritual—by Catholic scholars who nonetheless contributed to its formation (Morrow, part I). Even so, an unacknowledged Protestant bias, which identifies religion and theology with inner belief and regards "mere" rituals with suspicion, might lurk within even avowedly secular criticism that feels compelled to look past religious practices and assertions for what is "really" going on underneath the surface (Knight, part II).

In failing to acknowledge the extent to which this bias potentially influences our modern concepts of religion, scholars risk distorting the nineteenth-century literature and culture they analyze. Some might point out that a certain amount of distortion is unavoidable in any historicizing enterprise. Yet, as this volume illustrates, there are particularly high political and ethical stakes in leaving uninterrogated the "protestant" predisposition in criticism. Take, for example, the aforementioned tendency to regard the theological dimensions of working-class culture as false consciousness or as a convenient means of pursuing "real" political ends. Similarly, as Richa Dwor and Cynthia Scheinberg suggest in this volume, the tacit "protestant" orientation in literary studies encourages neglect or dismissal of theologies and religious expressions that rely more overtly upon ritual and the affective uses of texts. In this sense, the turn to religion perhaps necessitates a reevaluation of that "hermeneutics of suspicion" which for so long has been equated with criticism itself, as we begin to realize that any scholarly portrayal of religion inherently has political dimensions and implications.

This disregard for "mere" surfaces, textures, and rhythms of theology and religious practice also has profound implications in our treatment of poetry. Critics risk insensitivity to the ways in which a poet works out theological thinking and conviction in the intricacies of rhythm and verse craft, not just in the discourses paraphrased from his or her poetry or discovered in his or her historical context (Hurley, part III). More generally, the impulse to look beneath the surfaces of religion can blind us to the degree to which nineteenth-century religious experience, self-understanding, organization, and proselytizing were inseparably tied to material culture, whether church architecture and aesthetics (Janes, part II), the illustration and design of books (Carpenter, part II; Otto, part III), the hybridous and explosive market for novels (Burstein, part II), or open and publicized debates organized by secularist societies (Nash, part I).

III. CONTRIBUTION

Constructing Nineteenth-Century Religion primarily addresses literary scholars, religious studies scholars, and historians who concentrate on the Romantic and Victorian periods. Yet specific chapters are also valuable for postcolonial theorists, historians of the disciplines of religion and literature, and those studying the relationship between poetics, poetic practice, and modern notions of inspiration, the "religious," and the "secular."

As mentioned above, there has been a "turn to religion" in humanities scholarship, which has been marked by a critical reassessment of the significance of religion in politics, society, and culture. One need only look at the eager reception of Derrida's *Acts of Religion* (2002) or Charles Taylor's landmark *A Secular Age* (2007) to see this trend in action. More recently, *Religion and Literature,* one of the three flagship journals in its subject title,[4] dedicated a special issue to theorizing and practicing the study of religion and literature as a coherent area of intellectual inquiry (41.2, 2009) and followed this up with a forum on "Locating the Postsecular" (41.3, 2009; see discussion of "postsecular" above). Indeed, as John Caputo has observed, there seems to be a "desire for God" in humanities disciplines (118). Literary studies in particular has proved a fruitful site for these conversations. Some subfields have engaged with religion and religious issues longer than others, of course. For instance, as Nicholas Watson and others observe in the special issue "Literary History and the Religious Turn" in *English Language Notes,* "theology has, *mutatis mutandis,* been at the center of medieval literary studies for half a century" (Holsinger 1–3).

By and large, however, this has not been the case with nineteenth-century literary studies, which has been long dominated by narratives detailing the period's "crisis of faith," its secularism and secularization. Indeed, for a time, accounts of nineteenth-century religion seemed to attract interest in literary studies mostly insofar as they charted religion in an Arnoldian sense, demonstrating how poetry and literature took on the moral and ethical cultural functions of increasingly marginalized religious institutions and ebbing religious belief. So entrenched has been this "secularization narrative" that only

---

4. The other two major journals for the study of literature and religion are *Literature and Theology* and *Christianity and Literature.*

in the past fifteen years or so has there been concerted examination of the profound role that religion played in Romantic and Victorian literature and culture.

Constructing Nineteenth-Century Religion thus seeks to address a persistent gap between recognition of the inescapability of religion and its influences in nineteenth-century culture, on the one hand, and, on the other, a still-developing body of robust scholarship examining the myriad instantiations of this relationship in political movements, economic debates, reading practices, and novelistic and poetic forms. While rooted primarily in literary studies, then, this collection's interdisciplinary scope makes it relevant across disciplines.

Specific chapters and parts join conversations in fields including but extending beyond the nineteenth century. J. Barton Scott's chapter, for instance, offers an account of comparative religion valuable for postcolonial, transnational, and diasporic studies scholars who specialize in a range of eras and contexts. Moreover, drawing analogies between modern literary criticism and the Victorian Browning Society, Charles LaPorte asserts that literary studies remains preoccupied with theology, contributing to related analyses of the discipline by Tracy Fessenden ("'The Secular'" [2007]), Michael Kaufmann ("The Religious, the Secular, and Literary Studies" [2007]), and Lori Branch ("The Rituals" [2014]). Calling for literary critics to consider what it would mean to embrace, rather than deny, the seemingly ineluctable theological dimension of their devotion to texts, his chapter contributes to the final part of this volume, "Religion and Poetics in Postsecular Literary Studies," which also contains chapters from Cynthia Scheinberg, Michael D. Hurley, and Peter Otto. Thus, this part joins an ongoing scholarly conversation on the relationships among religion, poetic theory, and the particularities of poetic practice, one carried on in other periods by scholars such as Regina Schwartz (*Sacramental Poetics at the Dawn of Secularism* [2008]) and in the nineteenth century by a number of recent books too numerous to list here in full, including Colin Jager's *The Book of God* (2007), Kirstie Blair's *Form and Faith in Victorian Poetry and Religion* (2012), Karen Dieleman's *Religious Imaginaries* (2012), Jasper Cragwall's *Lake Methodism* (2013), and books by several contributors to this collection: Cynthia Scheinberg's *Women's Poetry and Religion in Victorian England* (2002), Charles LaPorte's *Victorian Poets and the Changing Bible* (2011), Michael D. Hurley's *Faith in Poetry* (2017), and co-editor Joshua King's *Imagined Spiritual Communities in Britain's Age of Print* (2015). The proliferation of these studies testifies to a widespread interest within nineteenth-century studies and beyond in the ways that form shaped and was shaped by theological debates and religious practices.

In its interdisciplinary scope, *Constructing Nineteenth-Century Religion* complements and extends contributions made by other recent collections without retreading the same ground. The high number of literary scholars in our collection reflects our emphasis on literature, of course, but it also mirrors a current scholarly trend. As Mark Knight, a contributor to this volume, recently observed in *The Routledge Companion to Literature and Religion* (2016), "Much of the recent intellectual energy behind contributions to literature and religion has come from those who identify with literary studies" (2–3). Knight's outstanding interdisciplinary volume of literary critics, theologians, historians, and scholars of religion is a case in point, as most contributors are from English departments. Yet only three of the forty essays in Knight's collection deal primarily or exclusively with nineteenth-century Britain. If this number is unremarkable, on the one hand, given that Knight's volume is intended to display a wide range of methods and topics, it is, on the other hand, surprisingly representative of the state of the field: while interdisciplinary collections on religion exist for literary scholars of the medieval and early modern periods, few collections on religion are available that prioritize nineteenth-century British literature in an interdisciplinary and comparative context. No existing collection takes the approach of this volume.

Akin to entries in *The Routledge Companion to Literature and Religion*, the discussions of religion here are weighted toward Christianity. Yet we follow the lead of the *Routledge Companion* in refraining from "suggesting that this faith retains control over where the conversation goes or becomes a requirement for those contributing to the conversation or ignores the considerable disagreements between those who identify with the Christian tradition" (Knight 8). Thus, we include several important contributions on faiths or movements other than Christianity, even though our breadth is comparatively limited by the priority given to nineteenth-century Britain. One could say that our collection supplements the encyclopedic approach of the *Routledge Companion* with a sympathetic investigation that is more thematically, theoretically, and historically focused. The relationship between *Constructing Nineteenth-Century Religion* and Susan M. Felch's *The Cambridge Companion to Literature and Religion* (2016) is much the same. Although Felch's collection contains nearly the same number of chapters as our own by literary scholars, scholars of religion, and theologians, it ranges widely, treating literary works from many eras, a number of broad thematic topics (e.g., "Ethics" and "Imagination"), and an array of religious traditions (e.g., one chapter each on "Hinduism," "Buddhism," and "Judaism," among others). Like the *Routledge* collection, *The Cambridge Companion to Literature and Religion* does not make the category of "religion" an organizing subject of analysis and conversation. Both collections point to a need for something like this volume, in which "religion" itself is recognized and treated as an ever-fluid construction, one perhaps best approached through an interdisciplinary examination of the multifarious ways it was enacted, practiced, and negotiated.

Reading the Abrahamic Faiths: Rethinking Religion and Literature (2015), edited by Emma Mason, occupies a territory between Knight's and Felch's collections. Mason's collection is, like Felch's *Cambridge Companion,* more deliberately comparative than either the *Routledge Companion* or our volume, focusing on comparative literature and containing equal numbers of chapters on Christianity, Judaism, and Islam. Yet it is at the same time arguably less interdisciplinary than both, as nearly all of the twenty contributors are from departments of English or Comparative Literature. *Reading the Abrahamic Faiths* engages many literary periods and national literatures, and therefore provides a wider lens through which to approach some of our chapters (especially those on comparative religion, Hindu reform societies, and Jewish poetics and fiction), even as our collection enables focused application of issues raised in *Abrahamic Faiths* to nineteenth-century (especially British) literature and culture.

Even closer to the historical period of our collection is *Shaping Belief: Culture, Politics and Religion in Nineteenth-Century Writing* (2008), edited by Victoria Morgan and Clare Williams.[5] Examining several literary genres, architecture, graphic art, and social reform, and pairing chapters on British subjects with two on American, this volume in some ways overlaps with ours—although the fact that all the contributors are literary scholars makes it less interdisciplinary. Yet the chapters are less intentional in sustaining a dialogue across the volume, and religion is more of a loosely assumed category (and almost exclusively identified with Christianity) than a concept that itself comes in for scrutiny. Collections such as Robert J. Barth's *The Fountain Light: Studies in Romanticism and Religion* (2002), Sheila A. Spector's *The Jews and British Romanticism* (2005), and Mary McCartin Wearn's *Nineteenth-Century American Women Write Religion* (2014) share our examination of nineteenth-century religion, even as their distinct temporal, geographical, and theoretical priorities mean that they form interesting extensions to chapters in our collection without impinging upon the uniqueness of these contributions or of the

---

5. Another related collection is *Religion in the Age of Reason: A Transatlantic Study of the Long Eighteenth Century* (2009), edited by Kathryn Duncan. *Religion in the Age of Reason* is less comparative than ours, as it focuses almost exclusively on forms of Christianity in Britain, with only two essays on American subjects bearing out the "Transatlantic" title. It is furthermore less interdisciplinary. Once again, the relationship between our collection and this one is complementary rather than competitive: it offers an eighteenth-century preface of sorts to our shared emphasis on literature and diverse historical constructions of religion.

volume as a whole. The same is true of collections aimed primarily at historians of religion, such as Sheridan Gilley's *Victorian Churches and Churchmen* (2005) and Hilary M. Carey's *Empires of Religion* (2008).

Although Linda Woodhead's collection *Reinventing Christianity: Nineteenth-Century Contexts* (2001) shares our concentration on Britain, its subject is "Christianity" rather than our deliberately broader term "religion." While most of our contributors also discuss Christianity, our overriding concern is less with Christianity alone than with the very category of "religion" and the diverse ways in which it was constructed and deployed by a range of figures—Christian, Hindu, Jewish, secularist, or otherwise. In addition to including religions other than Christianity, several of our chapters also foreground comparisons between religions, attending to the complex and problematic history of such comparison as much as its practice by present scholars.

Related to this interest in the history of comparison is the concern of many chapters in our collection not only with so-called objects of study—such as various nineteenth-century literary representations of religion—but also with nineteenth-century formulations of the disciplines that set the parameters of our inquiries, in this case literary criticism, religious studies, and modern historiography. Woodhead's *Reinventing Christianity*, like many of the collections mentioned above, does not undertake this kind of self-reflexive disciplinary history. Our comparatively greater interest in interrogating the category of "religion" and its disciplinary formulations is partly due to developments in scholarship since the publication of *Reinventing Christianity*. This is true of many other features that distinguish our volume from Woodhead's and most of those already mentioned—recognition of the institutional, political, ideological, and disciplinary contests played out through the concept of "religion"; treatment of the "secular" as itself a discourse and ideology with a history inextricably bound up with representations of "religion" and the "religious"; respect for denominational and sectarian peculiarities (e.g., evangelical, High Church, Moravian); interest in the material, market-driven, commodified dimension of religious practice and experience; and analysis of connections and tensions between colonial and metropolitan efforts to understand and compare religions. Many contributors to this collection have been formative to the development of these trends in scholarship.

IV. PARTS AND UNITING THEMES

Part I, "Reforming Religion and the Secular," concentrates on the ways in which religion was categorized, formulated, and invoked in nineteenth-century reform efforts, with several of the chapters uncovering underexamined political and reformist contexts for the emerging academic study of religion and comparative religion, and others demonstrating the complex reconfiguration of religious narratives, concepts, attitudes, and practices by major reformers and reform movements—such as Chartism, Marxism, and secularism.

Dominic Erdozain, for instance, questions the binary distinction between religion and the secular to show how Marxism, in fact, owes as much to theological conscience as to science, thus revealing the surprisingly religious nature of Marx's exposure of religion as false consciousness. J. Barton Scott—focusing on the Hindu reform society, the Brahmo Samaj—demonstrates that the modern discipline of comparative religion took shape as much in colonial religious institutions as in the metropolitan centers of academic study. Prominent practitioners of comparative religion within the Samaj, such as Keshub Chunder Sen and Protap Chunder Mozoomdar, reworked Hindu and Christian discourses in dialogue with protestant-Romantic notions of affect to promote an affective cosmopolitanism that defied national and religious divisions reinforced by European comparative religion and imperialism. Their struggle, and ultimate failure, to realize this global vision reveals a tension arguably characteristic of Victorian religion more broadly—that between affect and institution, and between a protestant-Romantic focus on inward experience and the modern nation-state's bureaucratic forms. Jeffrey L. Morrow places the work of Alfred Loisy, controversial Roman Catholic priest and scholar of religion, within a longer narrative about the debt of modern Western understandings of "religion" to state and imperial politics, arguing that Loisy's inheritance of these modern discourses, in turn, drove his politics: Loisy defied the Papacy and pursued secularization of French education precisely because he had come to accept religion as something that was inherently separate from, and best governed by, secular and public spheres. Mike Sanders, by way of the Methodist minister Joseph Rayner Stephens, examines how political theology legitimated working-class economic demands in the early nineteenth century. Turning to the originator of the term *secularism*, secularist reformer George Jacob Holyoake, David Nash demonstrates Holyoake's surprisingly subtle view of the relationship between secularism, secularization, and religion, one which complicates the narrative of a pitched battle between hardline secularists and monolithic religion that has until recently been sustained in scholarship on secularism. Together, then, the chapters of this part suggest that the institutions, discourses, and practices of an outwardly "secular" modernity have been constituted less by the absence of religion from public life than by debates and efforts to reform religion's public and social roles. Highlighting the complex ways that the "secular and religious depend on each other for meaning," this part looks to the nineteenth century to complicate the supposed "secularity" of reformers and reform movements, and to challenge simplistic stories about the decline of religion in the modern world (Kauffman 610).

Furthermore, in connecting various constructions of religion to reform efforts, each of these chapters offers a case study for the central role played in modern (Western-derived) understandings of religion by what Charles Taylor has called "Reform" in *A Secular Age* (2007). This is Taylor's term for the series of reform efforts—stretching back to late-medieval initiatives by ecclesiastical elites to raise the level of Christian devotion among the common people—that have resulted in now-widespread views of society as an order that is humanly (rather than divinely) constructed according to basic rights and for the mutual benefit of its members. This sense of human community—as an order built up by self-determining human agents in a mundane, contingent reality not necessarily mandated or guided by divine will—is central to most modern views of "secular" society. Each of these chapters complicates Taylor's assertion that this way of imagining society and our agency within it is both derived from and persistently engaged with religious history and constructions of religion. J. Barton Scott's chapter also demonstrates that this history was and is never simply "Western" and "Christian"; as José Casanova has argued, such concepts of secular society, reform, and religion might derive much of their original shape from developments within Latin Christendom, but they have long since become global, and have been reconfigured and redeployed in ways that reflect their new contexts around the world (62).

Part II, "Religion and the Materialities and Practices of Reading," carries forward two theoretical and historiographic concerns raised in part I. First, it extends the critical appraisal by Morrow and Scott in part I, which links the formation of the modern concept of "religion" to inward experience and belief in doctrines. Second, it builds on the challenge to simplistic divisions between "secular" and "religious" movements, practices, and texts posed by the remaining chapters of part I. These two concerns show themselves in part II through six chapters that examine the ways in which "religion," theology, and lived faith were constructed by nineteenth-century publishing practices, habits of reading, novel writing and reviewing, debates about church architecture and decoration, and (even semi-agnostic appropriations of) Christian rituals and disciplines. Though several of these chapters concentrate on Protestant readers, preachers, and reviewers who championed a modern view of "true" religion as something forged in the inner heart through commitment to core beliefs, each chapter ultimately shows the indebtedness of religious identity and meaning to material texts, forms, and reading practices.

Mary Wilson Carpenter opens part II by way of the overlooked genre of the "Family Bible," a nineteenth-century print phenomenon characterized by a host of competing functions and contrary impulses. On the one hand, as Carpenter notes, these were Bibles, intended to exalt the spirit and impart important religious and moral lessons. Yet these hefty and handsome Bibles, which were padded out with all sorts of additions to the scriptural text, invited readers to value them for the way they looked on the outside, not what was on the inside. Moreover, they were printed as much for profit as out of a sense of piety, and their many illustrations, chronologies, commentaries, and trivia sometimes seemed to encourage reading the Bible as literature or entertainment rather than as the "pure" Word of God. Carpenter's insights regarding the eclectic religious reading promoted by the "Family Bible" find resonance in the subsequent chapter by Michael Ledger-Lomas. Here, though, the locus of eclecticism is found not in a text but rather in the comprehensive reading habits of the foremost figure of the Victorian era, Queen Victoria herself. Examining Queen Victoria's voluminous (and rather humorously unreflective) reading as a case study, he provocatively suggests that while "print saturated Victorian culture with Christian messages, it also allowed lay readers to fashion magpie creeds of their own." Of course, such magpie creeds were never relegated solely to Christianity's competing sects; as Richa Dwor usefully reminds us, Jewish women writers, prohibited from participating in formal study of religious texts, explored new ways of representing religious feeling by blending midrashic structures of thought with conventional literary forms. What might appear as merely feminized sentimentality in Grace Aguilar's poetry, then, is revealed to be a subtle form of particularly Jewish feeling.

But if religious commitments and literary form combine nearly seamlessly in Aguilar's poetry—so much so that only careful reading reveals the former in the latter—Miriam Burstein's chapter shows that in the "hybridous monster" of the evangelical novel, the marriage between belief and form was decidedly less harmonious. No matter the criteria applied, Burstein demonstrates, the genre was regarded by critics as a failure. Religious critics found fault in the evangelical novel for *being* a novel: as a novel, it was inevitably multivocal and, as such, engendered the very desires it ostensibly was meant to repudiate. And "secular" critics found the often didactic, self-interrupting tendencies of the novel simply bad form. Yet, these novels refused to go away. Their success was troubling, as Burstein notes, for it implied that even evangelical faith, the "religion of the heart," could be successfully mechanized and marketed. So pressing was this concern that it extended to and profoundly influenced debates on Nonconformist architecture, as Dominic Janes demonstrates. Focusing on the popular preacher Charles Haddon Spurgeon, Janes illustrates how anxieties regarding the relationship of spirit and form manifested themselves not solely in literature, but in the question of church and chapel architecture and other instantiations of material religion. Concluding part II is Mark Knight's chapter. Here, Knight reads Wilde's *De Profundis* and "The Ballad of Reading Gaol" through the framework of theological ritual, which helps us to see Wilde grappling with forgiveness as an act that requires continual work rather than a state achieved by the elect. But perhaps even more, in revisiting what Wilde owed to (or inherited from) "religion" and its practices, Knight's chapter urges us, his readers, to take a hard look at our own invisible debts to religious traditions, to those religious forms—particularly those Protestant forms—that might shape the ways we ourselves comprehend and assess literary texts.

Thus, a second common thread unites the chapters of part II. Even as they show the diverse ways that material culture mediated understandings of "true" religion, they also demonstrate how texts, reading habits, and publishing practices often thought of as secular (e.g., popular novels) were literally bound up with sacred texts (e.g., the "Family Bible") and became fundamental to the articulation of religious feelings and habits of thought (e.g., Jewish women's novels that are often otherwise interpreted within a secular frame). With particular attention to relatively localized acts of interpretation—such as the relationship between Queen Victoria's reading habits and the "spiritual bricolage" of her personal faith, nineteenth-century critical responses to the "hybridous monster" of the evangelical novel, or Wilde's surprising evocation of Christian liturgy in *De Profundis*—part II considers how religion was defined, negotiated, and made culturally or politically meaningful outside the domain of religious institutions and hierarchies.

Part III, "Religion and Poetics in Postsecular Literary Studies," both responds to many of the issues raised in parts I and II and directly addresses the intersection of subjects highlighted in the book series to which this collection contributes, Ohio State's *Literature, Religion, and Postsecular Studies*. All the chapters in this final part continue, in some fashion, the focus of earlier sections on the fluid—rather than the fixed or innate—relationship between the secular and the religious in nineteenth-century literature and culture. Distinguishing these chapters from the preceding chapters are their shared concentration on the poetics of religion—that is, a poetics not only intended to convey religious meanings to readers, but one which also shaped Romantic and Victorian poetic forms as well as the emerging discipline of literary studies in profound ways.

To this end, Charles LaPorte's and Cynthia Scheinberg's chapters recover and take as their subject the often-neglected theological dimensions of literary theory and criticism, both as it emerged in the Victorian period and as it has been practiced since. While Christianity plays a major role in these discussions, Scheinberg's chapter also reveals the extent to which nineteenth-century English criticism of the Psalms as cultural icons of lyric poetry was inextricable from contemporary Jewish–Christian relations. Criticism of the Psalms at this period constitutes what Scheinberg, drawing from Mary Louise Pratt, calls a "contact zone," or social space where cultures meet and clash in asymmetrical relations of power. Emerging in dialogue with Romantic notions of the universality of lyric, Anglican and Anglo-Jewish criticism of the Psalms becomes a site of contest over the identity and presence of Jews and Jewishness at a moment when Britain's Jewish worshipping community was becoming unavoidably visible and politically active.

The final two entries, by Michael D. Hurley and Peter Otto, complement these discussions of poetics and literary criticism with fine-grained studies of practicing poets—William Blake and Gerard Manley Hopkins. Hurley, focusing on Hopkins and Blake, extends an interest, appearing also in several chapters in part II, in faith as a practice—in this case, a practice in which the finest motions of rhythm and patterns of sound are the means by which poets work out their understandings of inspiration, both divine and poetic. Otto, although differing from Hurley in his account of Blake's theo-poetics, similarly concentrates on the complex roles of religion and theology in Blake's artistry. Building on the richer knowledge of Blake's religious influences offered by recent advances in scholarship, Otto argues that we have yet to appreciate how powerfully Blake reread and reworked these influences in his illustrated books. Otto pursues Blake's subtle refashioning of these influences through a series of plates from across the poet-artist's career, focusing on Blake's engagement with the Incarnation to show how Blake ultimately articulates a view of imagination that defies and transforms fixed divisions between the "secular" and the "religious," the orthodox and the heretical.

Last, chapters in this part collectively reveal the deep connection between nineteenth-century (and later) formulations of the "poetic" and understandings of inspiration in its uniquely modern double meaning, as both divine gift and creative excellence or illumination. Debates between Anglican and Anglo-Jewish commentators over the Jewishness of the Psalms are, in Scheinberg's account, also contests over the divine and poetic inspiration of the Jewish poets who composed them—a contest that spills over into Romantic notions of the "inspired" poet whose language is supposedly universally relevant. LaPorte alerts us to the ways in which late-Victorian literary societies such as the Browning Society were eager to test their faith in the inspiration of poems, both as sources of religious illumination and as semi-sacred texts free from dogma. He further suggests that the discipline of literary studies has always since harbored a theological dimension, and that careful attention to Victorian criticism of poetry, with its investment in quasi-sacred secular poetry, therefore provides an opportunity to come to terms with this abiding fact and what it might mean for literary criticism at this postsecular moment. Hurley attends to the ways in which Blake and Hopkins negotiated the burden of inspiration in this multivalent sense, so that for them poetry was an art and a divine gift, and poetic practice was a test of faith in inspiration, divine and poetic. Blake, Otto's chapter indicates, provides one of the more unusual but surprisingly resonant examples of this mediation between poetic and prophetic inspiration, as he refashions his religious influences to represent imagination as a source of open-ended potential, whose creations can inspire efforts to supplement, compete with, or transform the existing world. In this account, Blake is perhaps already postsecular in his refusal to accept firm hierarchical or supersessional divisions between the given and the possible, the religious and the secular.

V. INTERDISCIPLINARY DIALOGUES

In constructing this volume, we draw inspiration from Mark Knight's introduction to *The Routledge Companion to Literature and Religion,* mentioned above. Knight proposes that scholarly work in religion and literature should be conceived as a "conversation rather than a field, an interest, or a specialty" (4). While the *Routledge Companion* deliberately "remain[s] in the world of literature and religion," he provocatively suggests that there could be "value ... in thinking about how conversation might become the means by which we configure a whole range of interdisciplinary relations" (5).

This book represents an effort to discover what "value" is yielded when we approach the study of nineteenth-century religion through such interdisciplinary conversations. Of course, many of the chapters in this volume have their origins in years of research and writing conducted mostly individually, as is typical in the humanities. Indeed, one of the strengths of this volume is that it marshals a group of scholars who are recognized experts in their subject. Yet in pursuing this project we wanted to explore the possibilities of seeing these subjects from new angles. We wondered, what might happen if literary critics, historians, and religious studies scholars were afforded the opportunity to bring their areas of research into meaningful conversation with one another?

Thus, every stage in the making of this book—from its initial formulation to the final version you hold in your hands—involved collaboration and exchange. In March 2016 contributors first met each other and exchanged ideas at the "Uses of Religion in 19th-C. Studies" conference at Baylor University. The conversations sparked at this gathering continued through August 2017 via Google Drive, with drafts of the chapters-in-progress uploaded, shared, and commented on not only by editors but fellow contributors as well. By means of this virtual scholarly community, the chapters were made to speak to each other, highlighting points of agreement with and divergence from other chapters; remarking on the emergence of overlapping interests and themes in outwardly divergent topics; and meditating on what is brought into view or obscured by various critical lenses.

We encouraged contributors to reflect upon this collaborative process when they submitted the revised chapters. They noticed the aptness of such an approach for this kind of project. "If one of the upshots of this volume is that religion in the nineteenth century was constructed via networks that were highly dispersed and that cut across diverse modes of knowledge and institutional practice," observes J. Barton Scott, "then the kind of collaborative work that went into making this volume becomes not only practically necessary, but also intellectually appropriate to mapping this historical terrain." Other contributors remarked on the ways that in-person and online conversations changed how they viewed and presented their own research interests. Mary Wilson Carpenter relates that her frame of reference for understanding the genre of the "Family Bible," which she first explored in her landmark study *Imperial Bibles, Domestic Bodies* (2003), was "richly complicated—or shall I say therapeutically confused"—by virtue of conversations with other contributors. Knight reflected on the "indirect value of writing with a real audience of brilliant scholars in mind." "It is easy for our idea of an audience to slip into the abstract," he explains, "but here, as I wrote my paper for the conference and then developed it for publication, the audience has been concrete." "How unique (and beneficial) it was to have our writing process made more transparent and material through the work of this volume!" Cynthia Scheinberg relates. "Consistent intellectual excitement and interdisciplinary engagement . . . helped me situate my specific research in larger contexts."

The result of this unique approach, we hope, is that this volume invites more than the typical scavenging that is often performed on collections, as readers hunt only for the morsel that interests them and leave the rest for others. Instead, readers are encouraged to recognize the ways that each chapter and part contributes to the next—and how, conversely, later chapters enter into meaningful dialogue with earlier ones. Throughout the volume, authors encourage readers to make such connections by highlighting them, whether through extended discussions of each other's work or parenthetical reminders that a point raised in their chapter is pursued or differently viewed in another. No doubt the work of "being interdisciplinary is so very hard to do" (to borrow Stanley Fish's oft-quoted phrase); but, as this volume models, this very difficult work perhaps is more achievable—indeed, perhaps is *only* achievable—when approached not in isolation but through conversation, through actually placing literary, historical, and religious studies in dialogue.

WORKS CITED

"American Piety in the 21st Century: Select Findings from the Baylor Religion Survey." *Baylor Institute for Studies of Religion.* Baylor Institute for the Studies of Religion, 2006. http://www.baylorisr.org/wp-content/uploads/American-Piety-Finall.pdf. Accessed 15 Aug. 2016.

Asad, Talal. *Formations of the Secular: Christianity, Islam, Modernity.* Stanford UP, 2003.

———. "Freedom of Speech and Religious Limitations." *Rethinking Secularism,* edited by Craig Calhoun et al., Oxford UP, 2011, pp. 282–97.

———. *Genealogies of Religion: Discipline and Reasons of Power in Christianity and Islam.* Johns Hopkins UP, 1993.

Barth, J. Robert, editor. *The Fountain Light: Studies in Romanticism and Religion in Honor of John L. Mahoney.* Fordham UP, 2002.

Blair, Kirstie. *Form and Faith in Victorian Poetry and Religion.* Oxford UP, 2012.

Branch, Lori. "Postsecular Studies." *The Routledge Companion to Literature and Religion,* edited by Mark Knight, Routledge, 2016, pp. 91–101.

———. "The Rituals of Our Re-Secularization: Literature between Faith and Knowledge." *Religion and Literature,* vol. 46, nos. 2–3, 2014, pp. 9–33.

Brown, Callum. *The Death of Christian Britain: Understanding Secularisation, 1800–2000.* 2nd ed., Routledge, 2009.

Caputo, John, and Gianni Vattimo. *After the Death of God.* Edited by Jeffrey W. Robbins, Columbia UP, 2007, pp. 114–60.

Carey, Hilary. *Empires of Religion.* Palgrave Macmillan, 2008.

Casanova, José. "The Secular, Secularizations, Secularisms." *Rethinking Secularism,* edited by Craig Calhoun et al., Oxford UP, 2011, pp. 54–74.

Cragwall, Jasper. *Lake Methodism: Polite Literature and Popular Religion in England, 1780–1830.* The Ohio State UP, 2013.

Derrida, Jacques. *Acts of Religion.* Edited by Gil Anidjar, Routledge, 2002.

Dieleman, Karen. *Religious Imaginaries: The Liturgical and Poetic Practices of Elizabeth Barrett Browning, Christina Rossetti, and Adelaide Procter.* Ohio UP, 2012.

Duncan, Kathryn, editor. *Religion in the Age of Reason: A Transatlantic Study of the Long Eighteenth Century.* AMS Press, 2009.

Felch, Susan, editor. *The Cambridge Companion to Literature and Religion.* Cambridge UP, 2016.

Felluga, Dino. *Critical Theory: The Key Concepts.* Routledge, 2015.

Felski, Rita. "After Suspicion." *Profession*, 2009, pp. 28–35.

Fessenden, Tracy. "'The Secular' as Opposed to What?" *New Literary History*, vol. 38, no. 4, 2007, pp. 631–36.

Fish, Stanley. "One University under God?" *The Chronicle of Higher Education*, vol. 51, no. 18, 7 Jan. 2005, p. C1.

Gilley, Sheridan, editor. *Victorian Churches and Churchmen: Essay Presented to Vincent Alan McClelland*. Boydell Press, 2005.

Hilton, Boyd. *The Age of Atonement*. Oxford UP, 1988.

Holsinger, Bruce. "Introduction: Literary History and the Religious Turn." *English Language Notes*, vol. 44, no. 1, Spring 2006, pp. 1–3.

Hurley, Michael D. *Faith in Poetry: Verse Style as a Mode of Religious Belief*. Bloomsbury, 2017.

Jager, Colin. *The Book of God: Secularization and Design in the Romantic Era*. U of Pennsylvania P, 2007.

———. *Unquiet Things: Secularism in the Romantic Age*. U of Pennsylvania P, 2014.

Kauffman, Michael W. "The Religious, the Secular, and Literary Studies: Rethinking the Secularization Narrative in Histories of the Profession." *New Literary History*, vol. 38, no. 4, Autumn 2007, pp. 607–28.

King, Joshua. *Imagined Spiritual Communities in Britain's Age of Print*. The Ohio State UP, 2015.

Knight, Mark, editor. *The Routledge Companion to Literature and Religion*. Routledge, 2016.

LaPorte, Charles. *Victorian Poets and the Changing Bible*. U of Virginia P, 2011.

Lemon, Rebecca et al., editors. *The Blackwell Companion to the Bible in English Literature*. Wiley-Blackwell, 2009.

Mason, Emma, editor. *Reading the Abrahamic Faiths: Rethinking Religion and Literature*. Bloomsbury, 2015.

McKeon, Michael. *The Origins of the English Novel, 1600–1740*. Johns Hopkins UP, 1987.

Morgan, Victoria, and Clare Williams, editors. *Shaping Belief: Culture, Politics and Religion in Nineteenth-Century Writing*. Liverpool UP, 2008.

Religion and Literature, vol. 41, no. 2, 2009.

———. vol. 41, no. 3, 2009.

Scheinberg, Cynthia. *Women's Poetry and Religion in Victorian England: Jewish Identity and Christian Culture*. Cambridge UP, 2002.

Schwartz, Regina. *Sacramental Poetics at the Dawn of Secularism: When God Left the World*. Stanford UP, 2008.

Spector, Sheila A, editor. *The Jews and British Romanticism: Politics, Religion, Culture*. Palgrave Macmillan, 2005.

Taylor, Charles. *A Secular Age*. Belknap Press of Harvard UP, 2007.

U.S. Religious Landscape Study. The Pew Charitable Trusts, 2014. http://www.pewforum.org/about-the-religious-landscape-study. Accessed 15 Aug. 2016.

Warner, Michael. "Uncritical Reading." *Polemic: Critical or Uncritical*, edited by Jane Gallop, Routledge, 2004, pp. 13–38.

Wearn, Mary McCartin, editor. *Nineteenth-Century American Women Write Religion: Lived Theologies and Literature*. Ashgate, 2014.

Woodhead, Linda, editor. *Reinventing Christianity: Nineteenth-Century Contexts*. Ashgate, 2001.

PART I

∼

Reforming Religion and the Secular

CHAPTER 1

Religion and the Secular State

Loisy's Use of "Religion" Prior to His Excommunication

JEFFREY L. MORROW

ALFRED LOISY (1857-1940) is well known to historians of modern Roman Catholicism as one of the leading figures at the heart of the Catholic modernist crisis in the early part of the twentieth century—a conflict between the papal magisterium of Pope St. Pius X and a number of Catholic intellectuals, primarily clergy, over the appropriation of modern philosophy and methods of biblical interpretation in Catholic theology. Although Loisy is less well known as a scholar of religion, his primary use of the term *religion* is significant in the larger historical context. Loisy's writing participates in the transition from premodern to modern views of religion, when the latter view was increasingly, but not yet fully for Loisy's Catholic readers, moving from rarified regions of scholarly debate into the territory it now enjoys of popular "common sense." His position on religion adopted the contemporary position of scholars like him, and his case illustrates that an understanding of religion is never merely academic but also has political dimensions and implications. In Loisy's case, his acceptance of the modern definition of religion drove his politics.

Thus, the chapter begins with a discussion of the way in which the word *religion* changed in the modern period, highlighting that transformation's connection with modern politics. I then turn to Loisy, the author who serves as this chapter's focus, providing a brief overview of his life and scholarship. In the third portion of this chapter, I examine the ways in which Loisy employed *religion* in his published books prior to his excommunication in 1908. His use of *religion* was fairly common among European scholars of religion at that time, but it differed greatly from its premodern usage. I conclude with some reflections on the significance of Loisy's use of *religion* in light of his broader social, religious, and political context, namely, that his use of *religion* supports a particular politics which he hoped would triumph.

In general, Loisy's usage of *religion* is quite similar to the modern concept of religion that continues today. That is, religion is an abstract generic category into which we place various belief systems or forms of worship, like Judaism or Islam. Loisy occasionally deviates from this usage, in 8 percent of the instances I studied, wherein he evidenced an earlier premodern usage. This secondary usage shows that, at least among the Catholics for whom Loisy wrote, religion still retained an earlier secondary definition. His primary modern usage of *religion*, however, carried veiled political intentions, namely, in support of the more secularizing trends within his contemporary France, embroiled as it was in the shifts from Catholic theological understanding of religion to the newer study of the history of religions (Hill, "Loisy's 'Mystical'" 76–77; Tavard). Loisy's primary usage of *religion* in this modern sense thus indicates one example of this modern definition, here expressed in Loisy's distinct form of biblical interpretation. This demonstrates how an understanding of religion is never merely academic: it can not only reflect political agendas but also determine them, shaping some of the most powerful institutions governing modern life. As Loisy's case shows, understanding the historical contexts of the terminology of religion and the "secular" illuminates modern debates over the nation-state, and how, in France, the separation of church and state was dependent upon the evolution of the modern term *religion*.

RELIGION AND EMPIRE: RELIGIONS AND STATES

When most modern Westerners discuss religion, they refer to a system of beliefs, perhaps involving a certain set of rituals, but they ultimately speak about it as something pertaining to the private sphere. Whatever religion may be, they say, it should not have any public authority—if it is present in public at all. Religion should be absent of any political power, or coercive violence, which belongs exclusively to the state government with its attendant police forces and armies. Modern Westerners distinguish between and attempt to separate religion and the secular. Historically speaking, these contemporary notions are modern and, in some cases, relatively recent.

John Milbank famously wrote, "Once, there was no 'secular'" (9). Milbank did not mean that the term *secular* was a modern invention. Rather, Milbank indicated the origin of the *new meaning* of "secular" in the modern period of Western Europe since the time of the sixteenth century. Before this era, people understood God to be operative in matters sacred as well as secular. The secular simply denoted the world and time, both of which God created. Moreover, although sacred and secular referred to distinct realities, they were not completely separate.

The secular was regarded as sacred. As Talal Asad notes, "at one time 'the secular' was part of a theological discourse" (*Formations* 192). This perspective continues in some theological circles, including in official documents of the Catholic Church, as when, for example, in the Second Vatican Council's Dogmatic Constitution on the Church, *Lumen Gentium,* in paragraph 31, we find "secular" as what typifies the Christian lay faithful, as in their secularity, their at-home-ness in the world, and also "secular" denotes the operating theater of the ordinary Christian (Morrow, "Secularization" 15–19; Tanner). Thus, in this earlier discourse, the "secular" belonged with the sacred, not in juxtaposition, but as something itself sacred, to the extent that Catholic priests not belonging to specific religious orders or communities could be identified as secular priests.

Andrew Jones convincingly demonstrates the complexity of this relationship in the medieval period. Jones relies upon copious primary sources from court hearings, various constitutions, and legal ordinances, and other such documents, showing with meticulous detail that the relationship between the Catholic Church and various political offices throughout Christendom was far more complex than previously has been grasped. Catholic clergy, including members of religious orders like the Dominicans, were often intimately concerned with what we would typically identify as matters of state, including the economy and virtually all temporal concerns. At the same time, local rulers, kings, princes, and nobles—all among the laity—were often equally concerned with matters we might think of as religious or spiritual, including enforcing excommunications and the decisions of heresy trials. This situation cannot be reflected adequately by our contemporary usage of the words *religious* and *secular.*

The contemporary understanding of religion is that religion is a universal abstract phenomenon separable from its concrete expressions. For many, religion is a category into which they can place various elements. Religion is a thing that exists, a general type of thing, which is instantiated differently. Thus, Buddhism is a religion—sometimes contested since some forms of Buddhism are nontheistic. Judaism, Christianity, and Islam are all religions.

These understandings of religion are the products of theoretical discussions in the sixteenth and seventeenth centuries, but their widespread acceptance is the result of the imperial and colonial pressures and cultural norms of the eighteenth and nineteenth centuries. In the modern period, particularly after the time we have come to call the Protestant Reformation, religion was redefined. This redefinition has been pointed out by a number of scholars (Asad, *Genealogies* 37–45; *Formations* 181–201; Cavanaugh, "Fire"; Feil, "From the Classical *Religio*"; Harrison 5–14; Morrow, *Three* 139–49; Pickstock 146–54). Largely unnoticed but of particular importance is Ernst Feil's four-volume work, *Religio*, which he published between the years 1986 and 2007, spanning 2,000 pages of main text, not including front matter and bibliography.

Feil's work confirms the main points made by scholars like Asad and Cavanaugh, but, unlike their works, Feil's represents a more comprehensive and focused historical study on the uses of the term *religion*. His thorough scholarship indicates that the modern usage of *religion* was not simply being redefined in the seventeenth through nineteenth centuries, but was becoming more normative among scholars and, increasingly, the intellectual classes, so that by the end of the nineteenth century, such understandings of religion were widespread beyond the small circle of political theorists and other intellectuals who contributed most to this new definition.

What Feil's work demonstrates is that initially, and all the way through the medieval period into the middle of the sixteenth century, religion primarily had to do with either the fulfilling of a duty one had to God—to the gods, in the case of the ancient Romans. More commonly, from the 600s and onwards, religion was an identifier for monastic life and discipline or of the kind of life lived in specific Catholic religious orders. Indeed, Catholic priests were (and still are) identified as secular or religious depending upon whether they were members of a religious order or not.

With the early modern period, however, this usage of *religion* began to change, especially among political theorists. In the sixteenth and seventeenth centuries, Jean Bodin (Feil, *Religio* 3:149–61, 278–314) and Thomas Hobbes (3:226–53) were transitional figures. Although Hobbes used *religion* primarily in more traditional ways, Bodin evidenced instances of the contemporary understanding. In the seventeenth and eighteenth centuries, however, with such people as Baruch Spinoza (3:416–31), John Locke (3:434–45), Jean-Jacques Rousseau (4:326–41), and others, the term *religion* had new shades of meaning, more like what we have come to expect. The modern usage of *religion* became widespread and hence normative in the eighteenth and the nineteenth centuries among intellectuals.

It is not mere coincidence that this initial shift occurred in the early modern period among figures who were political theorists. As Asad proposes, "The modern idea of secular society included a distinctive relation between state law and personal morality, such that religion became essentially a matter of (private) belief—a society presupposing a range of personal sensibilities and public discourses . . . emerged in Western Europe at different points in time together with the formation of the modern state" (*Formations* 205). This is where Cavanaugh's work, revisiting so-called wars of religion of the sixteenth and seventeenth centuries, is so beneficial, despite some oversimplifications in which his analysis might indulge and to which it could give rise (Shadle).

As Cavanaugh has emphasized, to define religion as pertaining to private sets of beliefs, perhaps uniting individuals in voluntaristic associations—as we moderns tend to do—and then to look back on the wars that ripped apart Europe in the sixteenth and seventeenth centuries and claim they were primarily fought over contested religious doctrines, is both anachronistic and overly simplistic. It is anachronistic in that religion, in our modern sense, was only then beginning to be redefined. The modern connotation of religion did not become normative until after those conflicts (Cavanaugh, *Myth* 57–122).

Furthermore, such textbook narrations obscure the utter complexity of the historical facts. It was easier to distinguish the sides along the lines of Catholic and Protestant affiliations prior to the St. Bartholomew's Day Massacre of 1572 (and perhaps Cavanaugh does not emphasize sufficiently these earlier conflicts in his work); afterwards, it is extremely difficult to make such neat and tidy distinctions. In many cases, these later conflicts were fought between Catholics and other *Catholics*—in what sense were they religious? Protestants often fought on either side of the conflicts. The Thirty Years' War is just one of Cavanaugh's prime cases in point, where the bloodiest last half of this, the most brutal so-called religious war, was waged primarily between the Habsburgs and the Bourbons, the two largest Catholic families of Europe. To assume that differing doctrines were the primary concern in these conflicts is to read modern assumptions back into the narratives, and to ignore the historical facts about the variety of Christian allegiances in these conflicts (Cavanaugh, *Myth* 123–80).

The new understanding of religion, as pertaining to private beliefs, was part of a larger program aimed at minimizing the authority of churches, and, in particular, of the Catholic Church. In Christendom, the Catholic Church had been the common unifying institution that affected virtually all aspects of society, culture, and family and work life, among others. European states after the Treaty of Westphalia (1648) attempted to replace Christendom's Catholic Church in each of their territories. Modern nationalism and secular nation-states were an attempt by the states to replace the authority that had previously been exercised by the Catholic Church in medieval Christendom, not spread across the globe, but within their controlled territories. Privatizing Catholicism, Calvinism, Judaism, and other such traditions and ways of life was one means of removing them from the newly created secular public sphere. The notion that these pre-1648 conflicts were fundamentally "religious" was a part of the new mythology that developed, serving to justify the privatization of commitments now deemed "religious." This new mythology contends that religions become violent when they enter the public realm, as in post-Reformation Europe. People kill one another because they believe different doctrines. Just look at the bloody wars of religion! Cavanaugh summarizes this narrative:

> The attempt to say that there *is* a transhistorical and transcultural concept of religion that is separable from secular phenomena *is itself* part of a particular configuration of power, that of the modern, liberal nation-state as it developed in the West. In this context, religion is constructed as transhistorical, transcultural, essentially interior, and essentially distinct from public, secular rationality. To construe Christianity as a religion, therefore, helps to separate loyalty to God from one's public loyalty to the nation-state. (Cavanaugh, *Myth* 9)

In the last several years, scholars have begun applying these and related genealogies of the modern concept of religion to the modern discipline of the academic study of religion. Two excellent examples of this are Brent Nongbri and Tomoko Masuzawa. Nongbri's text begins by underscoring the difficulties in defining religion (15–24). Like Feil, Nongbri explains that the ancients simply did not speak of religion the way we do; there never existed some generic phenomenological category out of which and from which culture, politics, economics, legal and juridical matters, among others, could be separated (25–45). Like other scholars, Nongbri identifies the transformation in the concept of religion as occurring in the early modern period (88–105). Nongbri concludes by demonstrating that the study of religion emerged in the seventeenth and eighteenth centuries (132–53).

Masuzawa's work has brought attention to the nineteenth-century colonial pressures that gave rise to the scholarly discussion of "world religions" (see next chapter in this volume, by Scott). Masuzawa's book concentrates on the emergence of "world religions" as a category, as well as on the pitting of Aryan versus Semitic, the de-Semitizing (over-Hellenizing) of Christianity—its Aryanization—and the re-Semitizing of Islam. Masuzawa observes that prior to the nineteenth century, Europeans tended to classify others as either Christians, Jews, or Muslims—whom they called Mohammedans—and everyone else as pagans, or idolaters, or something similar. In the nineteenth century, however, these groupings began to be categorized as "world religions" (xi).

The "reshuffling" of these categories is another instance of usefulness to early modern politics. Masuzawa notes this "was in fact part of a much broader, fundamental transformation of European identity" (xii).

One of the important figures in Masuzawa's narrative is Ernest Renan (171-78, 191-92), who was one of Loisy's most influential teachers. Masuzawa describes a process of nineteenth-century scholarly exaltation of things Indo-European, identified as racial Aryanism. At the same time, such scholars denigrated all things Semitic, focusing of course on Judaism. Philological work, like that of F. Max Müller, a "longtime correspondent" with Renan, played an important role here, supporting the colonial concerns of European nations (24-25, 172, 207-56). This shaped the European encounter with Buddhism, wherein Buddhism was valued as an Aryan religion (121-46). It also shaped European discussion of Islam, which was tied to practical colonial concerns, as Europe was in the process of carving up the Middle East. That is, re-Semitizing Islam, on implicitly anti-Semitic terms, helped justify European seizure of the lands of Muslim peoples (179-206). European scholars sought to "salvage" Christianity from its Jewish, and thus Semitic, heritage, by overly Hellenizing Christianity and de-Judaising it. This is where Renan played an important role (Masuzawa 191; Olender 112-29). As Masuzawa explains, "Renan's scientific interpretation of the biblical narrative thus relocated the generative moment of Hebrew history, lifting it away from the Garden of Eden (mythical origin) and away from Mount Sinai (sacrohistorical origin), and placing it squarely on the labor of several generations of prophets long after the fall of the Davidic kingdom" (192).

In part this nineteenth-century European scholarly emphasis, especially on East Asian religions, was directed against major "religious" institutions in Europe, as Masuzawa makes clear: "The image of the rational empire of the East was simply a very useful tool for sharply criticizing and denigrating, by means of contrast, what the proponents of the Enlightenment perceived as grievously benighted, hidebound institutions within their own society, in particular, the Catholic Church" (311).

ALFRED LOISY—*PRÊTRE*[1]

So where does Loisy fit into this narrative? Biblical interpretation is at the heart of the emergence of the modern nation-state and the origins of the con-

---

1. Despite his excommunication, and apparent abandonment of Christianity, Loisy's tombstone included the words: "Alfred Loisy, prêtre [priest]" (O'Connell, *Critics* 2). Loisy's friend, Maude Petre, depicted him as a deeply spiritual figure (Hill, "Maude" 834-51; see also Jacobs).

temporary usage of the word *religion*. Loisy has particular importance because he lies at the center of the conversation regarding the relationship of theology and biblical exegesis within the Catholic context. Loisy's life and work were a chief concern of the Roman Catholic modernist controversy at the dawn of the twentieth century. During this controversy, Catholic scholars who used modern historical biblical criticism were viewed with suspicion.[2] This historical context—both the controversial appropriation of such methods as well as the official and unofficial antimodernist measures taken in response—conditioned the development of Catholic use of modern biblical criticism down to the present moment (Morrow, "Fate"; "Modernist").

Moreover, the central debate about the relationship between faith and reason that emerged in the modernist controversy, and corresponding tensions between these Catholic scholars and the magisterium, were similar to the debates and tensions of the late 1960s and 1970s, which shaped a generation of scholars. Many older Catholic scholars of modernism find the struggles of the modernists to be relevant to their own struggles and tensions. William Portier captures well the broader significance of the controversy over modernism in the context of Catholic theology when he writes: "In the chronicle of Catholicism's protracted and ambivalent struggle with liberal secular states, the modernist crisis emerges as one in a continuing series of Catholic openings to the age. But it is the pivotal opening that gives shape to twentieth-century Catholic theology" (*Divided* 14).

Furthermore, Loisy represents an interesting case study because he was a scholar of ancient religion, among other related disciplines, and his once famous works have fallen into obscurity. A prolific scholar, he wrote on an incredibly vast array of topics in the development of Christian doctrine, biblical studies, Assyriology, and the history of religion, among other areas. At the time of his writing, his works were widely known, and he was notoriously controversial. His significance at his own time is a sufficient reason to return to his work today. Before examining his use of *religion*, it might be helpful to provide a brief sketch of his life.

Loisy was born in rural France in 1857.[3] The son of a farmer, Loisy felt inspired by a new parish priest to follow the path to priesthood when he was around the age of fourteen. At age fifteen he entered a Catholic secondary school, where he excelled in his studies in preparation for the seminary, which

---

2. On the modernist controversy, see Colin; García de Haro; Izquierdo; Jodock; O'Connell, *Critics*; Portier, *Divided*; Poulat, *Histoire*; Talar, "French"; *(Re)reading*.

3. To date, no critical biography exists of Loisy. Some helpful biographical sources include: Hill, *Politics* 12–35; Nichols 71–113; O'Connell, *Critics* 1–21, 62–69, 115–16, 126–40, 182–83, 234–54, 368–70; Poulat, *Alfred*.

he would enter two years later. Loisy enjoyed the five years of spiritual formation he received at the Seminary of the Diocese of Chalons-sur-Marne, but he was left unsatisfied with the low intellectual caliber of the classes. In 1878 his bishop sent him for further theological studies to the Institut catholique in Paris, where he learned more modern methods of historical enquiry from his church history professor, Louis Duchesne. With a brief hiatus after his ordination to the priesthood in 1879, Loisy returned to the Institut catholique in 1881. His mentor Duchesne arranged things in such a way that Loisy's earlier work counted towards degree requirements, and thus Loisy earned his bachelor's degree shortly after his return, and his licentiate in 1882. Already in 1881 Duchesne had arranged for Loisy to become an instructor of Hebrew at the Institut.

After receiving his license, Loisy began studying Egyptology (for only one year) and Assyriology (for four years) under internationally renowned scholars at the École pratique des hautes études. At the same time, he took courses in modern biblical criticism from Renan at the Collège de France. In 1889 Loisy successfully defended his Assyriology thesis on the royal annals of the Assyrian King Sargon II, but he had already added Assyriology to his Hebrew teaching requirements at the Institut ("Les Annales"). Upon the unexpected death of his thesis director a month later, he unsuccessfully attempted to replace him as Chair of Assyriology at the École. In 1890 Loisy successfully defended his doctoral dissertation in Scripture and became Professor of Sacred Scripture at the Institute. His new focus became the study of the Bible.[4] As others have noted, biblical criticism was at the very "heart of the modernist crisis" (Colin 115). In Loisy's scholarship, as well as in the classroom, he fully appropriated the methods of historical criticism. He read widely beyond the world of Francophone scholarship as the sources utilized in his footnotes indicate. His views on the nature of biblical inspiration as well as on historical matters, where he sided with the German Protestant historical critical scholars rather than with the Thomistic Catholic traditions of biblical interpretation, made him notorious in Catholic ecclesiastical circles, and landed him in trouble with the Pope as well as the Holy Office of the Inquisition, and some of his works were placed on the Index of Forbidden Books.[5]

In 1893, Pope Leo XIII issued his papal encyclical on Scripture, *Providentissimus Deus,* which, among other things, issued several cautions concerning

---

4. On Loisy's biblical scholarship, see Amsler 93–105; Baird 163–72; Colin 133–44, 151–63; Hill, *Politics* 59–89; Lahutsky; Morrow, "Alfred Loisy's Developmental"; "Loisy"; Talar, "Between"; "Innovation"; Théobald 391–92, 396–403, 418–21, 425, 432–38; Zumstein.

5. On his 1908 excommunication, as well as the controversies leading up to it, see Arnold, "Roman"; Arnold and Losito, *La censure*).

Catholic engagement with modern biblical criticism (269–92). Although not named explicitly, Loisy was one of the primary targets of Leo's encyclical (Hill, "Leo XIII" 40, 47, 51, 53, 56; O'Connell, *Critics* 133, 135). Loisy was forced to resign from his post at the Institut catholique the very same day *Providentissimus Deus* was issued. Loisy became a chaplain to a convent and continued to publish. By 1900 he began teaching again as a lecturer at the secular École pratique des hautes études, where a decade before he had graduated with a diploma in Assyriology. During the years leading up to the twentieth century, and in the immediate years that followed, Loisy published works of scholarship both in his name and pseudonymously. Matters were rapidly coming to a head, as Cardinal Richard of Paris began formally to censure some of Loisy's work and was submitting criticisms of Loisy's orthodoxy to the Holy Office. At the same time, the religious skeptic Prince Albert, the prince of Monaco, named Loisy as one of the three individuals he would be willing to nominate for the episcopal see of Monaco. Loisy was pleased at the thought of becoming a bishop and worked hard behind the scenes, albeit ultimately unsuccessfully, to make this a reality.[6]

In 1907 the Holy Office condemned sixty-five propositions it censured as "modernist," in its decree *Lamentabili sane exitu* (470–78), some of which were taken directly from Loisy's publications, and then, later that same year, Pope St. Pius X condemned modernism as "the synthesis of all heresies," in his papal encyclical *Pascendi dominici gregis* (593–650), also with the unnamed Loisy in mind.[7] The following year (1908) Pius X solemnly excommunicated Loisy. Loisy would then (1909) take up his post as Chair of the History of Religions at the Collège de France until his retirement in 1931. He continued to publish until 1939, the year before his death.

LA RELIGION IN LOISY'S WORK BEFORE HIS EXCOMMUNICATION

As such a prolific scholar, whose research pertaining to religion was so wide-ranging, Loisy serves as an interesting case study for nineteenth-century uses of *religion*. In what follows, I examine Loisy's use of *religion* in seventeen of his

---

6. On the ecclesiastical political background here, and how it affected Loisy's slippery writing at the time, see Hill, "French" 526; "Loisy's *L'Évangile*" 88–89; *Politics* 175–78; O'Connell, "Bishopric"; *Critics* 236–51.

7. For the background connecting Loisy's works to these documents, see Arnold, "Lamentabili"; Arnold and Losito *La censure*; *Lamentabili*. Loisy himself recognized that he was one of the main targets behind these documents (*Simples*).

books.[8] Although seventeen books might strike those unfamiliar with Loisy's literary corpus as extensive, they represent only a small fraction of his scholarly publications.

I limited the bulk of my study to Loisy's books prior to his excommunication. In these volumes under discussion, Loisy used the term *religion* 389 times.[9] Loisy is an excellent example of the narrative described at the beginning of this chapter in that the overwhelming majority of the instances in which he used *religion* (92 percent) were in some sense phenomenological, reflective of the modern shift in definition which reached its popular usage by the end of the nineteenth century. At one point Loisy explicitly identified Judaism, Christianity, and Islam as three distinct "religions" (*L'Évangile et l'Église* xvi). Loisy employed religion in this modern sense 358 times in the books I examined. Such plenteous examples included the following: "the religion of Moses" (e.g., *L'Évangile et l'Église* 47); "Israelite religion" (e.g., *Études bibliques* 45); "Babylonian religion" (e.g., *Les mythes babyloniens* 28); "the Jewish religion" (e.g., *La religion* 88); "the Christian religion" (e.g., *Histoire de canon de l'Ancien* 256); "pagan religions" (e.g., *Les mythes chaldéens* 1); "oriental religions" (e.g., *Les Évangiles I* 198); "monotheistic religion" (e.g., *Les proverbes* 35) or "monotheistic religions" (e.g., *La religion* 18); "polytheistic religions" (e.g., *La religion* 18); or even just the general category for study, "religion" (e.g., *Morceaux* 15) or "religions" (e.g., *L'Évangile et l'Église* 265); as well as the scholarly disciplines of "the history of religion" (e.g., *Histoire critique* 209) or "the history of religions" (e.g., *La religion* 5), and "the science of religions" (e.g., *Les mythes babyloniens* xiv). At one point, Loisy named Judaism and Christianity as religions in the context of a discussion of the Gospel of John. Here he contrasted Judaism as a "religion of ineffective symbols" whereas Christianity was a "religion of the spirit" (*Le quatrième* 371).

When Loisy defined "myth" he did so by way of reference to religion in its nineteenth-century context (Morrow, "Alfred Loisy"): "Myths are the dogmas of pagan religions" (*Les mythes chaldéens* 1). As was current in the study of religion at the end of the nineteenth century and early part of the twentieth century, Loisy addressed questions relating to the "development," "progress," or "evolution" of religion (*Le livre* 68; *La religion* 17–20). Loisy's resonance with modern understandings of religion as a generic category makes sense

---

8. I examined *Histoire de canon de l'Ancien*; *Les proverbes*; *Histoire du canon du Nouveau*; *Le livre*; *Histoire critique*; *Les mythes chaldéens*; *Les Évangiles II*; *Les mythes babyloniens*; *La religion*; *Études bibliques*, 2nd ed.; *Études évangéliques*; *L'Évangile et l'Église*; *Autour*; *Le quatrième*; *Le discours*; *Morceaux*; *Les Évangiles I*.

9. I am excluding here the instances of when he was quoting directly from someone else using the term *religion*, as well as when religion formed part of the title of a work he cited.

because he was a product of the nineteenth century. It is also significant, however, that Loisy was often in dialogue with scholars of religion who were influential in solidifying its contemporary meaning; scholars including Renan, Louis Auguste Sabatier, Adolf von Harnack, and later with Émile Durkheim (Cuchet; Loisy, *La religion* 16; "Sociologie" 45–76). Although this was not a focus of his work at this time, Loisy presumed the conclusions of contemporary scholars whose work solidified the modern concept of religion.

For Loisy, religion was social, communal, and involved ritual. He wrote, "History does not know of religion without cult [*culte*]" (*L'Évangile et l'Église* 221). This understanding of religion is what allowed Loisy to see Judaism, Christianity, and Islam as instances of religion; one can identify distinctive, communal rituals in each of these. Another instance of this understanding of religion can be found in two of his pseudonymously published articles (1898–1900), often referred to as his "Firmin" articles, because Loisy published them under his middle name, Firmin. The first article is entitled "The Individualist Theory of Religion," and the second one is "The Definition of Religion."[10] In these pieces one can see that, although Loisy shared in the modern understanding of religion, he was uncomfortable with the direction taken by some of his contemporaries.

In the first piece, "The Individualist Theory of Religion," Loisy wrote of the "religion of science"—the suggestion that science itself can be regarded as something akin to religion—and of the problem of the reduction of the notion of religion to the individual's personal and private spiritual needs, what Loisy calls "individualist" religion ("La théorie" 202). Loisy's main interlocutors here were Sabatier and Harnack, and he situated what he saw as their more Protestant-influenced focus on individualism within their critique of Catholicism. In the second article, "The Definition of Religion," Loisy returned to his critique of Sabatier and Harnack, underscoring how many others also viewed religion as basically about "religious sentiment" ("La définition" 193). For Loisy, religion was "private" in the sense that the degree of its presence in the public sphere should be determined by the appropriate secular authorities. Religion, for Loisy, was a private communal affair, not embodied in public governance. In contrast to many of his Protestant interlocutors, however, religion for Loisy was not "private" as in depending upon the individual person's invisible commitments. Religion involved communal ritual, and not just sentiment, nor merely faith; what distinguished the religion of Jews from the religion of

---

10. These were originally published respectively as Firmin, "La théorie"; Firmin, "La définition." English translations are available in Talar, *Prelude* 17–29, 31–44.

Christians was not simply their unseen religious sentiments and doctrinal consent but their differing visible rituals ("La définition" 200).[11]

Loisy also discussed the modern academic discipline of "history of religions" emphasizing again the communal nature of religion ("La définition," 194). Loisy wrote, "In every age and in every place, the idea of religion has been applied directly to the worship of divinity in the most extensive sense" ("La définition" 195). For Loisy, such religion was social, and of necessity included rites, morality, and specific beliefs. In his words, "Religion as it exists and has always existed is not conceivable without the symbols and the rites by which it is said to be described, created, maintained, and developed in the religious life common to the followers of the same cult" ("La définition" 196). As such, Loisy envisioned religion as a universal and essential part of being human, albeit expressed in different religions. His explanation was that "men are religious because they have within themselves the instinct of religion, as an innate respect for God and an innate need to confide in him" ("La définition" 206). This debate with Sabatier and Harnack should be viewed as an academic debate among those who presumed the modern conception of religion. Within that modern framework, Loisy chose to emphasize the external, social rituals denoting a religion, contra the Protestant move to view religion as primarily an unseen, private commitment to certain beliefs.[12]

Although, with the exception of his emphasis on communal as opposed to simply internal religion, Loisy's usage of *religion* matched the contemporary understanding of the term, it is noteworthy that there are thirty-one instances, accounting for 8 percent of Loisy's usage of *religion* in these texts, that bear more resemblance to the earlier premodern understanding of religion as a type of virtue. Occasionally, these uses of *religion* referred to an interior religious sentiment, but not one which was reductive; rather it was an interior disposition, specifically Christian in Loisy's usage. The contexts for most of these usages were in Loisy's comments on the New Testament. The other usages of *religion* in this nonmodern context pertain to virtuous works which please God.

In one of Loisy's works, his volume on the Sermon of the Mount, all five instances of his uses of *religion* were of this kind, as when he spoke of the religion of the publican, the humility of a repentant sinner (e.g., *Le discours* 72). At one point he described the Pentateuch as "a legislative work and a manual

---

11. See J. Barton Scott's chapter in this volume for the ways in which Protestantism—especially what he terms lowercase-*p* "protestantism"—reduces religion to private sentiment.

12. This distinction between modern academic uses of religion between Catholics and Protestants resonates with Mark Knight's discussion in this volume of a lingering Protestant bias in secular literary criticism of religion.

of religion" (*Études bibliques* 97). By *religion*, here, Loisy was not using it in the sense of a manual of the "Jewish religion" but rather of virtues pleasing to God. Throughout some of his volumes, Loisy returned to the same distinction between "the faith which one professes and the religion which one practices" (e.g., *Les Évangiles II* 38). Loisy wrote that God "proclaims that religion consists in respect and the practice of justice" (*La religion* 66). At times Loisy would write of "the religion of the heart" (e.g., *L'Évangile et l'Église* 103). In none of these instances was he focusing on religion as a generic category in which one can find instantiations in Buddhism, Judaism, Islam, Christianity, among others. The explanation for this particular usage is most likely the Catholic formation he received, including at the hands of members of religious orders, such as the Sulpicians, and also perhaps the emphasis on the thought of St. Thomas Aquinas during his years of seminary formation. That he could use *religion* in this way without any explanation for the seemingly dissimilar understanding indicates that other Catholics may have understood this usage as well; among such the previous usage had not yet fallen into complete disuse. This again demonstrates the narrative presented at the beginning of this chapter. Although religion had taken on a new primary meaning that was modern, there is indication that the traditional understanding still was a secondary definition in Catholic theological discourse. Loisy's uneven usage evidences the ending phase of this transition.

RELIGION AND THE SECULAR, CHURCH AND STATE

The intellectual habits of mind that facilitated Loisy's appropriation of modern categories for religion also informed his broader theological and political concerns. Loisy's scholarly work cannot be separated from his social, political, and historical context. Although his understanding of religion was representative of the period, it nonetheless influenced his decisions and actions beyond his scholarship. I therefore conclude this chapter with a final section examining one such context, Loisy's place in the debates over the Church's role in education in France. In brief, by the end of the nineteenth century, there was a growing movement in France bent on secularizing all of French education, so that even moral education would be taught as a secular subject, and thereby replacing the tradition of French Catholic moral education. Secularization of French education has a long history, even if we do not go back as far as the shift from the cathedral schools to the universities in the twelfth century (e.g., Quay 399–402). We find inklings of greater secularization in Napoleon's 1808 reconstitution of the entire French educational system under the French state.

Later nineteenth-century shifts saw the removal of the Catholic theology faculty from the Université de France in 1884, leaving only a Protestant theological faculty in its wake, which eventually would also be suppressed in the 1904 rulings prohibiting them from teaching, leading up to the 1905 French Law of the Separation of Church and State (Hill, "Loisy's 'Mystical'" 75–78; Tavard).

The ostensible push was for science to replace religion as the foundation of education. Loisy's teacher Renan was an important voice in this context before the latter's death in 1892. For a number of years in the last few decades of the nineteenth century, private schools were permitted to exist, with different degrees of oversight and restrictions—like Catholic institutions not being permitted to label themselves as universities, hence Institut catholique and not Université catholique. French scholarship within the history of religions emerged in this very context. As Harvey Hill explains, "The 'scientific' history of religions began to supplant Catholic theology in the secular university . . . The objective and historical investigation of religion at the secular university would, it was hoped, offer a corrective to the less scientific work done by theologians at Catholic institutions of higher learning" ("Loisy's 'Mystical'" 76–77). Thus, the French Parliament established a chair in the History of Religions at the Collège de France as early as 1879, a chair to which Loisy would be appointed in 1909. Needless to say, the Catholic bishops in France responded with their written protests. Pope Leo XIII tried to keep the peace with France's Third Republic, but he agreed with the French prelates on the matter of education.

Loisy's unpublished writings from the last several years of the nineteenth century provide a glimpse into his views, which differed sharply from Leo XIII's (e.g., *La crise* 35–504). Loisy's writings clearly showed his support for the secular autonomy of historical enquiry, including religious scholarship—and his thinking here predated his excommunication by more than a decade. Loisy likewise was in favor of the secularization of the public schools; the communal rites and theological teachings of religion did not belong in education sponsored by the government. One area where Loisy differed from the French secularizing trends, and which was closer to Leo's position, was on the matter of moral education, which Loisy thought remained in the Church's purview as it belonged to its religion. Loisy differed with Leo, however, on the state of moral education then current in the Church and found Leo's Thomism an unsatisfactory theological framework. Furthermore, Loisy found the Church too authoritarian; it was in dire need of decentralization, in his estimation.

Loisy saw an opportunity to implement his views with a bid for the episcopal see of Monaco. Recommended for the post by the atheist prince of Monaco, Loisy hoped to reform the Church and to relegate religion to a minimal role, compliant and submissive to state politics.[13] Hill explains, "Consistent with his support for separation and his opposition to the political pretentions of the pope, Loisy knowingly allowed himself to be used as a weapon against the Vatican in the developing struggle between Paris and Rome" ("Politics" 185). Loisy's episcopal candidacy was not approved by the Vatican, and after this failed attempt, as well as the battle of words between Pope Pius X and the French state in the wake of France's 1905 Law of Separation, Loisy published two anonymous articles attacking Pius X and the members of the Catholic hierarchy for their condemnations of the Laws of Separation, laws of which Loisy was an ardent supporter ("Réflexions"; "Sur l'encyclique"). Precisely because he shared in the contemporary view of religion as something instantiated in various religions that could be separated from "secular" life, Loisy was able to support the secularization process of traditionally Catholic French education. His view of religion, considered primarily in an academic setting, clearly had quite intentional reach beyond the world of scholars. This indicates the larger context pertaining to the evolving definition of religion. Loisy's is just one more instance demonstrating the political intentions (undermining Catholic authority) and practical impact (secularizing French education) underlying the definition of this term.

CONCLUSION

Given that Loisy's notion of a separation of church and state seems to fit the same sort of political context which gave rise to the modern definition of religion, coupled with the fact that his usage of the term *religion* is decidedly modern, one might assume that his political stance was chronologically prior. However, stating it in the reverse order is more accurate. Because he had the modern understanding of religion, it was consistent for Loisy to espouse a modern political stance that minimized the role of religion. Loisy's use of *religion* was conditioned by his scholarly reading, including the work of Renan; by Loisy's time at the end of the nineteenth century and early part of the twentieth century, religion had long been understood in the modern sense. The shift was far enough along that Loisy did not question it but assumed it, although the conventions of French society had not yet absorbed the modern dichotomy.

---

13. Episcopal appointments had long been a significant issue between the Catholic Church and states (Costigan; Morrow, *Three* 51–52; Portier, "Church Unity" 27–37).

Loisy's political leanings, particularly his position regarding the relationship between the church and state in France, were almost certainly strengthened by the modern notion of the essence of religion. This serves once again to demonstrate the initial narrative as to the change in the meaning of the term *religion*. This change in the understanding of religion set the stage for Catholic scholars such as Loisy to come into conflict with the magisterium of the Church. While in some early cases political convictions motivated an altered understanding of religion, in later cases such as this, the newly agreed-upon definition appears to have been the starting point for political convictions. The same intellectual habits and frameworks that influenced Loisy's political and theological positions coincided with those that make religion appear to be some abstract reality out there, of which Judaism, Christianity, Islam, Hinduism, among others, are but instantiations, variations of a theme separable from secular public and political spheres and, implicitly, best governed and held in check by the latter.[14]

WORKS CITED

Amsler, Frédéric. "Les sources des évangiles synoptiques de Loisy à la recherche actuelle." *Alfred Loisy cent ans après: Autour d'un petit livre: Actes du colloque international tenu à Paris, les 23–24 mai 2003*, edited by François Laplanche et al., Brepols, 2007, pp. 93–105.

Arnold, Claus. "'Lamentabili sane exitu' (1907). Das Römische Lehramt und die Exegese Alfred Loisy." *Journal for the History of Modern Theology / Zeitschrift für Neuere Theologiegeschichte*, vol. 11, 2004, pp. 24–51.

———. "The Roman Magisterium and Anti-Modernism." *Religious Modernism in the Low Countries*, edited by Leo Kenis and Ernestine van der Wall, Peeters, 2013, pp. 159–69.

Arnold, Claus, and Giacomo Losito, editors. *La censure d'Alfred Loisy (1903): Les documents des Congrégations de l'Index et du Saint Office*. Libreria Editrice Vaticana, 2009.

———, editors. *"Lamentabili sane exitu" (1907). Les documents préparatoires du Saint Office*. Libreria Editrice Vaticana, 2011.

Asad, Talal. *Formations of the Secular: Christianity, Islam, Modernity*. Stanford UP, 2003.

———. *Genealogies of Religion: Discipline and Reasons of Power in Christianity and Islam*. Johns Hopkins UP, 1993.

Baird, William. *History of New Testament Research*. Vol. 2: *From Jonathan Edwards to Rudolf Bultmann*. Fortress, 2003.

---

14. I owe Maria Morrow and Biff Rocha thanks for critiquing a draft of this chapter. This chapter was researched and, in an earlier form, written during my sabbatical leave while I was a visiting scholar at Princeton Theological Seminary during the 2015–16 academic year. I owe thanks to the administration and library personnel of Princeton Theological Seminary for their generosity, and to Seton Hall University's and Immaculate Conception Seminary's administration for granting me a sabbatical. I also owe thanks to the St. Paul Center for Biblical Theology for a generous sabbatical grant enabling me to complete this project.

Cavanaugh, William T. "'A Fire Strong Enough to Consume the House': The Wars of Religion and the Rise of the State." *Modern Theology*, vol. 11, no. 4, 1995, pp. 397–420.

———. *The Myth of Religious Violence: Secular Ideology and the Roots of Modern Conflict*. Oxford UP, 2009.

Colin, Pierre. *L'audace et le soupçon: La crise moderniste dans le catholicisme française (1893–1914)*. De Brouwer, 1997.

Costigan, Richard F. "State Appointment of Bishops." *Journal of Church and State*, vol. 8, 1966, pp. 82–96.

Cuchet, Guillaume. "La réception catholique des *Formes élémentaires de la vie religieuse* (1912) d'Émile Durkheim." *Archives de sciences sociales des religions*, vol. 159, 2012, pp. 29–48.

Feil, Ernst. "From the Classical *Religio* to the Modern *Religion*: Elements of a Transformation between 1550 and 1650." *Religion in History: The Word, the Idea, the Reality*, edited by Michel Despland and Gérard Vallée, Wilfrid Laurier UP, 1992, pp. 31–43.

———. *Religio: Die Geschichte eines neuzeitlichen Grundbegriffs vom Frühchristentum bis zur Reformation*. Vandenhoeck & Ruprecht, 1986.

———. *Religio Zweiter Band: Die Geschichte eines neuzeitlichen Grundbegriffs zwischen Reformation und Rationalismus (ca. 1540–1620)*. Vandenhoeck & Ruprecht, 1997.

———. *Religio: Dritter Band: Die Geschichte eines neuzeitlichen Grundbegriffs im 17. und frühen 18. Jahrhundert*. Vandenhoeck & Ruprecht, 2001.

———. *Religio: Vierter Band: Die Geschichte eines neuzeitlichen Grundbegriffs im 18. und 19. Jahrhundert*. Vandenhoeck & Ruprecht, 2007.

García de Haro, Ramón. *Historia teológica del modernismo*. Ediciones Universidad de Navarra, 1972.

Harrison, Peter. *"Religion" and the Religions in the English Enlightenment*. Cambridge UP, 1990.

Hill, Harvey. "French Politics and Alfred Loisy's Modernism." *Church History*, vol. 67, no. 3, 1998, pp. 521–36.

———. "Leo XIII, Loisy, and the 'Broad School': An Early Round of the Modernist Crisis." *Catholic Historical Review*, vol. 89, no. 1, 2003, pp. 39–59.

———. "Loisy's *L'Évangile et l'Église* in Light of the 'Essais.'" *Theological Studies*, vol. 67, 2006, pp. 73–98.

———. "Loisy's 'Mystical Faith': Loisy, Leo XIII, and Sabatier on Moral Education and the Church." *Theological Studies*, vol. 65, 2004, pp. 73–94.

———. "Maude Petre on Loisy's Religious Significance: Spirituality and Critical History." *Theological Studies*, vol. 69, 2008, pp. 834–51.

———. "The Politics of Loisy's Modernist Theology." *Catholicism Contending with Modernity: Roman Catholic Modernism and Anti-Modernism in Historical Context*, edited by Darrell Jodock, Cambridge UP, 2000, pp. 169–90.

———. *The Politics of Modernism: Alfred Loisy and the Scientific Study of Religion*. Catholic U of America P, 2002.

Izquierdo, César. "Cómo se ha entendido el 'modernismo teológico': Discusión historiográfica." *Anuario de Historia de la Iglesia*, vol. 16, 2007, pp. 35–75.

Jacobs, Joseph Harry. "The Last Modernist? The Spiritual Vision of Maude Dominica Petre." Dissertation, University of Dayton, 2003.

Jodock, Darrell, editor. *Catholicism Contending with Modernity: Roman Catholic Modernism and Anti-Modernism in Historical Context*. Cambridge UP, 2000.

Jones, Andrew Willard. *Before Church and State: A Study of Social Order in the Sacramental Kingdom of St. Louis IX.* Emmaus Academic, 2017.

Lahutsky, Nadia M. "Paris and Jerusalem: Alfred Loisy and Père Lagrange on the Gospel of Mark." *Catholic Biblical Quarterly,* vol. 52, 1990, pp. 444–66.

Leo XIII, Pope. "Litterae encyclicae De studiis scripturae sacrae." *Acta Sanctae Sedis,* vol. 26, 1893–94, pp. 269–92.

Anonyme [Loisy, Alfred]. "Réflexions d'un historien sur la letter précédente." *Libres entretiens,* 1905, pp. 438–52.

———. "Sur l'encyclique de Pie X." *Union pour la vérité,* 1906, pp. 162–75.

Firmin, A. [Loisy, Alfred]. "La définition de la religion." *Revue du clergé français,* vol. 18, 1899, pp. 193–209.

———. "La théorie individualiste de la religion." *Revue du clergé français,* vol. 17, 1899, pp. 202–15.

Loisy, Alfred. "Les Annales de Sargon, roi d'Assyrie." Thesis, École pratique des hautes études, 1889.

———. *Autour d'un petit livre.* 2nd ed., Alphonse Picard et Fils, 1903.

———. *La crise de la foi dans le temps présent (Essais d'histoire et de philosophie religieuses).* Edited by François Laplanche, Brepols, 2010.

———. *Le discours sur la montagne.* Alphonse Picard et Fils, 1903.

———. *Études bibliques.* 2nd ed., Alphonse Picard et Fils, 1901.

———. *Études évangéliques.* Alphonse Picard et Fils, 1902.

———. *L'Évangile et l'Église.* 2nd ed., L'auteur, 1903.

———. *Les Évangiles synoptiques I.* L'auteur, 1907.

———. *Les Évangiles synoptiques II.* L'auteur, 1908.

———. *The Gospel and the Church.* Translated by Christopher Home, Charles Scribner's Sons, 1912.

———. *Histoire de canon de l'Ancien Testament.* Letouzey et Ané, 1890.

———. *Histoire du canon du Nouveau Testament: Leçons d'Écriture sainte professées a l'École supérieure de théologie de Paris pendant l'année 1890-1891.* Maisonneuve, 1891.

———. *Histoire critique du texte et des versions de la Bible Tome I: Histoire du texte hébreu de l'Ancien Testament.* Rousseau-Leroy, 1892.

———. *Le livre de Job: Traduit de l'hébreu avec une introduction.* Rousseau-Leroy, 1892.

———. *Morceaux d'exégèse.* Alphonse Picard et Fils, 1906.

———. *Les mythes babyloniens et les premiers chapitres de la Genèse.* Alphonse Picard et Fils, 1901.

———. *Les mythes chaldéens de la création et du deluge.* Rousseau-Leroy, 1892.

———. *Les proverbes de Salomon.* Rousseau-Leroy, 1890.

———. *Le quatrième Évangile.* Alphonse Picard et Fils, 1903.

———. *La religion d'Israël.* Letouzey et Ané, 1901.

———. *Simples réflexions sur le Décret du Saint-Office Lamentabili sane exitu et sur l'Encyclique Pascendi dominici gregis.* L'auteur, 1908.

———. "Sociologie et religion." *Revue d'histoire et de littérature religieuses,* vol. 4, 1913, pp. 45–76.

Masuzawa, Tomoko. *The Invention of World Religions: Or, How European Universalism Was Preserved in the Language of Pluralism.* U of Chicago P, 2005.

Milbank, John. *Theology and Social Theory: Beyond Secular Reason.* Blackwell, 1990.

Morrow, Jeffrey L. "Alfred Loisy and les Mythes Babyloniens: Loisy's Discourse on Myth in the Context of Modernism." *Journal for the History of Modern Theology / Zeitschrift für Neuere Theologiegeschichte*, vol. 21, no. 1, 2014, pp. 87–103.

———. "Alfred Loisy's Developmental Approach to Scripture: Reading the 'Firmin' Articles in the Context of Nineteenth- and Twentieth-Century Historical Biblical Criticism." *International Journal of Systematic Theology*, vol. 15, no. 3, 2013, pp. 324–44.

———. "The Fate of Catholic Biblical Interpretation in America." *Weaving the American Catholic Tapestry: Essays in Honor of William L. Portier*, edited by Derek C. Hatch and Timothy R. Gabrielli, Pickwick, 2017, pp. 41–59.

———. "Loisy, Alfred Firmin." *Encyclopedia of the Bible and Its Reception Volume*. Walter de Gruyter, forthcoming.

———. "The Modernist Crisis and the Shifting of Catholic Views on Biblical Inspiration." *Letter & Spirit*, vol. 6, 2010, pp. 265–80.

———. "Secularization, Objectivity, and Enlightenment Scholarship: The Theological and Political Origins of Modern Biblical Studies." *Logos*, vol. 18, no. 1, 2015, pp. 14–32.

———. *Three Skeptics and the Bible: La Peyrère, Hobbes, Spinoza, and the Reception of Modern Biblical Criticism*. Pickwick, 2016.

Nichols, Aidan. *From Newman to Congar: The Idea of Development from the Victorians to the Second Vatican Council*. T&T Clark, 1990.

Nongbri, Brent. *Before Religion: A History of a Modern Concept*. Yale UP, 2013.

O'Connell, Marvin R. "The Bishopric of Monaco, 1902: A Revision." *Catholic Historical Review*, vol. 71, no. 1, 1985, pp. 26–51.

———. *Critics on Trial: An Introduction to the Catholic Modernist Crisis*. Catholic U of America P, 1994.

Olender, Maurice. *Les langues du Paradis. Aryens et sémites; un couple providential*. Gallimard, 1989.

Petre, Maude D. *Alfred Loisy: His Religious Significance*. Cambridge UP, 1944.

Pickstock, Catherine. *After Writing: On the Liturgical Consummation of Philosophy*. Blackwell, 1998.

Pius X, Pope. "Litterae encyclicae De modernistarum doctrinis." *Acta Sanctae Sedis*, vol. 40, 1907, pp. 593–650.

Portier, William L. "Church Unity and National Traditions: The Challenge to the Modern Papacy, 1682–1870." *The Papacy and the Church in the United States*, edited by Bernard Cooke, Paulist, 1989, pp. 25–54.

———. *Divided Friends: Portraits of the Roman Catholic Modernist Crisis in the United States*. Catholic U of America P, 2013.

Poulat, Émile. *Alfred Loisy, sa vie, son oeuvre*. Éditions du Centre national de la recherche scientifique, 1960.

———. *Histoire, dogme et critique dans la crise moderniste*. 3rd ed., Albin Michel, 1996.

Quay, Paul M. *The Mystery Hidden for Ages in God*. Peter Lang, 1995.

Shadle, Matthew A. "Cavanaugh on the Church and the Modern State: An Appraisal." *Horizons*, vol. 37, no. 2, 2010, pp. 246–70.

Supreme Sacred Congregation of the Holy Office and the Universal Inquisition. "Quo sub 65 propositionibus reprobantur ac proscribuntur praecipui errores reformismi seu modernismi." *Acta Sanctae Sedis*, vol. 40, 1907, 470–78.

Talar, C. J. T. "Between Science and Myth: Alfred Loisy on Genesis." *Mythos,* vol. 7, 2013, pp. 27–41.

———. "The French Connection: The Church's 'Eldest Daughter' and the Condemnation of Modernism." *U.S. Catholic Historian,* vol. 25, no. 1, 2007, pp. 55–69.

———. "Innovation and Biblical Interpretation." *Catholicism Contending with Modernity: Roman Catholic Modernism and Anti-Modernism in Historical Context,* edited by Darrell Jodock, Cambridge UP, 2000, pp. 191–211.

———, ed. *Prelude to the Modernist Crisis: The "Firmin" Articles of Alfred Loisy.* Translated by Christine E. Thirlway, Oxford UP, 2010.

———. *(Re)reading, Reception, and Rhetoric: Approaches to Roman Catholic Modernism.* Peter Lang, 1999.

Tanner, Norman P., editor. *Decrees of the Ecumenical Councils.* Vol. 2: *Trent to Vatican II.* Georgetown UP, 1990.

Tavard, George H. "Blondel's *Action* and the Problem of the University." *Catholicism Contending with Modernity: Roman Catholic Modernism and Anti-Modernism in Historical Context,* edited by Darrell Jodock, Cambridge UP, 2000, pp. 142–68.

Théobald, Christoph. "L'exégèse catholique au moment de la crise moderniste." *Le monde contemporain et la Bible,* edited by Claude Savart and Jean-Noël Aletti, Beauchesne, 1985, pp. 387–439.

Zumstein, Jean. "Alfred Loisy, commentateur de l'évangile selon Jean." *Mythos,* vol. 7, 2013, pp. 43–58.

CHAPTER 2

A Commonwealth of Affection

Modern Hinduism and the Cultural History of the Study of Religion

J. BARTON SCOTT

COMPARISON IN THE COLONIES

When Max Müller inaugurated his "Science of Religion" in the 1860s and '70s, he explained it with the slogan "He who knows one knows none" (qtd. in Sharpe 1; see also Molendijk). While scholars of religion have now left Müller and his comparative method mostly behind, something of his slogan's implicit impulse—a call to juxtapose seemingly divergent religious histories—remains an essential part of the field. Indeed, it is a method that can be applied quite fruitfully to Müller himself.

Victorian comparative religion sat at the intersection of at least three different histories. First, it was caught up with a late nineteenth-century shift in the meaning and usage of the term *religion* (see Morrow's discussion of this subject, and of related landmark scholarship, in this volume). Second, it coincided with the rise of the modern research university and the reorganization of the disciplines at the fin de siècle (Anderson and Valente 1–18). Third, it was implicated in empire. It is no coincidence that the German Müller spent most of his career in Britain: the East India Company agreed to underwrite his ambitious and expensive translation of the Vedas.

There was, at this time, a tactical alliance between empire and comparative religion. The grand theories promulgated by scholars like Müller helped colonial officials to, in David Chidester's words, achieve "local control in global terms" (*Savage Systems* 3). Metropolitan scholarship provided reliable data about religion that was crucial for colonial rule, dovetailing nicely with the more local forms of knowledge contained in gazetteers, legal manuals, censuses, and the like, as discussed by scholars like Chidester (*Savage Systems*) and Peter Gottschalk (*Religion, Science, and Empire*). It also provided ideological justification for empire, perhaps above all through the evolutionary paradigm that dominated comparative religion during the late nineteenth century.

But the connection between empire and comparative religion arguably went even deeper than this. As a number of scholars have argued, there is an intimate affinity between the comparative method and the regulatory impulse of modern colonialism. For comparative religion, as Chidester explains, "each religion has to be understood as a separate hermetically sealed compartment into which human beings can be classified and divided" (*Savage Systems* 4). To highlight the political stakes of this procedure, Chidester terms this mode of study "apartheid religion." Its logic of disjuncture underwrites the rule of racial cultural difference that was so central to empire.

The artificial tidiness of the comparative method was, however, belied by the complicated, transnational history of the discipline of comparative religion itself. As Chidester has recently shown in *Empire of Religion*, the beginnings of the discipline are to be found in Calcutta or Cape Town as much as in London or Leiden. Comparative religion took shape in the colonies as well as the metropole, and so its history needs to be studied contrapuntally (to use Edward Said's term), with close attention to the intimate connections between metropolitan centers of learning and the colonial field. In other words, comparative religion needs to pursue a methodological shift already being made by scholars of comparative literature, such as Pascale Casanova (*The World Republic of Letters*) and Rey Chow (*The Age of the World Target*), who are increasingly turning from the comparative "grid" to the study of historical networks of literary production.

Toward this end, this chapter asks what it would look like to situate Hindu reformism as part of the cultural history of the study of religion in the nineteenth century. It is already a well-established fact that India played an integral role in the emergence of the comparative human sciences, including the study of religion (see Halbfass). Building on this work, this chapter makes three interrelated arguments. First, and most minimally, I introduce scholars of Victorian literature to contemporaneous Indian intellectuals with whom they might be less familiar, as a means of arguing for the critical importance of the colonial world to nineteenth-century culture. Second, I encourage renewed attention in literary studies to the complex material entanglements of "religion" and "literature" as contested cultural fields inseparable from the history of institutions. Third, I draw attention to the transcolonial traffic in cosmopolitan affect that, I argue, was one important hinge for the construction of "religion" as a globalizing concept in the nineteenth century.

In what follows, I suggest that writings of the Brahmo Samaj, a nineteenth-century Hindu reform society, demonstrate a tension that is arguably characteristic of Victorian religion more broadly—a tension between affect and institution, between a protestant-Romantic notion of intense inward experience and the bureaucratic forms of the modern nation-state. While scholars of religion now widely recognize the extent to which protestant[1] preconceptions have shaped the field since Müller (if not longer), more work needs to be done to analyze the transnational reach of protestantism within the nineteenth century so that we might better understand how it was reinvented as it moved (cf. Scott). This chapter contributes to that larger effort by highlighting how Brahmo thinkers like Keshub Chunder Sen and Protap Chunder Mozoomdar reworked a protestant-Romantic interest in affect or sentiment in order to articulate a distinctive political project. Sen and Mozoomdar, I argue, sought to articulate a mode of affective cosmopolitanism that was destructive of difference per se and thus unsettling to the gridlines of apartheid religion. For these Brahmos, comparative religion was less a means of establishing universal truth than of proliferating cosmopolitan affective bonds that would eventually, Mozoomdar implied, come to form a global "commonwealth of affection." While this utopian project was never successfully translated into institutional form (and indeed perhaps never could have been, given its constitutive opposition to routinized institutions), it nonetheless calls our attention to one important axis around which "religion" was constructed in the nineteenth century—and, indeed, on into the twentieth.

AN INSTITUTIONAL HISTORY FOR "RELIGION"

By paying attention to how institutions like the modern research university shape and constrain religion, we as scholars can avoid the temptation to view religion as something radically deinstitutionalized—to view religion, in other words, in protestant fashion, as unconstrained inward faith or belief. Thanks to a generation's worth of robust critique, scholars working in religious studies departments are now acutely aware of the extent to which "protestant bias" has shaped the study of religion since Müller's time. During the conversations that went into making this volume, it became evident that this critique is perhaps less well known in literary studies. This would seem to pose a significant

---

1. See below for explanation of spelling "protestant/ism" with a lowercase *p*.

methodological problem, however, in that the study of religion and literature may be especially prone to protestant bias (on this topic, see also Knight's chapter in part II of this volume).

In spelling "protestant" with a lowercase "p," I follow Winnifred Fallers Sullivan. As she explains in her study of American legal secularism, this term designates "a set of political ideas that emerged in early modern Europe in and after the Reformation" to shape the practice and legal governance of religion. Religion, from the protestant perspective, is "understood as being private, voluntary, individual, textual, and believed." Lowercase "protestant" thus does not refer to a particular set of theological commitments (Catholics can be "protestant," and Protestants don't have to be); rather, it indicates one common configuration of the background conditions of religious belief in secular modernity (Sullivan 7–8; Taylor 13–14; see Morrow in this volume).

For the study of religion and literature, two of these traits seem most pertinent: protestant religion centers on (a) intensely inward individual experiences that are (b) triggered by texts. Both of these traits are quite evident in late nineteenth-century comparative religion—emblematized on the one hand by William James's *Varieties of Religious Experience* (1902) and, on the other, by the fifty volumes of Müller's *Sacred Books of the East*, published between 1879 and 1910. In looking for the essence of religion, one set of scholars turned to books (and imposed a scriptural model even on religious contexts in which texts had previously been peripheral); another turned to mystical experience.

On both fronts, comparative religion had strong literary precedent. In the early nineteenth century, Romantic poets like Coleridge had worked to align notions of inspired literary genius with ideas about religious inspiration (see the chapters in part III of this volume, especially those by Scheinberg and LaPorte). Literature, as a domain for the production and circulation of inspired texts, was carefully positioned as a possible complement to or replacement for a religion that was itself being rendered in literary terms as centering on acts of reading. For an example of this phenomenon, one might turn to William Howitt, a Quaker poet who in the 1830s and '40s left the Society of Friends to look for expressions of the inner light elsewhere, especially in Romantic poetry. For him, Wordsworth's poems in particular seemed a "very Bible of Quakerism" (qtd. in Scott 79). Howitt's ability to move between these two cultural fields (religion and literature) was enabled not only by a historically specific alignment between poetic and mystical inspiration but also by the broader protestant reduction of "authentic" religion to textually mediated individual experience. Nor was this protestant cultural space limited to confessing Protestants—as suggested, for example, by the precocious young Benthamite J. S. Mill's similarly inward encounter with Wordsworth in the 1820s.

In order to avoid falling into an overly protestant model of religion, then, we need to be careful not to abstract literary religion from its broader material and institutional contexts. These contexts could include the history of Victorian print culture and the religious uses of the book as physical object in the Victorian home (see Carpenter in part II of this volume; King). They could also include histories of organizations like the London Browning Society, which drew on the institutional forms of Victorian Christianity to position literature as the object of reverential group study (see LaPorte, part III of this volume).

It is especially important to emphasize the history of institutions in the early twenty-first century, at a moment when, as George Packer (*The Unwinding*) and Wendy Brown (*Undoing the Demos*) have argued, neoliberal policies and attitudes have substantially eroded institutional life. Religion played a significant role in shaping this mistrust of institutions, not least through the continued salience of the protestant ideal of the solitary believer to neoliberal thinkers like Margaret Thatcher, as Eliza Filby has shown (*God and Mrs. Thatcher*). To press at this ideal and to suggest its ideological instability is thus to push back against neoliberalism at a constitutive node in its ideological articulation. There is, of course, ample precedent for such work, ranging from Gauri Viswanathan's exploration of the institutional field that structures the ostensibly "individual" experience of conversion (*Outside the Fold*) to Janice Radway's studies of the institutional histories of reading and literary "taste" (*A Feeling for Books*). Here, my aim is simply to bring some of these tools to bear on the study of modern Hinduism and the Brahmo Samaj. The inward religious experiences prized by Brahmos were shaped and constrained by a variety of institutions, including the discipline of comparative religion itself.

As a scholar of modern South Asian religions, I am struck by the extent to which the Hindu "Orient" in English was, with respect to institutions, very much two-faced. On one side, Hinduism was seen as an oppressively absolute system of priestcraft that bound the Hindu masses to an institutional apparatus even more inescapable than the Catholic Church (see Scott 1–30). On the other, it provided a touchstone for the Romantics' interest in mystical interiority, for religion as radically liberated from institutions. This all-or-nothing approach to Hindu institutions pulls attention away from the very institutions that were redefining elite Hinduism in the nineteenth century. Chief among these, perhaps, were civic associations like the Brahmo Samaj that not only mediated Hinduism's relationship to the wider anglophone world but also worked to reshape Hinduism within India. It is to the Brahmos, then, that I now turn.

THE BRAHMO SAMAJ AND COMPARATIVE RELIGION

In the nineteenth century, Calcutta was the second-largest city in the British Empire and one of the largest and most cosmopolitan cities in the world. The sailors, merchants, intellectuals, and artists who roamed its streets and markets spoke not only Bengali but also English, Hindustani, Malay, Arabic, and Chinese, and they were plugged into the latest intellectual and cultural movements of Europe and Asia.

The Brahmo Samaj was at the crux of these competing currents. Founded in the 1820s, the society promulgated a rationalist religion that appealed to Calcutta's Hindu elite as well as Unitarians, deists, and others. By midcentury, the society had emerged as a major player within what is sometimes called the Bengal Renaissance, providing the template for a "bourgeois Hinduism" that shaped colonial public culture well beyond its own relatively circumscribed circles (Hatcher, *Bourgeois Hinduism* 3–18). Like any new religious movement, the Brahmo Samaj also had its fair share of internal tensions and schisms. The most important of these were related to Keshub Chunder Sen, the charismatic young leader who joined the society in 1857. Sen garnered a following of young men, whose resistance to traditional Hindu customs prompted a generational cleavage among the Brahmos that, in 1866, prompted the society to split into two competing groups. After the split, Sen continued to court controversy, including by founding his own syncretic religion, the New Dispensation, in 1881.

Even as they maintained strong roots in Calcutta, the Brahmos also looked outward to the rest of India and beyond. By the late 1840s the Brahmos had begun to missionize in rural east Bengal (now Bangladesh), where they met with considerable success. In the late 1860s and early 1870s they expanded across India, using English as their principal linguistic medium and Sen as their principal spokesperson. Between the 1870s and '90s Brahmo missionizing went global, largely via the work of Protap Chunder Mozoomdar, whom I discuss in depth below. Although the Brahmos retained their influence through the end of the century, their heyday was coming to a close. Membership in the society reached its peak around 1912 and declined thereafter, with younger progressives mostly losing interest in the Brahmos after the 1930s (Kopf 332–34).

Global Brahmoism was closely related to the discipline of comparative religion. In the 1860s, when Müller was promoting his "science of religion," Brahmos were using this very phrase to indicate something quite similar: a comparative method that could uncover the natural laws governing religion and thus facilitate the discovery of universal religious truth (Kopf 67). For example, in his *Defense of Brahmoism and the Brahmo Samaj* (1863), Rajnarain Bose suggested that Brahmoism had outpaced Christianity in the science of religion because it was able to combine "unity in essentials" with a tolerance for "variety in non-essentials"; applying the principles of "natural religion" to various scriptures, he suggested, would unite humanity in its feelings of piety while also allowing for variation in custom (Kopf 67–68). Bose continued his experiments in the science of religion into the 1870s, although he was not alone. Keshub Chunder Sen's 1880 promise "to apply the unity of science to God" was in much the same vein (Kopf 68).

It was Sen who made the connection to Müller direct and personal. The two men met on Sen's 1870 trip to England and, among other activities, paid a collective visit to Edward Pusey at Oxford. After this visit, the two seem to have lost touch for several years before striking up a correspondence in the early 1880s. In these letters, Müller offers advice to Sen about the scandals that had erupted around him by this time. Sen, meanwhile, explicitly aligns his New Dispensation with Müller's comparative religion: "We are giving effect to the 'Science of Religion' of which you are the most distinguished leader" (2 May 1881, qtd. in Müller, *Keshub Chunder Sen* 40). What comparative religion was doing at the level of theory, in other words, the Brahmos were doing at the level of practice—"giving effect" to comparative religion by writing it into the daily textures of devotional life.

The history of the Brahmo connection to comparative religion, however, began well before Müller. Brahmos had been writing about a "natural religion" that would unify races and nations since at least the time of Akkoy Kumar Dutt's work of the 1840s and '50s (Kopf 50–51). If the starting point is to be found anywhere, it is with the polymath Rammohun Roy, who founded the Brahmo Samaj and whose strongly Unitarian orientation led him to look for commonalities among Hinduism, Christianity, and Islam. Roy was close with several British Unitarians, and the Brahmo–Unitarian connection remained strong through the 1890s (Kopf 3–41). Christian Unitarianism shaped the Brahmo Samaj, and vice versa: Unitarianism, as Lynn Zastoupil argues, "came of age with the British empire," and its history is inseparable from the "triangular circuit" linking Britain, Bengal, and New England (23, 8). Unitarianism later went on to play a significant role in the rise of Victorian comparative religion, providing some of the key theological vocabulary for the discourse of pluralism that took hold by late century. Insofar as the Brahmos shaped Unitarianism, then, they were part of the history of the new discipline even before that discipline emerged as such in the 1860s.

Although Brahmos were integral players in this history, they were not therefore equal players. There was a necessary structural difference between comparison in the colony and comparison in the metropole. Already in the 1820s, Roy approached Christianity as the "standard" against which Hinduism had to be judged (Kopf 13). By later in the century, the Christian yardstick would become still more firmly established as the basis for religious comparison, especially within the evolutionary paradigm that dominated Victorian comparative religion—for which "Eastern" religions were merely progenitors of the more advanced monotheistic religions of the West (Masuzawa 1–36). Brahmo writers responded to such claims by resisting evolutionary classification. Thus, for example, in his *Comparative Studies in Vaishnavism and Christianity* (1899), Brajendranath Seal rejected the evolutionary paradigm by insisting that "historical comparison implies that the objects compared are of co-ordinate rank and belong more or less to the same stage in the development of known culture" (qtd. in Kopf 62). Comparison implies contemporaneity or, at least, coevality.

This colonial power imbalance is, however, only the beginning of the story. The Brahmo intervention into comparative religion went well beyond overt correctives to imperial ideology to include innovative reimaginings of what comparison could be and do. Much of this reimagination proceeded from a method that was often presented as a site of failure for the Brahmos but which became central to their distinctive idiom of comparison: eclecticism.

THE POLITICS OF ECLECTICISM

The Brahmo Samaj was routinely described (and, indeed, often described itself) as an "eclectic" religious movement (Hatcher, *Eclecticism* 3–21). One period chronicler glossed this designation as follows: "The word *eclectic* means choosing from. It was applied to certain philosophers in ancient times who did not attach themselves to any particular sect, but selected from opinions and principles of each what they thought true and good" (Murdoch 1). Despite its ubiquity, this word tended to produce ambivalence among the Brahmos. Eclecticism, it was said, established an inferior form of religion in that it failed to forge a new, higher religious truth, opting instead to simply cobble together the inadequate pieces of the old.

It was, however, precisely this indeterminate quality that was most generative for the Brahmos. Eclecticism permitted a mode of cosmopolitan thought that pulled away from particulars, but without ever leaving those particulars behind to constitute a new universalism.[2] Where Keshub Chunder Sen

---

2. The implicit distinction that I draw in this chapter between universalism and cosmopolitanism grows out of postcolonial theory's dueling commitments to cultural particularity

exploited this indeterminate quality to develop a distinctive spiritual hermeneutics (Scott 105–12), Protap Chunder Mozoomdar used it to structure his notion of the "commonwealth of affections"—a political body that almost, but never quite, amounts to more than a sum of its parts.

I develop my reading of Mozoomdar below. First, however, I want to note some of the other principal uses of Brahmo eclecticism. At least three of these have been explored in the existing scholarship. First, Brahmo eclecticism worked to align modern Hinduism with the Enlightenment ideal of individual autonomy. As Brian Hatcher suggests, eclecticism's emphasis on choice or "conscious selection" resonates strongly with one of the core tropes of high modernity: that the critical judgment of the individual is what liberates the individual from tradition. For the eclectic, it is the act of choosing, and not the object of choice, that matters most (*Eclecticism* 8).

Second, Brahmo eclecticism was a power play, a means of subordinating difference through inclusion (Hacker). All religions are equal, Brahmos implied, but some religions are more equal than others. While any of the extant faiths might be a viable path to the divine, only the neo-Vedantin theology of the Brahmos can adequately describe the interrelations among these faiths. Since the nineteenth century, such claims have played an important role in reinforcing the hegemony of India's Hindu majority, as well as providing grounds for erroneously contrasting "tolerant Hinduism" with "intolerant Islam" (Hatcher, *Eclecticism* 35; Adcock 1–22).

Third, Brahmo eclecticism fueled the emergence of the linguistic style that Srinivas Aravamudan has dubbed "Guru English." Its cross-cultural pastiche paved the way for the later linguistic experiments of a G. V. Desani or a Salman Rushdie and helped to move English from a language of imperial command to one of cosmopolitan experimentation.

I would add a fourth use to this list. Brahmo eclecticism was, at times, a means of trying to imagine a mode of universalism emptied of particularity. It leeched religious particulars of their significance, rendering them up as

---

and to global forms of political consciousness. As Leela Gandhi observes, universalisms are plagued by an "endemic particularism," a consistent failure of their advocates to "transcend their own interests. Universalisms are always French, German, British, American, Christian, and so on, and thence, Indian, Kenyan, Muslim, Chinese, as well" ("Pauper's Gift" 33–34). For postcolonial theory, then, the problem becomes one of how to articulate political collectivity across identity categories, but without thereby promoting one such identity to the status of an ostensible universal that is actually a crypto-particularism. Brahmo eclecticism, I am suggesting, offers one possible means of doing this—and one that resonates with the scholarly recuperation of "cosmopolitanism" as a sort of off-universalism, a situated globalism that refuses to efface the differences that it interlinks.

tepid pastiche, in order to rethink the problematic of religious difference per se. In 1820 Rammohun Roy expressed his hope that God would "render religion destructive of all differences" (qtd. in Scott 85). In the 1860s and '70s, I have suggested in *Spiritual Despots*, Keshub Chunder Sen tried to realize this hope by developing a distinctive religious hermeneutic based on the Christian missionary notion of prefiguration or fulfillment. Christian theologians had developed this notion as a means of Christianizing the Hebrew Bible; its Jewishness could be erased, in whole or in part, by rereading its major events as anticipations of Jesus (thus, the Passover lamb becomes a prefiguration of the crucifixion, which fulfills and subsumes it). In India some missionaries had applied the same hermeneutic to Hinduism, which was likewise said to find its fulfillment in Christianity.

Sen adopted this hermeneutic as the basis for his New Dispensation: all religions would find their fulfillment in his eclectic faith. One might think that this New Dispensation would simply put Hinduism in the hegemonic position once claimed by Christianity—that neo-Vedanta would become the master theology for the Brahmo eclectic. Without denying that this was one outcome of the New Dispensation, I suggest that it was not the only possibility implicit in Sen's work. Rather, as though pursuing Roy's call to reimagine the very problematic of religious difference, Sen developed a distinctive hermeneutic based around a technical usage of the word *spirit*. For Sen, "spirit" became a technology for putting the historical particularity of any given religion under erasure in order to gesture toward a mode of universality that exists—spectrally—only through the absent presence of these particulars (Scott 85–118). This project responded directly to the apartheid function of comparative religion. In Sen's hands the gridlines separating religions become unstuck. Like other Brahmos, he approaches religions as storehouses of convertible forces that can be rerouted to create new forms of human sociality (Scott 92). The utopian potential implicit in this project remained unrealized, however, and necessarily so, insofar as it relied on volatile flows of affect as the ground for the coming global community.

In his writings Sen uses the word *sympathy* to denote the affective bonds between persons. Sympathy, he writes, is the "electric fluid" that causes "little individualities" to "coalesce and combine" through the "natural affinity of spirits" (qtd. in Scott 106–7). Sympathy does to the self-possessed liberal individual what Sen's spiritual hermeneutic had done to self-contained religions: it undoes apartheid segmentation to produce more cosmopolitan cultural and social forms.

A July 1883 letter from Sen to Müller makes this connection quite clearly. Here, Sen uses the language of affect, and the conceit that affect can bring about a communion of spirits, to reimagine the discipline of comparative religion. Sen assures Müller that, although he does not write as often as he would like, his friend is often in his thoughts:

> The affinity is not only ethnic, but in the highest degree spiritual, which often draws you into my heart and makes me enjoy the pleasures of friendly intercourse. I forget the distance, and feel we are very near each other. These Himalayas ablaze with India's ancient glory constantly remind me of you, and as I read your lectures ... in the veranda of my little house in the morning, I feel so intensely the presence of your spirit in me that it seems I am not reading your book but talking to you and you are talking to me in deep spirit-intercourse. (qtd. in Müller, *Keshub Chunder Sen* 43)

At the heart of this passage is a sense of spiritual affinity as an electric current that can draw persons and nations together en route to utopian, transnational forms of collectivity. While the affinity between Sen and Müller is "ethnic" (that is, based on the shared Indo-European identity highlighted by Müller's linguistic research), it is also "spiritual"—based in a more personal ethic of affective connection and friendship (cf. Gandhi, *Affective Communities*). If the ethnic connection operates within the disjunctive logic of the racialized comparative disciplines, Sen's politics of affective connection is far less contained.

Sen calls Müller to mind in a way that echoes the mental "pilgrimages" he had encouraged among his followers a few years previously; adherents of the New Dispensation were to meditate on "saints" like Moses "to commune with them in spirit.... We enter into them, and they enter into us" (qtd. in Scott 110). Here, this spirit-intercourse betokens friendship, not worship, and it is mediated by the printed text. Sen's Himalayas become shot through with traces of Müller, with the play of textual absence (and the Orientalist reduction of India to text) inciting the love and longing of spiritual fraternity. The interleaving of text and world becomes an operator of friendship: it mixes subjects so that, caught in spiritual intercourse, they become difficult or impossible to disentangle. The end result of comparative religion, then, is not the truth of the book but affective connection or community.

A similar principle undergirds the work of Sen's friend and follower, Protap Chunder Mozoomdar. Where Sen seems interested mostly in spontaneous connection, Mozoomdar works to fit the affective bonds of spiritual affinity within a more elaborately philosophical narrative about the historical development of religion. It is to that narrative that we now turn.

TOWARD A COMMONWEALTH OF AFFECTION

In the late nineteenth century, Protap Chunder Mozoomdar was the Brahmo Samaj's major publicist outside of India. Between 1874 and 1900 he made a series of trips to Britain and the US, lecturing widely to religious and other groups, and meeting with prominent public figures ranging from Max Müller to John Henry Newman to Harriet Beecher Stowe. His status as the global face of Brahmoism was cemented in 1893, when he served as the Brahmo Samaj's delegate to the World's Parliament of Religions in Chicago.

Mozoomdar's spin on Brahmoism was strongly informed by Sen, his cousin and close friend. But where Sen had carefully maintained the ambiguity of the New Dispensation, refusing to align it clearly with any extant religious system, Mozoomdar tended to conflate it with Christian Unitarianism. This tendency, already evident in books like *The Oriental Christ* (1883), became more pronounced after Sen's death in 1884. Mozoomdar's Christian proclivities may have alienated his fellow Brahmos, but they were the secret to his success abroad (Kopf 18–23). Like Rammohun Roy decades earlier, he accrued an eager audience of Unitarians, smitten with a foreign visitor whose exotic mien became a visual icon for the religious cosmopolitanism to which both they and he aspired (cf. Dobe 109–46).

Mozoomdar's own effort to articulate a cosmopolitan religious politics is evident in two texts from the early 1890s. In the first of these, his lecture at the World's Parliament of Religions, he articulates his eclectic theology from within the institutional forms of Victorian liberalism. In the subsequent book, *The Spirit of God* (1894), he develops a narrative about the historical unfolding of spirit-affect that presents a challenge to liberalism as the basis for global politics. Both texts are structured around a tension that I take to be formative for religious movements of this period—a tension between affect and institution. Here, this takes the form of a constitutive contradiction between the connective powers of sentiment and the segmented bureaucratic forms of the modern representative state. Mozoomdar's attempt to reconcile connective sentiment and segmenting bureaucracy is deftly summarized in a phrase from *The Spirit of God*: Mozoomdar dreams of a "commonwealth of affection" that would harness spiritual affect to create a global political community that moves beyond the segmentation of religions and nations.

The tension between affect and institution is palpable in the 1893 lecture "The World's Religious Debt to Asia." This speech rehearses an idea that also featured prominently in Swami Vivekananda's Chicago address at the same Parliament of Religions—that the "Orient" would redeem the West by supplementing its materialistic civilization with otherworldly spirituality. Mozoomdar's distinctive twist on this tale is to insist on the innate link between Asia and affect: "Asia is the land of impulse. Religion there has always meant sentiment, joyousness, excitation, excitement in the love of God and man" (1087). For Mozoomdar, the apogees of Asian religions are figures like the madman-poet Hafiz, the entranced Prophet Muhammad, and the dancing "Hebrew Miriam." His ideal devotee "cries, he laughs, he sings, he dances, he falls into a trance," all from the rapture of divine love (1088).

There is, however, a certain situational irony in these words. What could be less madly ecstatic than a parliament? There was further irony—and, to my mind, considerably more of it—when Mozoomdar went on to insist that the "East . . . cultivates the habit of devotional silence" (1088). Victorian religion, whether in India or elsewhere, was many things; short on words it was not. For the loquacious Mozoomdar, as for so many of his contemporaries, the act of public speaking was inseparable from the practice of religion. Adapting a phrase from Walter Bagehot, I would term this mode of religiosity "devotion by discussion" (Bagehot 158).

If Mozoomdar registers discontent with the procedural ethos of liberal religion, this should come as no surprise. Within the history of the Brahmo Samaj, affect had been central to the Sen faction's rebellion against the society's sober senior generation. As Mozoomdar later reported of his early days with Sen: "With me and my companions, the prevailing feature of religious life was an extreme sentimentalism. There was no end to our weeping at the time of prayer and sermon" (Barrows xxx). In their pursuit of sentiment, the young Brahmos were, to some extent, class-slumming. They were appropriating the demotic religion of Bengal's Vaishnavas and using it to offend bourgeois mores. By the time it got to Chicago, Brahmo sentimentalism was also firmly entangled with a Romanticist-protestant interest in mystical inspiration. Across all of these fields, religion was conceived of as—to borrow a phrase from an 1883 Mozoomdar lecture—an "unutterable impulse" that is only later expressed through ceremonies and symbols ("Protestantism in India").

Of course, in setting himself up as giving utterance to the unutterable, Mozoomdar created a discursive game that was, by definition, irresolvable. Precisely in its constitutive irresolution, however, the tension between mad affect and sober parliamentarianism proved productive for Mozoomdar. I would suggest that it placed him at odds with the taxonomical logic of the World's Parliament of Religions and pointed him toward the (ultimately unsuccessful) attempt in *The Spirit of God* to rethink that logic.

As several scholars have argued, the World's Parliament of Religions exemplified the world religions discourse that was taking shape in the 1890s, in that it presumed that religions are discrete and reified entities that can be arrayed alongside one another in a representational grid. It was a museum of faiths, a visual presentation of cultural and religious difference that was perhaps more analogous to the spectacular displays of global goods and cultures available elsewhere at the Columbian Exposition than to the workings of an actual legislative body (Ziolkowski 1–22; Seager 1–19). The parliamentary trappings of the event were, however, more than a red herring. There was a deep structural affinity between the two different logics of representation behind this event, which I would term the *parliamentary* and the *museological*.[3] Delegates to the parliament were political representatives, speaking on behalf of implied constituencies, as well as symbolic representatives, standing in for a religious whole that is created partly through such acts of semiotic representation (in the same way that an ethnographic artifact in a museum represents a people or culture). These two sets of gridlines, each associated with a major nineteenth-century institution, worked in tandem to structure and, ultimately, to limit the parliament's aspirational cosmopolitanism. Although its organizers may have tried to use the mobile category "religion" to think beyond the divisions of nations and creeds, they were unable to do so. Instead, they underscored those divisions by endorsing a notion of religious pluralism that was indebted to both the taxonomies of the human sciences and the segmentations of the bureaucratic nation-state. In Mozoomdar's speech, by my reading, affective excess pushes against these constraints. It cannot, however, push past them. Brahmo sentimentalism remains trapped within liberal parliamentarianism, unable to produce a new mode of politics.

I read *The Spirit of God* (1894) as an attempt to move beyond this impasse. The book asks whether connective affect can transform liberal cosmopolitanism into a looser and more expansive mode of global alliance. *The Spirit of God* is a work of comparative theology that seeks to reconcile Hindu and Christian doctrines of "the spirit"—a term that, for Mozoomdar, connotes neo-Vedantic monism, the third person of the Christian Trinity, and the "unutterable experience" of the divine (7–8). It also recalls Sen's version of fulfillment theology,

---

3. I mean these terms partly as a historical specification of Gayatri Spivak's *Vertretung* and *Darstellung*, respectively. Spivak uses the German to draw a distinction between two different types of representation that tend to get conflated in English: political representation (*vertreten*, stepping in someone's place) and symbolic representation (*darstellen*, "placing there," proxy or portrait). Political representation, by Spivak's account, usually also entails some form of symbolic representation (in the same moment that one speaks for women, or Kansans, or Muslims, one also provides a portrait of that group); but, by keeping these two types of representation conceptually distinct, one reduces the level of epistemic confusion that such acts of representation often entail (Spivak 108–10). Here, by historicizing these terms via quintessentially nineteenth-century institutions (parliament and museum), I am trying to bring out something of their distinctive cultural logic at this particular moment.

as well as the popularized Hegelianism of late-century Bengal (Kopf 1; Sartori 85–87). For Mozoomdar, the divine spirit reveals itself progressively through a series of revelations, each of which alters how previous revelations should be interpreted. Jesus occupies a special place in this history, but even his revelation has yet to attain its full meaning. The final realization of spirit, which will synthesize and subsume all that precedes it in a fully global community, is yet to come.

"Commonwealth of affection" is one designator for this coming community. As Mozoomdar explains, Christ came to Earth to establish such a commonwealth, but it has yet to be achieved. It is, however, implicit in the divine governance of the world: "The sovereignty of the Spirit of God rules individual and national interests, and labors to combine these interests into a great spiritual commonwealth" (*Spirit of God* 291). The true "cosmopolitan" is the person who—like the poet or prophet, in our present age—lives in this "city of God" (26).

The seemingly interchangeable phrases *commonwealth of affection* and *spiritual commonwealth* reframe the tension between affect and institution that we have already seen in Mozoomdar's Chicago lecture. On the one hand, they anticipate the federation of discrete postcolonial nation-states that would, by early in the next century, become the default meaning of "Commonwealth" (Bell 1–30; Morefield 1–30). On the other hand, they call the discreteness of those states into question. In twinning "spirit" and "affect," Mozoomdar would appear to be following the lead of Sen. Although Mozoomdar's "spiritual commonwealth" might seem to indicate a simple coming together of discrete individuals on a classically liberal model, a slightly different picture emerges if the phrase is read as inflected by the affective commonwealth of a few pages before. Spirit-affect transgresses the boundaries of the liberal individual and the liberal nation-state to generate a more expansive mode of global community.

To be clear, Mozoomdar never says this outright. His cosmopolitan vision remains very much constrained by the segmented gridlines of religions and nations. Thus, in his narrative, Spirit matures the "distinctive qualities" of each individual nation and "every system of religion" (*Spirit of God* 278, 300). But this is not all it does. It is also a vitalist force, the "Life" that animates all beings, from the fungus on up (120–21; on vitalism as Romantic trope, see Gigante's *Life*). This vital force, he implies, lies behind the human capacity for sympathy. "The Holy Spirit is within a man's own self—the heart of his heart, the soul of his soul, bound to be felt and recognized in the innermost recesses where all is quiet" (61). Another term for this "Spirit of God in man" is "love" or "sympathy" (198), and it is the key to transpersonal connection. The "throb of sympathy" enlivens us to the suffering of strangers, giving rise to a "capacity for love [that] has neither limit nor end. This universal heart in the individual, this infinite sympathy in the finite . . . [is] the heart of God beating in man" (201). This "universal heart" is what broadens the "personal circle" until affection learns to "mak[e] its home among all mankind" (201).

These sentiments can be rendered consistent with a liberal politics of discrete individuals and nation-states. But they contain within them, I think, an implicit challenge to liberalism insofar as they transgress the boundaries of "little individualities" (to recall Sen's phrase). Rather than viewing the objects of the world as separate, Mozoomdar looks to Wordsworth to locate a "sense sublime" that can feel a "motion and a spirit" that "rolls through all things" (*Spirit of God* 122). If, in his text, this spirit seems to have grand systemizing tendencies, at other times its operations are much vaguer—like those of the weather. "The spiritual influences of systems and nations spread invisibly and mingle," he suggests, such that a "universal religion is always forming in the atmosphere" (302; on the atmospherics of religion, see Peters's *The Marvelous Clouds*). This nebulous coalescence of spiritual clouds is what marks Mozoomdar's commonwealth as distinctive. He is never quite content to let the commonwealth, as global political community, rest easy in the institutional forms of parliamentary liberalism. Instead, he destabilizes those forms by supercharging them with the connecting force of sympathy as transpersonal cosmopolitan affect.

This project cannot help but fail, however, if success is measured by translation back into institutions. Affect here is a Dionysian force that presses against the soberly Apollonian ethos of parliamentary liberalism. It cannot be routinized into a fixed institutional form without losing its disruptive charge. While Mozoomdar's turn to pop Hegelianism might appear an effort to reconcile spirit and system, affect and politics, it is an effort that (in his hands, at least) never quite gets off the ground. Rather, he finds himself in much the same place he had been in Chicago in 1893—dreaming of a more cosmopolitan world that he does not quite know how to realize, a potential that refuses to actualize. The Brahmos could imagine something like what we would now describe as "the global," but they were unable to express this imagined community in institutional form (in this, they are perhaps analogous to certain twenty-first-century religious movements, as discussed by Faisal Devji in *The Terrorist in Search of Humanity*).

THE INSTITUTIONS THAT CONSTRUCTED VICTORIAN RELIGION

These utopian yearnings would thus appear to be "juxtapolitical" in the relatively precise sense given that term by Lauren Berlant. As Berlant explains, nineteenth-century sentimental novels provided a space for an affective critique of political injustice, but this affect usually did not cross over into the domain of politics proper; rather, it created "a critical chorus that sees the expression of emotional response and conceptual recalibration as achievement enough" (x). To get a better sense of how "religion" related to "literature" in the nineteenth century, one could compare Berlant's sentimental novels to the World's Parliament of Religions. There are some grounds for considering the parliament juxtapolitical in Berlant's sense. Its organizers, after all, saw it as a spiritual antidote to the material achievements showcased at the nearby Columbian Exposition; the parliament, by their account, implied a moral critique of industrial capitalism. It stopped short, however, of taking concrete actions against its nemesis. Indeed, in very concrete ways, the Parliament of Religions depended symbiotically on the Exposition's grandiose displays of science and industry for its very existence. To this extent, then, the parliament created a classically juxtapolitical space, stoking critical affect but without channeling that affect into political action.

Where religion did differ from literature, however, and perhaps decisively so, was in its continued and necessary recourse to institutions. The literary book, as printed artifact, was inseparable from the publishing houses, literary societies, and other institutions that oversaw its circulation, just as the institution of the Brahmo Samaj was inseparable from its proliferating printed texts. In both cases Victorian print culture and Victorian institutional life went hand in hand. But, in the popular imaginary, the Brahmo Samaj could never be reduced to its books, whereas literature (however erroneously) could be. Something about the concept of religion in the nineteenth century kept returning the Brahmos to their samajes—that is, to the institutional form of the voluntary society. Thus, although protestant-Romantic ideas about textual inspiration did shape Brahmo religiosity (as Mozoomdar's citations of Wordsworth suggest), Brahmos consistently brought these poetic flights of fancy back to the mundane world of civic institutions, thereby loading these institutions with an affective excess that they could not contain.

Brahmo sentimentalism was therefore not juxtapolitical in quite the same way as literary sentimentalism, in that it inscribed affect into civil society institutions that were, according to liberal political theory, the very ground of political debate. Indeed, one might go so far as to say that Brahmo sentimentalism revealed the extent to which the Victorian state, or at least the British state in India, was itself an affective enterprise. Rather than simply existing alongside of the political, then, Brahmo sentimentalism worked to erode the segmentary lines that had separated the political from other social spheres to begin with, thus opening political affect toward new modes of global collectivity.

WORKS CITED

Adcock, C. S. *The Limits of Tolerance: Indian Secularism and the Politics of Religious Freedom.* Oxford UP, 2013.

Anderson, Amanda, and Joseph Valente, editors. *Disciplinarity at the Fin-de-Siècle.* Princeton UP, 2002.

Aravamudan, Srinivas. *Guru English: South Asian Religion in a Cosmopolitan Language.* Princeton UP, 2005.

Bagehot, Walter. *Physics and Politics.* New York, D. Appleton and Company, 1873.

Barrows, Samuel J. "Protap Chunder Mozoomdar: A Biographical Sketch." *P. C. Mozoomdar, Heart-Beats.* George Ellis [Boston], 1894, pp. iii–xlii.

Bell, Duncan. *The Idea of Greater Britain: Empire and the Future of World Order, 1860–1900.* Princeton UP, 2007.

Berlant, Lauren. *The Female Complaint: The Unfinished Business of Sentimentality in American Culture.* Duke UP, 2008.

Brown, Wendy. *Undoing the Demos: Neoliberalism's Stealth Revolution.* Zone Books, 2015.

Casanova, Pascale. *The World Republic of Letters.* Translated by Malcom DeBevoisem, Harvard UP, 2004.

Chidester, David. *Empire of Religion: Imperialism and Comparative Religion.* U of Chicago P, 2014.

———. *Savage Systems: Colonialism and Comparative Religion in Southern Africa.* U of Virginia P, 1996.

Chow, Rey. *The Age of the World Target: Self-Referentiality in War, Theory, and Comparative Work.* Duke UP, 2006.

Devji, Faisal. *The Terrorist in Search of Humanity: Militant Islam and Global Politics.* Hurst, 2008.

Dobe, Timothy S. *Hindu Christian Faqir: Modern Monks, Global Christianity, and Indian Sainthood.* Oxford UP, 2015.

Filby, Eliza. *God and Mrs. Thatcher: The Battle for Britain's Soul.* Biteback, 2015.

Gandhi, Leela. *Affective Communities: Anticolonial Thought, Fin-de-Siècle Radicalism, and the Politics of Friendship.* Duke UP, 2006.

———. "The Pauper's Gift: Postcolonial Theory and the New Democratic Dispensation." *Public Culture*, vol. 23, no. 1, 2011, pp. 27–38.

Gigante, Denise. *Life: Organicism and Form.* Yale UP, 2009.

Gottschalk, Peter. *Religion, Science, and Empire: Classifying Hinduism and Islam in British India.* Oxford UP, 2013.

Hacker, Paul. "Aspects of Neo-Hinduism as Contrasted with Surviving Traditional Hinduism." *Kleine Schriften*, edited by Lambert Schmithausen, Franz Steiner Verlag [Wiesbaden], 1978, pp. 580–609.

Halbfass, Wilhelm. "India and the Comparative Method." *Philosophy East and West*, vol. 35, no. 1, Jan. 1985, pp. 3–15.

Hatcher, Brian A. *Bourgeois Hinduism, or the Faith of the Modern Vedantists.* Oxford UP, 2008.

———. *Eclecticism and Modern Hindu Discourse.* Oxford UP, 1999.

King, Joshua. *Imagined Spiritual Communities in Britain's Age of Print.* The Ohio State UP, 2015.

Kopf, David. *The Brahmo Samaj and the Shaping of the Modern Indian Mind.* Princeton UP, 1979.

Masuzawa, Tomoko. *The Invention of World Religions; Or, How European Universalism Was Preserved in the Language of Pluralism*. U of Chicago P, 2005.

Molendijk, Arie L. *Friedrich Max Müller and the Sacred Books of the East*. Oxford UP, 2016.

Morefield, Jeanne. *Empires without Imperialism: Anglo-American Decline and the Politics of Deflection*. Oxford UP, 2014.

Mozoomdar, Protap Chunder. "Protestantism in India." *The Unitarian Review and Religious Magazine* [Boston], November 1883, pp. 399–473.

———. "The World's Religious Debt to Asia." *The World's Parliament of Religions*, edited by John Henry Barrows, vol. 2, Parliament Publishing Company [Chicago], 1893, pp. 1083–91.

———. *The Spirit of God*. Boston, George Ellis, 1894.

Müller, F. Max. *Biographical Essays*. London, Longmans, Green, and Co., 1884.

———. *Keshub Chunder Sen*. Edited by Nanda Mookerjee, Calcutta, S. Gupta and Brothers, 1976.

Murdoch, John. *The Brahma Samaj and Other Modern Eclectic Systems of Religion in India*. 1888. 2nd ed., Madras, Christian Literature Society, 1893.

Packer, George. *The Unwinding: An Inner History of the New America*. Faber and Faber, 2013.

Peters, John Durham. *The Marvelous Clouds: Toward a Philosophy of Elemental Media*. U of Chicago P, 2015.

Radway, Janice A. *A Feeling for Books: The Book-of-the-Month Club, Literary Taste, and Middle-Class Desire*. U of North Carolina P, 1997.

Sartori, Andrew. *Bengal in Global Concept History: Culturalism in the Age of Capital*. U of Chicago P, 2008.

Scott, J. Barton. *Spiritual Despots: Modern Hinduism and the Genealogies of Self-Rule*. U of Chicago P, 2016.

Seager, Richard Hughes. *The World's Parliament of Religions: The East/West Encounter*. Indiana UP, 2009.

Sharpe, Eric. *Comparative Religion: A History*. Scribner's, 1975.

Spivak, Gayatri Chakravorty. *The Postcolonial Critic: Interviews, Strategies, Discourses*. Edited by Sarah Harasym, Routledge, 1990.

Sullivan, Winnifred Fallers. *The Impossibility of Religious Freedom*. Princeton UP, 2005.

Taylor, Charles. *A Secular Age*. Belknap Press of Harvard UP, 2007.

Viswanathan, Gauri. *Outside the Fold: Conversion, Modernity, Belief*. Princeton UP, 1999.

Zastoupil, Lynn. *Rammohun Roy and the Making of Victorian Britain*. Palgrave Macmillan, 2010.

Ziolkowski, Eric J., editor. *A Museum of Faiths: Histories and Legacies of the 1893 World's Parliament of Religions*. Oxford UP, 1993.

CHAPTER 3

"God's Insurrection"

Politics and Faith in the Revolutionary Sermons of Joseph Rayner Stephens

MIKE SANDERS

THIS CHAPTER is intended as a contribution to an intermittent debate between labor history and its religious and theological counterparts. It begins with a general overview of the treatment of religion within labor history and continues with a discussion of E. P. Thompson's analysis of Methodism in *The Making of the English Working Class* (1963), which focuses on his notion of a "reactive dialectic" whereby Wesleyan Methodism's insistence on "submissiveness and the sanctification of labour" generated working-class rebels (437). The chapter then offers a sustained analysis of the "Chartist" sermons delivered by the Reverend Joseph Rayner Stephens between January and August 1839. Stephens's sermons, I argue, not only illustrate the operations of Thompson's "reactive dialectic" but, more importantly, can help us understand the particular ways in which religious and theological attitudes and ideas can variously generate, inform, and sustain forms of working-class radicalism. Thus, the chapter aims to bring labor history, theology (understood as a body of formalized ideas), and religion (understood as practical activity) into a (locally) meaningful dialogue.

I. LABOR HISTORY, RELIGION, THEOLOGY

Generally speaking, labor history has paid minimal attention to questions of religion and theology. The "religious" dimension of movements such as Chartism and Trade Unionism are frequently acknowledged in passing but do not usually provoke intellectual curiosity. Religion, like poor sanitation, is treated simply as an inescapable fact of Victorian working-class life, a part of the Victorian worldview which apparently requires no further exploration. There are exceptions to this rule. The religious aspects of Chartism, for example, have been explored by Eileen Yeo, Roy Vickers, and Eileen Groth Lyon. However, there is still no working-class equivalent to Boyd Hilton's *The Age of Atonement*, with its careful tracing of the complex ways in which theological ideas inform and motivate social policies and political philosophies.

In part, this is due to an understanding of religion "as an ideology of domination that reifies social reality into an unchangeable given and justifies the status quo" (Reed 239). Moreover, for much of the twentieth century most forms of Marxism assumed that atheism was the inevitable and appropriate endpoint of proletarian philosophy. The weight of historical evidence had convinced them, not unreasonably, that institutional religion (priestcraft and superstition) played an overwhelmingly reactionary role by opposing human emancipation. There were historical exceptions, figures such as John Ball and Thomas Müntzer who led liberation movements, but not only were these *historical exceptions,* they were also regarded as historical anachronisms; their historical value residing precisely in the extent to which they anticipated various aspects of socialism. The irony of using this essentially typological approach escaped most of its practitioners. Similarly, religious belief on the part of the wider working class tended to be regarded as evidence of ideological domination, indoctrination, or a form of "false consciousness." Similar commitments on the part of the working-class activists and leaders, while acknowledged, were often treated as if they were either religiously mystified renderings of essentially secular positions or a rhetorically convenient way of articulating socialist politics. The idea that the "theological" could constitute or generate the "political" was, and remains, for many an unthinkable proposition (see chapters by Morrow and Scott in this volume for related discussions of modern separation of the religious from the political).

In addition, because religious differences, especially denominational loyalties, were potentially divisive, most of the working-class movement's organizations practiced religious neutrality, thereby promoting a broadly secular view of religion as a "private" matter. Two factors (local to academe) may be added to this institutional presumption of the Labour movement. The first is the attraction of dissidence for leftist historians. This creates a predisposition to focus on freethinkers (and other forms of religious dissidence) rather than on more "conventional" forms of belief. Second, there remains the challenging nature of the working-class archive; the kinds of archival resources that made Boyd Hilton's work possible are simply unavailable to historians of working-class culture.[1]

However, as Dominic Erdozain's contribution to this collection suggests, there is a tendency to treat the undeniable hostility of both Marx and Engels to clericalism (organized religion, especially state churches) as an equally implacable opposition to religious values. As Erdozain notes, the work of Marx and Engels is marked by an ethical sensitivity which owes much to their respective religious backgrounds. Similarly, other commentators have noted the presence of alternative currents within Marxism which take a more positive view of the Judeo-Christian tradition and which can be seen as constituting a "critical theory of religion . . . [which understands] religion as both a source of *negative thinking,* that is, the *great refusal* of what is, and as a 'narrative form of human resistance and hope'" (Reed 241). It is this dimension of religious experience that has often been overlooked in accounts of Victorian working-class radicalism.

In making this argument, I am not seeking to install theology as a new master-code for the interpretation of Victorian working-class radicalism in general and Chartism in particular. However, I am arguing not just for the general recognition of religious belief as an important element of working-class culture (an uncontroversial, if not banal, observation) but for the necessity of thinking about the theological specificity of working-class culture. In some senses this is a reinflection and recalibration of aspects of the analysis offered by E. P. Thompson in his pioneering and, in many ways unsurpassed, study *The Making of the English Working Class.* Towards the end of the chapter entitled "The Transforming Power of the Cross," Thompson introduces his idea of a "reactive dialectic" and identifies three working-class, West Riding preachers—Ben Rushton, William Thornton, and Abram Hanson—who "made a contribution to the Chartist movement [which] it is *impossible* to overestimate" (438). Thus, a chapter largely concerned with documenting Methodism's repeated attempts to obstruct and frustrate the development of the working-class movement ends with a fulsome tribute to the significance of individual Methodists. As the following paragraphs will demonstrate, the brief "Chartist" career of the renegade Methodist preacher Joseph Rayner Ste-

---

1. Key problems confronting scholars interested in working-class culture in the first half of the nineteenth century are the fragmented and scattered nature of the archive. Despite the existence of a number of Chartist Churches and Democratic Chapels throughout the 1840s, none of their records appear to have survived. Similarly, it appears that only one of the hymnals produced by the Chartist movement has survived; for details, see Sanders.

phens illuminates the particular contribution played by theological ideas in the formation of Chartism.

II. THE REVEREND JOSEPH RAYNER STEPHENS

At the time of his arrest in December 1838, Joseph Rayner Stephens was, arguably, the most popular and the most controversial preacher in the United Kingdom. The son of an influential Methodist minister (his father was an ally of Jabez Bunting and president of the Methodist Conference in 1827), J. R. Stephens became a Methodist minister in 1825, served as a Methodist missionary in Sweden from 1826 to 1829, returned to England in November 1829, and was appointed to the Ashton-under-Lyne circuit in 1832 (Edwards 1–6). Ashton-under-Lyne, just outside Manchester, was part of the Lancashire cotton belt and noted for both its dissent and its radicalism.[2] In 1834 Stephens, under threat of immediate suspension and possible expulsion, resigned from the Methodist Connexion and became minister to a number of independent and overwhelmingly working-class congregations in and around Ashton-under-Lyne (Edwards 11–17). By 1836 Stephens was a staunch supporter of the Tory-Radical Richard Oastler and followed his mentor in opposing the New Poor Law (1834) and advocating Factory Reform. In 1838 Stephens (though not himself a Chartist) was closely associated with Chartism and was a popular speaker at many Chartist meetings. The ferocity of his speeches—for example, his oft-repeated slogan, "For child and wife, I will war to the knife"—and his calls for the people to arm themselves soon attracted the attentions of the government, which began to gather evidence against him. Following an arson attack on an Ashton mill in December 1838, Stephens was arrested on a charge of sedition (Edwards 55–58).

Between his arrest in December 1838 and his trial August 1839, Stephens preached a series of sermons. After his release on bail, the first sermon he gave to his congregations at Ashton and Stalybridge was published as *The Political Preacher*. This was followed by *The Political Pulpit*, a series of thirteen sermons preached at a variety of locations between February 10 and August 3, 1839.[3] This rest of this chapter explores the ways in which Stephens, in these sermons, presents political action as the necessary corollary of Christian faith.

---

2. For details of Ashton's political radicalism see Hall; for its religious radicalism see Lockley.

3. Both *The Political Preacher* and *The Political Pulpit* were reprinted in G. Claeys ed., *The Chartist Movement in Britain 1838–1850. Volume 1*, and all subsequent references to / quotations from these sermons are taken from this volume.

In particular, it focuses on four key aspects of these "revolutionary" sermons. First, it traces the ways in which Stephens uses biblical analogies to explain and analyze the economic, political, and social condition of the working classes. Second, it examines Stephens's use of the Bible to construct a vision of a just social order, thereby highlighting its positive program for society. Third, the chapter explores the social ramifications of Stephens's interpretation of the doctrine of "justification." Finally, it considers Stephens's belief in the possibility of a spontaneous, religiously inspired social transformation, which he termed "God's insurrection." This chapter, therefore, examines the ways in which religious and theological ideas contributed to the political and economic thinking of the Chartist movement. Ultimately, it argues that for Stephens and his Chartist congregants, one of the "uses of religion" was precisely its insistence on the necessity for political action as an expression of Christian belief; or, as Stephens himself put it in *The Political Preacher,* "unless a priest of the living God be . . . a politician in the pulpit, he has no business there at all" (184).

III. THE USE OF SCRIPTURAL ANALOGY

One of the most striking aspects of Stephens's "Chartist" sermons is the way in which he makes the Bible speak directly to the present situation of his audience/congregation. For example, in the first sermon Stephens preached following his release on bail, he offers a reading of Exodus in which the travails of Israel in Egypt are clearly analogous to those of workers in the textile mills of Northern England. Indeed, Stephens argues that the current sufferings of the working classes exceed those of their biblical counterparts:

> We are no where told that in Egypt the men were worked so hard or had to work so long as our fellow countrymen have; nor that the women were doomed to do man's work; nor that little children were driven to work at all as children and women are everywhere forced to do in the corn fields, the coal pits and the cotton mills of christian England. (193)

In Pharaoh's instruction to kill all male Israelite children at birth, Stephens finds equivalents for Malthusianism, the New Poor Law, and "Marcus," the anonymous 1838 pamphleteer whose Malthusian and Poor Law satire recommended gassing every poor child after the second-born to achieve population control (all key figures in Chartist demonology). Finally, in a manner that anticipates Latin American liberation theology, Stephens adduces from

Exodus both the promise of deliverance and "the duty of resistance in [such] circumstances" (193).

IV. THE LINEAMENTS OF A JUST SOCIAL ORDER

In his early sermons, Stephens clearly thinks that the time for resistance is now at hand. The first number in his *Political Pulpit* series begins:

> The world at this hour is set against the word of God. The struggle must be a deadly one: there is now no helping it . . . England is claimed by Satan as his lawful inheritance and prey . . . [it is possible that England shall] be destroyed . . . at a stroke. (197)

Despite the unmistakably apocalyptic tone of this and other sermons, it would be wrong to see Stephens as simply a politicized "fire and brimstone" merchant, since his sermons also emphasize the importance of social justice. If Exodus informs Stephens's critique of existing social conditions, it is Genesis that provides the lineaments of a just social order. In a sermon preached at Ashton-under-Lyne on 9 June 1839,[4] Stephens offers an exegesis of Genesis which begins by emphasizing the goodness of the created world. Next, he reminds his congregation that of all the creation only humankind was made in the image of God. Moreover, he notes that in the relevant biblical verse (Gen. 1:26), the fact of likeness includes dominion over the earth. Stephens argues that the implication of this verse is that God intended (and intends) the world to be "a common treasury for all" (to use the Diggers' formulation) and he challenges his opponents to find the biblical verse that countermands this first law.[5] Stephens's radical reading of Genesis is part of a long-suppressed "tradition" in English history dating back at least as far as the Peasants' Revolt of 1381 when John Ball asked the question, "When Adam delved and Eve span, who was then the gentleman?" It resurfaced again during the English Revolution in a variety of antinomian sects such as the Diggers and Ranters, and remained a marginal presence in English society thereafter. It is unclear whether Stephens knew himself to be working within this tradition, but the antinomian tradition was part of the popular religious culture of the indus-

---

4. This sermon was published as *The Political Pulpit No. 11*.

5. The Diggers or "True Levellers" were a radical Christian group during the English Revolution. Under the leadership of Gerard Winstanley, their attempts to form a communist society at various locations in England were thwarted by a combination of legal and physical challenges orchestrated by local landowners.

trial areas of Northern England. For example, when the Primitive Methodists first appeared in the Stalybridge area in the early nineteenth century, the place where they held their meetings became known as "Ranter's Court" (Hill 117).

Stephens continues by observing that God's second law was the instruction to "Be fruitful, and multiply" (Gen. 1:28) and similarly argues that despite Malthus and Marcus this injunction has not been abrogated. Thus, Stephens makes a strong defense not just of working-class domesticity, which was menaced by the New Poor Law, but also of working-class fecundity with a particularly trenchant defense of those early marriages, which were castigated as "improvident" by champions of the New Poor Law. Stephens goes yet further and argues that sensual pleasures are divinely ordained:

> All the powers of body, as well as of mind when healthy, the organs of the body when in a state of health, and the powers of the mind when reasonably exercised—those organs and those powers will contribute in the exercise of them to the pleasure of man who is possessed of them, to eat, to drink, to taste, to handle, to see, to enjoy sweet sounds, sweet smells, sweet tastes, sweet and soft touches, everything within, as everything around us, all that God meant us to do, communicates a pleasurable sensation to man, and therefore life is sweet. (319)

This promise that life is, or rather ought to be, "sweet" informs Stephens's effective re-visioning of Genesis 3:17–19 as constituting a promise as well as a curse. Stephens construes these lines as guaranteeing that "the sorrows to which we are heirs in our flesh are to be sweetened by our daily bread" (229). Stephens develops his exegesis by drawing his congregation's attention to the duration of this "curse-promise."[6] In particular, he ponders the significance of the phrase "all the days of thy life," and observing that man "cannot work much after he is 50 years old," he interprets this verse as guaranteeing a surplus to the laborer:

> If thou wilt work whilst thou hast power the 12 hours of the day—(there are 12 hours in which man is to work—eight to labour, and four to rest)—If thou wilt work so long as the sun of youth shines, thou shalt make, earn and gather enough in store, enough not only to keep thee, enough not only to make up for the wear and tear of strength in doing the work, but thou shalt reap and gather enough to serve thee all the days of thy life. (229)

---

6. Some fifty years after this sermon, Wilfrid Richmond in *Christian Economics* (1888) asks, "How did the words ever come to sound other than a blessing, 'In the sweat of thy brow thou shalt eat bread'?" (qtd. in Hilton 332).

Above all, Stephens argues, a man's labor ought to be enough to support a wife and family. He invites his hearers to read Leviticus and Deuteronomy, as there they will find that "God himself provided that every man . . . should have means in his own hand of amply providing for all the necessary wants, and for all the reasonable comforts of his family" (284). The affirmation of a right to "reasonable comforts" must have sounded pleasantly in the ears of those who had received endless lectures on the supposed "iron law" which meant that wages inevitably tended towards the level of subsistence. A little later in the same sermon he condemns "this diabolical system . . . which, prevent[s] a man from earning, by his own labour, enough to maintain himself and his family" (285). Indeed, Stephens argues that in a society where labor does not guarantee domestic security the commandment against theft is void:

> What if the bulk of Society cannot by constant labour earn enough for themselves and their households, letting alone that which they ought to be able to earn, over and above, for the supply of the necessity of others, then it follows that the command—"Thou shalt not steal," is superseded and set aside. (288)

Precisely because the guarantee of a proper reward for labor is one of the first promises made to humankind in Genesis, Stephens regards this guarantee as the primary covenant that grounds the entire social compact.

For Stephens, and his working-class congregation, the Bible underpins a form of political economy that is radically different from the "Christian political economy" championed by the Reverend Thomas Chalmers, which found widespread acceptance among the middle and upper classes. As Boyd Hilton observes, Chalmers argued for both laissez-faire and free trade on the grounds that these were consistent with divine law understood as "general providence." Moreover, for Chalmers, the travails and challenges associated with the "free market" constituted a form of moral and spiritual discipline that developed "character" in this world and prepared individuals for the next.[7] The crucial differences between Chalmers and Stephens are, first, that the former subscribes to a wholly Malthusian worldview, wherein scarcity and overpopulation are the default settings of the economic order. In contrast, Stephens emphatically rejects both Malthusian propositions and, as noted earlier, grounds these rejections on his reading of Genesis. Second, where Chalmers adopts an essentially "liberal" position centered on the individual (whether soul or property-owner), Stephens articulates an essentially "communitarian"

---

7. See Hilton 57–88 for a much fuller discussion of Chalmers and "Christian Political Economy."

position wherein individuals always (and only) exist within a network of relationships, of which the family is the most important. These philosophical/theoretical differences also correlate with theological differences in a manner that is broadly consistent with Hilton's schema: Chalmers believes in general providence, Stephens in special providence.[8] Moreover, there is a pronounced incarnational emphasis in Stephens's thought that anticipates later developments in Victorian theology.[9]

V. STEPHENS ON JUSTIFICATION

Stephens also makes the question of the proper reward for labor central to his discussion of the doctrine of justification in the fourth and fifth numbers of *The Political Pulpit*. Stephens begins by complaining of the deliberate mystification and obfuscation of the Christian creeds by self-interested preachers. Stephens remarks that while most of his audience will have heard of "Justification," very few indeed will have any clear understanding of it. He then offers his own definition: "To be justified means, in a few plain words, to be set right; to be set right with God, to be set right with man; God setting us right with himself, with our own heart, and with one another" (239). Stephens clearly considers this an uncontroversial definition and invites his hearers to ask their own ministers whether they are prepared to dispute this definition. Controversy arrives with Stephens's suggested follow-up question: if this is an accurate definition, then "put it to them whether any mill-owner in their society is justified by faith" (239).

As far as Stephens is concerned, this is not an open question. The only possible answer, he declares, is that

> [the mill-owner] cannot be justified . . . All is wrong, all is crooked between him and God; all is wrong between him and the people; and so long as he continues a mill-owner in the present state, and under the present system of trade, he must be; however he may fancy himself; justified by faith, and sanctified, and adopted into the family of God, elect by the foreknowledge of God into eternal salvation; he is, and he must be on the high road to everlasting damnation. (240)

---

8. "General providence" refers to the idea that God continuously maintains the existence and order of the universe, whereas "special providence" refers to the idea that God makes extraordinary interventions into the lives of people.

9. Hilton notes the move from Atonement to Incarnation as the central concern of Victorian theology from the 1850s onward (320–27).

Again, in radical departure from Chalmers's "Christian political economy," which, aside from a few anxieties about cupidity and fraudulent speculation, had few qualms about current commercial activity (Hilton 54, 117–23), Stephens condemns the entire "present system of trade" as one of intense sinfulness. The factory system is seen as a massive dislocation of the moral cosmos—"All is wrong"—akin to a second Fall. The main sins committed by the mill-owners consist in the harm that they do to the bodies and souls of their workers by overworking them. In Stephens's opinion this makes each, and every, mill-owner "a robber from God" (240). In short, in Stephens's political economy, the claims of the laborer take priority over the claims of private property.

Stephens offers a distinctive, if not idiosyncratic, version of the doctrine of justification here. To a certain extent, Stephens shares Augustine's sense of justification as both "the 'right-wising' of the God–man relationship" (to use Alister McGrath's term) and "the restoration of the entire universe to its original order" (McGrath 34, 36). However, Stephens places as much emphasis on the interpersonal (human to human) axis as he does on the transcendental (individual to God) axis: "all is crooked between him and God; all is wrong between him and the people" (240). Justification, for Stephens, then, is not simply a question of private belief but something that requires social action.[10] In order to be justified, Stephens argues, the mill-owner must ask no more than eight hours daily labor of his employees. For Stephens, the demand for excessive hours of labor is sinful, and it must be "forsaken" by mill-owners if they are to become justified.[11]

VI. GOD'S INSURRECTION

For Stephens, as noted earlier, the social compact depends on labor receiving an appropriate reward. Societies that violate this compact are essentially sinful because they violate divine law. Throughout his sermons, Stephens affirms the superior claims of divine law and legitimizes resistance to unjust laws by arguing that such resistance is a sacred duty. Indeed, the idea of a justified resistance is everywhere in Stephens's "Chartist" sermons and is frequently accompanied by sanguinary or martial imagery:

---

10. In this respect, Stephens anticipates important aspects of Dietrich Bonhoeffer's attack on "cheap grace" in *The Cost of Discipleship* (1937). I am grateful to Joshua King for making this connection.

11. "... repentance means also the forsaking of sin by shutting up his mill after it has run eight hours" (242).

> Whenever I find a law opposed to the law of God, then I will not obey it—then will I oppose it, then will I resist it. By argument[,] I have done so; by reasoning, I have done so; by petitioning, I have done so; by remonstrating, I have done so; by rebuking, I have done so; by threatening, I have done so; and if reason, and argument, and remonstrance, and prayers, and tears, and entreaties, shall all be ineffectual—then, as God has shown me, as God has taught me, and, as God will empower me, I will go on resisting it, even though I shall be called to resist it unto blood. (Loud cheers.) (288)

These words seem to suggest the inevitability of a violent collision between oppressor and oppressed—and in 1839 some Chartists were indeed arming themselves in readiness for what they believed was an inevitable confrontation with the government. Indeed, Ashton was one of the most bellicose localities, with some local Chartists claiming that membership was only by means of a "steel certificate" (i.e., a pike-head).

Speaking in Wigan, Stephens appears to sound an unmistakably insurrectionary note:

> To have arms in his house . . . and to be prepared for their use (loud and continued cheering)—and not only prepare to use them, but actually to use them for the very purpose for which they were made, for the reason why God gave us cold lead and sharp steel was to put an ounce of the one, and six inches of the other into the bodies and brains of any men . . . call them magistrates, if they liked, or Commissioners, or Powers, or principalities, or thrones . . . having tried all the means he had beforehand, then was the time for the people to prepare for war . . . It was God's insurrection—it was God's rebellion—it was a divine revolution, a revolution in favour of truth and righteousness through the spirit of God and by means of the right arms of men (Loud cheers). ("Great Radical Demonstration" 6)

In his sermons, Stephens repeatedly affirms the right to resist unjust law, frequently deploys violent and martial imagery, and often invokes the complete destruction of cities and societies as examples of divine judgment. For Stephens, scripture demonstrates that hopelessly corrupt societies deserve to be, and historically have been, destroyed by God. Stephens's analysis of his own society is that it too is a dangerously corrupted society. One possible understanding of Stephens's position is to view his propositions as constituting two-thirds of a syllogism: God destroys hopelessly corrupt societies; Britain has become a hopelessly corrupt society; therefore, Britain (understood as the current social order) deserves to be destroyed. How many of Stephens's auditors "heard" this implicit syllogism and inferred the missing final term themselves? Another possibility is that Stephens is suggesting that although Britain is perilously close to deserving divine wrath, there yet remains a final opportunity for repentance. In turn, the possibility of repentance requires the working classes to exercise patience, to wait a while for their deliverance.

A similar ambiguity attends the question of agency. Is the divine wrath of God to be understood as a supernatural intervention, or do human beings become the witting or unwitting tools of the Lord? In short, is there a political strategy informing Stephens's sermons? At times, Stephens appears to be advancing a strategy based on the escalation of resistance if demands are not satisfied. For example, in his 12 May 1839 Kennington Common sermon, Stephens outlines a program of graduated resistance, "by reasoning, . . . by petitioning[,] by remonstrating[,] by rebuking[,] by threatening[, and if these all fail, then] as God will empower me, I will go on resisting it, even though I shall be called to resist it unto blood" (288–89). One possible reading of these lines is that Stephens is offering himself as a political martyr, prepared to shed his blood for the cause if necessary. Another possible reading is that Stephens, having rehearsed all the actions taken by Chartism thus far (the first petition had been made ready for presentation to the House of Commons by May 7), was preparing his auditors for the possibility of a violent confrontation with the state if the petition was rejected.[12]

In his tenth sermon in *The Political Pulpit,* Stephens offers an extended analysis of New Testament accounts of Christ's arrest in the garden. He begins his exposition with Luke 22:35 (the instruction to buy swords) and continues by exploring Luke 22:49–51, John 18:10–11, and Matthew 26:51–53. Stephens argues that Christ approved rather than reproved Peter's use of physical force and also contends that in Matthew 26:51–53 the words "all they that take the sword shall perish with the sword" are directed against the men who come to arrest Christ. Stephens dwells on Matthew and Christ's claim that he could, if he wished it, call on "twelve legions of angels" to assist him in his hour of need. Stephens follows this scriptural quotation with a rhetorical question: "And how many [angelic legions] could the people of England have?" (336). Stephens contrasts the earthly powers of state force with the transcendental powers at God's command:

> Ah, how poor, how paltry, how beggarly, how miserable, how pitiful, and how pitiable, is yonder brick barracks, and the few, raw, half-starved lads of

---

12. Because of the "Bedchamber crisis," the petition was not presented until June 14.

the 10th. God bless them and fatten them. How paltry all this is—all those policemen, these pensioners, those meetings and marchings of the poor fellows backward and forward! How paltry it is! Why, if the hour of God's vengeance and your redemption were fully in, as I said before, twelve legions of troops from heaven would come down to honour it. (336)

It is difficult to determine precisely what Stephens counsels here. His emphasis on a Christ who instructs his disciples to buy swords and approves their using them might be seen as a coded call for Chartists to arm themselves. However, Stephens's decision to end his exegesis by focusing on divine intervention ("twelve legions of troops from heaven") introduces an element of uncertainty. It is not difficult to see the attractions of this trope: divine intervention would testify to the righteousness of the workers' cause. In addition, as a military force, angels are clearly superior to the forces of the state. Yet Stephens also claims that divine intervention signals "the hour of . . . your redemption." Thus, if the arrival of angelic legions (which would negate the need for fighting) signals the hour of working-class redemption, then their nonarrival must mean that neither the hour of redemption nor the time for fighting has yet arrived.

This ambiguity recurs in his final pretrial sermon, when Stephens warns against any attempt at calculated, premeditated agency, arguing instead for a spontaneous, divinely inspired insurrection:

My friends, never put your trust in, and never follow after, men who pretend to be able to manufacture a revolution. A revolution, a rolling away of the whole from evil to good, from wrong to right, from injustice and oppression to righteousness and equal rule, never yet was manufactured, and never will be manufactured. God, who teaches you what your rights are . . . will, in his own good time, if that time should come—God will teach your hands to war, and your fingers to fight. (354)

There is, then, a fatal ambivalence in Stephens's preaching. He insists that oppression must (and will) end. He affirms the right of armed resistance to oppression but insists that the time for fighting, though close, has not yet arrived. On one level, this ambiguity might simply reflect the genuine political and strategic uncertainty within Chartism in 1839. Alternatively, the "not yet" might be seen as an attempt by Stephens to restrict violence to the field of rhetoric alone, to provide a symbolic outlet for working-class anger. This, in turn, might be regarded as an attempt by Stephens to restrain his supporters from a potentially disastrous course of action or, more cynically, as an attempt to row back from his earlier invocations of violent reprisal while retaining the favor of the crowd.

All of these possible explanations privilege an underlying political logic. The meaning of Stephens's words is to be found by calculating their possible political ramifications. Given the political nature of Chartism, this is not an unreasonable assumption. However, in the case of Stephens it is insufficient. For if we consider the structure of Stephens's thought—the way in which his sermons are oriented on the "now" of oppression which is contrasted with a "then" of deliverance, and the way in which his invocations of violence are generally organized around a "not quite" or "not yet" formula—we find a family resemblance to what Elizabeth Phillips calls the "eschatological tale of the already and the not yet" of Augustine's theology of the two cities (277).

With the introduction of an eschatological lens, certain aspects of Stephens's thought attain a clearer focus. For example, Stephens's understanding of justification as a reordering of the moral cosmos clearly draws on those traditions within Christian theology that interpret the eschaton or apocalypse as fulfilling "the finality of the created universe rather than simply destroying and negating it in a final conflagration" (Phillips 279). Indeed, Stephens interprets Mark 1:3 ("Prepare ye the way of the Lord, make his paths straight") not as a prefiguration of the day of judgment but as applying to all "those periods of time in which the great purposes of Heaven" become manifest. Stephens clearly believes that the present moment is one such period of time. Stephens is not announcing the eschaton but he does understand the present moment as possessing an eschatological dimension. Given such a situation, Stephens's call for forbearance elides the "not yet" of the insurrectionary moment with the "*not yet* of the Kingdom of God." In other words, not only is there a theological as well as a political logic operating throughout Stephens's sermons, but it is also possible that the "slippage" between these two logics is not always immediately apparent to either Stephens or his auditors.

I would like to conclude by considering another example of the uncertainty that attends the movement between the theological and the political in Stephens's sermons. In his last Chartist sermon, Stephens opposes what he calls "the delusion of a National Holiday" (or General Strike) because it "means a national fight." On hearing this, his auditors could be forgiven for wondering what Stephens had meant previously by invoking resistance of oppressive laws "unto blood" and "Revolution by force . . . by blood . . . by the sword . . . by the musket . . . by the cannon" (288, 220).[13] Indeed, some of

---

13. In fairness to Stephens, it must be noted that he did oppose the National Holiday and that many of his objections to it—that it would provoke an armed confrontation for which the

his auditors did voice their surprise at, and opposition to, Stephens's apparent change of position: "Now you know that I am not a Radical. ('Would to God you were,' from several voices.)" (351). Nonetheless, Stephens repeats his claim that the National Holiday would inevitably fail and tells his audience that if they embark on it:

> I shall have the satisfaction of recollecting that I gave you the best counsel I had to give you—I washed my hands of your blood, and left it upon your own heads, and upon the heads of your dear children[.] (352)

Stephens's words here clearly allude to Matthew 27:24–25, Pilate's handwashing and the transfer of responsibility for Christ's death to the Jerusalem crowd.[14] Stephens is too well versed in the New Testament for this to be an accidental allusion. However, it is an overdetermined allusion insofar as blood will only be spilled (and thus require cleansing) if the people attempt insurrection (the National Holiday). Yet in the New Testament narrative it is Christ's blood that is spilled, and for which Pilate seeks to absolve himself of any responsibility. Thus, while Stephens equates his renunciation of the National Holiday (working-class insurrection) with Pilate's act of disclaiming responsibility, and his allusion identifies his listeners with the Jerusalem crowd (responsible for the bloodshed), the poetic logic at work also identifies his audience as (potentially) the Christ whose blood will be shed. This reads like a symbolic acknowledgment of the multiple betrayals that are being played out in the historical moment. Just like Pilate, Stephens recognizes the justice of the cause he is about to betray. The unspoken knowledge carried by the sermon's poetic logic is the redemptive possibility of working-class insurrection, that "God's insurrection" of his earlier sermons. It is in an effort to repress this knowledge that he casts the people in the role of the Jerusalem crowd which rejects the messiah.

---

workers were unprepared, that it would threaten working-class unity and would, therefore, require the intimidation of workers reluctant to participate in the strike—are perfectly valid.

14. The relevant verses read: "[24] When Pilate saw that he could prevail nothing, but *that* rather a tumult was made, he took water, and washed *his* hands before the multitude, saying, I am innocent of the blood of this just person: see ye *to it*. [25] Then answered all the people, and said, His blood *be* on us, and on our children."

WORKS CITED

Claeys, Gregory, editor. *The Chartist Movement in Britain 1838–1850*. Vol. 1, Pickering and Chatto, 2001.

Edwards, Michael S. *Purge This Realm: A Life of Joseph Rayner Stephens*. Epworth Press, 1994.

"Great Radical Demonstration at Wigan." *The Northern Star*, 17 Nov. 1838, p. 6.

Groth Lyon, Eileen. *Politicians in the Pulpit: Christian Radicalism in Britain from the Fall of the Bastille to the Disintegration of Chartism*. Ashgate, 1999.

Hall, Robert G. *Voices of the People: Democracy and Chartist Political Identity, 1830–1870*. Merlin Press, 2009.

Hill, Samuel. *Bygone Stalybridge*. Printed for the author, 1907.

Hilton, Boyd. *The Age of Atonement*. Oxford UP, 1988.

Lockley, Philip. *Visionary Religion and Radicalism in Early Industrial England: From Southcott to Socialism*. Oxford UP, 2013.

McGrath, Alister E. *Iustitia Dei: A History of the Christian Doctrine of Justification*. 2nd ed., Cambridge UP, 1998.

Phillips, Elizabeth. "Eschatology and the Apocalyptic." *Cambridge Companion to Christian Political Theology*, edited by Craig Hovey and Elizabeth Phillips, Cambridge UP, 2015, pp. 274–95.

Reed, Jean-Pierre. "Religion as Custom and Political Resistance: An Unorthodox Interpretation of E. P. Thompson's *The Making of the English Working Class*." *Critical Sociology*, vol. 39, no. 2, 2011, pp. 239–58.

Sanders, Michael. "'God is our guide! Our cause is just!' *The National Chartist Hymn Book* and Victorian Hymnody." *Victorian Studies*, vol. 54, no. 4, 2012, pp. 679–705.

Stephens, Joseph Rayner. *The Political Preacher* (1839) and *The Political Pulpit* (1839). *The Chartist Movement in Britain 1838–1850*. Vol. 1, edited by Gregory Claeys, Pickering and Chatto, 2001.

Thompson, E. P. *The Making of the English Working Class*. Penguin, 1980 [1963].

Vickers, Roy. "Christian Election, Holy Communion and Psalmic Language in Ernest Jones's Chartist Poetry." *Journal of Victorian Culture*, vol. 11, no. 1, 2006, pp. 59–83.

Yeo, Eileen. "Chartist Religious Belief and the Theology of Liberation." *Disciplines of Faith: Studies in Religion, Politics and Patriarchy*, edited by Jim Obelkevich, Lyndal Roper and Raphael Samuel, RKP, 1987, pp. 410–21.

———. "Christianity in Chartist Struggle, 1838–1842." *The People's Charter: Democratic Agitation in Early Victorian Britain*, edited by Stephen Roberts, Merlin, 2003, pp. 64–93.

CHAPTER 4

George Jacob Holyoake, Secularism, and Constructing "Religion" as an Anachronistic Repressor

DAVID NASH

THIS CHAPTER examines and contrasts the ways in which "religion" was categorized, and often portrayed as anachronistic, in the thought of leading nineteenth-century secularists in Britain and, to a lesser extent, America. Roughly speaking, it re-examines the bifurcation between those vehemently opposed to religion per se and those dissatisfied with its prevailing foundations and formulations. Traditional historiography saw this as a division between "eliminationists" (seeking the destruction of religion) and "substitutionists" (seeking to supplant religion with something supposedly more enriching and edifying) (Schumaker 62). However, this chapter builds on recent reappraisals of both secularism and secularization to offer new insights into—and, hopefully, a reevaluation of—both concepts and the two analytical stances. As such, it suggests that by looking more closely at the thoughts and approaches of George Jacob Holyoake (1817–1906), the most famous advocate of what was previously classed as "substitutionism," it becomes possible to see beyond this dichotomy of religion's supposed "value" or "worthlessness." From this analysis more nuanced arguments, such as those offered by Holyoake, begin to grow in coherence, while religion itself no longer seems to be the unnuanced, unmoving construction sometimes portrayed in previous histories of secularism.

ELIMINATIONISTS AND SUBSTITUTIONISTS DEFINE RELIGION AND THE SECULAR

George Jacob Holyoake is quite pivotal for this task since he was the originator of the concept of "Secularism" in the middle years of the nineteenth century. His life and ideological contributions also span three-quarters of the century, reaching from the end of Jacobin radicalism right through to the Edwardian period. This "Secularism" explicitly denied the claims of religion and the state's official establishment of a religion that claimed to influence the lives and practices of its citizens. His original conception of "Secularism" in 1851 argued that the unproven nature of the Christian conception of the universe justified an explicit focus upon this world. This effectively denied the hegemony and authority of the speculative spiritual dimension, yet it did not utterly reject all that religion had created or spawned. Holyoake's early experience was as a Social Missionary for the Rationalist Society, which engaged him with views that were antagonistic to religion. The Rationalist Society was the brainchild of Robert Owen, Britain's foremost Enlightenment-inspired utopian thinker who motivated a rainbow coalition of radicals, people who sought answers to the structures of oppression confronting them—whether these resulted from market forces or from the tyrannical pretensions of revealed religion enforced by the state. While Owen argued against the "Old Immoral World"—regularly blaming it for incursions upon his "New Moral Worlds"—his conception of the latter remained resolutely utopian (Harrison 11–192). This stands in contrast to the vaguer and unformed conceptions of religion's demise by eliminationists like the early Jacobin-inspired Richard Carlile. Individuals like Carlile were prepared to be imprisoned for charging the religious establishment with misinformation and the promulgation of fraudulent doctrines, as explored by Joel Wiener in *Radicalism and Freethought in Nineteenth-Century Britain* (1983) and by Edward Royle (*Victorian Infidels* 31–43). This consideration is also pertinent in relation to the later-century secularist leader Charles Bradlaugh, who established a national campaign (the National Secular Society) that emphasized the need for a frontal assault upon religion's claims and privileges. As Walter Arnstein argued in *The Bradlaugh Case* (1965), Bradlaugh was also a liberal individualist who took his agenda to the heart of Victorian society in becoming, after a protracted battle, the first openly atheist Member of Parliament—ushering in the right to affirm rather than swear an oath in Parliament. One reason for this bifurcation in strategy (frontal assault vs. Owenite emphasis on dialogue between perspectives) is because religion seemed such a totalizing system and the need to transcend it appeared obvious and self-evident, even if emphases and approaches differed. Carlile's struggles to publish Enlightenment critiques of religion, and Bradlaugh's attempts to gain citizens' rights for all freethinkers, are secular narratives that foreground conflict, aggression, iconoclasm, and languages of the oppressed. However, we can also see Carlile and Bradlaugh's efforts positively as quests for freedom, self-determination, modernization, and the progressive promotion of the "spirit of the age." This emphasis on conflict and stuggle made contemporaries, and some earlier historians, see the Victorian religious landscape as a monolithic establishment. Until comparatively recently, such accounts of secularism portrayed religion as unnuanced, inflexible, and an apparently immovable wall. As Michael Rectenwald has noted, this aggressive picture of secularism was the one that came to predominate in later analyses (190–97).

This narrative of secular debate and questioning as a conflict model has also been undermined when religion has been seen as rather less of an oppressive obstacle and instead as an open door. This has complicated portrayals of it as the antithesis of liberal civilization. When it has opened itself to discussion and argument, thereby relinquishing its claim to be the "only truth," it has also ceded the justification for tyrannically clamping down on the unorthodox and the heretical in earlier and less enlightened ages. The people thus far described in my brief survey of the nineteenth-century boundaries of secularism and atheism were in the business of holding the monolithic conception of religion up to modern, and often self-consciously liberal, values in their own search for an end time to its influence.

Nonetheless, the quiet negotiations and bridge building of Holyoake were scarcely visible to the bulk of secularists who episodically, and understandably, were carried away by the apparent courage and crusading of Charles Bradlaugh, which provided an intoxicating species of populism for many. Moreover, deeper and more sober contemplation could easily be outpaced by events. The sporadic blasphemy prosecutions of the nineteenth century created a different scenario whereby defendants in blasphemy cases such as George William Foote struggled against religion as a state-enshrined anachronism, upheld by spurious and malevolent stakeholders acting against the "spirit of the Age" (Nash, *Blasphemy in Britain* 107–66). Even those much closer to Holyoake's dialogue with religion—Ethicist/Positivists, such as Edward Spencer Beesley and F. J. Gould—saw religion in league with industrial urban society to demean human fellowship and cooperative impulses (Nash, *Secularism, Art and Freedom* 152–56). Meanwhile, America's leading secularist, Robert Ingersoll, similarly had a strident message in which he railed against Christianity's inability to offer any kind of truth, repeatedly pleading for Christianity to offer him "just one fact" (Ingersoll 51).

Too often, all these individuals acted as though they spoke for a stable and homogenous movement, and their various narratives generally espoused a collective "we." Historians of secularism have been caught between the personalities that appeared to "run" movements and the diffuse culture created by movements, which stretched, albeit in weaker form, into the provinces. Thus, these historians often speak of a nineteenth-century secular "movement" within England that was in fact often protean, evasive, and opaque.[1] The idea of unified movements persuaded contemporaries that they were destined for something called "victory" over religion. However, "victory" involved actively engaging with the phenomenon of secularization and whether it would deliver a society free from religion and its influences in areas such as education and the law. The desire to extricate the law and education from religion eventually proved to be problematic since religious moral and symbolic influence continued in both these areas into the twentieth century. Combative secularization models argued that religion should surrender its role in education and welfare, mirroring the later classic model of secularization offered by Peter Berger in *The Sacred Canopy* (1967), which envisioned secular victory over, and subsequent colonization of, institutions previously controlled and influenced by religion. Relatedly, conceiving of secularism as a movement headed toward "victory" focused attention on removing milestones of oppression such as blasphemy laws, affirmation in court, the right of inheritance for secular purposes, and parliamentary oaths. This vision of secularism's victory also required imagining a plausible "end time" for religion.

HOLYOAKE'S "SECULARISM" AS CONFLICT RESOLUTION

George Jacob Holyoake's thinking was influenced by a mixture of instinct, experience, and his affinity with the autodict lifestyle and education that had brought many to Secularism, and this combination of qualities would perpetually appear in his writing. For example, in his *Principles of Secularism* he commenced with a description of autodidact intellectual bewilderment, of people denied the force of structured and supervised comprehension:

> They do not understand the worth of contested points; names have no associations for them, and persons kindle no recollections. They hear of men,

---

1. Historians who have remarked upon this trend in scholarship include Royle (*Victorian Infidels*; *Radicals, Secularists, and Republicans*) and myself (*Secularism, Art and Freedom*).

and things, and projects, and struggles, and principles; but everything comes and goes like the wind; nothing makes an impression, nothing penetrates, nothing has its place in their minds. They locate nothing: they have no system. They hear and they forget; or they just recollect what they have once heard, they cannot tell where. (5)

Influenced by the fluid nature of much autodidact education, it was natural for Holyoake to nullify conflict models, which often encouraged entrenched positions and ideas that had stopped testing their utility against real circumstances. Moving away from such intransigence spurred in Holoake and others an autodidact, eclectic acquisition of knowledge that would later be an important part of Millite Liberalism. This was also a part reaction stemming from Holyoake's absorption of Owenism's utopianism, and his subsequent rejection of millenial aspiration eventually developed into a narrative of accomodation and compromise. Holyoake's eclecticism, therefore, inclined him to examine religious practices and beliefs for the value that could be found within them. However, experience of organized and vocal opposition demonstrated that such forms of inquiry had to be protected. When promoting Secularism, Holyoake adopted sectlike organizational structures, so that his local secularist groups in some ways resembled Nonconformist congregations. Such structures were aided by the introduction of quasi-religious idioms, preaching styles and a "circuit" of itinerant lecturers. This was a defensive pragmatic approach that enabled and nurtured quietism. The eliminationists might have scoffed or poured scorn upon what they saw as softer accommodation, but Holyoake had some unappreciated and centrally important points to make with this agenda. It is worth considering some of these in depth. His ideology of Secularism argued that it was as ridiculous to deny religion as it was to affirm it actively (Holyoake, *Principles of Secularism* 8–12). Such attitudes foregrounded a more benign form of inquiry that differed from the hostile iconoclasm heralded as the alternative by figures such as Bradlaugh. Was it the case that Holyoake, in his mind, left the pursuit of freedom from religion and its ties to the state to others more skilled in strident agitation, something for which he himself had neither taste nor aptitude? Moreover, Holyoake's experience with ideology meant that he was used to seeing ideas at least partly discredited, and perhaps even in pieces. His track record, after all, clearly indicates that he was prepared to sift through the wreckage of each ideological disaster in search of what could be retrieved and recycled.

Holyoake even readily suggested that he was prepared to do this with Christianity (Holyoake, *Principles of Secularism* 14–15). It seemed foolish to reject out of hand all components of Britain's religion and its past in search of what was a fitfully disturbing revolution. Holyoake noted this very late in life in some of his restatements of Secularism's nature and goals. In *English Secularism; A Confession of Belief* (1896), he is unwilling to dismiss the value of Christianity entirely, even as he criticizes rigid orthodoxy for refusing selective adaptation of Christian principles. He objects to the inflexibility of something monolithic seeking to maintain its illusory impregnability.

> Christianity does not permit eclecticism—that is, it does not tolerate others selecting portions of Christian Scriptures possessing the mark of intrinsic truth, to which many could cheerfully conform in their lives. This rule compels all who cannot accept the entire Scriptures to deal with its teachings as they find them expressed, and for which Christianity makes itself responsible. (Holyoake, *English Secularism* 3)

Here Holyoake notes the intellectual inflexibility of confessional religious systems while inviting the genuine pursuit of answers to moral questions craved by his autodidact artisan readership and audience. If, Holyoake believed, all those who earnestly sought for a higher morality could speak and exchange their views, then such individuals could unite around campaigns (such as his Anti-Persecution Union) and a wider sense of freedom. Beyond seeking allies among believers, it seemed realistic to Holyoake that this quest was what the bulk of those in Victorian society who were moral but skeptical were doing within their own lives.

This climate of tolerant debate could readily be divorced from the strident campaigns of national figures seeking to change laws and wider attitudes. These agitations would help, but they never could comprehensively represent that for which the secular-minded could and should be striving. But this was, for Holyoake, without doubt a teleological journey. In the often-expressed idiom of the age, the achievement of his vision of Secularism was to happen in stages, in this case, three of them. The first cornerstone was the right of independent thought (Holyoake, *English Secularism* 9–16). As befitting someone from an artisan background, Holyoake believed that the failure to realize this right was what so frequently silenced people, thus retarding social and cultural progress. Once established, this faculty needed to be used to critically scrutinize theology in the quest to establish "life according to reason." As he saw it, "disputation becomes the passion and the higher state of life" (*English Secularism* 2–3, 17–21). His third stage argued for the transfer of ethical sensibility away from its connection with religion, which he held to be a primary function of Secularism: "supplying . . . secular reasons for duty is Secularism, the range of which is illimitable" (*English Secularism* 2–3).

IMPACT, FOLLOWERS, AND FELLOW TRAVELERS

Holyoake was not alone among secularists in holding these views, and he had many artisan followers in the provinces. Tracing these provincial connections can be difficult since local societies that followed his lead were notoriously unsuccessful. However, this should alert us to a potentially wider audience hidden from history. Secularism, as Holyoake articulated it, was a defensive strategy that removed the necessity for a head-on confrontation with religion (Micklewright 226–27). Removing the time and energy wasted on conflict would empower individuals to continue their own search for truth and ethical principles, aided and abetted by a secularist press that readily reached the outlying parts of provincial Britain. Where Holyoake's provincial Secularism did take root successfully, it reveals a much firmer picture of the constituency attracted to his ideas, and precisely how they put their understanding of secularism to practice. When the Leicester Secular Society completed the building of its Secular Hall in 1880, it furnished its frontage with its five apostles of religious criticism. Alongside Paine, Voltaire, Owen, and Socrates was a bust of Jesus, effectively demonstrating the efficacy of Holyoake's search for what was valuable within all religious teaching and philosophy. At the Hall's opening, Holyoake argued for an extension of thinking and thinkers to produce species of independence from both dogma and dogmatic positions. He cemented this with further liberal principles, declaring at the opening of the Leicester Secular Hall that "the habit of thought was the greatest form of independence" and that free speech and its audiences "could contribute to the great stream of public truth" (qtd. in Nash, *Secularism, Art and Freedom* 46). While championing free thought and speech among local supporters at the opening of the Leicester Secular Hall, Holyoake allowed followers of his brand of Secularism to regard as a theatrical distraction the latest events around Bradlaugh's attempts to enter Parliament (*Secularism, Art and Freedom* 43–47).

Thereafter, the society at Leicester saw itself as firmly integrated into the wider landscape of local religious groups. This was partly evidenced by their decision to place a bust of Jesus on the front entrance of their hall, allowing him to take his place as a central figure in philosophical thought. As such, it also once declared that the society's purpose was not to remove prayer from public life but to work hard to enhance its message and quality. In this way, grassroots secularists in provincial England implemented Holyoake's message about the utility of belief and opinion tested through discussion and intellectual engagement. From this point onwards, the society at Leicester enshrined the power of the liberal Millite platform, which championed the principle of free speech, by having an increasingly heady mix of speakers from all corners of the political and religious ideological map. Holyoake's own ideological clash with Bradlaugh was frequently played out with members of the national wing of secularism, epitomized by Bradlaugh's National Secular Society. During their frequent visits, some members of the National Secular Society scarcely hid their exasperation in noting just how far Holyoake's Secularism had negotiated the nonnegotiable—culminating in one of them suggesting that the Leicester Secular Society had "effectively signed a peace treaty with the Christians" (Nash, *Secularism, Art and Freedom* 133).

REASSESSING HOLYOAKE WITHIN VICTORIAN RELIGION

Viewing Holyoake in greater depth means that we must now fit him and his ideological stance into a longer conception of the rise of the secular and its meaning to British society and culture, considering the outcomes of Holyoake's approach and the longevity of secularism's philosophical trajectory. In fact, such a reassessment chimes more readily with the actual outcomes of secularization for an envisioned "end time" for religion, which has more recently been described as incomplete, messy, inconclusive, or illusory (Stark 252–73; Nash, "Reconnecting Religion" 307–18). In his apparent agreement with the messy results of secularization, Holyoake's Secularism perhaps contrasts with the eliminationists' bipolar conceptions of victory and defeat. In other words, focusing upon Holyoake and his pragmatic negotiation and accommodation more readily resembles the fate of the secular in the West, which has discredited the linear and mechanistic models of secularization. As such, Holyoake's acceptance that the late history of religion does not fit with crude secularization grand narratives tells us far more than the theories of absolutist eliminationists committed to the end of religion, both those in the nineteenth century and in our own moment.

Holyoake's undogmatic approach, which itself actively avoids grand narratives, can also be traced back to particular elements he learned from Robert Owen. Not for nothing has Owen been so readily identified with socialism. Owen consistently believed his schemes were striving for a better collective world. This stood in some contrast to the solitary individualism espoused by the "hard secularist" eliminationists. Bradlaugh's quarrels, in particular, with socialism and his fears of it are well documented. Holyoake thus inherited Owen's own sense of mission and optimism, something that sprang from the latter's espousal of a prototype of the labor theory of value. As J. F. C. Harrison has suggested in *Robert Owen and the Owenites in Britain and America* (1969), Owen hoped that human fellowship would be realized in a utopia that had addressed economic problems as the essential by-product of economic underconsumption. This again differed from what Owen and Holyoake respectively would have seen as Carlile and Bradlaugh's capitulation to the dismal science, with their ready (and individualist) adoption of Malthusianism and its attendant litany of potential misery.

Thus, Holyoake was more readily able to appropriate small changes in thought and ideology, and such optimism sustained a lingering sense of micro-victory, alongside what became the great liberal motif of embarking on an educational journey. Holyoake instinctively subscribed to a Whig view of progress, and this explains his later flirtation with Comtean Positivism. Comteanism, which elevated the achievements of humankind to the status of the sacred, also contained essential elements of transcendence and, once again, a theory of evolution in stages that could be mistaken for an Owenite-style "science of society," according to which rational principles—when put in place of religious doctrines—would become the motor of social development. So it is no surprise when, later in the nineteenth century, Holyoake-style secular societies in England's provinces readily adopt Millite lecturing platforms, in which all opinions were invited to appear and be heard. This directly tested the social and functional utility of each slab of knowledge or new idea. No fledgling thought or aspiration would ever be thrown out with the ideological bathwater while such open minds were encouraged to flourish. Nonetheless, this had the potential of encouraging religious and ideological eclecticism, in which strong views could be episodically and weakly held.

In getting himself and his followers to this position, Holyoake had recognized that Owen's utopianism was also readily dismantled in the mind by those who had more pragmatic and specific agendas. It was a feature of Owen's thought and the phases it went through that he could attract followers to each manifestation without them subscribing to his whole system. This meant that the more prosperous artisan was attracted by Owen's trade-union phase, made concrete in the formation of the Grand National Consolidated Trades Union of 1833. The less prosperous flocked to Owen's Labor Exchanges, where the cycle of sweated labor was broken by a system of credit notes used to exchange the products of labor directly, without the imposition of capital profit evident in the outside world. Such institutions were able, at least for a time, to stave off the damaging effect of falling prices for the goods that their handiwork produced. Those still closer to destitution would find themselves inexorably drawn to Robert Owen's communitarian schemes that would do battle with the "Old Immoral World"—with unfortunate results, such as the failure of the Queenwood community in 1845. Given that Owen's grand programs rarely succeeded and were in any case so often adapted piecemeal by Owen's followers, Holyoake unsurprisingly avoided a programmatic utopian agenda.

Instead, he pursued what Owen occasionally suggested: that secularism might provide alternatives to dominant religious sensibilities. Holyoake was aware that such a quest for individual liberation from religion would be appealing to many educated artisans and skilled workers in urban mid-Victorian England.

In this spirit, Holyoake created his Anti-Persecution Union in 1843, an organization designed to protect the conscience of the individual and persuade religion to stop acting in conjunction with secular authority. This union tried to nullify the conflict models by helping both the secular and the religious who had fallen foul of religious laws at home and abroad. The Anti-Persecution Union also reveals Holyoake's defense, not of atheism or the irreligious, but of social progress through free discussion. Ironically, this was the sounding board for Holyoake's eventual move into advocating noncombative, quietist ideas that would eventually surface fully formed as the ideology of Secularism. In the twelfth issue of the Anti-Persecution Union's newspaper, *The Movement and Anti-Persecution Union Gazette* (1844), Holyoake found himself advocating quietism in the face of talking to the religious and to socialists ("A Lesson to Atheists" 89–90). Attempts to appease Christians by interacting with their sensibilities apparently resulted in accusations of hypocrisy from the radically irreligious, while discussions of atheism's apparent value and importance resulted in an accusation of irrelevance from socialists who felt such investigations lacked economic analysis of exploitation. Although obviously not consciously created as such, these approaches offered two versions of what would later be recast as the secularization thesis. The first, Holyoake's effort through the Anti-Persecution Union to disconnect religion from secular state power, equates with the older Berger sacred-canopy version of secularization, in which unraveling religious control of cultural life and institutions would have inevitably positive effects. Control of knowledge, schooling, and access to the medical and welfare systems would come into secular hands, allowing rational social goals to be pursued. Holyoake's quietism—his encouragement of Secularism to demonstrate tolerance of Christian sensibilities so that it was characterized by dialogue and discussion rather than combat and colonization—aligns with a second anticipation of the secularization thesis. This version acknowledges progress towards a greater secularization of life without thinking about what an end time for religion means or entails. In both cases, liberal progress is imagined to place religion in retreat.

When secularization came to be characterized as a numbers game in the 1960s, it created a third view of secularization, affirming the unequivocal retreat of religion that Victorian secularists were often certain they could observe. But religion's apparent waning instead now looks different with the enduring power of religious narratives (as Holyoake eventually realized and gave up trying to deny), which has been evident in three primary ways in the modern West. First, since the nineteenth century, religion has adapted and reused its own narratives rather than simply fading away or becoming more secularized. But it is perhaps much less appreciated how, second, religion has also borrowed secular narratives and told narratives about the secular over this same period. Third, rather than merely fading away in a numbers game, religion has learned the power of becoming and speaking as the oppressed minority. While religious influence might have waned from its once powerful cultural position, I have argued in *Christian Ideals in British Culture* (2013) that there is sufficient evidence to suggest that religious narratives have retained utility for individuals who have seen them as tools to shape and frame life experiences. Despite Holyoake's enthusiasm for exploring religious narratives and his desire to remove cultural hiostility to them, he never envisiaged that religious narratives would have such enduring utility in the modern world. All three developments in religion's modern status indicate how far religion has moved from the monolithic status that elminationist secularists cast for it in the early and, for that matter, late nineteenth century. Likewise, Charles Taylor's description of Christianity's own dismantling of pagan subcultures as a force for disenchantment similarly undermines traditional associations between secularization and disenchantment (425–26).

Holyoake and his compatriots would be surprised that much of the secular world has been constructed without the destruction or removal of religion and its institutions, which were still visible in the physical, emotional, intellectual, and psychological landscape of Victorian Britain. Moreover, Holyoake and friends might be likewise perplexed at how religion may not have chosen to do pitch battle, but instead was more prepared to retreat to defensive positions. Effectively, Victorian secularists would be surprised, or even shocked, at how compliant Christianity was capable of becoming for its longer-term survival. The recent research priority around the concept of the religious "nones" (those with little or no knowledge of religious culture) asks questions about quietism, individual responses to surveys of religious affiliation, and the whole notion of religious indifference (see Quack and Schuh, alongside their contibutors, in *Religious Indifference*). This is an area that both nineteenth-century and contemporary activists accustomed to categories of oppositional thought, such as "agitation" and "movement," find difficult to comprehend.

NEW CONTRIBUTIONS TO THE MODERN DEBATE ABOUT THE SECULAR

With this set of theoretical and analytical problems on the agenda, it is no surprise that Holyoake has begun to be the center of renewed interest among some scholars, and this is for several interesting and interlocking reasons. Religion itself now appears to be a target that has moved, and in some respects it has been instrumental in removing some of the grievances that modernizing society laid at its door (such as prosecution of blasphemy, and issues around sexuality and gender equality). A liberalizing religion has made the blunter, more confrontational, versions of secularism look combative and somehow "unfair," thus reawakening interest in figures like Holyoake who were associated with dialogue. He has equally been reappraised by scholars wanting to return him to the historical record, which has tended to overemphasize the more strident and visible secular agitators and campaigners of Victorian England. This has been the central focus of Michael Rectenwald's recent work (*Nineteenth-Century British Secularism*, 2016), which takes us into the more contemporary world and offers some wider historiographical arguments about the secular and its trajectory.

Certainly, it is pertinent to ask just how far Holyoake's approach to secularism and secularization offers a Victorian prototype of the secularization thesis. If we consider this as a possibility, then such a suggestion must become rather more nuanced. Part of Holyoake's thought might be construed as resembling the cruder and older Peter Berger sacred-canopy version of secularization, where religious influence withers under liberalizing pressure. Yet Holyoake's vision also entailed acknowledging progress in the first instance without thinking about what an end time for religion means. The original Berger thesis and its derivatives obviously are now considered to have fissures and cracks in their conception of religion's end time. The sacred-canopy thesis had no definition of an "end" for religion and could equally never explain what happened when its processes stalled or were reversed, even if temporarily. This perhaps now illuminates the belief held by Holyoake that the ongoing process of liberal progress would be placing religion in something they felt was surely visible retreat. This was something that was far more important than a vaguely theorized "end time" for religion. This was because, for Holyoake and his supporters, negotiatied progress with religion was better than combative destruction, since the former could retain elements of religion useful to future societies while transcending what was not valuable.

But, again, was religion actually in retreat? Secularization, when predominantly examined by postwar social scientists, especially in the 1960s, became a numbers game that quickly came to answer in the affirmative. But religion's waning does look significantly different if we think less about numbers and instead acknowledge the enduring power of religious narratives (indeed as Holyoake himself frequently did). As indicated above, my own recent *Christian Ideals in British Culture* (2013) has investigated the effective power of religious narratives, revealing how religion has continued adapting and reusing its own narratives. In doing so, religion borrows secular narratives and recreates and tells narratives about the secular. Religion has also learned, within the contemporary world, to express the power of becoming and speaking as the oppressed minority. Ironically, this is the ultimate lesson learned from George Jacob Holyoake—the man who ideologically grew up within defensive and sectlike structures, using this experience to promote an ideal of quietist peaceful coexistence with religion.

Both coexistence and religion's adoption of sectlike minority aspirations constitute hopes for the desirability and the possibility of a full and lasting religious re-enchantment stemming from the individual's more passionate embrace of religious belief, rather than religious views being dispensed, as in previous historical moments, from an institution to a mixed reception. This version of re-enchantment was something that Holyoake's conception of progress and its direction never envisaged. Moreover, it is tantalizing to speculate whether Holyoake would wave an accusing finger at the eliminationists, both old and new, whose totalitarian urge to replace an apparent evil actively persuaded religion to reboot and revivify itself. Beyond this, we should also ask whether this re-enchantment was aided and abetted by the critiques of secularization that discredited some of its explanatory power. Certainly, removing an end time, and even suggesting that movement in this direction has effectively stalled, has led to narratives of re-enchantment. Equally, it is possible to observe spaces and places where the religious have commenced using the secular narrative to re-enchant or even to enchant for the first time those who never knew the "original" religious enchantment discarded by the secular and secularization (Nash, *Christian Ideals in British Culture* 185–57, 191–92).

A number of contemporary events potentially persuade us of some of this. We might think of the success and profile of the Alpha Course in Britain, which advocates religious solutions to life's questions by adapting a secular therapy model of observing a need and tapping into the language and idioms of that need as expressed in secular terms. Individuals are persuaded that they are suffering a malaise because they are weighed down by the false promises of the secular and instead should cast these off in pursuit of God and what he can offer—"in order to enjoy these treasures, we have to leave behind the rubbish in our lives" (Gumbel 224). The twentieth century also saw the emergence of the ideas of subsidiarity in the hands of the theologians Dietrich Bonhoeffer, Paul Tillich, John Robinson, and Don Cuppit with the idea of religion now permanently subordinated to the pressures and demands of daily life. It is tempting to suggest that Holyoake might approve of this development, but once again he might prefer to see this as religion in retreat and merely changing its communication strategy, rather than altering its fundamental principles and assumptions. Last, we might think of the Archbishop of Canterbury Justin Welby expressing pious honest doubt in the wake of the Paris atrocities. His misgivings about a moral world emerged in an interview in which he said, "I ended up saying to God 'Look this is all very well but isn't it about time you did something—if you're there'" (Staufenberg).

These trends in modern religious practice and narrative might indicate how far Christianity has moved from a monolithic status. However, when combined with the language of oppressed status at the hands of the secular, the adaptations above might equally look like opportunism, an effort to portray the agenda of the New Atheists as combative, making them look like playground bullies. This perhaps resembles the intransigently pious that Holyoake's ideology was designed to protect people from. But adopting the status of the oppressed may not necessarily lead to religious re-enchantment on a wide scale. That is because the success of such religious adaptations depends on how viable they or competing secular narratives will become, how successfully they each become self-contained, and how personally satisfying they become to populations at large.

Holyoake's more obviously subtle view of the relationship between secularism, secularization, and religion, a view so central to the intellectual history of secularism, allows us to draw the following conclusions. Ultimately, we should reinstate Holyoake into a more widely nuanced history that has a place for gradualist consideration of religion's achievements alongside its faults. Such historiography should not encumber the history of secularism with a blinkered view of its supposed intransigent opposition to religion, or with the monolithic and oppressive models of religion entailed in this view—models inherited from the Paine-Carlile-Bradlaugh eliminationist tradition.

Moreover, Holyoake's aspirations and those of his Victorian followers complicates confrontational visions of secularization, which so often used the language of liberation for the secular-minded. Holyoake lost sight of, and inclination for, the very idea of an end time. This was driven primarily by both his ideological heritage as an Owenite and his embrace of fundamental principles of liberal free discussion. At its heart, Holyoake's involved and discursive position sat at odds with a more strident national culture whose campaigns and personalities did not permit such wordy or suggestive discussion. Inevitably, reconsideration of Holyoake and growing appreciation of his thought suggests a link with ideas of the postsecular, produced by the apparent failure of secularization models.

Holyoake's eclecticism, his avoidance of dogmatic polarized positions, his openness to religious idioms and ideas, and, last, avoidance of an end time to religion's influence—this all tempts one to envisage him as a potential prophet of Charles Taylor's ideas. At first the comparison appears quite seductive. The failures, misgivings, and dissent that seem to have characterized the recent history of secularization theory created a space in which a new synthesis could flourish in the shape of Charles Taylor's *A Secular Age* (2007). Taylor's opinions and conclusions appeared constructed to fit in with an age that was tolerant, attentive, multicultural, and appreciative of difference—in ideological terms, an age that might just have already passed. Beyond this, *A Secular Age* recognized a post-Fordist, post–Dietrich Bonhoeffer age, where time constraints and choices had supplanted the religious duties and imperatives of previous centuries. Taylor provided support and succor to all sides of the argument and protected each of them from the claims and assaults of each other.

Thus, it is supremely tempting to see components of Taylor's arguments as modern updated versions of the intentions and original thoughts of George Jacob Holyoake, as formulated by him at the start of the 1850s. Holyoake's pragmatism, the apparent openness, and the decision to back away from combative creations of the religious and the secular seems, at first sight, to correlate rather well with some readings of Taylor's. However, it is a little too easy to depict Holyoake as a prophet of the secular age and postsecular compromises and accommodations.

Taylor's agenda does contain an *enduring* and sustained, if sometimes covert, undermining of the secular. Taylor regularly suggests the ultimately unfulfilling nature of the "schizophrenic" secular, and its failure to provide satisfactory answers to the increasingly complex questions posed to it by modern and postmodern populations (726–27). His answer is to see the capacity for religious renewal in the current mode of secularity, moments and places when secular fancies flee away. For Taylor, God appears to have permitted secularization to happen and therefore it must unequivocally have a purpose. It is as though the permitted rise of the secular lured humankind into a belief in its own destiny before this would invariably falter and stall. Instead, individuals might now turn from their dissatisfaction to recognize a "transcendent reality" that Taylor believes offers the attraction of a "broader field" of meaning and leads to a sense of deeper "fullness" (768–69). For Taylor, what he calls "minimal religion," or "being spiritual without being religious," occurs within private spheres such as the family. Its openness and "ecumenism" disarm secular criticism, and it remains a possible replacement for discontentment with the mainstream masternarrative of secularism about the desirability of religion's eclipse (534–35). This is a religion born out of a retreat from a failure of the modern and of secular narratives that are questioned and, according to Taylor, become "less plausible over time" (770).

In this Charles Taylor is not at all like Holyoake, whose liberalism wanted perpetually to move forward in a Whig-inspired acceptance of what human discussion and social utility would bring forth for humankind. Both religion and the "hard secular" would eventually become redundant under Holyoake, although the quest for an end time would remain tantalizingly vague, even arguably becoming superfluous. Again, this was perhaps because for Holyoake participation on the journey would arguably be as important as, if not more important than, thinking clearly about the precise nature of the destination. Holyoake might well have taken something of a jaundiced view of Taylor's sleight of hand, however slight Taylor might want it to appear. Ultimately, Holyoake would find Taylor's potential for enchantment anew deeply problematic. For Holyoake, re-enchantment held out the prospect of humankind being filled anew with assertions and propositions that uncomfortably defied logic. He equated these with the supernatural and superstitious that could simply not be tested or revealed with the tools of proof, or the quest for social utility.

CONCLUSIONS

Holyoake might not have wanted to destroy (eliminate) religion, as Bradlaugh did. However, he endlessly wanted to improve the quality of the beliefs that religion espoused and hoped that doing so would jettison the more obviously archaic, selfish, and vengeful ones. Embracing re-enchantment would remove the fundamental role of questioning and its centrality to life. This would scarcely enshrine the concept of "life according to reason"; nor would "disputation" become the "passion and the higher state of life" (Holyoake, *English Secularism* 5). Questioning, and the right to it, had pulled Holyoake and hundreds like him both to challenge religion's relationship with the state and to agitate for a cheap and honest press. Likewise, it was questioning that was central to the Owenite search for a new view of society and the Millite testing of social utility. A focus on social utility so easily saw religion, and more importantly the actions of the religious, as brakes on social progress. Insights from both Owen and Mill were uncompromising cornerstones of Holyoake's Secularism, as defined in his pronouncements of the early 1850s and demonstrated by his followers in succeeding years.

By all means, it is incumbent upon all of us to trace ideological lineages, but regular scrutiny is needed to ensure that the comparison does not stray too far from the historical context of each individual. Careful consideration will often drive us to note that individuals are products of their age. Intransigence or pragmatism can be produced by individual historical contexts. In this case, the life of an artisan attracted to Owenism, Chartism, and autodidact lifestyles is, and remains, fundamentally different from the Canadian Catholic college professor whose intervention served notice that an intellectual juggernaut of a theory had massively outstayed its welcome.

Last, we should carefully distinguish between earnest cravings and sober predictions. Both Holyoake and Bradlaugh had been high-profile individuals and had considerable numbers of followers who had personally experienced the uncompromising end of religion in their own lives. The two leaders acted differently in their approaches to religion but ultimately wanted the society of their age to be reformed and to give a fair deal to those who critiqued religion. Holyoake wanted discovery and dialogue while Bradlaugh wanted religion to come to an end. Yet neither were in the business of predicting and theorizing about what was likely to happen at the hands of social change and the first advocates of secularization theory. Ironically, if they were alive today, like Charles Taylor, they might seek to confine the theory of secularization to the realm of things past. The difference would be that while Taylor would see the possibility of something like a widespread resurgance of longing for "transcendent reality," both Bradlaugh and Holyoake would look forward to liberal progress and the realization of social utility—with Holyoake emphasizing that critical engagement would always be more fruitful than conflict.

WORKS CITED

Arnstein, W. L. *The Bradlaugh Case: Atheism, Sex, and Politics among the Late Victorians*. U of Missouri P, 1965.

Berger, Peter. *The Sacred Canopy: Elements of a Sociological Theory of Religion*. 1967. Anchor Books, 1990.

Gumbel, Nicky. *Alpha: Questions of Life*. London, Kingsway, 2010.

Harrison, J. F. C. *Richard Owen and the Owenites in Britain and America: The Quest for the New Moral World*. Routledge, 1969.

Holyoake, George Jacob. *English Secularism; A Confession of Belief*. London, Watts and Co., 1896.

———. "A Lesson to Atheists." *The Movement and Anti-Persecution Union Gazette*, no. 12, 1844, pp. 89–90.

———. *The Principles of Secularism*. London, Austin and Co., 1871.

Ingersoll, R. G. *The Gods*. Washington, DC, C. P. Farrell, 1879.

Micklewright, F. H. Amphlett. "The Local History of Victorian Secularism." *Local Historian*, vol. 8, no. 6, 1969, pp. 221–27.

Nash, David. *Blasphemy in Britain: 1789–Present*. Ashgate, 1999.

———. *Christian Ideals in British Culture: Stories of Belief in the Twentieth Century*. Palgrave Macmillan, 2013.

———. "Reconnecting Religion with Social and Cultural History: Secularization's Failure as a Master Narrative." *Cultural and Social History*, vol. 1, no. 3, 2004, pp. 302–25.

———. *Secularism, Art and Freedom*. Pinter Press, 1992.Quack, Johannes, and Cora Schuh, editors. *Religious Indifference: New Perspectives from Studies on Secularization and Nonreligion*. Springer International, 2017.

Rectenwald, Michael. *Nineteenth-Century British Secularism: Science, Religion and Literature*. Palgrave Macmillan, 2016.

Royle, Edward. *Radicals, Secularists and Republicans: Popular Freethought in Britain, 1866–1915*. Manchester UP, 1980.

———. *Victorian Infidels*. Manchester UP, 1974.

Schumaker, J. F. "Mental Health Consequences of Irreligion." *Religion and Mental Health*, edited by J. F. Schumaker, Oxford UP, 1992, pp. 54–69.

Stark, Rodney. "Secularization RIP." *Sociology of Religion*, vol. 60, no. 3, Autumn 1999, pp. 249–73.

Staufenberg, Jess. "Paris Attack: Archbishop Justin Welby Admits 'Doubt' over God's Presence after Tragedy." *The Independent*, 22 Nov. 2015. Accessed May 28, 2018.

Taylor, Charles. *A Secular Age*. Harvard UP, 2007.

Wiener, Joel. *Radicalism and Freethought in Nineteenth-Century Britain: The Life of Richard Carlile*. Praeger, 1983.

CHAPTER 5

Karl Marx and the Invention of the Secular

DOMINIC ERDOZAIN

BORIS PASTERNAK'S novel *Doctor Zhivago* (1957) contains a spirited discussion between the young Zhivago and his uncle, Nikolai, a philosopher and former Orthodox priest who now works for the publisher of a progressive newspaper. "Uncle Kolia" was a representative of the "new Christianity," a religion of life and action, rather than creed. He was determined to establish Yura Zhivago into such a faith—if that is quite the word.

> As I was saying, one must be true to Christ. I'll explain. What you don't understand is that it is possible to be an atheist . . . and yet believe that man does not live in a state of nature but in history, and that history as we know it now began with Christ, and that Christ's Gospel is its foundation.
>
> Now what is history? It is the centuries of systematic explorations of the riddle of death, with a view to overcoming death. That's why people discover mathematical infinity and electromagnetic waves, that's why they write symphonies. Now, you can't advance in this direction without a certain faith. You can't make such discoveries without spiritual equipment. And the basic elements of this equipment are in the Gospels.

The sermon continued while Uncle Kolia worked on some proofs. His colleague and companion complained that metaphysics was bad for his stomach, and that his doctor had forbidden such discussions. Yura, however, was spellbound as his uncle unveiled the majestic heresy that Christianity was not an ethic but an energy, an outlook, a glint in the eye. What was this spiritual equipment?

> To begin with, love of one's neighbor, which is the supreme form of vital energy. (Pasternak 10)

But it was more—Uncle Kolia unleashed another, rising homily:

> But don't you see, this is just the point—what has for centuries raised man above the beast is not the cudgel but an inward music . . . It has always been assumed that the most important things in the Gospels are the ethical maxims and commandments. But for me the most important thing is that Christ speaks in parables taken from life, that He explains the truth in terms of everyday reality. (Pasternak 42)

Christ was not a teacher so much as one who lived, transfiguring the mundane into a realm of supreme importance. When he appeared, "emphatically human, deliberately provincial, Galilean, at that moment gods and nations ceased to be and man came into being" (Pasternak 43).

Apart from its poetic brilliance and tireless dissidence, one of the virtues of Pasternak's novel is its capacity to deprovincialize Christianity as the exclusive possession of orthodoxy, and to destabilize the secular as a sphere of imagined independence.

Christianity appears in surprising places. The Soviet mind is shown to be a welter of hopes, fears, and taboos. Conventional distinctions between the religious and the secular dissolve. Some of the more intriguing characters in the book are as conversant with the *Communist Manifesto* as with the works of Dostoevsky, and equally fond of both. It is, Pasternak writes, "only in mediocre novels" that people are crudely separated into the categories of good and evil, heroes and villains (Pasternak 298).

Pasternak's masterful blurring of the sacred and the secular provide an inviting introduction to the nineteenth-century ferment that arguably created the Soviet experiment. And his playful yet respectful rendering of Marxism as something closer to prophecy than science offers a window into recent debates over secularization and the very possibility of the secular. In a fascinating discussion of Jeremy Bentham and Michael Oakeshott, Simon During has recently posted the question: "Is absolute secularity conceivable?" (During). And it is a question we may also ask of Marx. Just as Bentham's concept of happiness turns out to be a complex of ideas borrowed from the religious mind he so vigorously "censured," Marx's robust secularism may be interpreted as a smokescreen for an awkward debt, a radical dependence that flies in the face of the triumphant notion of secularization that he and Engels espoused. If, to borrow Denis Janz's phrase, the modern period's "dominant form of secularism" is understood as the smoldering, Judeo-Christian compound that it was, the tidying presumption of the secularization narrative may take a further blow (Janz 3–4). Secularism may not be secular. To conceive of Marxism as the historical triumph of a secular outlook is to confuse propaganda with history. My claim is that Marx's philosophy owed as much to conscience as to science, and it is to this concept that we should turn for more fruitful understandings of the shared ecologies of "religion" and the "secular." Others have acknowledged Marx's debt to prophetic traditions of religious thought, but it is this dynamic concept of conscience—a hybrid of Judeo-Christian thought and internal moral reasoning—that I wish to emphasize in this chapter.

Conscience was a concept employed by Pasternak in *Doctor Zhivago*, as he explored the erosion of inner certainties by a culture of compulsive, desperate duplicity, and it is one that is rich in interpretive potential. There is a school of thought, often associated with Kantian philosophy, that the dictates of conscience are fixed, permanent, and largely immune to historical conditioning: a natural law, in the literal sense of the term. But there is a contrasting, more historical view closer to the perspective of John Locke that consciences are made, not given. Moral sensibility and ethical frameworks, to this school of thought, are forged in the friction of human encounter and lived history. They are not timeless features of the human condition. My conviction is that the intellectual culture of the West supports this latter view, and that much of what we take for granted in terms of natural law or human rights discourse is historically sedimented, rather than convincingly natural—which of course is Simon During's point about Bentham, and the nakedly utilitarian philosophy that is in fact as culturally textured as any other (for a more developed discussion of conscience, see Erdozain; Boobbyer). Which brings me to Marx: one of the great inventors of the secular who nevertheless drew many of his most dynamic ideas from the "misty regions" of thought that his political teleology had theoretically trounced. Marx offers the paradox of a secularism that cannot escape religious conceptuality even as it assails the delusions of faith. To examine this paradox, however briefly, is to ask questions about the basic dichotomy of the religious and the secular to which scholarship still often defers (for more on this point, see chapters by Morrow and Scott in this volume).[1] In "conscience" I do not propose a full solution to the problem

---

1. See also David Nash's discussion of one of the first figures to use the term *secularism*, George Jacob Holyoake, in this volume. Holyoake, as Nash explains, eludes the "eliminationist"

of normative, shepherding language. But as a word that literally suggests a "co-knowing"—a confluence of spiritual and natural reasoning—it is a helpful antidote to this conventional dichotomy. Marx tried to transcend the deadening vapor of religious imagination, yet the energy and timbre of his protest revealed something of Pasternak's "inward music" of faith.

This was something scholars began to recognize with increasing sensitivity in the mid-twentieth century, as tensions between Marx's philosophy and Soviet ideology became ever more apparent. This is not to say, as Jonathan Sperber claims in a recent biography, that there was minimal to no relationship between the brutal communist regime and the writings of Marx himself (Sperber 560). Clearly there was. But there was a moralism and humanism in the movement's founding literature that jarred with the sharper claims of dialectical materialism and economic determinism by which Marxism came to be known. Marx was a moralist before he was a materialist. One of the remarkable aspects of the era of Perestroika was the degree to which Marx's early writings contributed to unraveling of a Soviet ideology premised upon his official teachings. As Philip Boobbyer has demonstrated in *Conscience, Dissent and Reform*, assessments of the Soviet failure were universally ethical (75–113), and among the materials with which a totalitarian experiment was sternly indicted were Marx's *Economic and Philosophic Manuscripts*, written between April and August 1844 and only rediscovered in the 1920s. One dissident of the late-Soviet era insisted that the "real humanism" of Marx and Engels was founded on the principle of the freedom and spiritual autonomy of the individual. As Boobbyer notes, "The very study of the early Marx was a subtle indication of discontent with the regime" (150). The reignition of conscience that Boobbyer's study describes, arguably beginning with *Doctor Zhivago* and gathering pace with the publication of Solzhenitsyn's *One Day in the Life of Ivan Denisevich* in 1962, drew sustenance from Marx's prophetic humanism. This cannot be counted among the ironies of history.

In a brilliant introduction to the *Communist Manifesto*, written in 2002, Gareth Stedman Jones has questioned whether Marx and Engels ever really believed in the uncompromising economic determinism with which they became associated. He quotes a letter in which Engels backtracks from the cruder interpretations of historical materialism, explaining,

---

account of secularization as a decisive overcoming of religious "oppression." Rather, he retains and exudes an esteem for elements of religion, an esteem that, as Nash contends, might seem to anticipate—though it does not in truth coincide with—the "postsecularization" (my quotation marks) secularization narrative of Charles Taylor in *A Secular Age*.

Marx and I are ourselves partly to blame for the fact that the younger people sometimes lay more stress on the economic side than is due to it. We had to emphasize the main principle vis-à-vis our adversaries, who denied it, and we had not always the time, the place or the opportunity to give their due to the other elements involved in the interaction. (qtd. in Stedman Jones 114)

Other scholars have suggested the oddity of a doctrine of economic necessity finding expression in the apocalyptic idiom of the *Communist Manifesto*, with its "Specters," hidden "Powers," and its dark warnings of a coming warfare between two, elemental forces: the cruel bourgeoisie, on one side, and "the revolutionary class, the class that holds the future in its hands," on the other (Brown 93–104). Marx's advice for the former: "tremble."

As a blow for cool, scientific materialism, *The Manifesto* leaves a lot to be desired. Like Marx's unfinished treatise on *Capital,* the modus operandi was to shame and expose the dark secrets of the capitalist system. As Marx prefaced the German edition of *Capital*:

Should the German reader shrug his shoulders, like a Pharisee, at the conditions of the English industrial and agricultural workers, or optimistically calm himself by thinking, that in Germany things are . . . not yet so bad, then I must call out to him: *De te fabula narratur!* ["It is your story being told!"] (Sperber 437)

Stedman Jones is surely right to dispute the purity of the economic reasoning to which Marx and Engels appealed in defense of their mission. Stung, in 1844, by Max Stirner's accusation that the humanism of the Young Hegelians was yet another incarnation of the Judeo-Christian ethic—"only the last metamorphosis of the Christian religion"—Marx and Engels offered what Stedman Jones terms the "thermo-nuclear response" of denying that their ideas had any history at all (Stedman Jones 143). Indeed, they denied that any ideas have a history apart from the close, tethered, all-controlling parentage of economic conditions.

Horrified by the contention that they had reprised the moralizing dilettantism of the French Christian socialists, Marx and Engels rebranded not just their own philosophy but history itself. Intellectual culture, they now declared, is a servant, not a master. It is always the effect, never the cause. As they write in the *German Ideology*:

Morality, religion, metaphysics and all the rest of ideology as well as the forms of consciousness corresponding to these, no longer retain the semblance of independence. They have no history, no development. (qtd. in Jessop and Wheatley 372)

And most famously of all, in chapter 1 of the *Communist Manifesto*, they write: "The history of all hitherto existing society is the history of class struggles" (Marx and Engels, *Communist Manifesto* 219).

Such statements amount to the invention of the secular: a great reordering of the economy of historical agency to leave religion and morality empty-handed. It is an idea that has dominated social history, until perhaps the 1990s, and its traces are found in myriad discussions of religion and modernity (see Sanders, in this volume, for an account of similar trends in histories of working-class culture). But it was a theory built upon a cobbled denial of an unsettling fact: that Marxism itself was the progeny of that despised soft tissue of morality, religion and metaphysics. Stirner was right. Feuerbach, Bauer, Marx and their friends were theologians in denial. Their inward music was thunderous and grave, but it had little relationship to some all-controlling economic "base."

Marx was never a man of conventional piety or personal faith. His religious criticism lacks the personal, almost lachrymose intensity of Feuerbach's, for example. He was an atheist by the time he finished his doctorate on Greek philosophy, complete with defiant epigraphs from Epicurus and Prometheus. Yet he shared Feuerbach's in-house protest against the disintegration of ethics and theology in the Protestant tradition, he quoted the Bible freely by way of correction, and he drew on a suspiciously spiritual cast of Enlightenment icons in his critique of confessional authority.

Indeed, Marx's shift from an epistemological or intellectual critique of religion to practical or political analysis heightened his dependence on Judeo-Christian criteria of judgment. As Marx often admitted, his critique of democracy, liberalism, and the free market was an extension of his religious criticism: namely, the exposure of a system that claims one thing and does another. The criticism of earth, he explained, begins with the criticism of heaven—or the theology that spuriously ennobles and excuses terrestrial injustice. And it was from this caustic, triumphant exposure of the ideological activity of religion that he moved, in his *Critique of Hegel's Philosophy of Right* (1844), to a wider indictment of the failed promises of liberal modernity. To crack religion, as Feuerbach had apparently done in *The Essence of Christianity*, in 1841, was to crack the code of a still-theologizing modernity. As Marx put it with his inimitable, presumptive precision: "The task of philosophy . . . [,] once the holy form of human self-alienation [i.e., religion] has been discovered, is to discover self-alienation in its unholy forms," that is, politics, economics, and their ideological accomplices. "The criticism of heaven," Marx continues, "is thus transformed into the criticism of earth, the criticism of religion into the criticism of law, and the criticism of theology into the criticism of politics" (Marx 72). Marx's ability to throw a critical light upon the strutting unrealities of democracy and liberal economic theory rested on a mode of criticism forged and tested on religion—for Marx, the original ideology. Yet the method and the mode of exposure was (for Marx as well as Feuerbach) itself religious. The driving knowledge that Marx brings to every discussion of these failing icons of modernity is always ethical, and often strikingly biblical. Marx's philosophy may be described as a rage for integration, a revolt against the alienation engendered and justified by the disappointments of liberal modernity. Marx saw clearly that the inequities of industrialism were structural, rather than accidental. Yet the economic analysis was preceded and perhaps transcended by a moral disquietude that raged against the barbarities that a liberal philosophy was prepared to count among the running costs of industrialism. Marx's hardheaded verdict that money and egoism are the real gods of a self-styled Christian civilization was an initially moral, even spiritual insight. His materialism actually emerges from his moralism, placing him inside that sacred company of religious reformers, such as William Weitling or Charles Fourier, that he was so eager to disown.

Erich Fromm was surely right to place Marx within a lineage of spiritual reformers: "What is common to prophetic, thirteenth-century Christian thought, eighteenth-century enlightenment, and nineteenth-century socialism," he wrote, "is the idea that State (society) and spiritual values cannot be divorced from each other; that politics and moral values are indivisible" (Fromm 95–96). In demanding some sort of consistency between ideal and action, aspiration and reality, Marx was issuing a complaint kindred to an English Methodist firebrand such as Joseph Rayner Stephens, discussed by Mike Sanders in this volume. Like Stephens, Marx was uneasy with any theology or philosophy that privileged thought over deed, or theory over practice. Indeed, Stephens's account of "justification," as Sanders puts it, as "not simply a question of private belief but something that requires social action," captures the substance of Marx's position—as does Stephens's ability to tap the liberation narratives of the Old Testament as a rationale for organized, and if necessary violent, resistance. To say, for example, that Marx's vision is intrinsically un-Christian for its violent eschatology—secular, for its sanction of armed resistance—is to level the same charge at figures of unquestioned spirituality, such as Stephens. Both the putatively secular Marx and the Methodist Stephens—at the time of his arrest for seditious activity in 1838 among the most popular preachers in Britain—urged a salvation that transcended the private self to encompass a reordering of the whole "moral cosmos." Whatever differences remain, the kinship of such indictments of "the coal pits and the cotton mills of christian England" is clear (Stephens 193). Marx and Stephens felt empowered to arraign the injustice of an industrial system because they knew what "justice" was. And their models of justice were religious in origin if not outcome. Marx's religious criticism is not so much a staking out of secular terrain against religious illusion as a revolt against religiously sanctioned failure or inconsistency. The problem, for Marx, is not hypocrisy or deliberate evasion of moral duty. It is the more subtle and insidious phenomenon of religious alignment with secular power. The complaint is that religion, through a combination of social complacency and theological invention, has served to baptize an unjust secular order: projecting justice into a heavenly future while living, in the meantime, off the benefits of the delay. Marx is almost complaining that religious people are not religious enough. Indeed, secularization is an accusation, for Marx, before it is an aspiration or a verdict upon history. His critique of a power-friendly Christianity is one that presupposes that Christianity is meant to be something different. "You want to base the state . . . on faith," he challenges the Prussian authorities in 1842, "religion being for you the general sanction for what exists" (Marx and Engels, *Collected Works* 117–18).

It was, he suggested, a rather feeble version of Christianity that nineteenth-century theocrats wished to enshrine in law. As he challenged: "He who wants to ally himself with religion owing to religious feelings must concede it the decisive voice in all questions, or do you perhaps understand by religion the cult of your own unlimited authority and governmental wisdom?" It was, in other words, a selective and somewhat bleached account of Christianity that Prussian Protestants wished to preserve. To the claim that the "Christian state" embodied the true spirit of Christianity, Marx responded with a preacher's indignation: "Does not every moment of your practical life brand your theory as a lie?" As he continued, with the New Testament as his witness: "Do you consider it wrong to appeal to the courts if you have been cheated? But the apostle writes that it is wrong. If you have been struck on one cheek, do you turn the other also, or do you not rather start an action for assault? But the gospel forbids it" (Marx and Engels, *Collected Works* 191, 198, 199).

Marx's suspicion that modern faith is "simply a sacred cloak to hide desires that are . . . very secular" gains its power, its epistemological edge, in a moral stance that contains disappointment as well as rage (Marx 22). Marx knows that the Prussian Protestant establishment is secular because he believes it should be something else. To one untrained in any economy of virtue the critique would carry no force. So, while he does move toward a materialist analysis of religious motivation, it is an ethical sensitivity that gets him there. Indeed, his economic analysis surfaces from the same, expository fury. Berating the would-be guardians of the "Christian state," he asks: "Are not most of your court cases and most of your civil laws concerned with property?"(Marx and Engels, *Collected Works* 199). The sobering yet electrifying insight that property, money, and egoism are the real drivers of human activity—religious or otherwise—rests upon a diagnostic moralism: a critical conscience. And as he moves from religious criticism to economics, this religious tonality only strengthens.

Marx's analysis of the profaning, truth-altering power of "money" is a striking example of a theological conscience at war with a strutting idol of modernity (Marx and Engels, *Collected Works* 324–26). Not that the worship of Mammon is new, but it is newly vindicated by a surging, unrepentant bourgeoisie. Money, Marx rages, is a godlike agency that turns everything into its opposite: it changes love into hate, vice into virtue, and stupidity into intelligence. "I am ugly, but I can buy myself the most beautiful women. Consequently I am not ugly," Marx writes. "I am a wicked, dishonest man without conscience or intellect, but money is honored and so also is its possessor." Money, Marx laments, is a "perverting power," "the enemy of man,"—sundering and destroying even as it claims to bind and heal. It was a "divine power," "distorting and confounding . . . all human and natural qualities," transforming "the real essential powers of man and nature into what are merely abstract notions and therefore imperfections and tormenting chimeras." Money, he concludes, as society's "existing and active concept of value . . . confounds and confuses all things." It turns "the world upside-down"—a clear, biblical allusion. Money was alienation masquerading as liberation. As a theological critique, the only word Marx lacked was *sin*. But such was his diagnosis. Money was the corruption of what was formerly good: a foreign, interrupting, beguiling force in the affairs of humanity (324–26).

Once again: Marx's critique can only register in one who shares his commitment to concepts like "love," "virtue," and "conscience." Unless the reader values such things, the protest rings hollow. Marx is demystifying a system of worship with beliefs of his own: convictions that look and feel like beliefs. All of this would later be denied or incorporated within the immanent logic of an economic theory, but the source of the protest was native to the religious culture he assailed.

Marx's reflections on the alienating effects of labor are better known. Modern work patterns turn us into objects and commodities, Marx protests, "mortifying" mind and body. The word he uses for this stripping of human dignity recaptured the language of the Epistle to the Philippians, where Christ is described as "emptying himself" to assume the condition of a slave. Marx's ability to attach a promise of emancipation to such language of alienation, writes Stedman Jones, "recaptured much of the drama attached to the original Lutheran reading of Christ" (Marx and Engels, *Communist Manifesto* 136). But where Christ's renunciation was voluntary, deliberate, and profound, the worker's is forced, mean, and degrading, reducing him to a nonbeing: a repudiation of his true self. It may be remarked that Marx knew little of the actualities of industrial life when he drew such conclusions—less than Engels, certainly. Yet his basic insight that industrial labor constituted a new phase of (in)human existence, in which a person exchanges his or her very being for the meager price of their labor, was powerful and influential. What compassion Marx felt for workers he neither knew nor personally encountered is hard to perceive. But his protest rests upon what may be termed a sacred anthropology—a belief in the sanctity of human life and work, corrupted and violated by an arbitrary, unnatural industrial system. *Manu*facturing—working with your hands—was yesterday's concept. For now, men had become machines.

The prophetic idiom was nowhere more arresting than in the *Communist Manifesto*: a simmering, eschatological promise of a brighter future, with the details to follow. The Communist League had been previously known as the "League of the Just," united around the motto "All Men are Brothers." Marx and Engels rebranded it, adopting a more aggressive and divisive tone, but the metamorphosis from prophecy to science was again uncertain. The industrial economy had crushed and commodified all that was once sacred in human culture, drowning religion, morality and filial sentiment "in the icy water of egotistical calculation" (Marx and Engels, *Communist Manifesto* 225, 258, 222).

The market-corrupted bourgeoisie, they complained, has "resolved personal worth into exchange value, and in place of the numberless and indefeasible chartered freedoms, has set up that single, *unconscionable* freedom—Free Trade." This was moral reasoning, fierce and unapologetic, one moment raging, the next, lamenting the crashing progress of a market economy. As they continue: "The bourgeoisie has stripped of its halo every occupation hitherto honoured and looked up to with reverent awe. It has converted the physician, the lawyer, the priest, the poet, the man of science, into its paid wage labourers." Even the family had been reduced, by a merciless factory system, into "a mere money relation." For the market, write Marx and Engels with language taken straight from the book of Genesis, "creates a world after its own image" (Marx and Engels, *Communist Manifesto* 223, 224).

The two key influences on Marx's conversion to communism were Moses Hess's essay "The Essence of Money" (1845) and an article by Engels himself,

"Outlines of a Critique of Political Economy." The mystical, millenarian Hess became an embarrassment to Marx, and he was written out of the narrative. Like Engels, he was the son of a successful industrialist whose journey toward socialist remedies was animated by a mixture of guilt, disgust, and intimate knowledge of the industrial system. Unlike Engels, Hess retained his (admittedly unorthodox) religious convictions, preaching socialism as emancipation from greed (Hess, *The Holy History of Mankind and Other Writings*; Hess, "The Essence of Money"). Marx, it seems, was prepared to endorse (or borrow) almost everything Hess had to say about the worship of money, while otherwise alienating Hess with savage disdain. The treatment of Hess, Sperber writes, was nothing less than cruel, and it again suggests that in severing ties with spiritual versions of socialism Marx and Engels protested too much. For Engel's assault on political economy was ultimately no less theological than Hess's essay on money. As a seminal influence on Marx's conversion to communism, its biblicism is historically significant. Once again, it is the explicit association of economic "freedom" with sin that is most striking.

Inspired in turn by Thomas Carlyle, the English Chartists, and a range of Christian socialists, Engels eviscerated Adam Smith's gospel of free trade as a creed of destruction and estrangement:

> "Have we not overthrown the barbarism of the monopolies?" exclaim the hypocrites. "Have we not carried civilisation to distant parts of the world? Have we not brought about the fraternisation of the peoples, and reduced the number of wars?" Yes, all this you have done—but how! You have destroyed the small monopolies so that the one great basic monopoly, property, may function the more freely and unrestrictedly. You have civilised the ends of the earth to win new terrain for the deployment of your vile avarice. You have brought about the fraternisation of the peoples—but the fraternity is the fraternity of thieves. You have reduced the number of wars—to earn all the bigger profits in peace, to intensify to the utmost the enmity between individuals, the ignominious war of competition!

"When," he challenged the high priests of political economy, "have you done anything out of pure humanity . . . ? When have you been moral without being interested, without harbouring at the back of your mind immoral, egoistical motives?" (Marx and Engels, *Collected Works* 439, 422, 423).

This prophetic intensity is sustained over long sections of Engels's essay: an angry, zero-sum clarity that can have no compromise with the egoism of trade. And the point about *political* economy was that the raging market now had the backing of the state.[2] The English Poor Law of 1834 had institutionalized this gospel of avarice—a theory that, Engels protested, "ill conforms with the Bible's doctrine of the perfection of God and of His creation; but," he added in sarcastic deference to the logic of the new science, "it is a poor refutation to enlist the Bible against facts." "Am I to go on any longer," he finally interjects, "elaborating this vile, infamous theory, this hideous blasphemy against nature and mankind?" (Marx and Engels, *Collected Works* 437).

To place Marx and Engels within a history of conscience is not to say either was conventionally religious. The value of conscience as a historical category is that it can outlive personal belief. This was Pasternak's point. Consciously or not, Marx and Engels each carry a potent theology of creation, of the natural goodness of the world and human relations, and the sinful, destructive role of industrial capitalism in damaging a holy order. Their humanism is theological, even as it castigated the rationalizations of "Christian economics" and the "heart-burnings" of tinkering, middle-class moralists. It is more than a rhetoric of comparison that draws them back to the Bible and concepts of avarice, blasphemy, and alienation. This is the substance of their critique of a liberal system that had literally sanctified the injustices of the market economy. And Marx was sometimes explicit about his debts. When he gravitated toward radical philosophy in Berlin in the summer of 1837, the first set of lectures he attended was on the prophet Isaiah. "Criticism," he then believed, was prophetic work, breaking out of the cloistered holiness of the monk to the public ministry of philosophy. "What was inner light has become consuming flame," he wrote with menace and grandeur. Was this a deliberate appropriation of the Protestant theology of the inner light or simply the language he knew and understood? Marx leaves us constantly unsure as to his own stake in the language that he employed. "The religion of the workers has no God," he wrote to a friend in the early 1880s, "because it seeks to restore the divinity of man" (qtd. in Lubac 41). There are continuities. Marxism, as Paul Ricoeur has written, was "an event" of "western theology" (275).[3]

To speak, then, of the invention of the secular is to say that there was disingenuousness in Marx's claim to have escaped the blundering romanti-

---

2. As Boyd Hilton has exhaustively demonstrated, this retributive theology effectively became the working principle of the emerging liberal state, between the age of Pitt in the late eighteenth century, and the premiership of Rober Peel, culminating in the Repeal of the Corn Laws, in 1846. Engels, in other words, was not exaggerating when he spoke of the reign of Christian economics. The key figure in this connection was Thomas Chalmers. In this volume, Sanders also discusses the "Christian political economy" championed by Chalmers and analyzed by Hilton, demonstrating how clergy associated with Chartism, such as Joseph Rayner Stephens, interpreted the Bible to support a radically different political economy.

3. I am grateful to Charles LaPorte for this helpful reference.

cism of theology for the firm ground of science and economics. Marx continues to operate within an idiom of social prophecy, and his ability to expose organized religion, politics, and bourgeois "ideology" as covers for egoism and self-interest rests upon still-religious criteria. The irony is that it takes a certain knowledge of what a religion should be to declare that it isn't. Marx's great assertion that spirituality is but the aroma of capital, as Merold Westphal has written, the "deodorant" of the acquisitive society, remains an unhappy accusation (166). His program of emancipation from the unfree market is an eschatology of its own. It is, to borrow a Weberian term, a "this-worldly" transcendence, and one that sits uneasily with language of secularization. The power that Marxist concepts would command among his followers would continue to betray this heritage: the appeal to absolutes, the incapacity for compromise, the rooting out of the uncommitted or impure. Like the rights discourse of the democratic West, concepts nominally secular would acquire an instant, invocatory resonance (Glendon 18–47). So in practical function, as well as historical origin, notions of cool, practical disenchantment fail to do justice to what some would consider the excessively reverential, almost cultic dimensions of modernity.[4] This was Wendy Brown's point about the *Communist Manifesto*, in relation to Charles Taylor's uncharacteristically flat acceptance of Marx's supposedly "materialist" outlook. That may be the theory or the claim, Brown protests, but we have to think more about how an idea is proclaimed (Brown 94–95). Even within the generous and undogmatic sophistication of a study such as *A Secular Age*, there is, she suggests, an editorializing instinct that is too quick to proclaim the verdict of secularization as a kind of pan-historical reality. Confessional or faith-based histories inevitably balk at the idea that "godless" political philosophies represent any authentic continuity with their own theological traditions. The point, however, is not about authenticity or even integrity so much as historical candor: Where do ideas come from? How do cultures emerge? As I have argued elsewhere, modernity is understood better as a war of religious ideas than as a war upon them (Erdozain). G. K. Chesterton wrote in 1908 that "the modern world is full of the old Christian virtues gone mad" (233). Whether that is said in comfort or grief, it may in fact be true.

---

4. For an interesting discussion of Russian intellectuals on this theme, see Zernov.

WORKS CITED

Boobbyer, Philip. *Conscience, Dissent and Reform in Soviet Russia*. Routledge, 2005.

Brown, Wendy. "The Sacred, the Secular, and the Profane: Charles Taylor and Karl Marx." *Varieties of Secularism in a Secular Age,* edited by Michael Warner et al., Harvard UP, 2010, pp. 83–104.

Chesterton, Gilbert Keith. *The Collected Works of G. K. Chesterton*. Ignatius Press, 1986.

During, Simon. "Is Absolute Secularity Conceivable?" *Intellectual History Review,* vol. 27, no. 1, Jan. 2017, pp. 151–69.

Erdozain, Dominic. *The Soul of Doubt: The Religious Roots of Unbelief from Luther to Marx*. Oxford UP, 2015.

Fromm, Erich. *Marx's Concept of Man*. Ungar, 1961.

Glendon, Mary Ann. *Rights Talk: The Impoverishment of Political Discourse*. Reprint ed., Free Press, 1993.

Hess, Moses. "The Essence of Money." *Rheinische Jarhrbücher Zur Gesellschaftlichen Reform,* translated by Adam Buick, 1845, https://www.marxists.org/archive/hess/1845/essence-money.htm.

———. *The Holy History of Mankind and Other Writings*. Edited by Shlomo Avineri, Cambridge UP, 2004.

Hilton, Boyd. *The Age of Atonement: The Influence of Evangelicalism on Social and Economic Thought, 1795–1865*. Clarendon, 1988.

Janz, Denis. *World Christianity and Marxism*. Oxford UP, 1998.

Jessop, Bob, and Russell Wheatley. *Karl Marx's Social and Political Thought*. Taylor & Francis, 1999.

Lubac, Henri de. *The Drama of Atheist Humanism*. Ignatius Press, 1995.

Marx, Karl. *Karl Marx: Selected Writings*. Oxford UP, 2000.

Marx, Karl, and Friedrich Engels. *Collected Works*. Vol. 3, Lawrence and Wishart, 1975.

———. *The Communist Manifesto*. Edited by Gareth Stedman Jones, Penguin, 2002.

———. *Karl Marx, Frederick Engels: Collected Works*. Vol. 1, Lawrence & Wishart, 1975.

Pasternak, Boris Leonidovich. *Doctor Zhivago*. Pantheon Books, 1991.

Ricoeur, Paul. *The Philosophy of Paul Ricoeur: An Anthology of His Work*. Edited by Charles E. Regan and David Stewart, Beacon Press, 1997.

Sperber, Jonathan. *Karl Marx: A Nineteenth-Century Life*. Liveright, 2013.

Stedman Jones, Gareth. Introduction to Marx and Engels, *The Communist Manifesto,* Penguin, 2002.

Stephens, Joseph Rayner. *The Political Preacher* (1839) and *The Political Pulpit* (1839). *The Chartist Movement in Britain 1838–1850*, vol. 1, edited by Gregory Claeys, Pickering and Chatto, 2001.

Westphal, Merold. *Suspicion and Faith: The Religious Uses of Modern Atheism*. Fordham UP, 1998.

Zernov, Nikolai Mikhailovich. *The Russian Religious Renaissance of the Twentieth Century*. Darton, Longman & Todd, 1963.

PART II

Religion and the Materialities and Practices of Reading

CHAPTER 6

From Treasures to Trash, or, the Real History of "Family Bibles"

MARY WILSON CARPENTER

AGAINST ALL ODDS, the Andover-Harvard Theological Library has recently acquired a collection of consumer Bibles of a genre confusingly titled "Family Bibles." The generic title is confusing because most people think of "Family Bibles" as Bibles with a handwritten family genealogy on the flyleaf, a proud family heritage demonstrating ancient family lineage, romantically imagined as being discovered in an old trunk in the attic.[1] Readers of Victorian literature are likely to think of them as the kind of Bible from which the "Master of the family" read aloud to the assembled family of wife, children, and servants—most famously described in the well-known passage in *Jane Eyre*, where Jane writes rapturously that "never did his [St. John's] fine voice sound at once so sweet and full—never did his manner become so impressive in its noble simplicity . . . as he sat there, bending over the great old Bible" (Brontë 42).[2]

But the consumer Bibles called "Family Bibles" are not simply "great old Bibles." Their most important distinction is that, in addition to the King James translation known as the "Authorized Version," or AV, they are "picture" or illustrated Bibles. They also contain many other features such as commentar-

---

1. See Carpenter for an account of this myth as found in Taylor's *The Family Bible Newly Opened: With Uncle Goodwin's Account of It* (1853) (3).
2. See McDannell for a representative selection of paintings and even a posed photograph of such family Bible–reading sessions, in which the Bible reader is always the patriarchal head of the family (75–79).

ies, printed pages for "Family Record" or "Family Register" inserted inside the Bible, dictionaries, and chronologies that chronicle dates of specific events in "history" from the Creation to the Millennium. They sport titles intended to appeal to consumers, such as *The Universal Bible; or, Every Christian Family's Best Treasure . . . Containing the sacred text . . . illus. With notes and comments . . . By S. Nelson, D. D.* (London [1758, 1759]). They were published in many different editions from the early eighteenth century through the late nineteenth century, and a few have continued to be published right up until the present day, but the heyday of their publication was the Victorian era. They were most often published in affordable parts or serial numbers, and families or individuals who bought the parts could have them bound later in whatever binding they chose. Some remain in reasonably good condition with obviously expensive and ornamental covers, perhaps even with gold-tipped pages, but many of those that survive—and it is probable that this is only a small fraction of those that were published—are beaten up, covers falling off, inside covers perhaps scrawled on by semiliterate writers, illustrations sometimes colored over unevenly as if by a childish hand. They have not been, and are not, prized as collectors' objects. You can find them on Google offered perhaps for as much as $500 or as little as $35. You will not find them displayed in glass cases in rare book libraries.

In fact, you are likely not to find them even in comprehensive research libraries or, if you do, there will be only a few examples. Research libraries commonly do not accept these "Family Bibles,"[3] (hereafter referred to as Family Bibles) save for a select few that were owned—and donated—by some illustrious family. For in addition to their space-hogging character (they are typically large and heavy, sometimes very large and heavy) and frequently dilapidated condition, these self-proclaimed Bible "treasures," padded out with all sorts of additions to the biblical text, are viewed by scholars more as the "trash" of the Bible trade. Their illustrations are seen as largely cheap reproductions, their commentaries a collection of trivia copied from previously published commentaries, their chronologies a mass of long-discarded fictions about history. Even in the nineteenth century, these Bibles were disdained in their elegant bound form. Leah Price comments, "The great realists did loathe anyone who loved the look of books—who displayed 'a great, large handsome Bible, all grand and golden, with its leaves adhering together from the book-

---

3. The notable exception is the British Library, which, as the original deposit library in Britain, received many copies deposited by publishers as required by law. Some university research libraries, notably the University of St. Andrews in Scotland, hold a significant number of "Family Bibles." Yet these Bibles were not purchased and are not cataloged as separate collections of the genre but are included with many other editions of the Christian Bible.

binder's press,' or whose 'splendidly bound books furnished the heavily carved rosewood table'" (2). Unlike the novel, it was believed, the great, large handsome Bible was prized especially for the way it *looked* from the outside, not for what was inside it.

These are some of the reasons why I describe the Andover-Harvard Theological Library's recent acquisition of a large collection of Family Bibles as a momentous event in the history of the Bible as a book, taking place against all odds. For still other odds against such Bibles had emerged early in the nineteenth century. Bible societies such as the British and Foreign Bible Society (1804) and the American Bible Society (1816), which launched campaigns to publish "cheap Bibles" with the aim of having every individual possess his or her own Bible, excluded everything except "pure" text. That is, the Bibles were to include no notes or comments, nothing but the text of the AV. Leslie Howsam and Scott McLaren comment that this "simple restriction was designed to set aside doctrinal differences" (53). However, as Timothy Beal characterizes it, this also materialized the "Puritanic Biblicist ideal"—the fundamentalist principle that the Bible should be read as the literal Word of God, its meaning to be divined only from private prayer and public preaching (*Rise and Fall* 8). The material format of Family Bibles ran directly counter to this principle, for though they contained the full AV, they contained much that was not authorized as well. Not only were multiple interpretations of the text offered, but as Howsam and McLaren explain, there were illustrations of a kind that some found positively "disturbing" (60). In one illustration of the Fall, for example, Adam appears more tempted by Eve's round-as-an-apple breasts than by the apple from the Tree of Knowledge (Brown, *The Self-Interpreting Bible* [1814] 13). Frontispieces featuring a naked Adam and Eve—especially Eve—abound. Also, as Dominic Janes demonstrates in his chapter in this volume on Charles Spurgeon's ambivalence toward Gothic architecture, the illustrations in Family Bibles, some of which featured cathedrals and even icons of saints, were subject to Protestant suspicions of association with popery.

Looking at the nineteenth-century Family Bible as the religious trash of the Victorian family's library, the commodity once so popular that one edition proclaimed itself to be the "Eightieth Thousand," places it in a new and productive perspective (Henry, *The Family Devotional Bible* [185–?]).[4] Like the religious novels discussed by Miriam Burstein in this collection, they have been largely overlooked by scholars as not worthy of serious consideration

---

4. The University of St. Andrews (Scotland) holds a copy of *The Family Devotional Bible . . . Matthew Henry*, London & New York: The London Printing and Publishing Company, described on the title page as "One hundred and forty-seventh thousand." This copy is tentatively dated as [1880?].

today, despite or because of their extraordinary popularity in the past.[5] These were the bestsellers of the Bible market, and like all bestsellers, they are also ephemera despite the decidedly non-etheral quality of those that remain. Scholars seem to have shared the same skepticism of them as being but "surface" aspects—mere appearances—of Victorian religion in the manner that Mark Knight describes in his discussion of critical resistance to Oscar Wilde's explicitly written Catholic theology.

I will argue, however, that neither the "treasures" nor "trash" views of the "Family Bibles" represent their real history. More accurately seen as that of large picture Bibles sold in cheap serial numbers, so that they might be purchased by the working classes, they were also explicitly intended by commentators *for* working-class families. As John Brown (1722–87) was to put it in his address "To the Reader," his *Self-Interpreting Bible* was designed to exhibit the "principal substance" of earlier commentaries "in a manner that might best comport with the ability and leisure of the poor and labouring part of mankind." A working man himself, Brown intended his Bible to be accessible to those with little formal education and little leisure. His *Self-Interpreting Bible*, first published in 1778, went through countless editions.

A study of actual "Family Bibles" further testifies to their unexpected appeal to Jewish families because, as Richa Dwor points out in her chapter in this volume, Jewish women lacked access to study of the Torah or the Hebrew language, and therefore turned to English Bibles. Family Bibles frequently included the Apocrypha, or a part of the Jewish scriptures often excluded from Bible Society versions.[6] And as Cynthia Scheinberg demonstrates in her study of Christian struggles either to deny or somehow to resolve the problem of the Jewish origin and character of the Psalms, which intensified as the Anglo-Jewish community in England increased in both size and political presence, Family Bibles also deploy various strategies for at once constructing biblical origins as fascinatingly exotic, "Oriental," or even "peculiar to the Jews," while nevertheless maintaining the Bible as the official scripture sacred to Christianity. The real history of Family Bibles is much more culturally diverse than "appearances" suggest.

That history can only be assessed by examining a real—material, not virtual—collection of them.[7] The Andover-Harvard Theological Library collec-

---

5. For what has been written on Family Bibles, see McDannell 67–102; Carpenter 3–67; De Hamel 254–69; Bottigheimer; Gunn.

6. See Howsam, especially pp. 13–16, for an account of sectarian differences over the Apocrypha.

7. The only other collection originally identified as Family Bibles that I know of is that in the British Library, which as a deposit library acquired many as serial numbers and had them later bound in the standard British Library binding. This collection was named Family Bibles

FIGURE 6.1. *The Illustrated Family Bible with Explanatory, Critical and Devotional Commentary* . . . London, Edinburgh and Dublin, A. Fullarton & co. [1876].

tion is the donation of a private collector who acquired over 120 editions of these Bibles, the Mortimer B. Zuckerman Collection of Family Bibles.[8] This extraordinary collection, on which this chapter is based, includes a complete fourteen-number set of paper-covered parts (fig. 6.1).[9] With only fourteen numbers, these were priced rather high at a cost of 4 shillings each. The Prospectus, however, advises that the Bible could be purchased in twenty-eight

---

as a subject category in the catalog and was held in large bound volumes in the round Reading Room of the British Museum. However, it is no longer accessible as such in the digital catalog.

8. I thank Nell Carlson, Curator of Historical Collections at the Andover-Harvard Theological Library, for her invaluable expertise and generous assistance in my work on this collection.

9. The *Illustrated Family Bible* [1876]. The Houghton Library (Harvard University) holds another set of Family Bible parts: *Harper's Illuminated New Pictorial Bible* (New York: 1843–46) in fifty-four paper-covered parts. The Houghton Library also holds a bound copy of this same Family Bible, published in 1846.

parts at only 2 shillings each. The paper covers are obviously made from a cheap, disposable kind of paper which is in the process of disintegrating, although the paper in these serial parts is not.

What can we learn from looking at these Family Bibles, so evidently designed to be looked at, *not* just read? William St. Clair proposes that if we are to learn how mentalities were shaped by reading, it is essential to consider "the print which was actually read, not some modern selection" (2). We can learn from these Bibles how the AV was contextualized for readers poor enough to be able to afford only a penny a part and also for those able to pay 4 shillings a part for classier versions, or even able—especially in the later nineteenth century—to buy an entire volume at once. One can also speculate from examining these Family Bibles what they meant to families and why they became so popular. The Zuckerman collection is especially valuable to scholars because the Bibles included in it were privately owned. Each copy is bound with a binding chosen by an individual or family member, many have "Family Registers" that have been at least partially filled in, and they show other signs of having been both heavily used and highly prized, such as a title page ripped in half, a binding taped back together with duct tape, and dried flowers pressed between pages (fig. 6.2). Although few of these Family Bibles include marginal notes written by owners, these Bibles have been *used*—they are not collectors' items in themselves, they are Bibles that display the marks of having been consumed, and are therefore valuable artifacts in the history of Bible reading.[10]

HOW THE FAMILY BIBLE BUSINESS GOT STARTED, OR KNOWLEDGE AS COMMODITY

It is important to recognize that from its earliest beginnings, the Family Bible business was just that—a business. The primary motive for publishing these Bibles was to make money. From the time of the completion of the King James translation in 1611 it had been illegal for anyone in Britain or the colonies to print the AV except the Oxford and Cambridge University presses or the King's (or Queen's) Printer in London. But a Family Bible that included pictures,

---

10. Digitized versions of some Family Bibles are now available, but while a digitized version is certainly better than no Family Bible at all, such versions also make clear why the Family Bible as a physical object, a material book, is superior for research purposes. Because the Bibles are so large, images of individual pages may have to be split in half, giving a distorted perception of image size and proportions. Digital versions, moreover, bear little evidence of how they were used.

FIGURE 6.2. *The Self-Interpreting Bible* ... John Brown. Bungay, T. Kinnersley, 1814.

maps, commentary, and other materials, and that just happened to include the text of the AV as well, might be able to get around the law and allow other printers to get into the lucrative Bible-printing business. But, of course, this was not what publishers wanted potential customers to know. To look at the title pages of Family Bibles published in eighteenth-century Britain, therefore, is to see what lies they told—but also what truths those lies exposed. The first one published was titled *The Compleat History of the Old and New Testament; or, a Family Bible, . . .* (1735, 1737) with S. Smith, D. D., listed as its "Author" and W. Rayner as the printer. Whether S. Smith existed or not is questionable. The important name on the page is Rayner's (1699–1761). He was a printer who had been in trouble with the law more than once for various crimes such as libel and piracy (Lupas 16; Black 463; Carpenter 5, 166 n3). Printing a Bible called a "Compleat History" or "Family Bible" was an innovative strategy to avoid further legal penalties. His "Family Bible" apparently did sell well, since it went into a second edition later. Its sale was doubtless aided by the wonderful engravings of Noah's Ark, expanded into a fold-out version in the later edition and reused many times in later "Family Bibles," as will be discussed.

The Zuckerman collection does not include that particular Family Bible, but it does include a number of others published from 1761 up through the first quarter-century of the 1800s that follow in its train. It so happens that that 1761 Family Bible was also published by someone who'd been jailed more than once, mostly for indebtedness, and was in need of money. But Leonard Howard (1699?–1767) was a clergyman, not a printer, and an actual historical person. Rayner called his Bible a "Compleat History." Howard's *Royal Bible* did not include that claim, being titled only as "A Complete Body of Christian Divinity: containing The Holy Scriptures at large," but went on to assert in addition "a Full and Clear Explanation of all the Difficult Texts, from the various Readings of Authors Antient and Modern . . . A Work Highly useful and Necessary for all Families and private Christians." Howard did not claim to have actually written all the notes himself: he acknowledges that he will "compile, collect, and with my own opinions and remarks give the notions and thoughts of such preceeding annotators" but will always "give place to their better opinions." He hopes by this means to strike out "something new and entertaining, as well as edifying and instructive" ([i]).

"Something new and entertaining"—yes, these Bibles meant to entertain, as well as instruct and improve their readers, not to mention enrich their printers and "editors," often identified as "the Author" with a capital *A*.[11] Family Bibles thus made clear that many Bible texts were indeed "difficult" and in need of explanation, especially "new and entertaining" explanations that would appeal to less educated readers. These Bibles also emphasized the truth that the AV was a translation, not words transcribed directly from God or even identical to those written by the inspired writers of the Holy Bible. This was not a lie—but it might well have been a new idea to some Bible readers.

Consider the title of a Family Bible published around 1790: *The Christian's New and Compleat Family Bible: or, Universal Library of Divine Knowledge*. The title page further promises that in this volume, the "most difficult passages are rendered clear and familiar; the seeming contradictions removed; the mistranslations rectified." This "Family Bible" is to be "a treasury of Divine Revelation," which in addition to "Notes and Annotations, Historical, Chronological, Biographical, Geographical, Theological, Moral, and Practical," will further provide "A Chronological Index of Transactions from Adam to the Time of our Blessed Saviour; A Geographical Index of Places mentioned in the Holy Scriptures; A Brief Account of the Apostles and their Successors . . . etc."

---

11. David Norton quotes from "S. Smith" (more probably Rayner, the printer) about the "Family Bible" providing "amusement" for children, and also describes Sarah Trimmer's objections to allowing children to read "promiscuously" in Bibles (215, 217).

In short, this Bible and others promised readers a *completeness* of knowledge not available to them elsewhere: readers would find a "divine library of universal knowledge" in them. From the earliest published in the eighteenth century through many published in the first quarter of the nineteenth century, printers and/or editors harped on how much *knowledge* was included with the complete text of the AV. Ann M. Blair comments that the lust for "information," meaning "the collection and arrangement of textual excerpts, designed for consultation," goes back for centuries (1). But the eighteenth century, which saw an unprecedented increase in the quantity and quality of printing, was particularly characterized by what Blair terms "info-lust."

Family Bibles, by including all sorts of "consultative works," or reference works compiled from other reference works and meant to be consulted rather than read through—unlike the biblical text itself—could give readers the sense of being part of a new age of information, comparable in some respects to our sense of a new age of "information technology" produced by computers and digital information. This was, after all, the age of the first printed encyclopedia, the first printed dictionary. Jonathan Rose describes the burgeoning of an autodidact culture in the late eighteenth and early nineteenth centuries, especially in the Lowlands of Scotland and the north of England, where weavers and other working-class men strove to educate themselves through the newly acquired skill of reading (11, 19). Family Bibles that described themselves as "universal libraries" containing all knowledge, ancient and modern, divine and human, must have had particular appeal for these eager learners.

The engravings of Noah's Ark that appeared in the first Family Bible, and that showed up again and again in later editions, illustrate this lust for knowledge—perhaps especially *new* knowledge. When I first wrote about this engraving in *Imperial Bibles*, having studied only the Family Bibles as available in the British Library collection, I suggested, following McDannell, that the weird design of this ark—which looks as though it surely would never float—represented values of order, symmetry, harmony, and stability (Carpenter 16–17; McDannell 92). In the Zuckerman collection, however, I discovered that the engraving was reproduced in a number of nineteenth-century Family Bibles, including at least one American Family Bible, the *Columbian Family and Pulpit Bible* (1822). This image here, from an 1816 British Family Bible, published by J. Gleave in Manchester, included a plan of several floors of the Ark (fig. 6.3).

This time, with the aid of the computer and the vast new image-data files available, I was able to identify the image as the work of a seventeenth-century German Jesuit monk, Athanasius Kircher (1602–80), who produced an entire

FIGURE 6.3. *The Holy Bible ... Complete Commentary ... Apocrypha ... and the New Testament.* Embellished with Elegant Engravings. Manchester, printed and published by J. Gleave, 1816.

book on Noah's Ark, complete with the plan of the three floors as reproduced in the 1816 Family Bible, drawings of all the creatures that would have been stalled in it, calculations of the food they would need and how much space it would take, and so on. Discovering the origin of the Ark—which was also reproduced in Diderot's *Encyclopédie* (1751–72)—upended my interpretation of why Rayner had included it in his path-breaking edition of the AV known as "the Compleat History." Yes, Kircher's design of the Ark certainly is symmetrical, ordered, well planned. But more significantly, it was an entirely new kind of naval design. Kircher was interested in technology of all kinds, and he was an inventive genius. Rayner, like other Bible printers following him, probably included it because it represented *new* knowledge. It must have fascinated Bible readers in his day and for a hundred or more years following, none of whom had surely ever seen a boat like it and for whom this seventeenth-century architectural design remained a curiosity.

THE FAMILY BIBLE FOR THE WORKING-CLASS MAN

The Zuckerman Collection of Family Bibles demonstrates a sudden jump in publication after 1800, moving from nine editions published from the 1760s to the 1790s to eighteen editions published between 1806 and 1838. This doubling in number correlates well with St. Clair's statement that in the years between the 1790s and the 1830s, "the number of men, women, and children who read printed texts began to grow rapidly," and that for the first time, "lower-income groups, whose reading had long been the English-language Bible, short chapbooks, and ballads, now had access to other print including book-length literary texts" (10, 11). Moreover, the Family Bibles published in the early decades of the nineteenth century were increasingly published in places other than London: they were printed in Liverpool, Newcastle upon Tyne, Manchester, and Bungay (a market town in Suffolk). These statistics suggest that the installment-plan Family Bible did indeed become an important part of what was actually read by lower-income groups in Britain at this time. How do these Bibles reflect the interests of this newly literate segment of the population? A close look at one of the many editions in the Zuckerman collection of John Brown's *The Self-Interpreting Bible* provides insight into the readers and their readings of this Family Bible.

John Brown was a Scottish weaver who became a Presbyterian minister and, as undoubtedly one of those autodidacts described by Rose, produced not only an annotated Bible but a Bible dictionary and concordance, as well as a metrical version of the Psalms. His *Self-Interpreting Bible,* as mentioned earlier, went through numerous editions in Scotland and England. It was also picked up in the fledgling US and published by Hodge and Campbell in New York in 1790 as *Brown's Self-Instructing Folio Family Bible,* and renamed in 1792 as *Brown's Self-Interpreting Family Bible* (Lacey 80). In Britain, long after John Brown's death, his grandsons John and Alexander Patterson, also ministers, printed editions from the late 1860s on. Many editions, perhaps most, were printed in installments and may have vanished, never reaching the stage of binding.

There are seventeen editions in the Zuckerman collection of John Brown's *Self-Interpreting Family Bible.* The one I look at here states on its title page that it was printed for T. Kinnersley in Bungay, 1814. Brown begins his address "To the Reader" with the reservation "Not to depreciate the valuable commentaries of *Pool, Patrick, Clark, Henry, Burket, Gill, Doddridge, Guyse, etc., etc.*" but to exhibit them in a manner best fitted to "the ability and leisure of the poorer and labouring part of mankind" has been his intention (italics original). Although he provides a "copious Introduction," he believes that the sacred books are themselves an "accurate, full, and explicatory representation of their subject." If the reader properly attends to these, he may "easily . . . find out or explain whatever passages of scripture he may desire." Thus, Brown includes only what he considers simplified or easier commentaries than those he himself has consulted. The title page of this edition states that it contains "A Paraphrase on the Most Obscure or Important Parts." This is not a Bible for university-educated men. It is a Bible for the more ordinary sort who might need some plain, clearly written help with the more obscure passages, and so find the whole easier to read. It is a Bible for the working-class man. (It was probably assumed that most working-class women could not read.)

The covers associated with this particular copy, both entirely detached, are rotted at the edges and have holes in the surface of whatever material was used to bind them. Julia Miller comments that the use of cheaper materials for bindings—sheepskin instead of calfskin, for example—and the introduction of acid tanning caused "a real falling off in quality" of book bindings in the nineteenth century, ultimately producing the condition known as "red rot" (Miller 107 n178). Books with this condition must be placed in special containers to isolate them. The covers of this Bible, however, appear not so much rotting as just beaten up by frequent handling. The bottom of the "Table of the Offices and Conditions of Men," which appears to be the last page, has been ripped off. This Bible does not look as if it was shown off in solitary splendor on a parlor table. It looks as if it's been *read*, its pages turned many times by many hands.

It has also been written on, and by at least three different hands. On the greenish paper pasted to the inside cover, someone has partially written, partially printed in block letters, an inscription that is only partially legible: "Andrew Murray Born 5 of November 1857 . . . Andrew Murray . . . steal this book at 9 years of age . . . Sunderland is my dwelling place and Heven is my home In Christ Murray WIH I DEAD AND IM MY GRAVE PRAY DOMT STEAL THIS BOOK FOR THE LORD WILL BE LIKE MY LAST WILL." For this apparently semiliterate person, the Bible was not only a prized possession but a place where a written statement might take on the authority of a will. It reminds one of the similar curse in George Eliot's *The Mill on the Floss*, where Mr. Tulliver insists that his vow of vengeance against Wakem be written in the great Bible (248).

Inside the book, beneath an engraving of the Madonna and Child, identified by their halos and flanked by two worshipful angels, captioned "Hebrews. Chap. I.V, 6" though positioned next to the first page of the Second Epistle to Timothy, someone has written in good black ink in a carefully tutored hand, "And blessed are the pure in hart [sic] for they shall see God." The sentence runs across the page as straight as if on a ruled line. This annotator is not struggling to write, but appears awed by the Renaissance-like portrayal of the holy mother and child.

On the white page pasted to the inside of the back cover, a third hand has written a partial genealogy and history, beginning with George Henry Ellis born November 1873 (the date is illegible). It continues with births up through 1899, the entries separated by wavery lines drawn across the page. Halfway down the list of births, this family registrar writes: "My dear Mother Mary Jane Barwick 3 th [13th?] June 1809 Cristned at Cent Margret Walmegate York," and this is followed by "George Ellis Started in the carrage Shop November 13—1893." The handwritten notes in this Family Bible surely exhibit the limited education of that poorer and laboring part of mankind, yet these writing readers also make their mark in this book across the nineteenth century. Perhaps it was passed down through generations of the same family. Perhaps it was bought and sold, bought and sold again. Perhaps it was thrown away because a cover or both covers had come loose, and then a bookseller supplied the missing cover(s).

A later nineteenth-century editor, the Rev. John Eadie (1810–76), proclaimed his *National Illustrated Family Bible* (1876) to have been "originally designated the WORKING MAN'S FAMILY BIBLE" and that this "large and interesting class especially . . . will find that their advantage has been consulted in the choice of materials." Eadie, however, was not himself a "working man." He studied at the University of Glasgow and also at the Divinity Hall of the United Secession Church and was a professor of biblical literature and hermeneutics at Divinity Hall. He became minister of the Cambridge Street Secession church in Glasgow in 1835, and in 1863 moved with part of his congregation to the new Lansdowne United Presbyterian Church, which was in a much better part of town than the Cambridge Street church. His income was probably considerably augmented by his many editions of a Family Bible, of which there are ten in the Zuckerman collection.

His fairly lengthy preface—ten pages in the edition I examine here—celebrates the "Protestant liberty of studying and diffusing sacred truth," which he salutes as "a prime element of our national greatness," for Christian civilization not only leads to "liberty, fraternity, and equality" but "soothes and elevates the temporal condition of man" (v). His preface attacks "RITUALISM" and "RATIONALISM" equally, condemning the "revival of the architecture and the sacerdotal forms of the Middle Ages," and also those "boasts of superior reason" that "take away from the Bible its Divine authority" (vi).

His Bible is based on the commentaries of Matthew Henry (1662–1714) and Thomas Scott (1747–1821), from both of which he quotes extensively in his preface. He quotes Henry as intending "to make it [the Bible] as plain as

I could to ordinary capacities," and Scott as noting that "some comments are far too learned for common people" (xiii, xiv). Scott "purposes to adopt something of a new method. Not indeed entirely *new*; for Brown's *Self-Interpreting Bible* suggested the idea" (xiv).

Eadie is most fascinated, however, by the profits associated with the Family Bible. He cites in detail not only the numbers but the pounds associated with "Scott's Commentary":

> The first edition, which was begun in 1788, and was published in numbers, consisted of five thousand copies; the second edition, in 1805, was one of two thousand; an edition of similar size was published in 1810; a fourth, of three thousand copies, in 1812; and another was stereotyped in 1822 . . . Many issues have been made since his death, and thousands of copies have also been sold in the United State of America. During the author's lifetime, the sales amounted to nearly £200,000. Scott's Commentary thus continues to "praise him in the gates." (xiii)

In an 1858 addendum column, Eadie gloats over the already greater sales of his edition: "The sale of thirty-six thousand copies of the previous folio edition within seven years, is a proof that the book has met a deep and extensive want, especially among the classes for whom it was originally intended. Thousands of working men have now, through Mr M'Phun's enterprise, got possession of a cherished Family Bible . . . The present edition, in more convenient quarto size, has been thoroughly revised" (xv). It is obviously true, as he has said earlier in his preface, that "in consequence of Anglo-Saxon Protestantism and enterprise, the sun never sets on the English Bible" (vi).

THE "GRAND AND GOLDEN" AGE: EXPANDING SALES AND BIBLES

From the 1840s on through the 1880s, Family Bible editions soared in both number and kind.[12] The Zuckerman collection has as many as forty editions from this period—the exact number cannot be given, as many Family Bibles from the mid-nineteenth century on omit the date of publication. Place of publication, however, is specified, showing that Family Bibles were increasingly published internationally, listing not only London and New York but

---

12. McDannell notes, for example, that in the decade of the 1850s alone, "almost three hundred *new* editions of the Bible and New Testament were published" (99).

Paris and Melbourne. Publishers reached out for new markets with new features such as many more types and kinds of illustrations and additional supplementary materials: metrical versions of the Psalms, indexes to translators of the Psalms, lists of illustrations, enlarged Family Registers, a selection of hymns, and enlarged Bible dictionaries and concordances. *Cassell's Illustrated Family Bible*, which inaugurated its first edition by sales of weekly numbers at one penny each, later published in bound volumes as well (Ledger-Lomas 331). This extremely popular Family Bible, claiming more than nine hundred engravings, integrated its illustrations into the text, most pages having at least one illustration and many two or more. They have an almost comic-book-like appearance, very appealing to the eye and accompanied by similarly appealing commentary, written to highlight curious, interesting, and even amusing aspects of the text. They seem designed to lure children especially into reading the Bible.

But to at least some adults, these Family Bibles when bound took on an almost heavenly aura in their grand and golden form. A schoolteacher living in Shetland, Andrew Dishington Mathewson, experienced a "ruinous fire" that destroyed most of his precious library in 1860. But as he wrote to a friend some six years later, "about a fortnight before I had sent the value in Stamps to London for a Copy of the first Vol. of Cassel's Illusterated [*sic*] family Bible and to my great relief the following Mail & Posts brought me this very interesting Book, Large Beautiful and gilded. It became as a Messenger for relief and as if sent from on high with the Glad tidings of greater Joy than Earth and Time afford" (26 January 1866).

THE FAMILY BIBLE FOR JEWISH FAMILIES

It was particularly during this period that the "Family Bible" as a genre shows modifications to meet the needs of an increasingly diverse religious culture. The Zuckerman collection, for example, includes two editions of "Family Bibles" in the Douay-Rheims translation from the Vulgate for Catholic readers.[13] Even more significantly, it also includes what may be the first "Family Bible" explicitly designed, as stated in the preface, for "Jewish families": *The Holy Bible, containing the Pentateuch, the Hagiographa and the Former and Latter Prophets* . . . [1880?]. The preface, signed "The Publisher," states that this edition "has most carefully been corrected and revised by the REV. H.

---

13. A translation from the Vulgate for Catholic readers was published in the United States in 1790 by Matthew Carey.

GOLLANCZ, London, a Clergyman of their own body," but specifies that "the point in which this Bible differs most especially from Bibles hitherto published, lies in the alterations effected in the heads of the Chapters and the headings at the top of pages, revised so as to conform with the interpretations usually put forth by Hebrew Commentators." In fact, the text of this Family Bible is the standard King James translation and the black-and-white illustrations—such as the frontispiece of Moses with the tables of the law, here inscribed on the stone tablets in English—largely those that had been printed in various earlier Family Bible editions.

The Rev. H. Gollancz (1852–1930) was actually a Jew who had obtained a doctor of literature degree at London University in 1876 and begun preaching at that time. As there was then no rabbinical training program in England, he returned to Eastern Europe (he had been born in Bremen, Germany) and received his rabbinic ordination in 1897 from the chief rabbis of Galicia. Only after that was he called "Rabbi" rather than "Revd." He produced his translation "for Jewish families" by adhering "'as closely as possible to the excellent Anglican version of the 17th century'" (qtd. in Paul 93). It was published in 1880 and reprinted in 1882. Gollancz produced many scholarly works, became a professor of Hebrew at University College London, and in 1923 became the first rabbi to receive a knighthood.

Gollancz was not alone among Anglo-Jews in respecting the King James translation (AV or KJV). Dwor describes how Grace Aguilar repeatedly directed Jewish women, who were debarred from Jewish textual materials, to "'their *English* Bibles'—that is, to the King James Version" (60). Aguilar insisted that a heartfelt religion could "'only be obtained by *teaching* [the Jewish poor] their *English* Bibles,'" suggesting that Jewish identity could be fostered through the KJV, but only if readers were trained to recognize that the God in the KJV is "first and most powerfully the Mosaic God of the Jews" (69). In fact, Leonard J. Greenspoon argues that the seventeenth-century translators of the KJV were "deeply indebted to Jewish scholarship," that "the cadence, vocabulary, and overall structure of the KJV strongly resemble the Heb[rew] original," and that this translation "apparently served the needs of England's growing Jewish community for the first c. [late seventeenth to late eighteenth centuries] of its post-expulsion existence" (2097).

Although English translations of the Hebrew Bible by Jewish scholars were published in England from the 1780s on, their availability to the Anglo-Jewish population, especially women, is uncertain. What was commonly available during Aguilar's lifetime was the KJV, both in editions with no supplementary materials, such as those published by the British and Foreign Bible Society, and Family Bibles, which invariably included illustrations. As Aguilar emphasized the mother's importance in reading the Bible with her children in such a way as to "develop the child's mechanisms of feeling so that it may learn the spirit, as well as the forms, of religion," it does not seem improbable that Jewish mothers might have found the illustrated Family Bible highly suitable for reading with their children (Dwor 63). McDannell notes that the same turn to teaching the Bible as a *maternal* rather than a *paternal* function can be seen in American representations of mothers reading the Bible with their children (80–86).

HOW THE IMAGE OF WOMEN CHANGES IN FAMILY BIBLES

Illustrations in Family Bibles document this shift from women represented chiefly as objects of the male gaze to women as subjects in their own right, and also from anglicized types to actual Jewish women, suggesting that publishers were increasingly aware of the influence of the Jewish population in both the UK and the US. A look at three images of women in Family Bibles suggests a gradual—and by no means consistent—change in views of the role of women in both Christian and Jewish religions over the course of the nineteenth century. The first image shown here is "The Sacrifice of Jepthah's Daughter," representing the narrative in Judges 11:30–40 in which Jepthah has promised to make a sacrifice of whatever he sees first after the battle if God makes him victorious. That first sight is his daughter coming dancing out of the house to greet him, and it is that moment that is represented in many illustrations in Family Bibles. However, some Family Bible editions include instead an image of the daughter being sacrificed. The one shown here is from a Bible with Scott's commentary (*The Holy Bible . . . Thomas Scott*) (fig. 6.4). Although date of publication is not listed, it has been dated by library catalogers as [1844?] or [1849?].[14] The Cornish painter John Opie (1761–1807) represents the daughter as sexually vulnerable, breasts bared and exposed to the High Priest's phallic knife, the father Jepthah crouching behind her. This melodramatic visual interpretation of the biblical text would not have been out of line with Christian commentary in the nineteenth century, but it surprises readers today as having been thought appropriate for a Family Bible. However, the painter was well known, and publishers must have thought it would be appealing to a nineteenth-century readership. I have found this illustration in more than one

---

14. The Claremont College of Theology library dates this "Family Bible" as [1844?] and notes that the plates are dated 1841–44. St. Andrews University (Scotland) library catalog dates it as [1849?].

FIGURE 6.4. "The Sacrifice of Jepthah's Daughter." *The Holy Bible containing the Old and New Testaments according to the Authorized Version . . . by Thomas Scott.* London, Fisher, Son, & Co., n.d. [1844? 1849?].

Family Bible. It is characteristic of Family Bible images of women from the eighteenth through the later decades of the nineteenth century, representing women as sexual objects.

My second example of Family Bible images of women is from the one shown in the paper-covered part published by A. Fullarton & Co., of London, Edinburgh, and Dublin in 1876 (fig. 6.5). The visual representation of women in this work eschews the violent and the sexual, and moves into a new perspective that often focuses on women only in the presence of other women. One, for example, from a painting by Ary Scheffer (1795–1858), depicts Ruth and Naomi and carries the biblical text "Entreat me not to leave thee, nor to return from following after thee." The image and the text emphasize the relation between two women, as compared to many earlier Family Bible illustrations of the Book of Ruth that show Ruth with Boaz.

Other images in this Family Bible show Leah and Rachel with a baby but no Jacob, the finding of the infant Moses by women, and "the Maries at the

FIGURE 6.5. *The Illustrated Family Bible with Explanatory, Critical and Devotional Commentary* . . . London, Edinburgh, and Dublin: A. Fullarton & co. [1876].

Sepulchre." To be sure, illustrations with male subjects appear as well, but it's a new undertaking to show biblical women solely in the company of other women, not as the object of the male gaze.

My third and last example of Family Bible images of women is from a 1900 American edition, and one that has dropped the term "Family" from its title: *The Pronouncing Edition of the Holy Bible*. This edition includes both the Authorized and the 1884 Revised Standard versions of the Bible in parallel columns. The KJV was no longer the sole authoritative text. This Family Bible is held at the Baylor University Library, and I include it here for only one reason: it includes two images of biblical women that are highly unusual, "Queen Esther" and "Daughter of Jepthah." Both images appear to be photographic images of contemporary Jewish women enacting the biblical characters.

Here is "Queen Esther" (fig. 6.6):

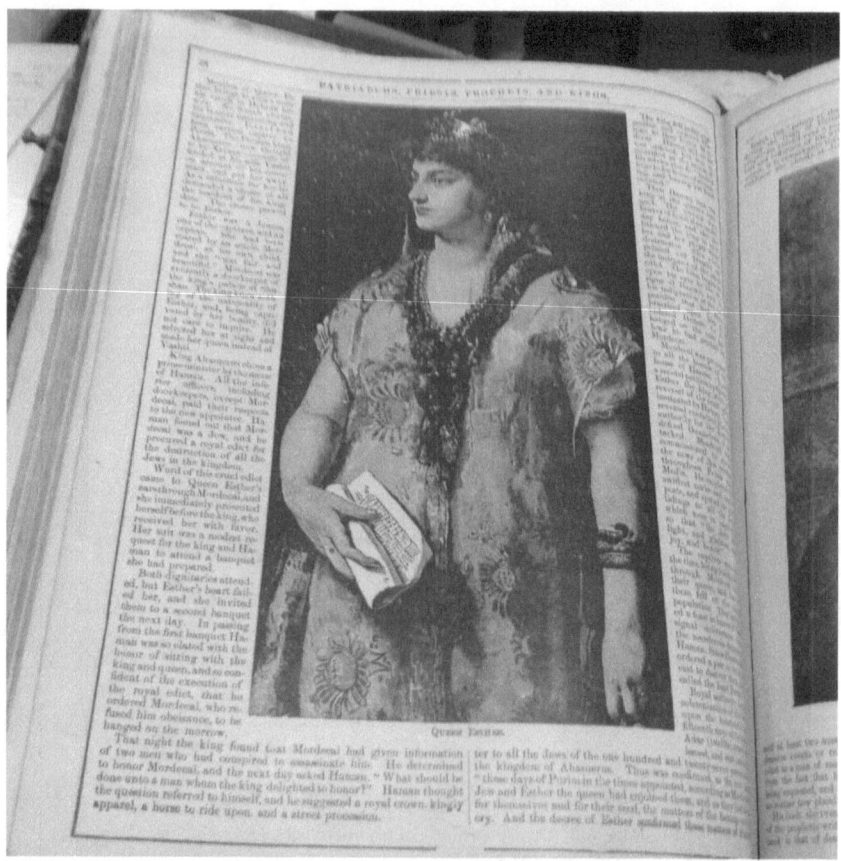

FIGURE 6.6. "Queen Esther." *The Pronouncing Edition of the Holy Bible* . . . [Philadelphia, A. J. Holman & Co., 1900? C1890]. Baylor University Library copy.

Whereas earlier biblical illustrations of Esther most commonly show her as fainting in the presence of King Ahasuerus—a posture often interpreted by Christian exegetes as conveying her recognition of the King as typological image of Christ—here she represents Esther as Queen. The rolled-up text in her hand probably represents the "decree" of the feast of Purim, which she is said to have instituted. The image thus reverses her usual portrayal as a fainting female to that of a powerful Queen. The image of "Daughter of Jepthah" shows an enticingly beautiful young Jewish woman, also in contemporary dress, and includes no male figure nor any suggestion that the young woman is about to become a sacrificial victim. Both images, but particularly the one of "Queen Esther," suggest the publisher's awareness of the important, even powerful, presence of Jewish women in American culture.

CONCLUSION: THE FAMILY BIBLE AS HOLIDAY BOOK

McDannell comments that the number of new editions of Bibles declined from the 1890s on, though it's not known whether the actual number of Bibles printed declined (99). Those Family Bible editions that continued to be printed in the twentieth century became more and more like one-volume encyclopedias, including an increasing number of scholarly essays which, in the United States, were often copyrighted by the author. The Family Bible genre as I have described it here apparently ceased to be produced.

Why did the Family Bible in its Victorian format disappear? Perhaps simply because the need for it had disappeared, along with the "poor and labouring part of Mankind" as it existed in John Brown's time and the more middling classes into which most of them moved during the nineteenth century. George Eliot gives us a very close-up look at the Family Bible and the needs it served in her novel *Adam Bede,* set in 1799. Lisbeth Bede, Adam's mother, refers repeatedly to "Adam's new Bible." To Dinah, a Methodist preacher at this time when women were still allowed to preach, she says, "'Ye've got a' most the face o' one as is a-sittin on the grave i' Adam's new Bible'" (Eliot 10:121). Lisbeth refers to this picture twice more. "'I could be fast sure that picture was drawed for her i' thy new Bible—th' angel a-sittin on the big stone by the grave," she says to Adam as they watch Dinah departing, and much later, as Adam is reading his "new picter Bible" on a Sunday morning, and turns over the page to that picture, Lisbeth comments, "'That's her—that's Dinah'" (14:153, 51:544). Lisbeth, like most of the people of her generation, cannot read. The narrator comments on the church congregation that "none of the old people held books—why should they? Not one of them could read" (18:215). But from the pictures in that Bible, Lisbeth learns a Bible lesson familiar to Eliot's readers: how to see the divine in a human face.

For Adam, who had learned how to read in Bartle Massey's night school for laborers, his "large pictured Bible" was something he turned to on Sunday mornings. "You would have liked to see Adam reading his Bible," the narrator tells us. "He never opened it on a week-day, and so he came to it as a holiday book, serving him for history, biography, and poetry" (51:543). But after the 1872 Education Act most people learned to read, and by the turn of the twentieth century, most had a little more leisure time. And books, books with pictures, and all kinds of illustrated materials, had become ubiquitous—available to everyone in one form or another. The Family Bible was no longer a working man's "holiday book" or a school teacher's "very interesting Book, Large Beautiful and gilded . . . a Messenger for relief and as if sent from on high." Family Bibles still in existence in this twenty-first century are for the most part no longer read or looked at, but instead lie unopened in attics. But a few of them, though in greater or lesser stages of deterioration, have reached such destinations as the Zuckerman collection or the British Library, where they may once again become treasures—treasures for scholars, serving as unique sources in the history of the Bible as a book.

WORKS CITED

Family Bibles Cited

Cassell's Illustrated Family Bible. London, Cassell & Co. [1859–63].

The Christian's New and Compleat Family Bible: or, Universal Library of Divine Knowledge. By the Rev. Thomas Bankes, London, Printed for J. Cooke, No 17, Pater-Noster Row; and sold by the Booksellers of Bath, Bristol, etc. [ca. 1790].

The Columbian Family and Pulpit Bible; Popular English Family Bible; with concise notes and annotations . . . Poole, Brown, Doctors A. Clarke, Coke, Scott, Doddridge, etc. Boston, published by Joseph Teal, 1822.

The Compleat History of the Old and New Testament; or, A Family Bible, with . . . annotations, extracted from the writings of the most celebrated authors. Together with maps, cuts &c. By S. Smith, D. D., London, Printed by W. Rayner, 1735, 1737. 2 vols.

The Family Devotional Bible . . . Matthew Henry. London and New York, The London Printing and Publishing Co., Ltd., London and New York, [185?]. "Eightieth Thousand."

The Holy Bible . . . Complete Commentary . . . Apocrypha . . . and the New Testament. Embellished with Elegant Engravings. Manchester, printed and published by J. Gleave, 1816.

The Holy Bible containing the Old and New Testaments according to the Authorized Version, with Explanatory Notes, Practical Observations, Copious Marginal References, Indexes, etc. by Thomas Scott, Rector of Aston Sandford, Bucks. A New Edition, in Three Volumes. Illustrated with Engravings on Steel, from Historical Designs of the Old Masters: and a series of views of the principal places mentioned in Scripture, from drawings on the Spot. London, Fisher, Son, and Co. n.d. [1844? 1849?].

The Holy Bible, containing the Pentateuch, the Hagiographa and the Former and Latter Prophets; Translated out of the original tongues; and with the former Translations diligently Compared and Revised. London, John G. Murdoch [1880?].

The Holy Bible: . . . notes and practical observations selected from . . . The Rev. Matthew Henry. London: J. M'Gowan and Son . . , 1827.

The Holy Bible translated from the Latin Vulgate. Edited by Rev. George Leo Haydock, London, George Henry & Co., n.d.

The Holy Bible translated from the Latin Vulgate . . . Dublin, James Duffy and Co., n.d.

The Illustrated Family Bible with Explanatory, Critical and Devotional Commentary . . . London, Edinburgh, and Dublin, A. Fullarton & co. [1876].

The National Illustrated Family Bible, The Holy Bible with the Commentaries of Scott and Henry . . . condensed and the whole edited by the Rev. John Eadie, D. D. , LL. D. Liverpool, [1876].

The Pronouncing Edition of the Holy Bible: containing the Authorized and Revised versions of the Old and New Testaments: arranged in parallel columns . . . [Philadelphia, A. J. Holman & Co., 1900? C1890]. Baylor University Library copy.

The Royal Bible or a Complete Body of Christian Divinity . . . *critical notes and observations* . . . *A Work highly Useful and Necessary for all Families and Private Christians.* [Revd. Leonard Howard], 2nd ed., London, I. Pottinger, 1761.

The Self-Interpreting Bible . . . By John Brown, Bungay, T. Kinnersley, 1814.

The Universal Bible; or, Every Christian Family's Best Treasure . . . *Containing the sacred text* . . . illus. With notes and comments. By S. Nelson, D. D., London, printed for J. Coote [1758, 1759].

Other Works Cited

Beal, Timothy K. *The Rise and Fall of the Bible: The Unexpected History of an Accidental Book.* Houghton Mifflin Harcourt, 2011.

———, editor. *Oxford Encyclopedia of the Bible and the Arts.* Vol. 1, Oxford UP, 2015.

Black, M. H. "The Printed Bible." *The Cambridge History of the Bible.* Vol. 3: *The West, from the Reformation to the Present Day,* edited by S. L. Greenslack, Cambridge UP, 1963.

Blair, Ann M. *Too Much to Know: Managing Scholarly Information before the Modern Age.* Yale UP, 2010.

Bottigheimer, Ruth B. "Family Bibles." Beal, pp. 313–19.

Brontë, Charlotte. *Jane Eyre.* Penguin Books, 1996.

Carpenter, Mary Wilson. *Imperial Bibles, Domestic Bodies: Women, Sexuality, and Religion in the Victorian Market.* Ohio UP, 2003.

De Hamel, Christopher. *The Book: A History of the Bible.* Phaidon Press Ltd., 2001.

Dwor, Richa. *Jewish Feeling: Difference and Affect in Nineteenth-Century Jewish Women's Writing.* Bloomsbury Academic, 2015.

Eliot George. *Adam Bede.* Edited by Margaret Reynolds, Penguin Books, 2008.

———. *The Mill on the Floss.* Edited by Gordon S. Haight, introduction and notes by Juliette Atkinson, Oxford UP, 2015.

Greenspoon, Leonard J. "Jewish Translations of the Bible." *The Jewish Study Bible,* edited by Adele Berlin and Marc Zvi Brettler, Jewish Publication Society, Oxford UP, 2014, pp. 2091–2106.

Gunn, David M. "Illustrations, Bible." Beal, pp. 435–57.

Howsam, Leslie. *Cheap Bibles: Nineteenth-Century Publishing and the British and Foreign Bible Society.* Cambridge UP, 1991.

Howsam, Leslie and Scott McLaren. "Producing the Text: Production and Distribution of Popular Editions of the Bible." *The New Cambridge History of the Bible.* Vol. 4: *From 1750 to the Present,* edited by John Riches, Cambridge UP, 2014, pp. 49–82.

Kircher, Athanasius. *Arca Noë, in tres libra digesta, quorum* . . . Amstelodami, 1675.

Lacey, Barbara E. *From Sacred to Secular: Visual Images in Early American Publications.* U of Delaware P, 2007.

Ledger-Lomas, Michael. "Mass Markets: Religion." *Cambridge History of the Book in Britain*, edited by David McKitterick, vol. 6, Cambridge UP, 2009, pp. 324–58.

Lupas, Liana. *The Book of Life: Family Bibles in America*. Rare Bible Series vol. 4, New York, Museum of Biblical Art, 2011.

Mathewson, Andrew Dishington. Letter to Wm. Edw. Turner. 26 January 1866. Shetland Archives, Lerwick, UK: D23/150/24/1.

McDannell, Colleen. *Material Christianity: Religion and Popular Culture in America*. Yale UP, 1995.

Miller, Julia. *Books Will Speak Plain: A Handbook for Identifying and Describing Historical Bindings*. The Legacy Press, 2010.

Norton, David. *A History of the English Bible as Literature*. Cambridge UP, 2000.

Paul, William E. *English Language Bible Translators*. McFarland & Company, Inc., 2003.

Price, Leah. *How to Do Things with Books in Victorian Britain*. Princeton UP, 2013.

Rose, Jonathan. *The Intellectual Life of the British Working Classes*. Yale UP, 2001.

St. Clair, William. *The Reading Nation in the Romantic Period*. Cambridge UP, 2004.

Taylor, Jeffreys. *The Family Bible Newly Opened: With Uncle Goodwin's Account of It*. London, 1853.

CHAPTER 7

Rereading Queen Victoria's Religion

MICHAEL LEDGER-LOMAS

ON 7 MAY 1865, the weather was unpropitious for churchgoing: "Heavy rain: It was even too bad to get to Church.—Read Prayers & a sermon by Dr Stanley with Lenchen" (Victoria 7 May 1865). For Queen Victoria, the author of this diary entry, reading was not just an auxiliary to religious practice but often constituted it. Dutiful in attending church whenever she could, she considered the reading of prayers and sermons by her favorite preachers to be a perfectly adequate substitute for it. What might the study of Queen Victoria's exceptionally well-documented reading habits tell us about her religious experience? And how, furthermore, might a reading of the Queen's religious reading advance our broader understanding of changes in Victorian religion that a historiography dominated by secularization has not yet fully captured? This chapter, which derives from my forthcoming spiritual biography of Queen Victoria, offers some answers to those questions by mapping the adventitious, but lifelong, engagement with books as recorded in the pages of her journals.

Although Victoria was the most celebrated of Victorians, her reading, her religion, and the relationship between them still await satisfactory explanation. This investigation therefore starts by asking what historians have said about her religion, then suggests how paying attention to reading practices might assist both in understanding it and the ways in which it was representative of broader transformations in lay piety. Walter Arnstein settled the outlines of Victoria's faith long ago. She came to the throne a diligent student of the practices and orthodoxy of the Church of England. Her marriage to Prince Albert, a rationalist Lutheran who patronized liberal churchmen such as Charles Kingsley, strengthened a tendency to Low Church views. Their purchase of the Balmoral estate in the Scottish Highlands brought them into close contact with liberal ministers in the Presbyterian Church of Scotland, who inculcated in her a nonsacerdotal religion of ethical striving. Their counsel proved important after Albert's death plunged Victoria into a restless search for consolation, which put pressure on orthodox Christian explanations. As her initial grief faded, her religion changed in other unpredictable ways. Her fondness for her Presbyterian servant John Brown and her awareness of the *Kulturkampf* between the Catholic Church and Continental governments inflamed her Low Church opinions. Never keen on Anglican clerical pretensions, she was an instigator of the 1874 Public Worship Regulation Act, which curbed Ritualism in the Church of England. Yet her intolerance of crypto-Catholicism did not prevent a mounting appreciation for Roman Catholicism, particularly as practiced in the female religious communities she encountered on Continental holidays. Diverse friendships strengthened these broadening sympathies: with Napoleon III's widow Eugénie, whose Catholicism was as flamboyant as her clothes, and with her manservant Abdul Karim, an Indian Muslim (Arnstein, "Challenge"; "Queen Victoria"; *Queen Victoria*).

While Arnstein's test drills into Victoria's personal piety remain invaluable, this chapter takes a different approach. It presents Victoria's changing religion as indicative of broader transformations in Victorian religiosity, transformations that helped to create a new, demotic kind of monarchy. Royal biographies often distort their subjects by taking their intellectual or spiritual lives (such as they are) out of their cultural and religious context. Yet there can no more be a private religion than a private language. In framing a religion that paid diminishing heed to the dictates or orthodoxies of the Anglican clergy, the Queen was representative of her subjects, who increasingly used print and material culture to create identities that were less often consciously unorthodox than they were careless of orthodoxy. Exemplified at its apex, such spiritual bricolage was widespread throughout Victorian society. Yet the historiography of Victorian religion had relatively little to say about it until recently, because it was less interested in the pieties of individuals than in the statistical life signs of churches (Brown; Morris). Moreover, historians were content to let the clergy determine what beliefs constituted Victorian Christianity and agreed with them that levels of churchgoing were the best indicator of its vitality. The clerical perception that Victorian cities were godless spaces made dechristianization the remorseless reality to which churches had to respond. That self-fulfilling fear explained why the commitment to philanthropy, the building of churches, and the liberalization of theology should be fervent yet futile. Victorian believers were, on this reading, Canutes in reverse: powerless to stop the ebb tide of secularization, yet deafened by its long, melancholy, withdrawing roar.

More recent historiography contends, though, that we must not confuse the undeniable attrition in the cultural and intellectual authority of the clergy with religious decline. If *secularization* remains a helpful word for the transfer of power from clerics to other thinkers, doers, and tastemakers, notably men of science, then that process pluralized more than it menaced Victorian religious experience (Morris; Harris 150–79). By the end of Victoria's reign, we could understand Christianity less as a "doctrinal category" than as a pluriform "religious culture," a "rich and malleable vehicle," at the disposal of creative eccentrics as much as of church leaders (Knight 4, 226). Dominic Erdozain has rightly suggested that many ecclesiastical responses to the ethical or artistic imperatives of modern culture inadvertently advanced secularization by stripping Christianity of its soteriological and transcendent character ("Secularisation"). Yet the result was nonetheless not a secular void but a cluster of rival but cross-fertilizing pieties, a religion in aggregate found outside as well as within churches.

Reading was vital in this proliferation of the meanings of "religion" in the lives of ordinary people, both in Britain and further afield (Priest). Yet religious historians have tended to pay less attention to the consumption than to the production of reading matter. Their eyes have been drawn to evangelicals who in late eighteenth and early nineteenth-century Britain identified the mass printing and distribution of cheap Bibles and homiletic texts as a means of manufacturing like-minded believers: anxious consumers of text led by evangelical words to salvific encounters with the Word (Stubenrauch). Yet it proved easier to stereotype tracts than Christians. Mass literacy in a Protestant culture encouraged the investigation, negotiation, or subversion of Christianity rather than simply its reproduction. Even though Bibles like those discussed in Mary Wilson Carpenter's chapter in this volume were a fixture in every Victorian home, people read them in strikingly different ways (Larsen, *People of One Book*). Moreover, evangelical print never conquered the marketplace. Unable to supplant fiction or popular science, Christian propagandists wrote variants on it, such as the novels discussed in Miriam Burstein's chapter in this volume. These "hybridous monsters" did more to dilute than to serve conversionist or catechetical aims, ramping up the cultural static that made it ever harder to attend to the word of God. If clerics and Bible-bashers produced most religious literature, then the expanding universe of religious print encouraged new types of authors to pose as spiritual authorities. The poets mounted invisible pulpits, extracting "religion" from the grip of historic churches and locating it instead within imagined spiritual communities bound together by shared affect rather than by submission to Bible or creed (King; LaPorte; Blair).

If print saturated Victorian culture with Christian messages, then it also allowed lay readers to frame magpie creeds of their own. Victoria's habit of comprehensively recording what she read and what she thought of it during the sixty-three-year reign that gave "Victorian" culture its name affords a rich illustration of this process. It may of course seem perverse to present Victoria as a woman who lived to read, because to a post-Victorian generation she embodied anti-intellectualism. H. G. Wells acidly described the "merely deadening" influence exercised on Britain by "the Court of an alien-spirited old lady . . . court taste was a joke, court art was a scandal; of English literature and science notoriously the court knew nothing" (Wells 17). His "alien-spirited old lady" was certainly not much of a reader by the standards of the leading Victorian intellectuals with whose reading habits historians are familiar. William Ewart Gladstone read about 20,000 titles by 4,500 authors over his lifetime, making it possible to track the evolution of his religious opinions along his bookshelves (Windscheffel 1; Bebbington). Even if the Queen did read some of the works in Gladstone's library, her diaries do not reveal the anguished grappling with them that are a staple of intellectual and cultural histories of Victorian religion. To take one instance, she recorded on 8 August 1852 that "Albert told me much about an interesting book he is reading, the 'Life of Jesus' by Strauss." That is, to put it mildly, the most minor footnote to what we know of Strauss's explosive and varied reception by plebeian and elite readers alike (Larsen, "Biblical Criticism"). The verdicts on books scattered throughout her diaries make today's Amazon reviewers look like paragons of fluency and penetration: "pretty," "interesting," "thrilling." She did not often read alone with fixed attention but was read to—by tutors, family members, or courtiers, who often chose what she read.

Yet we should not dismiss the spiritual charge of the Queen's reading because it was inattentive, uncritical, and intermittent. Just as Mark Knight's chapter in this volume suggests that unexamined Protestantism can narrow scholarly visions of true or authentic spirituality, so scholars must avoid adopting a narrow test of what counts as committed reading or as religious reading. When Jonathan Rose insisted that the British working classes had an intellectual life, he did not have to argue that they read with the assiduity of assistant professors. Indeed, he emphasized accidental encounters with texts and the disruption of study by hard work or illness. Books were borrowed or handed down to his working-class readers, who often them read aloud to others or listened as others read them out just as often as they engaged in solitary study (Rose). Mary Wilson Carpenter reminds us that even the Protestant study of the Bible was a social, domestic, and leisured act. Illustrated family Bibles were designed to be gazed on, riffled through, or read aloud by the paterfamilias, rather than studied by some abstract ideal reader. This chapter also argues that what looks like a softening in intellectual intensity in the autumn of the Queen's life—a turn from theological works to fiction—may have helped her develop a freer piety, one shared with and communicable to her subjects. Burstein's chapter in this volume begins with William Thackeray's disapproving observation that religious novels were supplanting theology as vehicles for religious argument, transferring power from church to the marketplace. Victoria's example suggests that not just avowedly religious novels but also fiction and poetry in general could assume that role.

That shift counts as secularization only in the limited sense that secular genres were invading space once reserved to sacred ones. As Dominic Janes reminds us in this volume, Victorian culture was constantly puzzled to determine where the sacred stopped and the profane began. A shift in that frontier did not amount to a shrinkage or privatization of religion. In Victoria's case, it fostered a transformation in her standing from head of the Church of England to the chief member of an imagined spiritual community bound together by affect rather than doctrine (King). Wells sneered that the "real England, dissentient England," saw through the "pathos of her widowhood," but for many Victorians that pathos, which Victoria explored and framed through reading verse and fiction, brought the otherwise distant "roof of church and state" under which they lived into touching distance (Wells 17). While historians of "democratic royalism" such as William Kuhn have pointed to the ceremonial of the Jubilees as the means through which such a connection was forged, this chapter closes with the suggestion that texts were just as important.

Victoria's reading life began under discipline. Authority figures hovered over young female readers in the early nineteenth century, and it was no different for Victoria (Vallone). The constraints on her were the more pronounced because her mother, the Duchess of Kent, and her governess, Baroness Lehzen (1784–1870), were anxious to train her as a future head of the Church of England. The consequence was that clerical texts offering systematic instruction in the doctrines and worship of the Church dominated Victoria's reading. A diary entry from 12 August 1835 describing her studies with her tutor George Davys (1780–1864) captures how such reading was crammed into her schedule: "I read in Smith's Theology when I came home and also sang. At ½ past 11 came the Dean [of Chester] till 1. I read first in the New Testament with him, then in Russell, and finished with Evans on the Sects." These texts instilled in her the doctrines of her church and the means of defending them. To take one mentioned here as an example, the Reverend John Bainbridge Smith's *A Manual of the Rudiments of Theology* (1830) was dedicated to that Tory ogre the Duke of Newcastle, a "firm and consistent supporter of the Church of England ... the staunch uncompromising opposer of every measure, however specious, calculated to diminish her deserved pre-eminence, or to weaken her salutary influence in the nation at large" (Smith iv). Smith wrote not for lively young women like Victoria but for "persons preparing for holy orders" or junior clergymen ("Preface"), and as a result he offered them copious extracts from old divines, which both presented evidences for the truth of Scripture and argued that the Church's articles were the best exposition of it. Victoria soon gave up on what was "more a book to refer to, than to read all through" (Victoria 27 August 1835), but it was striking that she should have read it at all.

The Queen's reading emphasized not just doctrines, but right worship and good conduct. 28 August 1835 found her reading "the Bishop of Chester's Exposition of the Gospel of St. Matthew. It is a very fine book indeed. Just the sort of one I like; which is just plain and comprehensible and full of truth and good feeling. It is not one of those learned books in which you have to cavil at almost every paragraph." John Bird Sumner (1790–1874), then bishop of Chester, had published expositions on the Gospels, which were the latest contribution to the long-standing Protestant genre of helps to "family religion" (Cambers and Wolfe). An evangelical Anglican as well as a quickly promoted servant of the Hanoverian court, Sumner turned the Gospels into conduct literature for comfortable families. He noted for instance, in a passage that Victoria might have read, that Jesus's origins in Nazareth, a lowly town, were an indication that "it often happens that those who do seek that honour [from God alone] simply and consistently, are unexpectedly rewarded, in the end, by the good opinion of men" (Sumner 16).

Lehzen had given Victoria this book just after she had received the sacrament. It is a reminder that her youthful religion was not just scriptural but deeply sacramental, and that this had an impact on her reading. She often turned to user manuals for public worship to instill the right attitude for the reception of the Eucharist. On 22 May 1836 she "got up at 8. Read in 'Cornwallis on the Sacrament,' while my hair was doing." She supplemented Mary Cornwallis's *Preparation of the Lord's Supper, with a Companion to the Altar, for the Use of Ladies* (1826) with Pacificus Baker's *The Devout Communicant* (1813), a compendium of meditations compiled at a lady's request to "entertain her pious thoughts, and raise up in her a spirit of fervent devotion towards the holy sacrament, and Jesus Christ therein truly and really present" (iii). If Baker's writings extolled the real presence, then some of Victoria's devotional reading was still more conservative. On 31 July 1836, Victoria found the *Ikon Basilike*—the supposed meditations of Charles I, which Davys had passed to her with the qualification that its authorship had been disputed—to be a "very good and pious book."

When Victoria became Queen in June 1837, she wriggled free from maternal direction: her reading and the place occupied in it by religious texts consequently underwent a shift. She had always read history, travel literature, and poetry—it helped that Davys was, "s'il est permis de le dire, poetry-mad"—but her absorption in imaginative literature greatly increased once she was freer to make her own choices (Victoria 18 November 1836). When she "read aloud to Lehzen Walter Scott's novel of the Bride of Lammermoor" on 9 January 1838, it was "the <u>first novel</u> I have ever read!" Her love affair then marriage with Prince Albert, a passionate admirer of Walter Scott whose arrival decisively sidelined the controlling Lehzen, increased that preoccupation with the romantic fiction to which respectable young women were often denied access.

Victoria's religious reading turned from didactic guides to the liturgy to works by clergymen who advocated reform of their Church. The liberal Anglican authors she favored insisted on the distinction between Scripture, which was authoritative, and the fallible and contingent conclusions that historic churches had drawn from or imposed upon it. That distinction notably suggested that it should be possible to conciliate Protestant Dissenters by classing the aspects of the Church's worship or government they disliked as negotiable, even optional (Brent). From January 1838 for instance, Victoria embarked on a regular reading of sermons by Thomas Arnold (1795–1842), the doyen of liberal Anglicans. On 8 December 1839, "It was so cold & raw that I settled not to go to Evening Service, as I was not feeling very well. Read Prayers, & a very fine sermon by Arnold." There was plenty of time for such reading with the serious Albert. On a "peaceful, happy evening" in December 1844, they dined alone "& afterwards I read to Albert, whilst he was drawing, out of Archbishop Whately's 'Kingdom of Christ,' which interested him very much." In *The Kingdom of Christ: In Two Essays* (1841), Richard Whately (1787–1863) had employed a plain reading of the New Testament to contend that Christ and his Apostles had founded a spiritual society whose "great fundamental Gospel-doctrines and moral duties" were clear but the details of whose government had been left providentially vague (30). The implications were clear. The New Testament did not support the view that "Church-of-England principles" were the only possible realization of Christ's kingdom (117). Moreover, because it was not of this world, it was abhorrent to use force to settle disputes about it. It showed a "sinful distrust,—a want of faith in Christ's wisdom, and goodness, and power,—to call in the aid of the arm of flesh" on Christ's account. Those whose "own conscience is tender, and . . . sense of religion deep-felt and sincere," would "seek for the genuine conviction of others, and not their forced conformity" (47, 46).

These texts imagined an enlarged church and a tolerant state that would be truly representative of Britain's religious diversity. Victoria's embrace of these dreams of spiritual community derived from a real community: her droll, Whiggish court, whose leaders chaffed pretension and obscurantism. Lord Melbourne (1779–1848) pointed her to Arnold and Whately as well as to liberal histories of the English nation by Henry Hallam, François Guizot, Thomas Babington Macaulay, and Charles de Montalembert, which she read with Albert. These authors brought a cosmopolitan, stadial sensibility to national history, stressing that economic prosperity and political stability were not only goods in themselves but processes which were curing the bigotry and fanaticism that had disfigured the past. Victoria had initially found Hallam's *The Constitutional History of England* (1827) to be "very difficult" (Victoria 5 October 1839) but was quickly absorbed in its developmental reading of the English past. On 8 October 1842, she read to Albert Hallam's account of Charles II's Parliaments and was struck by "their great *bigotry then,*—so different from *now,* & their cruel persecution of the unfortunate nonconformists." These readings suggested a discerning Christian patriotism in which the monarchy should foster the already impressive advances in enlightenment and charity (Parry). Indeed, Hallam's name was mud with Tories precisely because of his desire not just to chart the growth in English liberty, but liberty *from* what had once been a persecutory Church of England (Bentley 466–67). Enjoying Montalembert's *L'Avenir de l'Angleterre* in 1856, she felt that this Catholic but liberal Frenchman had pinpointed England's continued weaknesses "while, at the same time appreciating our immense internal strength & stability" (Victoria 21 January 1856).

Victoria's reading expanded her understanding of religion in other ways, instilling for instance the importance of philanthropic activism. Harriet Beecher Stowe's sentimental onslaught on slavery overwhelmed her as it did so many of her subjects (Huzzey 21–39). On 23 March 1853, Albert and Victoria "glanced" at the recently published factual key to *Uncle Tom's Cabin,* "& saw enough to make one's hair stand on end. The accounts of real *facts,* trials, evidence, &c—are much worse, than anything in the book. Mrs Stowe would, very properly; not put in these details, but every incident in the book can be verified from facts." Such reading supplied an ethical lingua franca for discussions with liberal politicians. She lent the key to Lord Aberdeen (1784–1860) and found him "fully aware to the horrors of Slavery & to the necessity of every nerve being strained to put a stop, & a final one, to the *Slave Trade*" (Victoria 27 March 1853).

Victoria had not simply replaced a clerical and sacramental conception of Anglicanism with a commitment to credal and philanthropic meliorism. Neither reading nor religion works so linearly in individual lives. The reception of the Eucharist remained vital to the Queen as a symbol and guarantor of her family's spiritual well-being, and she valued literature that prepared her for it, from whatever quarter. On 19 December 1841, for instance, she "read in a very pretty little book (which I had already read in last night) called 'The Eucharistica,' compiled by Archdeacon Wilberforce, from the very old Divines." The son of a renowned evangelical, Samuel Wilberforce (1805–73) was a royal favorite, an ardent high churchman who prefaced his anthology of early modern divinity with a passionate rebuttal of those who considered that the "inner life of piety" could flourish without sacramental "means of grace" (Wilberforce xi). It had a striking effect after Wilberforce had presented it to her. On 9 April 1843, "After reading in Wilberforce's 'Eucharistic' [sic] which is very fine, we went to the Chapel ½ p. 9, where seats were prepared for us directly in front of the altar, & we took the Holy Communion. It was very impressive, quiet & solemn." Echoing her mother's practice, she instructed her daughter from the *Eucharistica,* and it came to color the language she used about communion: "may the reception of our blessed Saviour's Body and Blood bring me real strength," she remarked to her diary on 10 April 1845.

Indeed, if Victoria's sympathies in church politics remained firmly on the side of liberal reformers in the Established Churches of England and Scotland, then her religious reading remained eclectic. As Burstein notes in this volume, critics of religious novelists often scolded them for promoting sectarian or confessional objectives. Yet Victoria's experience shows that readers might be indifferent to, and almost oblivious of, "party" considerations, reading whatever suited their needs best at any given moment. In the spring of 1846, she enjoyed both a "German Devotional Book" that Albert read aloud to her and a sermon by the seventeenth-century French Jesuit Louis Bourdaloue (27 December 1845).

The death of Albert in December 1861 greatly accelerated the interlinked process of emancipation from clerical oversight and the personal search for texts that made sense of life—and death. Historians have already given us detailed accounts of Victoria's grief, which notice that it was as innovative as it was immoderate, fostering new kinds of material religiosity, such as the passion for mourning jewelry in Whitby jet (Rappaport). The point worth emphasizing here was that it was not merely a material but also a literary process, in which the Queen used literature to confront her loss while also erecting literary monuments to her dead husband. While clerics such as Gerald Wellesley (1809–82), the Dean of Windsor; Norman Macleod (1812–72); and Arthur Penrhyn Stanley (1815–81) advised the Queen how it was proper for a Christian to grieve, poets rather than preachers were still more useful to her. Because her grief was so immoderate as to challenge Christian explanations of loss, she dealt with it through intense literary bricolage, cladding her pain in texts by fellow sufferers. Tennyson's *In Memoriam* was the most important of these works: a shrine to Arthur Hallam, but also a monument to the "spectral doubt" that he was gone forever, in ways that Christianity could not extenuate (Lutz 125). As a textual reliquary (Lutz 113), *In Memoriam* lent itself to the production of the Queen's reliquaries, such as the album assembled by her daughter Alice of "Poems and Extracts—January 1862—collected after dear Papa's death" and now preserved in Darmstadt. This volume shows how poetry might sit beside and improve upon Scripture as a consoler. The epigraphs to the volume cite Tennyson—"My paths, are in the fields I know, / And thine in undiscovered lands"—alongside Scripture: "Blessed are they that mourn, for they shall be comforted" (Matthew 5:4); "Sorrow endureth for a night, and joy cometh in the morning" (a rendering of Psalm 30:5); "Oh rest in the Lord—wait patiently for him—for he shall give thee thy heart's desire" (Psalm 37:7) (Alice 1–2).

This coupling works because the Tennyson of the Darmstadt album is the sermonic Tennyson (King 162): the poet of hard-won faith rather than doubt. The first long extract from *In Memoriam* in the album puts grief into a Christian context, apologizing for immoderate sorrow: "Forgive my grief for one removed / Thy creature, whom I found so fair / I trust he lives in thee, and there / I find Him worthier to be loved. . . . I sometimes hold it half a sin / To put in sounds the grief I feel; / For words, like Nature, half reveal / And half conceal the Soul within" (Alice 3). Not only does this book show the Queen and her family exploring the shock of death in verse: it also represents that grief not as private but as communicable. The Darmstadt volume contains texts and extracts from texts that make that point more forcibly, because more crudely, than Tennyson. W. H. Latchmore's *The Widowed Queen* describes how "Eyes sorely weeping, hearts strained nigh to breaking / Over the Land are seen / Of thy deep grief thy people are partaking / Our Queen, our Queen! / O that our souls could ease thee in thy sorrow, / Could bear away / The grief that will be keener on the morrow / Than it is today. . . .Let not thy faith in the All-wise be shaken, / But may the prayer be heard: / Thou Lord hast given and again hast taken / Blest be thy name, O Lord" (Alice 83–84).

Latchmore's verses personally and corporately implicate their readers in the trial of the Queen's faith. In the final decades of the reign, the demotic heart religion they evoke became ever more important in her life and in the representation of her reign. A change in reading supported that shift. That is not to say that her taste for serious books died with Albert. Scripture and sermons remained a Sunday staple, while Stanley came to occupy Melbourne's role as a Whiggish guide to progress in theology (Victoria 13 April 1864). She also shared her daughters' passion for Frederick William Robertson (1816–53), an evangelical turned broad churchman and a favorite of Albert, whose sermons envisaged the Christian life as an untiring struggle to improve both one's self and the world (Victoria 13 March 1864, 25 March 1864). Victoria also kept up with publications from the liberal Anglican and Church of Scotland clergymen she still patronized, such as Frederic William Farrar (1831–1903) and John Tulloch (1823–86).

Yet with these qualifications, there was no mistaking the rise of fiction. With Albert, Victoria had usually picked up novels still widely read today. On 21 March 1857, she "read to Albert out of that melancholy, clever interesting book 'Jane Eyre,'" while on 17 October 1857 she embarked on *Adam Bede*, "which Albert likes & is much interested in." By the seventies, this high-minded fare gave way to less canonical if still familiar fare, notably novels by Margaret Oliphant (1828–97), Dinah Mulock Craik (1826–87), and George Macdonald (1824–1905). Other favorite authors, such as the Scots William Black (1841–98) and George Whyte-Melville (1821–78), are now obscure. Female, often titled authors of historical fiction or lachrymose romances predominated, such as Lady Rachel Butler (1826–98) and Edna Lyall (1857–1903). Although the Queen developed favorites among these authors, her initial encounter with them was haphazard, owing much to the initiative of ladies-in-waiting who read them to her. Given the suspicion that they were a kind of mental filler or aural wallpaper, it is helpful to identify ways in which they represented less a diminution than a change in how reading supported her religion.

Varied as these novels were, the Queen evinced a preference for those set in the Scottish Highlands. That explains why on 28 June 1869 Jane Ely read to her from Grace Aguilar's *Days of Bruce: A Story of Scottish History* (1852). Aguilar was otherwise an unusual match for the Queen, given that as Richa Dwor argues she used historical, poetical, and fictional modes to express and defend distinctively "Jewish feeling" (Dwor, *Feeling*; "Jewish"). Victoria's *Leaves from the Journal of our Life in the Highlands from 1848–1861* (1868) and *More Leaves from the Journal of a Life in the Highlands, from 1862 to 1882* (1884) presented Scotland as the habitat for the godly simplicity that had disappeared from

England. In Oliphant, Craik, and Macdonald's novels, the Highlands were a Tartan *Gemeinschaft* of upright elders and kindly ministers. One of the heroes of Macdonald's *Sir Gibbie* is typically an autodidact peasant, one of that "class coming up to preserve the honour and truth of our Britain, to be the oil of the lamp of her life, when those who place her glory in knowledge, or in riches, shall have passed from her history as the smoke from her chimneys" (Macdonald, *Gibbie* 1:142).

These novels idealize the simple Scottish Kirk. The heroine of Oliphant's *Margaret Maitland* returns from England preferring to hear "the simple folk of Pasturelands sing one of David's magnificent Psalms, to some such plaintive and moving tune as Martyrs or Montrose, than by the chanting of all the liturgies that were ever set to music" (Oliphant, *Passages in the Life* 3:163). Yet these novels had no time for Calvinist martinets—unsurprising, given that Oliphant had abandoned the prickly Free Church for the Church of England, while Macdonald had abandoned Congregational ministry. The Queen found his *Alec Forbes of Howglen* (1865) to be full of "religious feeling & good principles,—very powerfully written, but at times rather unnecessarily coarse" (10 June 1870). It was in large part the story of its hero's struggle against the "corrupt Calvinism" of his schoolmaster Murdoch Malison (1:63). Such stances echoed the preaching of the Queen's favorite Scots, such as Oliphant's friend R. H. Story (1835–1907), which defined the Kirk's strength not as its doctrinal rigor but its historic success in embodying Scottish national virtues.

Loneliness and bereavement haunted the Queen's last decades. It was therefore significant that her Scottish novels repeatedly presented pain as a heathery via dolorosa, a path to spiritual improvement. The motto of Craik's *A Noble Life* (1866), the story of a crippled laird who bears his sufferings with Christlike resignation, even when his cousin seduces the only woman he ever loved, is *Fiat Voluntas Tua*. On his deathbed, he cites the words of Paul "to which many an agonized doubter has clung, as being the last refuge of sorrow—the only key to mysteries which sometimes shake the firmest faith—'For now we see through a glass darkly, but then face to face; now I know in part, but then shall I know even as also I am known'" (2:293). His tombstone in the village churchyard is inscribed with "Thy will be done on Earth as it is in Heaven" (2:302). Other works of Craik devoured by the Queen repeatedly return to the moral expressed by the epigraph to *Christian's Mistake* (1865): "In the awful mystery of human life, it is a consolation sometimes to believe that our mistakes, perhaps even our sins, are permitted to be instruments of our education for immortality." The heroine of *The Unkind Word* (1870) waits years to discover why her betrothed suddenly vanished on a hike: years, later it transpires that he was killed by falling into a sinkhole. His discoverers identify him from the Psalter on his corpse, its leaves turned down at her favorite Psalm, number 121: "I will lift up mine eyes unto the hills, from whence cometh my help" (1:53).

If Craik and Oliphant's novels preach Christian fortitude, then it is often women, often single women, who are most called upon to manifest these virtues (Newnum). Victoria undoubtedly often consumed these novels simply as entertainments, enjoying having her tears jerked as much as anyone. William Black's *Madcap Violet* (1876) was "dreadfully" and thus delightfully "sad": "The principal male person dies of a heart complaint, & poor Violet goes mad, after having gone through terrible trials, just when all her hopes seemed to be realized" (Victoria 4 November 1879). But to borrow the title of one of Craik's nonfictional works, they were also *Sermons out of Church* (1875), which taught women their duty. Although the Presbyterian manse was the natural home for such sermons, they could come from many sources. Victoria became a keen reader of Pauline de la Ferronays after the latter sent a copy of *Le Récit d'une Soeur* (1866) to court, even going on to request books that Ferronays had considered "too controversial" in their Catholicism to send at first. Ferronays, who published under her married name as Madame Augustus Craven, was a romantic Catholic and like Victoria a sympathizer with the ill-starred Bonapartes. Catholics across Europe had hailed the *Récit* on its appearance as a family memoir that could be read both as an epistolary novel and a devotional work, a "manual for those who suffered" (Harrison 180). No wonder it appealed to Victoria: bearing a startling dedication "To God," the *Récit* described Alexandrine's blissful marriage to Pauline's brother Albert before it was terminated by his untimely death. It explored in Tennysonian terms the mingled pain and sweetness involved in remembering and craving reunion with the dead (Harrison 154–58).

If the Queen recognized herself in these works, then their authors reciprocated, writing of her as a suffering helper of sufferers: a Queen of broken hearts. In 1864 Oliphant too had suffered a trial of faith when her daughter had died suddenly at Rome. "I ask myself why, why, and I cannot find any answer." She struggled to find an answer to this "terrible enigma" in the words of *In Memoriam* and through a fervent devotion to Christ. In 1887, the year of Jubilee, feeling "really touched and sensitive and extremely sympathetic with her," she sent some verses to the Queen, receiving a medal from her in return (Oliphant, *Autobiography* 4, 7, 11, 157). Craik's *Fifty Golden Years: Dedicated by Permission to the Queen* (1887) was similarly a pious Jubilee offering, its opening hymn claiming that both women had "known life's change and loss, / Both taken up its heavy cross, / Its bitterer and yet better part." Deploying the Christocentric symbol of the pelican, Craik hailed the Queen as a "generous

Heart, that, bleeding, fed / Her people 'neath her sheltering wings, / Taught pity for all suffering things / Out of the very breast that bled" (Craik, *Fifty Golden Years* 10–11). One chapter, entitled "She 'Weeps with Them that Weep'" and illustrated with an engraving of the Queen in black, presented her distaste for state ceremonial as a virtue: the less time spent on it, the more there was for loving visits to stricken cottages or firing off supportive telegrams to widows (Craik, *Fifty Golden Years* 45–48).

This chapter has then suggested that the Queen's reading encouraged a piety that evaded ecclesiastical definition and doctrinal tests but was synonymous with charity, sympathy, and the endurance of suffering. It was nourished by Victoria's eager consumption of the stories that pious Victorians told about themselves. A subject that now awaits investigation is how Victoria's power came to be expressed and imagined in stories her subjects told about her. As Craik's Jubilee tract concluded, the world would "never cease to reverence that kingship, or queenship, 'by the grace of God,' which proves that it has the grace of God by possessing sweet human graces, and by showing throughout a whole lifetime, as our Victoria has done, that to be a true man or woman is the Royalest thing on earth" (Craik, *Fifty Golden Years* 62).

WORKS CITED

Alice, Princess. "Poems and Favourite Extracts—Jan. 1862—collected after dear Papa's death." Hessisches Staatsarchiv, Darmstadt. D24 No. 1813.

Arnstein, Walter L. *Queen Victoria*. Palgrave Macmillan, 2003.

———. "Queen Victoria and Religion." *Religion in the Lives of English Women*, edited by Gail Malmgreen, Croom Helm, 1996, pp. 88–128.

———. "Queen Victoria and the Challenge of Roman Catholicism." *The Historian*, vol. 58, no. 2, 1996, pp. 295–314.

Baker, Pacificus. *The Devout Communicant*. London, 1813.

Bebbington, David. *The Mind of Gladstone: Religion, Homer, and Politics*. Oxford UP, 2004.

Bentley, Michael. "Henry Hallam Revisited." *Historical Journal*, vol. 55, no. 2, 2012, pp. 453–73.

Bishop, Maria Catherine. *A Memoir of Mrs. Augustus Craven-Pauline de la Ferronays*. London, 1894.

Blair, Kirstie. *Form and Faith in Victorian Poetry and Religion*. Oxford UP, 2012.

Brent, Richard. *Liberal Anglican Politics: Whiggery, Religion and Reform, 1830–1841*. Oxford UP, 1987.

Brown, Callum. *The Death of Christian Britain: Understanding Secularisation, 1800–2000*. Routledge, 2001.

Cambers, Andrew, and Michelle Wolfe. "Reading, Family Religion, and Evangelical Identity in Late Stuart England." *Historical Journal*, vol. 47, no. 4, 2004, pp. 875–96.

Craik, Dinah Mulock. *Christian's Mistake*. London, 1865.

———. *Fifty Golden Years: Incidents in the Queen's Reign*. London, 1887.

———. *A Noble Life*. London, 1866. 2 vols.

———. *The Unkind Word and Other Stories*. London, 1870. 2 vols.

Dwor, Richa. *Jewish Feeling: Difference and Affect in Nineteenth-Century Jewish Women's Writing*. Bloomsbury Academic, 2015.

Erdozain, Dominic. "The Secularisation of Sin in the Nineteenth Century." *Journal of Ecclesiastical History*, vol. 62, no. 1, 2011, pp. 59–88.

Harris, José. *Private Lives, Public Spirit: A Social History of Britain, 1870–1914*. Oxford UP, 1993.

Harrison, Carol E. *Romantic Catholics: France's Postrevolutionary Generation in Search of a Modern Faith*. Cornell UP, 2014.

Huzzey, Richard. *Freedom Burning: Anti-Slavery and Empire in Victorian Britain*. Cornell UP, 2012.

King, Joshua. *Imagined Spiritual Communities in Britain's Age of Print*. The Ohio State UP, 2015.

Knight, Frances. *Victorian Christianity at the Fin de Siècle: The Culture of English Religion in a Decadent Age*. I. B. Tauris, 2016.

Kuhn, William M. *Democratic Royalism: The Transformation of the British Monarchy, 1861–1914*. St. Martin's Press, 1996.

LaPorte, Charles. *Victorian Poets and the Changing Bible*. U of Virginia P, 2011.

Larsen, Timothy. "Biblical Criticism and the Crisis of Belief: D. F. Strauss's *Leben Jesu* in Britain." *Contested Christianity: The Political and Social Contexts of Victorian Theology*, Baylor UP, 2004, pp. 44–58.

———. *A People of One Book: The Bible and the Victorians*. Oxford UP, 2011.

Lutz, Deborah. *Relics of Death in Victorian Literature and Culture*. Cambridge UP, 2015.

Macdonald, George. *Alec Forbes of Howglen*. London, 1865. 3 vols.

———. *Sir Gibbie*. Leipzig, 1880. 2 vols.

Morris, Jeremy. "Secularization and Religious Experience: Arguments in the Historiography of Modern British Religion." *Historical Journal*, vol. 55, no. 1, 2012, 195–219.

Newnum, Anna Stenson. "Single but Not Solitary: Dinah Mulock Craik's Vision of a Protestant Female Community." *Women's Writing*, vol. 20, no. 3, 2013, pp. 308–24.

Oliphant, Margaret. *The Autobiography of Margaret Oliphant: The Complete Text*. Oxford UP, 2002.

———. *Passages in the Life of Mrs Margaret Maitland*. London, 1849. 3 vols.

Parry, Jonathan. "Whig Monarchy, Whig Nation: Crown, Politics and Representativeness 1800–2000." *The Monarchy and the British Nation, 1780 to the Present*, edited by Andrei Olechnowicz, Cambridge UP, 2007, pp. 47–75.

Priest, Robert D. "Reading, Writing, and Religion in Nineteenth-Century France: The Popular Reception of Renan's *Life of Jesus*." *Journal of Modern History*, vol. 86, no. 2, 2014, pp. 258–94.

Rappaport, Helen. *Magnificent Obsession: Victoria, Albert and the Death That Changed the Monarchy*. Hutchinson, 2011.

Rose, Jonathan. *The Intellectual Life of the British Working Classes*. Yale UP, 2001.

Smith, John Bainbridge. *A Manual of the Rudiments of Theology*. London, 1830.

Stubenrauch, Joseph. *The Evangelical Age of Ingenuity in Industrial Britain*. Oxford UP, 2016.

Sumner, John Bird. *A Practical Exposition of the Gospels of St. Matthew and St. Mark: In the Form of Lectures, Intended to Assist the Practice of Domestic Instruction and Devotion*. London, 1831.

Vallone, Lynn. *Becoming Victoria*. Yale UP, 2001.

Victoria, Queen. *Queen Victoria's Journals*. Bodleian Libraries, Royal Archives, *ProQuest*, http://www.queenvictoriasjournals.org/home.do.

Wells, H. G. *Joan and Peter: The Story of an Education*. New York, 1918.

Whately, Richard. *The Kingdom of Christ: In Two Essays*. London, 1841.

Wilberforce, Samuel. *Eucharistica: Meditations and Prayers, with Select Passages, on the Most Holy Eucharist from old English Divines*. London, 1839.

Windscheffel, Ruth Clayton. *Reading Gladstone*. Palgrave Macmillan, 2008.

CHAPTER 8

Jewish Women's Writing as a New Category of Affect

RICHA DWOR

IN 1840 two sisters from Portsmouth in the south of England named Marion and Celia Moss published a type of book that had not quite been written before. *The Romance of Jewish History* tells the stories of the Jews "as they were while yet an independent people," using all the characterization and narrative drive of a novel, while also displaying the careful presentation of sources and concern for accuracy increasingly found in academic works of history (Moss ix). It sold well enough to be followed three years later by *Tales of Jewish History*, which traces the fortunes of the Jews into Roman times and their ensuing diaspora. The aim of the Moss sisters (who later married and became known as Marion Hartog and Celia Moss Levetus) was to make the Jews known to their Protestant countrymen in England, in the optimistic expectation of improved mutual relations and expanded civil liberties.[1] Meanwhile, their works inaugurated a new genre of writing by Jewish women, one that dealt with topics viewed as masculine. The Moss sisters were alive to the gen-

---

1. Both sisters read widely in fiction and poetry during their youths, and *The Romance of Jewish History* was dedicated to the diplomatist and popular author Edward Bulwer Lytton. Celia Moss Levetus (1819–73) moved to Birmingham, where she had five children, and in 1865 published *The King's Physician and Other Tales*. Marion Hartog (1821–1907) also had several children. She ran schools in London and published occasionally. She also founded the first Jewish periodical edited by a woman, *The Jewish Sabbath Journal: A Penny and Moral Magazine for the Young* (1854–55), which failed after a harsh review in the *Jewish Chronicle*.

dered nature of certain forms of writing, explaining, "Our men of genius have neglected the lighter branches of literature" in favor of "theology, metaphysics, and philosophy" (Moss iv). They proposed to take up the "tale" and the "romance" as tools to represent Jewish identity, and they were keen to maintain formal, and thus gendered, categories:

> We do not intend this production to be considered in the light of a history; our wish is to call the attention of the reader to the records of our people; to awaken curiosity—not to satisfy it. (Moss ix)

By awakening curiosity rather than satisfying it, however, and by opening up new experiences of feeling rather than resolving enquiries with definitive resolutions, they were in fact deploying distinctly Jewish ways of thinking and of reading. And though they took care to advertise the gendered boundaries observed in their works, it remains the case that by engaging in an affective exploration of diverse sacred and historical source material, they intervened in a theological practice that had traditionally been the preserve of men.

I argue that writing by some nineteenth-century Jewish women deploys religious affect in secular literary forms, and as such, constitutes a unique theological genre.[2] While the formal study of Jewish sacred texts historically has been practiced solely by men, identifying Jewish affect—or what I will henceforth call Jewish feeling—can recover religious aspects of Anglo-Jewish women's writing in the nineteenth century.[3] Newly emboldened by the popularity of other (Christian) female novelists and poets and with a receptive evangelical press to publish their works, Jewish women sought to articulate a contemporary Jewish identity, generally without the benefit of formal religious education. The use of Jewish feeling as a framework for the study of Marion and Celia Moss's writings or those, say, of the better known Anglo-Jewish writer Grace Aguilar (1816–47), reveals Jewish structures of thought in literary works that hitherto have been placed in a secular frame.

---

2. This chapter reprises some of the argument from my book *Jewish Feeling: Difference and Affect in Nineteenth-Century Jewish Women's Writing* (2015) but extends it to new material.

3. The terms "affect" and "feeling" have distinct meanings. The former is unstructured and unconscious, while "feeling" is personal, conscious, and historical. Eric Shouse defines feeling as "a sensation that has been checked against previous experiences and labelled." In this chapter, "feeling" is used in a slightly different way than is conventional in affect studies, as meaning something closer to "a non-conscious experience of intensity," or affect (Shouse). A fuller explanation of these concepts is below.

The authors discussed here—the Mosses and Aguilar—were writing in Britain in the decades before Jewish emancipation, which occurred in 1858.[4] During this period, there was much to be gained by presenting Judaism in a way that could make emotional sense to Christian readers, as doing so might help pave a path for Jews to citizenship. As Bryan Cheyette has argued, this stance changed in the latter decades of the century when Jewish women and Jewish writers began to have greater access to formal education and so could write about religion in a more direct way, rather than adopting belles-lettristic modes (260).[5] The argument I am advancing here thus works well for a particular moment of midcentury Victorian Britain. However, as Jonathan Hess, Maurice Samuels, and Nadia Valman's *Nineteenth-Century Jewish Literature: A Reader* (2013) suggests, we might expect to find similar dynamics across the whole of the century and in other countries, thereby recovering women's theological thought which might otherwise go undetected.

I approach Jewish feeling as a set of affects produced through midrashic modes of interpretation found in Jewish communities, writings, and cultural practices. In particular, I look to the interpretive method of midrash as a practice developed to generate a distinctive mode of feeling. Jewish feeling enters the secular world when it underpins the creation of literary texts written by authors who have internalized or are deploying it. The Hebrew word *midrash* both designates a rabbinic method of narrative exegesis and describes the genre of literature that employs it. It is a way of thinking about the Hebrew Bible as well as the body of texts produced by the publication of this thought. There are two categories of midrash. Midrash *Halakha* are rabbinic interpretations of the Hebrew Bible (excluding Deuteronomy) that derive points of law governing religious practice from the sacred books. Midrash *Aggadah*, by contrast, uses narrative to fill "gaps" identified by the interpreter in ways that open up ethical and theological questions. The unending finding of gaps is as important as their filling, as to have filled all the gaps would be to conclude the search for meaning in the sacred text—impossible and not to be wished for.

Consider, for instance, the Book of Esther, in which a young Jewish woman is brought by her relative Mordecai before King Ahasuerus, who is in search of a new wife. Esther's Jewish identity, as well as her birth name Hadas-

---

4. Further advancements in civil liberties followed, such as the Universities Tests Act in 1871, which allowed Jews, Catholics, and Nonconformists to take up Fellowships at Oxford, Cambridge, Durham, and the University of London.

5. Nonetheless, even as Judaism pluralized, literature remained a site of religious thought for female authors. Lily Montagu, for example, wrote several novels exploring Jewish subjectivity alongside her work as a founder of Liberal Judaism and as a magistrate. I have written about this in "Lily Montagu and Liberal Judaism."

sah, are initially concealed, and Mordecai anticipates that by placing her in the palace, she can in time become an advocate for the Jews. Soon enough, the King authorizes a massacre of the Jews on the advice of his adviser Haman. On learning of this, Esther seeks to know more:

> Then called Esther for Hatach, one of the King's chamberlains, whom he had appointed to attend upon her, and give him a commandment to Mordecai, to know what it was and why it was. (Caroll and Prickett [eds.] 4:5)

The authors of the aggadic midrash on the Book of Esther, composed in Hebrew between 400 and 600 CE, not only read between the lines of this passage but also insert other voices into that interlinear space (prooftext below is rendered in caps):

> THEN CALLED ESTHER FOR HATHACH (*ib.* 5). Our teachers there say that Hatach is the same as Daniel, and because he was cut down (*hatkuhu*) on affairs of state. TO KNOW WHAT THIS WAS, AND WHY IT WAS. She told him: "Go and say to Mordecai that never in their history have Israel been in such a crisis as this. Have Israel perhaps denied [Him of whom they said], *This is my God, and I will glorify Him* (Ex. XV, 2), or have they perhaps denied the tablets of which it is written, *On the one side and on the other* [lit. "on *this* and on *this*"] *were they written* (*ib.* XXXII, 15)?" (Rabinowitz 105)

Formally, this commentary is anchored to the text, but it also shuttles freely between other registers and topics. There is the wordplay which, in a seeming non sequitur, relates the name of the king's servant to the figure of Daniel and thus invokes another instance of Jewish persecution earlier in the Babylonian exile. The voice of Esther is interpolated so that she goes from merely seeking information to drawing associations between the present moment and the text of Genesis.

By their use of allusion and quotation, these interventions place the narrative in a far wider Jewish textual history. They also probe the meanings of the episode by posing questions that are absent in the prooftext, questions that also constitute a commentary on the authors' own era. As Maurice Simon points out, the authors of this midrash "unhesitatingly read the conditions of their own time into the Biblical text" (vii). In this sense, their musings on whether Israel had brought about a cataclysm by disregarding God's commandments may pertain as much to Jewish conditions under Roman rule during the fourth century CE as to the massacre feared by Esther and Mordecai under Persian rule in the sixth century BCE. Midrash therefore draws contemporary relevance and, often, moral instruction from biblical prooftexts. Typically relying on the atomization of words and phrases and the juxtaposition of quotations from many other sources, it looks always to extend, interrupt, question, or challenge existing interpretations rather than provide a singular or definite meaning. Indeed, as Simon Schama pithily notes, "Jewish reading refuses to close the book on anything" (35).

A brief genealogy of affect, meanwhile, can begin with Baruch Spinoza (1632–77), the Dutch philosopher.[6] In his philosophical treatise *Ethics* (*Ethica, Ordine Geometrico Demonstrata*), published posthumously in 1677, Spinoza defines affect as a change in the body's power of acting as well as the "ideas" that prompt or result from this change: "By affect I understand affections of the body by which the body's power of acting is increased or diminished, aided or restrained, and at the same time, the ideas of these affections" (70; D3). Spinoza uses two terms to explain the interactions between the self and the world that produce affect: *affectus* and *affectio*. While these two terms are often collapsed into simply "affect" in translations of *Ethics* from Latin into English, in fact they have distinct meanings. The political philosopher Brian Massumi defines *affectus* in a well-known formulation as "a prepersonal intensity," a moment of potential that corresponds to "the passage from one experiential state to another" (xvi). *Affectus*, in other words, is prior to and outside of consciousness. It is the capacity to enter into "experiential [states]" rather than the specificity of those states themselves. *Affectio*, by contrast, refers to changes that occur as the result of "an encounter between the affected body and a second, affecting, body" (Massumi xvi). Affect for Spinoza, then, refers to the body's powers of acting (*affectus*) coming into contact with the world and the resulting change (*affectio*) caused by that encounter.

Midrash and affect come together if we may view a text, particularly one believed to be divinely authored, as an externally originating stimulus to affect.[7] Engaging in the Jewish interpretive strategies characterized by midrash facilitates and amplifies this affective response. The way that midrash is presented on the page (with many voices intercutting one another, blocks of text

---

6. A member of the Portuguese Jewish community in Amsterdam until the age of 23, Spinoza was famously excommunicated as a heretic in 1656.

7. Massumi makes the important proviso that the idea of a body—both an affected and an affecting body—must be "taken in its broadest possible sense to include 'mental' or ideal bodies" (xvi). This view is upheld by other recent theorists of affect, notably Lawrence Grossberg, Eve Kosofky Sedgwick, and Teresa Brennan, who have sought both to decenter the individual subject and to radically expand what might be considered as an affecting body.

surrounded by further commentaries, and notations indicating other texts to read alongside the one under discussion) emphasizes a multiplicity of voices arranged without evident hierarchy, a feature that Emmanuel Levinas refers to as "the characteristic pluralism of rabbinical thought" (62). This multiplicity has a formal similarity to the intensity and openness of affect, in which a static expression of personal feeling has not yet occurred. Put another way, we may use Spinoza to explain how midrash works on the emotions of its producers and readers. Midrashic multiplicity is akin to Spinoza's *affectus* in exhibiting an essentially neutral capacity to act or be "in motion." The playfulness and polyvalence characteristic of this mode has led in recent years to studies of the literariness of midrash and the presence of midrashic modes of thought in literary texts. In their 1986 volume *Midrash and Literature,* Geoffrey Hartman and Sanford Budick describe a "pressing need" for contemporary literary studies to look closely at midrash and its implications, thereby challenging conventional distinctions between the religious and the secular (ix).

I suggest here, as in my earlier work, that we can answer the call raised by Hartman and Budick by examining Jewish women's writing of the nineteenth century. Michael Galchinsky argues that while Victorian Jewish women did look to both Sephardic and Ashkenazic forms when writing in English, they also turned to the novel in significant numbers, indicating an interest in "forming bonds with the dominant culture that went beyond submission to or resistance against coercive measures" (33). In writing literary works for Jewish and non-Jewish readers, these female authors deployed midrashic structures of thought and thus participated in the formation of a distinctly Jewish form of affect. Reading their works to detect deliberate and innovative Jewish thought rebuts the common assumptions among their contemporaries (and ours, too) that because Jewish women were prevented from formal religious study they engaged in none and that because they were the targets of campaigns for their conversion, they merely replicated and assimilated the language of evangelical Protestantism.

As Miriam Burstein points out in her chapter in this volume, for many Protestant Victorians, religious formalism or "excessive" attention to ritual was associated with Judaism and Catholicism. Moreover, these readers tended to believe that formalism rid religious belief of its affective qualities. Burstein further notes two key anxieties held by nineteenth-century reviewers: first, they worried that biblical "truths" might be transformed through literary writing into "a *form,*" and second, they were concerned that realistic representation of exotic religious practices implied the absence of "spiritual essence." Such prejudices, no doubt, were a barrier to female Jewish authors, many of whom used the genre of domestic fiction to record didactic accounts of their daily lives, including religious practices. Their engagement with popular genres, one imagines, made them vulnerable to accusations of embracing those types of religious and literary formalisms that seemed to indicate spiritual vacuity.[8]

As we have seen, however, one of the main characteristics of Jewish reading practices is its flexibility—flexibility of interpretive strategies, and flexibility in developing a range of genres for the expression of diverse interpretations. Viewed in this light, Jewish women's authorship of novels, poetry, and drama can be understood not as abandoning but rather as extending Jewish reading practices, using the textual forms and publication networks available. Consequently, their writing is anything but form-bound and vacuous, underpinned as it is by a tradition of flexibility that is actually generative of religious affects—of Jewish feeling, in other words.

Mark Knight offers a corollary to my argument in his chapter in this volume on Wilde. He observes that our current critical practice in literary studies is informed by a Protestant viewpoint, which insists on penetrating surface appearances. Yet, as he notes, the surface itself can be the site of "theological acts." Something similar certainly holds true in Jewish practice, in which reading and writing in the service of religious thought both records and provides stimulus to religious feeling. Rather than searching for a singular truth, midrashic thought probes the surface, subtext, hypothetical counternarratives, and unrelated texts precisely in order to continue the process of searching. Even more importantly, Knight's argument reminds us that detecting historical religious difference relies not only on sensitive knowledge of a period but also on self-reflexive critical practices. With an expanded definition of midrash as an affective exchange and a wider sense of how Jewish epistemology may be manifested in literary form, we may trace the influence of Jewish thought even in works that do not appear to fit into a classical Jewish theological genre, thereby locating the presence of distinctively Jewish feeling in nineteenth-century Jewish women's writing.

Of course, women's literary and theological writing was not limited to Jewish authors alone. Rebecca Styler has shown how Christian women used literature throughout the nineteenth century "as a means to engage in theological discourse" while circumventing barriers, including the denial of "any formal theological role in the church and academy" and "cultural prohibitions regarding the assumption of spiritual authority" (1). Jewish women in England at this time were also largely excluded from sites of religious learning and study.[9]

---

8. Or to risk the sarcasm of George Eliot, who would satirize such productions as the "*white neck-cloth* species" of so-called silly novels by lady novelists (196).

9. For an overview of Jewish women's writing that encompasses the early nineteenth century to the present, see Valman.

Open to them, however, were evangelical periodicals, radical Scottish newspapers, London presses printing three-volume novels, and a growing Jewish market in the US with a publication center in Philadelphia. As Galchinsky and others have shown, this combination of exclusion and opportunity gave rise in the 1840s to the social phenomenon of the Jewish woman writer. Many scholars now view their novels, poetry, and essays as either assimilationist or apologetic, particularly in the authors' adoption of gendered conventions regarding female domesticity and emotional piety.[10] However, what might appear to be conventionally feminized sentimentality is also, and more significantly, a form of affect stemming from midrash.

Take, for instance, Grace Aguilar. Born in 1816, she was the descendant of Portuguese Jews who had arrived in England after fleeing the Inquisition three centuries earlier. Previous generations of her family had lived as *marranos*, or Jews who outwardly professed Catholicism to evade persecution while conducting Jewish study and ritual in private. England in the early nineteenth century therefore represented a place of measured tolerance. Jews had few civil liberties, but they could at least practice their religious life and form community organizations without concealment.[11] Aguilar inherited from her parents loyalty towards Protestant tolerance in Britain and a tradition of matrilineal cultural transmission. Aguilar's oeuvre includes novels and short fiction—including several historical romances that revisit the Spanish Inquisition—lyric poetry and prayers, a collective biography of women in the Bible, polemics, theological explications, and the first history of the Jews in England written by a Jewish person. Across these works, she calls for the formation of a Jewish literary tradition in English. Aguilar and her contemporaries were responding to the concerted attempts of conversionists who looked to Jewish women as likely targets for their millennial zeal. In addition to being the most popular Jewish author of her time, she is thus paradigmatic of other female Jewish authors who highlighted their exclusion from both Jewish learning and the English literary tradition, while using the publishing opportunities available to them to negotiate a qualified entrée to both.

Cynthia Scheinberg deftly accounts for Aguilar's self-fashioning by arguing that she "exploits" the emerging paradigm of women's theological poetry while also deliberately resisting "the ways Christian woman writers appropriate Jewish/Biblical women in the service of their own Christian and artistic authority" (149). Scheinberg rightly argues that literary writing forms a part of Aguilar's wider "religious project," a project that involved circumventing

---

10. See, for example, Beckman.

11. For historical works on Jews in Britain during the nineteenth century, see Endelman; Alderman; Feldman.

the rabbinic authorities that prohibited women from participating in theological discourse (148). In her work, Aguilar advanced an idea of Jewish spiritual renewal and also critiqued Christian modes of presenting Jewish women's spirituality. As an alternative, she posited a personal and unmediated connection to sacred texts and Jewish history. This borrowing from Protestant theology was nonetheless designed to enable Jewish women to read the materials available to them—often, the King James Bible—in order to develop religious identities that could withstand the attempts of evangelical conversionists.[12] We can build on Scheinberg's reading of Aguilar's "project" by showing that a further expression of Aguilar's theology lies in her uses of affect. Aguilar deploys Jewish feeling in her writing in a way that both gives voice to a new iteration of Jewish thought and refashions the literary forms in which she writes.

An often overlooked poem called "The Importance of Religion to Genius" exemplifies this dynamic. It does so by borrowing from English poetic traditions while also registering the speaker's irreconcilable alienation from that world. Even more, when read alongside Aguilar's later works it can be seen to establish a key idea which is then developed via repeated examinations of a biblical prooftext (in this example, the Book of Esther). That idea is the collapse of an epistemological distinction between emotion and intellect and the resulting sense that feeling is the ultimate way of knowing.

The poem was written in 1839 and copied out by Aguilar into one of the handwritten booklets of her best poetry and short fiction that she prepared each year. Each of these books has a carefully prepared title page that replicates printer's conventions of type, ornamentation, and information about place and year of publication (Aguilar's volume for 1838/39 was produced by

---

12. There is some irony in arguing that Aguilar deploys rabbinic structures of thought even as she outwardly decried "the trammels of rabbinism" ("History" 344). Indeed, her views are in keeping with a western Sephardic tradition, which was historically antagonistic toward rabbinic exegetical practices. However, in works such as "The Spirit of Night, Founded on a Hebrew Apologue" (published posthumously in 1852) and *The Women of Israel*, Aguilar is clearly practicing midrash aggadah. English-language Jewish periodicals such as the *Hebrew Review* (founded 1835) and the *Voice of Jacob* (founded 1809) published similar midrashic works by men and women, and Aguilar was reviewed in or had involvement with both, just as she was a contributor to *The Cheap Jewish Library*, founded in 1841 by the heiress Charlotte Montefiore and run by Rabbi Abraham de Sola, a Sephardic community leader. In this sense, then, her "Jewish feeling," as I am calling it here, emerges in large degree from contemporary Anglo-Jewish print culture as much as it does from familial inheritance or formal religious education. We might further note that in the study of women's histories, it is often impossible to reconstruct the same paper trail that offers the material evidence of men's lives. It is important that in the absence of documentation of education or professional activities in the public realm, we do not assume that women did not lead social, intellectual, professional, or, indeed, religious lives.

her in London).¹³ The books often include a dedication, table of contents, and numbered pages. The titles of each poem are written out with characteristic flourish. The pleasure and care in the production of the books thus evinces an interest in the reception of the works contained therein. What began as the project of a precocious young woman (the earliest extant fair copies of Aguilar's work in her hand are from 1831, when she was fifteen and living with her parents in Teignmouth, Devon) became a form of professionalism on her return to London and her subsequent search for a readership beyond her family. This particular poem eventually found its audience in 1846, when it was published in *The Occident*, a Philadelphia-based Jewish periodical.¹⁴

In "The Importance of Religion to Genius," the pains of "Genius" and a frustrated desire for renown animate the poem (2). Religion—unspecified, untheorized religion—is presented as the ultimate "balm" to the speaker's "o'erwhelming pangs" (5, 18). The pangs themselves, however, as well as the speaker's misguided yearnings toward "fame" and "love," haunt the poem from beginning to end, undermining any succor offered by the "Spirit of peace" (25, 33, 89). The pain is relentless, characterized by wakefulness and troublingly intense emotions: hope, the desire for fame, anger, and ungovernable resentment. On the surface, the speaker describes a process of consolation through conversion. Where once she was tormented by unbearable yearnings, religion brings peace. The subtext of this happy solution, however, implies that the real tension is between a desire for worldly fame and, in its place, self-abnegation. Descriptions of "The poet's sure, yet hidden wreck" and her "never-spoken woe" indicate the pain of going unseen and unheard (34, 70). Believing that "love, or fame, or joy, / That earth can give [will] too soon alloy" (41–42), the speaker looks to religion to address a struggle *within* the self, rather than the struggle *between* the self and the world:

Oh, what but thou can lull to rest
The throbbing of a bleeding breast,
And still the soul too oft oppress'd
By its own force;
Can break the dull and heavy chain,
That soaring pinion would restrain,

---

13. Permission to quote from the Aguilar papers has kindly been granted by the Jewish Museum, London, and UCL Library Services, Special Collections.

14. Aguilar had a long-standing professional relationship with the editor of *The Occident*, Rabbi Isaac Leeser. In 1842 he had edited and brought out an American edition of her book *The Spirit of Judaism*. Her poems appeared frequently in *The Occident*, as did a moving obituary by Leeser after she died in 1847.

> Yet scarce their prisoner can retain,
> Or curb his course! (57–64)

The "thou" addressed here is religion itself, which alone can break the self-made chains by which the genius makes a prisoner of herself. The breaking of these chains implies a refashioning of subjectivity, now released from inner turmoil: religion "brings relief to all who bring / A childlike heart" (79–80). No longer seeking admiration for her abilities, the speaker, her thoughts thus purified, instead glorifies the "blessed spirit" (81). Peace, then, is attained when yearning gives way to the regressive purity of a childlike state. The only release from direst torment is to surrender the thinking, feeling, adult self. The ambivalence of this rescue is underpinned by the dread fascination the speaker feels for "that peculiar sense, / Shrinking and deep, and wild, intense, / The poet's doom" (65–67).

The poem is savagely direct and richly intertextual. It deploys the type of balladic stanza similar to the one favored by Robert Burns, also called the Scottish stanza. While the latter uses six lines and rhymes the fourth and the sixth, Aguilar's stanza is eight lines, with a rhyme scheme of AAABCCCB, in which A and C lines are iambic tetrameter, B lines are iambic dimeter. The interruption effected by the foreshortened fourth and eighth lines mimics the speaker's irresolvable gestures toward surrendering self-expression. Aguilar's allusions range from John Donne to William Blake, those exemplars of religious grappling. The speaker's idea of herself as a "prisoner" (63) in need of divine release from a "dull and heavy chain" (61) invokes Donne's "Holy Sonnet 14" (ca. 1609), in which the speaker similarly experiences confinement within the prison of the self and implores God to grant release through destruction:

> That I may rise and stand, o'erthrow me, and bend
> Your force to break, blow, burn, and make me new. (3–4)

Aguilar's "chain" furthermore recalls the malign "hammer," "chain," "furnace," and "anvil" that manufacture a fearsome counterpoint to lamblike innocence in Blake's "The Tyger" (1794). In addition, the speaker is variously referred to as a "genius" and a "poet," one whose soul is "too oft oppress'd / By its own force" (59–60). In this, the protagonist replicates a decades-old Romantic tradition of the genius-tormented creative figure, notably the Poet in Percy Bysshe Shelley's *Alastor: or, the Spirit of Solitude* (1815). Aguilar's speaker dearly wishes to avert the "abject and inglorious" destiny that Shelley claims awaits those who have been awakened to a "too exquisite perception," but like his

Poet, her speaker "thirsts for intercourse with an intelligence similar to itself" (Shelley iv–v). Aguilar draws on a deep English poetic tradition to articulate an attempt to abandon the desire for poetic renown and personal fulfillment. Her poem thus declares allegiance to English poetry and poetic subjectivity while also registering irreconcilable alienation from both.

Just as "The Importance of Religion to Genius" has a surface and a deeper meaning with respect to the possibility of religion calming the torment of genius, so, too, does it have deep intertexts with the Hebrew Bible. Six years after writing this poem, Aguilar retraced the struggle described here in her discussion of the Book of Esther, one of the longest entries in her collective biography called *The Women of Israel; or, Characters and Sketches from the Holy Scriptures and Jewish History, Illustrative of the Past History, Present Duties, and Future Destiny of the Hebrew Females, as Based on the Word of God* (1845).[15] Esther occupies a special place in this volume, which builds on the popular genre of prosopography to acquaint readers with exemplary Jewish female figures and to draw from these Jewish narratives didactic relevance for a contemporary readership. Esther's crucial moment occurs when she must approach her husband the King to sue for protection of the Jews, a move that risks her execution for petitioning him without invitation and also the exposure of her concealed identity as a Jew. There are two apocryphal versions of the Book of Esther, the Hebrew and the Greek, and Aguilar uses both as sources. In the latter Esther prays to God for "eloquent speech" (Esth. 14:13) and deliverance of the Jews from annihilation as well as herself from her own weakness:

> O thou mighty God above all, hear the voice of the forlorn, and deliver us out of the hands of the mischievous, and deliver me out of my fear. (Esth. 14:19)

Upon entering the throne room Esther faints twice, once even as she is speaking. Aguilar picks up on this emotional crisis:

> It is the still undercurrent of deep feeling, . . the absence of all trust in her own gifts of beauty and elegance, unless so blessed by Him as to soften the heart of the king towards her—the courage, not *natural*, but acquired through prayer . . . these are the traits which surely must rivet our interest and our love. (Aguilar, *The Women of Israel* 349)

---

15. The events of the Book of Esther are celebrated in the Jewish holiday of Purim. One commandment for the observance of this holiday is that all Jews should hear the Book read out loud, in its entirety, twice.

Like the speaker in "The Importance of Religion to Genius," Esther in *The Women of Israel* gains strength through prayer to vacate the self and let God enter. While Esther achieves this aim, so ensuring the safety of a Jewish minority within a powerful empire, neither the speaker of her earlier poem nor Aguilar herself can ultimately do the same. *The Women of Israel* is widely viewed as an example of literary midrash. Like the rabbinic sages before her, Aguilar returns to biblical prooftexts to fill in gaps and to consider these narratives through the lens of contemporary priorities. Underpinning this exercise is the belief that the Bible contains all these meanings and more and that expanding on its original sense in this way merely unfolds its depths.

What is harder to detect is the Jewishness of a poem like "The Importance of Religion to Genius," which appears to replicate, invoke, or assimilate emotional postures of British Christianity. Yet we should pay attention to what the speaker describes as her "dearest hopes in mental breast" (13), a phrase that implies that the intellect can reside in the passions (in "the breast") and that the speaker's desire for recognition is linked to her intellectual performance. That "still undercurrent of deep feeling," which Aguilar saw in the story of Esther, thus seems initially to have found expression in this earlier poem. In both works Aguilar makes an epistemological distinction: to feel something is to know it, and to know is to reread it, many times, forever.

Aguilar was still thinking of Esther during the year that *The Women of Israel* was brought to press, and in 1845 she published "Dialogue Stanzas: Composed for, and Repeated by, Two Dear Little Animated Girls, at a Family Celebration of the Festival of Purim." Purim is the carnival-like festival that marks the Jews' escape from a massacre recounted in the Book of Esther. It is an occasion on which Jews are customarily obliged to celebrate and be happy. In Aguilar's poem, the livelier of the two girls implores her more contemplative friend to put away her book (the Book of Esther, we assume) and join the celebrations, which the latter girl eventually does but not before seeking to understand the events of the book and to meditate on the ongoing presence and protection of the God of Esther and Mordecai:

> Sweet sister! let me think awhile, and then I'll merry be,
> Should we not think a grateful thought e'en in our sunny glee?
> It was not *only* Esther's words—but Israel's God was there,
> The king of Persia's heart to turn—His chosen ones to spare.
> And we should bless Him, sister dear, that He protects us still—
> And such kind friends bestows on us, to guard us from all ill
> ("Dialogue" 19–24)

Karen Weisman notes that the poem calls to mind William Wordsworth's "Expostulation and Reply" (first published in *Lyrical Ballads* in 1798) but rewrites the stakes. While Wordsworth presents a dichotomy between scholarship and nature, Weisman points out that in the Jewish tradition of Purim, the joy is in the text itself and in the act of reading it publicly. Thus while the two girls ultimately put down the book and take up a garland for their mother, their re-entry into the natural world remains encumbered by the distant threat of violence as in Esther's time, and it occurs in a symbolic pastoral landscape "that was never [theirs] anyway" (Weisman 280). In this way, while Aguilar's work often appears to take up popular English forms and tropes, it is also underpinned by a sense of difference and often an act of revisiting and rereading sacred texts.

Attention to the presence of Jewish feeling helps us to detect the distinctiveness of Jewish thought and to recover the theological work of women. Doing so requires understanding the conceptual underpinnings and effects of midrashic interpretation. In midrashic thought, acts of reading and writing take on theological status because they can extend the encounter with the divine Word. In a sense, this holds true even when carried over into secular forms. If, as Spinoza posits, affect is composed of the body's powers of acting (*affectus*) and the resulting change (*affectio*) caused by coming into contact with the world, then Jewish affect (or Jewish feeling) can potentially arise in the encounter between a pluralistic way of thinking and a text of any kind. It was women during the nineteenth century who carried Jewish feeling into forms that were not explicitly religious precisely because they were excluded from those which were.

Too often, current examinations of nineteenth-century religion cleave to the dominant Christian readings that were advanced during that period without considering other interpretive frameworks. Focusing on Jewish forms of reading, writing, and interpretation is important if we are to detect the wider complexity of religious thought. This is particularly the case when analyzing commentaries on the Hebrew Bible, but it also extends to the study of apparently secular texts. If Jewish women's writing is indeed a theological form that makes cultural interventions across a range of literary styles, then it falls to scholars today to pay careful attention to the ways that Jewish thought, spirituality, and practice might revise our understandings of nineteenth-century religion. Doing so can effect the recovery of a minority subjectivity experienced during the period. Even more, it can prevent critics from adopting and replicating the prejudices of clergy in the period, such as the evangelical Anglican leader Charles Simeon, who declared that Judaism lacked a "vital principle" and instead possessed merely "empty" form, as Burstein notes in her chapter in this volume. Finally, considering formal experimentation in Jewish writing expands our investigation of the interplay between the secular and the sacred, as well as the ultimate interrelatedness of Jewish and Christian thought and feeling in identity formation during the nineteenth century.

WORKS CITED

Aguilar, Grace. "Dialogue Stanzas: Composed for, and Repeated by, Two Dear Little Animated Girls, at a Family Celebration of the Festival of Purim." *Grace Aguilar: Selected Writings,* edited by Michael Galchinsky, Broadview Press, 2003.

———. "The Importance of Religion to Genius." Book 7. 1838–39, UCL Library Services, Special Collections, London, MSS Notebooks 378 A/1–2iii.

———. *The Spirit of Judaism.* Edited by Isaac Leeser, Jewish Publication Society of America, 5602 [1842].

———. *The Women of Israel; or, Characters and Sketches from the Holy Scriptures and Jewish History, Illustrative of the Past History, Present Duties, and Future Destiny of the Hebrew Females, as Based on the Word of God.* 1845. George Routledge and Sons, [1890?].

———. "History of the Jews in England." 1847. *Grace Aguilar: Selected Writings,* edited by Michael Galchinsky, Broadview Press, 2003, pp. 313–53.

Alderman, Geoffrey. *Modern British Jewry.* Clarendon Press, 1992.

Beckman, Linda Hunt. "Leaving 'the Tribal Duckpond': Amy Levy, Jewish Self-Hatred, and Jewish Identity." *Victorian Literature and Culture,* vol. 27, no. 1, 1999, pp. 185–202.

Blake, William. *William Blake: The Complete Poems.* Edited by Alicia Ostriker, Penguin, 1977.

Brennan, Teresa. *The Transmission of Affect.* Cornell UP, 2004.

Caroll, Robert, and Stephen Prickett, editors. *The Bible: Authorized King James Version.* Oxford World's Classics, 2008.

Cheyette, Bryan. "From Apology to Revolt: Benjamin Farjeon, Amy Levy and the Post- Emancipation Anglo-Jewish Novel, 1880–1900." *Transactions of the Jewish Historical Society of England,* vol. 29, 1985, pp. 253–65.

Donne, John. *The Varorium Edition of the Poetry of John Donne.* Edited by Gary A. Stringer, 7th ed., Indiana UP, 2005.

Dwor, Richa. *Jewish Feeling: Difference and Affect in Nineteenth-Century Jewish Women's Writing.* Bloomsbury, 2015.

———. "Lily Montagu and Liberal Judaism." *The Edinburgh Companion to Fin de Siècle Literature, Culture and the Arts,* edited by Josephine M. Guy, U of Edinburgh P, 2017, pp. 345–60.

Eliot, George. "Silly Novels by Lady Novelists." 1856. *The Essays of George Eliot,* edited by Nathan Sheppard, Funk Wagnalls, 1883, pp. 178–204.

Endelman, Todd. *Radical Assimilation in English Jewish History, 1656–1945.* Indiana UP, 1990.

Feldman, David. *Englishmen and Jews: Social Relations and Political Culture, 1840–1914.* Yale UP, 1994.

Galchinsky, Michael. *The Origin of the Modern Jewish Woman Writer: Romance and Reform in Victorian England.* Wayne State UP, 1996.

Grossberg, Lawrence. "Affect's Future: Rediscovering the Virtual in the Actual." *The Affect Theory Reader*, edited by Gregory J. Seigworth and Melissa Gregg, Duke UP, 2010, pp. 309–38.

Harris, Daniel A. "Hagar in Christian Britain: Grace Aguilar's 'The Wanderers.'" *Victorian Literature and Culture*, vol. 27, no. 1, 1999, pp. 143–69.

Hartman, Geoffrey H., and Sanford Budick, editors. *Midrash and Literature*. Yale UP, 1986.

Hess, Jonathan, Maurice Samuels, and Nadia Valman, editors. *Nineteenth-Century Jewish Literature: A Reader*. Stanford UP, 2013.

Levinas, Emmanuel. "On the Jewish Reading of Scriptures." *Literature and the Bible: A Reader*, edited by Jo Carruthers, Mark Knight, and Andrew Tate, Routledge, 2014, pp. 62–74.

Massumi, Brian. "Notes on the Translation." *A Thousand Plateaus: Capitalism and Schizophrenia*. 1980. Edited by Gilles Deleuze and Felix Guattari, translated by Brian Massumi, U of Minnesota P, 1987, pp. xvi–xix.

Moss, Celia, and Marion Moss. *The Romance of Jewish History*. Saunders and Oatley, Conduit Street, 1840.

Rabinowitz, L., translator. *The Midrash Rabbah: Lamentations, Ruth, Ecclesiastes, Esther, Song of Songs*, edited by H. Freedman and Maurice Simon, vol. 4, The Soncino Press, 1977.

Schama, Simon. *The Story of the Jews: Finding the Words, 1000 BCE–1492 CE*. The Bodley Head, 2013.

Scheinberg, Cynthia. *Women's Poetry and Religion in Victorian England: Jewish Identity and Christian Culture*. Cambridge UP, 2002.

Sedgwick, Eve Kosofsky. *Touching Feeling: Affect, Pedagogy, Performativity*. Duke UP, 2003.

Shelley, Percy Bysshe. *Alastor: or, the Spirit of Solitude*. Reeves and Turner, 1885.

Shouse, Eric. "Feeling, Emotion, Affect." *M/C Journal*, vol. 8, no. 6, 2005, http://journal.media-culture.org.au/0512/03-shouse.php. Accessed 27 March 2018.

Simon, Maurice, translator. *Midrash Rabbah*. 1939. Edited by H. Freedman and Maurice Simon, vol. 9, The Soncino Press, 1961.

Spinoza, Benedict de. *Ethics*. Translated by Edwin Curley, Penguin Classics, 1996.

Styler, Rebecca. *Literary Theology by Women Writers of the Nineteenth Century*. Ashgate, 2010.

Valman, Nadia, editor. *Jewish Women Writers in Britain*. Wayne State UP, 2014.

Weisman, Karen. "Anglo-Jewish Romantic Poetry." *The Blackwell Companion to British Romantic Poetry*, edited by Charles Mahoney, Blackwell, 2011, pp. 268–84.

Williams, Raymond. *Marxism and Literature*. 1977. Oxford UP, 1986.

Wynn, Mark R. *Emotional Experience and Religious Understanding: Integrating Perception, Conception and Feeling*. Cambridge UP, 2005.

CHAPTER 9

Hybridous Monsters

Constructing "Religion" and "the Novel" in the Early Nineteenth Century

MIRIAM ELIZABETH BURSTEIN

IN 1832 W. M. Thackeray complained in "Madame Sand and the New Apocalypse" that in the "age of duodecimos," fiction had supplanted traditional controversial forms, resulting in "detestable mixtures of truth, lies, false-sentiment, false-reasoning, bad grammar, correct and genuine philanthropy and piety—I mean our religious tracts, which any woman or man, be he ever so silly, can take upon himself to write, and sell for a penny, as if religious instruction were the easiest thing in the world" (205). Thackeray's polemic attacks how religious controversy has been both commodified and dangerously democratized, handed over to writers outside structures of church authority and disseminated cheaply to the public. Although Mary Wilson Carpenter has documented elsewhere in this volume the popularity of big family Bibles, for Thackeray these books are strangely small: the "touching histories and anecdotes of little boys and girls" that somehow encapsulate the entirety of "church history, church catechism, church doctrine" (Mrs. Sherwood) to the "three-and-sixpenny duodecimo volume" that attempts to demolish the "stately structure" of Catholicism (Grace Kennedy) to the "little half-crown trumpet" directed against Protestantism (E. C. Agnew). All these novels stand in contrast to the "folios" that once dominated religious controversy (Thackeray 205). The modern religious book is both spiritually and materially diminutive, reducing the once-solid and prestigious genre of the controversial text to the form best suited to the modern consumer.

Thackeray's critique emerged from the heated struggle to make sense of the genre's increasing popularity during the first half of the nineteenth century, sparked by a growing uneasiness about the very fact that readers could recognize the genre as such. Although writers like the evangelical Hannah More intended their works to combat the spread of potentially subversive secular reading for female, working-class, and young audiences, critics publishing in the dedicated religious press argued that the religious novel combined two incompatible goals: entertainment, which lacked an immediately detectable purpose and frequently inspired the reader to work *against* the grain of the text; and religious instruction, which needed to both constrain the reader's interpretation and lead to transformative, real-world effects. But the genre's viability as such was not the only issue. Even though early nineteenth-century "Protestant book and tract production flooded the marketplace with its explicitly religious wares" (Morgan 142), so that distributing the Word was always imbricated in selling words, reviewers nevertheless worried that novels threatened to disrupt an already-disrupted boundary line between commercial fungibility and eternal truth. Both self-defined Christian and more secular critics questioned the relationship between narrative form and religious content; both, defining "religious truth" as something with universal meaning (but actually Protestant), questioned how marketing it to specific consumers affected its dissemination. And both feared the result of transforming biblical "truths" into a recognizable (and portable) collection of genre conventions—that is, a *form*.

"HYBRIDOUS MONSTERS"

Early responses to religious fiction were anxious about the novels' possible sectarianism, which threatened to undermine an idealized Christian unity in an age when religion itself seemed endangered by radicals. Sectarianism not only revealed that the religious was also the political; it undermined the project of forming a cohesive Christian (Protestant) community, by celebrating the more restricted public sphere enabled by adhering to specific doctrines and practices. While conservative critics like those writing for the *Anti-Jacobin Review* called for religious novels that would "be moulded into that popular form, which most attracts the popular attention" ("*Infidel Father*" 41), the possibility of such a reconciliation seemed dubious.[1] Even the phrasing hinted at the way in which "religion" would be reshaped (literally) by such an act. Thus,

---

1. Novel titles in quotation marks indicate an anonymous review.

in a deeply ambivalent review of John Satchel's *Thornton Abbey: A Series of Letters on Religious Subjects* (1806), the critic for the *Eclectic Review* complains that the novel fails because of its "spirit of positivity and infallibility," directed against the Established Church, that will likely have a "fatal effect" on those already inclined to doubt (*"Thornton Abbey"* 1030). To be too partisan, that is, emphasizes *adiaphora* (things indifferent) over biblical doctrines of Christian faith (a Protestant definition); religious partisanship highlights the proliferation of denominations, inviting the doubting reader to confuse the endless production of difference with the actual stability at Christianity's center.[2]

Critics seized on these difficulties when faced with Hannah More's *Coelebs in Search of a Wife* (1808), one of the first religious novels of the nineteenth century to receive extended critical attention. As Christine L. Krueger points out, it seems contradictory for an author like More to try to combine "multivocality" with "authoritarian closure" (118), but early reviewers disagreed about whether there was too much of one and not enough of the other. On the one hand, writing in the Whiggish *Edinburgh Review*, Sydney Smith denounced *Coelebs* for being too obviously monologic. Like the reviewer of *Thornton Abbey*, Smith faulted *Coelebs* for its partisanship, complaining that "if, instead of belonging to a trumpery faction, she had only watched over those great points of religion in which the hearts of every sect of Christians are interested, she would have been one of the most useful and valuable writers of her day" (1:210). Smith thus downgrades evangelicalism to yet another example of adiaphora that foregrounds localized difference over Christian unity, squashing the universal in the favor of the particular. But the sympathetic reviewer in the *Monthly Review* had the opposite complaint: they sighed "that young people will be repulsed instead of being attracted to imitation by the character of Lucilla; that the cause of Methodism, though such is evidently not the intention, will be rather promoted than retarded by the religious dialogues contained in these volumes; and that many professors will be misled to adopt the cant of humility for humility itself" (*"Coelebs"* 136). The reviewer finds More's attempts to foreclose on alternate interpretations of the text inherently unstable. Not only will the target demographic resist rather than embrace the text, but also the novel's own dialogic qualities open up a space for a Dissenting reading nowhere anticipated by More's "intention." Kevin Gilmartin has suggested that in the Cheap Repository Tracts, More negated the perils of working-class reading by "control[ling] how books are distributed and where they are read" (92), but the critic for the *Monthly Review*, by contrast, finds

---

2. In practice, readers (and the parents thereof) did not purchase books solely in accordance with their own affiliations; see, e.g., Grenby 88; Brown 133–37.

that *Coelebs* evades More's strategic guidance. Insofar as it brings multiple perspectives into the narrative, the conversation format legitimates alternative interpretations in the act of refuting them. The reviewer's praise for the novel's admirable qualities thus collapses into the fear that readers will be alternately confused, misled, or antagonized by a narrative that seeks to educate, clarify, and inspire. Even for a reviewer inclined to agree with More's project, then, the religious novel threatens to produce unintentional, unanticipated effects upon the "young" reader, who may opt to imitate the wrong thing as opposed to the right.[3]

Indeed, in the early nineteenth century, it was not apparent to readers that the "religious novel" existed or *could* exist. Granted that the ideal Christian reader would still feel a yen for "imaginative entertainment," it was still the case that such yearnings ought to be fulfilled by morally improving literature "with a focus on the kingdom of God"—like missionary and travel narratives, as Benjamin L. Fischer has recently argued (239–40). But the problem extended beyond fact versus fiction. Critics, no matter how evangelical, "frequently tired of relentless sermonising when it appeared in novels" (Killick 89; cf. Pickering 36–37); it is symptomatic that when reviewing *Coelebs* in the evangelical *Christian Observer*, Zachary Macaulay began by denying that More's novel was a novel at all, before conceding that even if it *were* a novel, "Who ever reads the didactic parts of an attractive novel? Who *can* read them?" (109, 115). (Indeed, as Samuel Pickering points out, denying that the novel under review *was* a novel was the *Christian Observer*'s original justification for attending to fiction in the first place, beginning with John Cunningham's *A World without Souls* [1805] [35].) For Macaulay, *Coelebs* is not a novel *because* it is didactic; a didactic text that had more of the novel about it, or vice versa, would merely fail to combine irreconcilable genres. Worse, he warns that didactic fiction, far from taming readers, provokes them into *resistant* reading. Presented with a moral work, even the most Christian reader reads against the grain—a point made even more drastically by the *Eclectic Review*, which warned that Protestantism could not be encoded in fiction at all.

During the same year as the *Review* mused on the failures of *Thornton Abbey*, it offered a stirring defense of Hannah More's *Hints toward Forming the Character of a Young Princess* that critiqued her call for religious fiction.

---

3. Although critics tended to focus on the novel reader as someone potentially subordinated to the didactic text, Adrian J. Wallbank points out that while the evangelical dialogue form often identified the reader as the uninstructed figure in need of "'conversion,'" it might just as well cast them as a potential "mentor in a shared religious project" (110). Novel criticism usually obscured the latter in favor of the former.

More had praised *The Arabian Tales* for the knowledge to be gained about the religious beliefs of its characters:

> But we beg leave to ask, whether the prominent appearance, which the Mahometan religion makes in the compositions referred to, may not be the necessary consequence of its low, ceremonial character? A religion of this kind, necessarily shews itself in common life; because it prescribes rules for so many common actions:—and there is nothing in vice, however gross, to keep such a religion at a distance; as ceremonial observances have, at all times, been intermingled with the most immoral conduct. We do not, therefore, literally concur in Mrs. M's. wish, respecting the *novels* of our country. It is indeed our earnest desire, to see the Spirit of our Divine Religion transposed into every species of useful writing; and we lament sincerely, that this has very rarely taken place: yet, still, we feel satisfaction in the thought, that our religion is such as must be introduced *in the spirit of it,* or not at all. This is our glory as Christians; and it is still more especially so, as Protestants. A novel, describing the actions of Roman Catholics, might have references to religion, where an English novel could have none; because the religion of Rome has in it so much of ceremonial observance, and of course, so much that admits of being intermingled with a life of profligacy. Genuine Christianity, on the contrary, can never be made to blend either with vice or folly; so long, therefore, as either of these evils prevails in any description of human manners, that very prevalence implies, by a happy necessity of nature, a corresponding absence of our pure and undefiled religion. ("*Hints*" 120–21)

As the reviewer notes, More's *Hints* (here slightly misquoted) skips over the fantastic elements of the *Arabian Nights* in favor of recuperating it as "useful instruction" for the future ruler (More 2:174). The Christian reader ignores the *Arabian Nights*' excesses by translating it into an unselfconsciously realist representation of Islamic mores—unselfconscious because an accident of the author's own historical circumstances and identity. It is up to the active reader to extract the storyteller's unmediated reproductions of Islamic life. The reviewer isolates this accidental realist mode in terms of religious difference: "ceremonial character" and "rules" both collapse Islam into Catholicism and, more importantly, suggest that the only aspects of religion that can be integrated into fictional narrative are its rituals. If Islam and Catholicism can be rendered realistically and adequately, then by definition they have no spiritual essence *beyond* the everyday repetition of rituals that structure "common life."

Protestant anxieties about the role of Catholic ritual date to the Reformation period, and frequently reared their heads in conflicts between the Established churches and Dissenters. One of the most frequent charges against Roman Catholicism during the Reformation was that it practiced "idolatry," by which was meant not only its use of the crucifix and icons but also its ritualized modes of worship. In the sixteenth and seventeenth centuries, Dissenters were deeply suspicious of the Book of Common Prayer, which they felt reinstated the Roman Catholic Church's formalism—"vain repetitions" that effectively reduced set prayers to acts of "rhetoric, magic, and idolatry" (Yelle 107)—and imposed another dangerous level of mediation between the worshipper and God. Anglicans like Richard Hooker, by contrast, insisted that liturgical form stabilized the religious community and protected it from "the performative aberrations of either the minister or the congregation" (Targoff 55). This quarrel continued at white heat through the nineteenth century. One of the objections to evangelicals, for example, was that they abjured set forms of prayer in favor of extemporaneous prayer and preaching, thereby associating "authentic" Protestant spirituality with heartfelt emotion. Hence, by the late eighteenth century many Protestants believed that insofar as liturgy is both "legally imposed" and "repetitious," it "is taken to stultify genuine, spontaneous emotional response" (Branch 45). But ritual did not just squash the immediacy of the believer's response to God. It also reinforced fallen desires. As Kirstie Blair points out, evangelicals criticized Catholic "formalism" for its "excessive use of ritual and ceremony and by an emphasis on aesthetic, sensuous pleasures in worship, as well as by excessive attempts to regulate the individual's thoughts, feelings, and modes of behavior" (23). For that reason, formalism was linked to non-Christian practices; the important early evangelical Charles Simeon was not alone in warning that the Jews were "destitute of that vital principle, without which their religion was a vain ceremony, an empty form" (15:48). Formalism evacuated the affective qualities of religious belief, which many Protestants held to be essential, and replaced them with mechanized repetitions of language and body that erased individuality altogether.

If we return to our book reviewer, then, a Catholic novel would be permeated by religious ritual, and yet in the act of representing that ritual, the novelist would reveal Catholicism's empty formalism, which points to nothing beyond itself. Significantly, the reviewer holds up such ritual repetition as the *wrong* way of maintaining spiritual community. Catholicism's corporate body emerges not from individuals harmoniously unified by their love of God but from bodies and minds regimented into conformity. By contrast, the reviewer associates Protestantism with an excess that both escapes genre conventions (it doesn't "blend") and is at odds with its own historical moment ("vice and folly"). Protestant experience simultaneously conflicts with empirical realism and with the educated reader's imperative to decode fiction for its "useful knowledge"; its absence from contemporary fiction indicates not fiction's neglect of Christianity but rather realism's entrapment in a fallen world. If the fictional signifier can truly represent the religious signified, then that is a mark not of realism's success but of the religion's *failure*. Or, to put it differently, there should be no way to resolve Protestantism into a marketable fictional form, as the nature of Protestant religious experience is antithetical to the order of everyday life.

The argument that Protestantism was antithetical to the very possibility of religious fiction reappeared in anxieties about the religious novel's inability to produce transformative effects. Such issues preoccupied the evangelical *Christian Observer*, which in 1815 and 1816 hosted an impromptu debate between correspondents "A. A." and "Candidus"—the latter actually T. B. Macaulay, still within the evangelical fold—on fiction's power and potential. A. A. took the classic position, based on man's total depravity, which made it advisable "to avoid reading matter which could in any way imperil the soul" (Altick 110). For A. A., realism's idealized scenes and plot structure conceal the "dull mediocrity" of mundane experience (513). The novel reader becomes caught up in a simulacrum, in which "virtue, religion itself, becomes a mere play of the imagination, influencing neither the heart nor the conduct" (A. A. 514). Thus, A. A. opposes fiction on the grounds that it produces a "fictitious acquaintance" (514) with the reader's own subjectivity and her everyday life; unlike the ideal reader who extracts "useful" material from dross, the reader of novels narcissistically communes with her own imaginative projections from the text. Instead of promoting "domesticity, family and community" (Pearson 96), reading fiction generates the equivalent of those empty rituals earlier decried by the *Eclectic Review*. The novel as a form is born from the depraved imagination, and is therefore innately fallen, capable of working evil but not good. Even "good novels," A. A. insists, are unacceptable: "The foundation of the building is radically wrong, and the superstructure and ornaments are of little consequence" (516). In this metaphor, proper morality constitutes an extraneous ornament irrelevant to the building's stability, implying, yet again, that the essence of the novel's form militates against integrating the genre with anything of the spirit.

Macaulay's counterargument, by contrast, paints a grand picture of religious fiction's empirical success on the world stage. Having conceded his opponent's points about bad fiction, he nevertheless insists that fiction was the heart of Protestantism: "What were the writings which revived the age of literature in Europe, which shot the first ray of light upon the gloom of papal darkness, which unmasked the disgusting vices of the clergy, which prepared the way for the greatest event in the religious history of the world—the Reformation?" (Macaulay 784–85). Macaulay transforms fiction into a world-historical agent of (Protestant) religious transformation that leads to a literal re-vision ("shot the first ray of light," "unmasked") of human depravity. In his hierarchy of novelistic forms, constructed according to their spiritual intentions and effect, there are the "foolish and pernicious"; the "harmless and entertaining"; the "novels of Fielding and Smollett" (*sui generis,* apparently); the "moral novel"; and, finally, "religious novels" (785), now understood to be fiction's crown jewel. Ironically, given his father's insistence several years previously that *Coelebs* was *not* a novel, Macaulay argues that, far from being a "hybridous monster," *Coelebs* exemplifies how representing Christians "in so true and so pleasing a light" must necessarily produce at least a "momentary impulse in its [Christianity's] favour" (786). Notably, Macaulay insists on the possibility of melding technical craft and religious messages within the same text. More to the point, encountering these characters is a pleasurable experience, with the pleasure reinforcing the religion. Far from leading readers to creatively rework religious texts in pursuit of their own wayward pleasures, high-quality religious novels lead readers to associate enjoyment with faith. In this interpretation, the right kind of novel can transform subjects at the individual level and reconfigure entire continents at the social level.

THE RELIGIOUS NOVEL IN THE MARKETPLACE OF LETTERS

Although arguments about the possibility of religious fiction recurred throughout the nineteenth century, the genre's existence as a stubborn fact was obvious enough by the 1820s.[4] In the 1820s critical awareness of religious novels as such outstripped the actual production of them: the Religious Tract Society would not enter into the religious novel market until midcentury, and denominational publishing had not yet emerged as a widespread phenomenon.[5] Nevertheless, the genre's visibility raised anxieties about the place of the religious novel in an increasingly specialized market for fictional prod-

---

4. Simon Eliot calculated that religious books made up 20.3 percent of all published in the period 1814–46, but it is not clear how many of the over 3,100 novels and over 2,600 children's works published during that time frame would have fallen into the "religious novels" category. See Eliot 44–45.

5. Denominational publishing houses became widespread by the 1840s; see Scott 220–22.

uct—and therefore, by extension, between commodification and community-building. Opening a "puff" of Robert Plumer Ward's *Tremaine, or the Man of Refinement* (1825), Henry Colburn's *New Monthly Magazine* offered a comical survey of the current novel market:

> We have classical novels, and romantic novels, and domestic novels; theological novels and geological novels; biographical novels, and topographical novels; educational novels, and conversational novels; natural novels, and supernatural novels, and unnatural novels; philosophical novels, and historical novels, and political novels, and religious novels, and moral novels—to say nothing of the irreligious and unphilosophical and immoral ones—and we have every conceivable variety of all these species of novels, together with another species more various and more extensive than any of the above, but which can only be described negatively, as being novels that are any thing but a novel. (*"Tremaine"* 321)

Breathlessly acknowledging that it is impossible to enumerate every "species" of fiction in the marketplace, the reviewer locates "religious novels" amidst a taxonomy so complex that the concept of "novel" per se finally implodes. At the same time, the reviewer suggests the concurrent multiplication of niche markets, even though the purchaser of religious novels may also be interested in the "irreligious and unphilosophical and immoral ones"—further implying that a religious novel may be interchangeable with *other* kinds of novel. Certainly, the rolling periods and coordinating conjunctions hint that the rapidly diversifying forms of the novel are, when understood as commodities in a growing literary marketplace, all alike. As a genre, the hyperspecialized novel now exists in formats suited to the taste of any given reader, whose wants are targeted to parodic specificity.

Having classified the novel's many forms, though, it remained to define what a religious novel's difference *was,* and the *New Monthly Magazine*'s occasional attempts to do so—perhaps an example of its tendency to seek out "cultural straws in the wind," as Jon Klancher puts it (62)—are instructive. Faced with *Influence* in 1822, the magazine sourly suggested that "this is one of the anomalous productions which late years have been fruitful in bringing forth—an Evangelical novel, or in other words, a covert vehicle for the conveyance of certain theological opinions, and rules of life; among which is generally to be found a caveat against reading novels, as in the present instance, v. I. p. 81, and consequently we should have thought against writing them" (*"Influence"* 26). Evangelical novels are both oddities and all-too-common, their projects not only not aesthetic but also self-defeating. Despite the "anomalous" quality of such texts, the reviewer is quite clear that he can define them by their contents and intentions, which, as he goes on to note, are intended to set them apart from novelists like Ann Radcliffe. The religious novel advertises its own acceptability, along with its formal prescriptions for practice. Moreover, having indicted the novelist for self-contradiction, the reviewer then proceeds to lecture the novelist on the dangers of her "ostentatious display of particular opinions"—in other words, on both her and the novel's qualifications for the title of "Christian" or "evangelical" novel in the first place. The professional critic thus takes on the task of gatekeeping for a more liberal Christian readership that shuns such performative "display" of the author's spiritual peculiarities.

Four years later, the magazine was even less charitable when faced with *The Story of Isabel* (1826):

> We suppose this must be called an evangelical novel: for under a plentiful acquaintance with worldly principles, an easy delineation of general manners, and no mean knowledge of all the avenues by which fascination finds its way to man, a spirit of straitest intolerance, combined with all the usually associated doctrines of that party, erects its unyielding neck perpetually— catching our eye, and meeting our steps, and disappointing our hopes in the midst of scenes and conversations, which but for this ingredient would irresistibly chain the interest, and compel the admiration of the reader.
>
> Reasoning,—by which we understand a debate upon some unascertained question by opponents, who rest on mutually acknowledged axioms, is entirely set at nought, and made foolishness of, by a sect, who will allow of no test of worth and ability, but the profession of a certain set of notions. ("*Story of Isabel*" 427)

The novel's secular formal and aesthetic attractions conflict fatally with the eruptions of "straitest intolerance," which the critic implicitly associates with Judaism (the "unyielding neck"). This "intolerance" swaps one form of power for another: ideally, the reader would enjoy being *mastered* by the novel's contents ("chain," "compel"), but instead, the evangelical "notions" interrupt this process by being intellectually and formally out of place ("catching," "meeting," "disappointing"). "Notions" conflict with "scenes" and "conversations," suggesting that they are immovable objects strewn amidst moments of dialogue and activity; indeed, they aspire to being pure monologue. Whereas the earlier critics complained that More's dialogues smuggled dangerous alternatives into the text, here the critic insists that the novel interferes with all voices other than its own, making its claims to power too obvious.

In these instances, the religious novel is both a recognizable commodity and, again, a form consistently defined by its *failure*. To borrow from Jack Downs's assessment of the later Victorian critic David Masson, the *Monthly Magazine* reviewers diagnose the evangelical novel with a bad case of rhetorical *im*propriety: "For the belles lettres–influenced critic, great art explores the tension between ethics and aesthetics without ever giving precedence to one or the other" (8) (that balance being an example of rhetorical propriety). Moreover, the evangelical novelists' aesthetic failings also offend the magazine's liberalism, which avoided "overt partisanship" (Sweet 153) in order to maintain alliances across a range of political and social positions. The evangelical novel fails, that is, not simply because it is evangelical but because it rejects the possibility of compromise. Notably, the nondenominational literary review tries to speak for a public that prefers its Christianity to come without any assertions of one particular form's truth. "We scruple not to confess, that we entirely disapprove of religious novels," snapped the *Edinburgh Literary Journal,* "for, besides a quantity of whining cant and raving enthusiasm, they are likely to contain a considerable mixture of erroneous religious opinions." The result, as in the case of *The Modern Martyr,* was invariably "trash" ("*The Modern Martyr*" 273).

This objection to a form of unpleasant mastery over the reader speaks to the problem of *effect*. Debra Gettelman's point that "mid-Victorian novel critics were seeking to shield taste for the 'literary' from the encroachment of the 'popular' by making literary distinctions based [not?] on a work's intrinsic qualities, but on the reading experiences the work generated" (61) can be extended back to the 1820s. But not all critics were concerned with effect in the same way. For the critics of the *New Monthly Magazine,* these novels were frustrating because their aesthetic effects *as novels* were frustrating—not just formalism, but bad form. What increasingly concerned religious critics, however, was that the effects of religious novels were no *different* from those of their secular counterparts. That is, whereas secular critics insisted that they could isolate both the contents and effects of religious fiction as a distinct genre, religious critics referenced the effects of "the novel," *tout court*, worrying that reading religious fiction would have "the same ill-effects as ordinary novel-reading" (Rosman 143). To that end, the *Christian Observer* returned to the novel fray with a paradoxical review of the anonymous *May You Like It!* (1822), devoted to the proposition that there was no point in reviewing religious fiction. By the 1820s the reviewer could think of religious fiction in literary-historical terms, tracing its origins to *Coelebs* and J. W. Cunningham's allegorical *World without Souls* (1818). The reviewer finds that religious fiction has already become targeted to consumers' niche tastes: *Coelebs* spawns the novels of Barbara Hofland and Emily Brunton, among others, as well as the "*'juvenile*' religious novels" of Jane Taylor and Mary Martha Sherwood; *World without Souls* the "sentimental religious tales" like those of the story under discussion ("*May You Like It!*" 646, 648). The novels descended from *Coelebs,* which the reviewer describes as "theological," rely on "judgment and understanding" to convey religious concepts, whereas the "sentimental" novelists draw on "incidental touches and appeals to the sympathies of the heart," not dramatized expositions of dogma (648–49). This important division highlights both effect and intention: if the novel relies on representing and thereby evoking religious feeling in order to effect spiritual change, then how can the novelist control such feelings? Patricia Demers suggests that early didactic novelists assumed that "the process of the reader's reception was uncluttered with new twists and overreaching effects; what they intended, as moralists, was what the reader, as a receptive vessel, perceived" (130). Critics like this one were not sure that such passive reader reception was the case. Indeed, the reviewer hints that a less than "pure mind" reading *May You Like It!* might arrive at "associations not by any means *intended* to be conveyed" (649). The inadvertent conjunction of religious writer and irreligious reader produces unfortunate, possibly erotic, results. As in some earlier worries about *Coelebs,* the reviewer points to the ever-present danger of multiple interpretations that might transform a religious novel into something else entirely.

The difficulty, though, was that even a religious novel was always already something else—it was a novel. As the reviewer admits, the spread of religious fiction seemed to demand corresponding attention from a religious periodical, and yet it is precisely that spread that leads the *Christian Observer* to ignore the new products. "We own, with all due penitence," the reviewer admits, not very penitently, "that we see from ten to twenty religious novels advertised, not one of which have we reviewed" ("*May You Like It!*" 646). The very fact of a popular market for both religious fiction and religious nonfiction is the sticking point. Given the choice between reviewing a religious novel and something "combining *truth* with amusement and instruction" (647), the *Christian Observer* opts for the latter as a higher form of moral prose. Not only that, but pleasure and religious "instruction" here return as qualities more likely to be harmonized in nonfiction. In that sense, the *Christian Observer* ignores religious fiction the better to shape the morality of their audience's taste. More than that, though, after a "month" or so, the dropped religious novels have become "old fashioned or obsolete," and must give way to a crowd of yet "newer tales" (647). Here, the reviewer positions religious fiction within the new pace of literary publishing, in which books are rapidly dated commodities purchased according to the fashion, like Gothic chapbook literature and other similarly cheap texts.

Thus, the reviewer proceeds to dissolve the boundaries between the religious novel and all other forms of fiction:

> For what is at present in many instances almost exclusively the reading of our nurseries?—*miniature* novels! What the reading of our parlours?—*full-grown* novels! What the reading of our kitchens?—novels both miniature and full-grown! The process is varied indeed in different families: the religious preferring religious novels, as the irreligious prefer irreligious ones. But still, in either case, may there not be danger of a super-saturation of excitement? Must not a *habit* of *religious* novel reading be attended with *some* at least of the injurious effects which accompany an undue indulgence in works of fiction, even of a laudable class? Our children now will read nothing unless it comes in the shape of a tale. The poor throw aside all the old-fashioned tracts, many of them truly excellent, which were formerly distributed by the clergy in their parishes, and will accept of nothing unless dressed up in fictitious narrative. ("*May You Like It!*" 647)

In this nightmarish vision of a novel-reading polity, the novel entraps everyone from children to adults to servants—a "textual infantilizing of the working classes" (Nelson 145).[6] The critic admits that the novel has multiple audiences to which it is targeted, as the distinction between "religious" and "irreligious" families further concedes. Moreover, the emphasis on reading within the household itself is important, reflecting the evangelical push to "aggressively exploit[] the permeability of household boundaries" (Atkins 340) by swapping out harmful novels and swapping in morally beneficial reading matter.

Thus, having granted that novels have penetrated every region of the household, and that novels have niche markets, the critic pulls back to the big picture. Like any other novel, religious novels lead to this "super-saturation of excitement," a paradoxically self-canceling excess probably leading to, as Wordsworth might say, "a state of savage torpor." This climaxes in the spectacle of "the poor" buying into a faceless mass consumer fad for fiction and denying the significance of local relationships (along with clerical authority). Notably, the reviewer retroactively strips tracts of their relationship to "fictitious narrative," even though early tracts from such sources as the Cheap Repository and the Religious Tract Society were frequently just that. (That tract distribution might, ironically enough, have led working-class readers to be more leery of evangelical projects, not less, is not something that the writer envisions; Wallbank 67.) But instead of a "far-flung network" of Christian believ-

---

6. The concatenation of child and working-class readers is common in the early nineteenth century, where readerships were defined by "social status" rather than "numerical age"; see Michals 26.

ers, "a print remediation of oral, face-to-face communication" (Morgan 150), the novel dissolves, diffuses, and dissipates Christian community without any hope of reintegration. Tract distribution involved hierarchical management that sought to control working-class reading, whether it was the clergyman buying in bulk to distribute tracts to his parishioners (as here) or the Religious Tract Society fixing prices in order to make their products more appealing to the hawkers than less improving material (Stubenrauch 555–60). Instead, ironically anticipating Benedict Anderson's famous claim about newspapers, novel-reading here produces a dangerously declassed readership, united in its hunger for fiction, that subverts social hierarchies founded in immediate personal connections.[7] The Religious Tract Society itself had distinguished between the charitable act of *giving* tracts, which developed community via direct interaction, and the actual work of *reading* tracts, in which the tract's didactic success depended on its being "read apart from him who gave it," and thus producing the illusion that the reader was "teaching himself" instead of being on the passive receiving end of a lecture ("An Address to Christians" 5). But the flip side of this strategy was that the working-class reader was reading independently, yet not necessarily with the right qualifications. Such readers thus threw a spanner in the interpretive works, as not only might they read the wrong books for pleasure, but also they were presumed to lack the evaluative abilities that might at least keep their employers clear of the most dangerous material (if only because it was unenjoyable). As the Protestant controversialist William McGavin would observe of the Catholic novel *Alton Park* a few years later, "persons of taste" were in no danger from the book; the "poor and illiterate, who are ignorant of the gospel," however, would be ripe pickings for Catholics (96). The cultured and educated might resist (or, in this case, contemptuously ignore) a spiritually and aesthetically bad book, but the poor, who might receive the book "gratuitously" (McGavin 96), would happily consume the product without thinking seriously about its implications, and be inspired to imitate what they did not understand.

This, then, is the central problem: to read a religious novel is to seek a wayward form of pleasure, irrespective of the author's (and novel's) original intentions. The reviewer of *May You Like It!* is anxiously aware that "when readers become buyers, every producer has to come to terms with the reader's essential autonomy" (Warner 288). The right doctrinal content is no match for

---

7. Kelly J. Mays argues that "like railway travel with which it was so often compared, reading endangered a number of crucial social boundaries—between man, machine, woman, and animal; between Occidental and Oriental, civilized and primitive, man; between laborer, doctor, and manufacturer" (180). For specifically religious critics, the breakdown of respect for the professional clergy was just as important.

the wrong discursive form. If, like Macaulay, the reviewer subdivides fiction into different types (he only has three), with "those written with an obvious view to the public benefit" at the top (*"May You Like It!"* 648), it is nevertheless the case that the audience for religious fiction behaves instead like an audience for fiction. Alas, "the readers of religious tales and novels, as of most other tales and novels, read, we fear, for the sake of the incident, and not of the moralizing,—and are often able, with the lubricity of an aquatic bird in a storm, to repel every particle of the author's intended instructions" (*"May You Like It!"* 648). This complaint brings us back to the *New Monthly Magazine*'s formal complaints about the religious novel, but in a different key: no matter how well the author integrates "incident" and "moralizing," the audience dissolves the relationship between the two and simply reads for the plot. "Too much narrative," in Doreen Rosman's words, "was regarded as not only inappropriate but also counterproductive" (141). Instead of submitting to the author's moral authority, the audience constructs (or deconstructs) a secular novel out of the original text, using their fallen wills to wrest novels into the shape that gives them the most pleasure.[8] The reader in quest of entertainment simply pretends that the instruction isn't there.

Perhaps excited in part by this review, another pro-religious novel correspondent who signed themselves Λογοφιλοι ("Logophiloi," that is, "Debater") tried to make a final stand. After citing the religious parable as an example of biblically approved fiction, the author appeals to universal human nature to demonstrate that "narrative, by the generality of the species, will ever be preferred to didactic composition" ("Logophiloi" 95). By rooting the argument in anthropology as well as theology, the correspondent suggests both that complaints about readership are misguided and that it is only the *elite* to whom didactic works can be expected to appeal. The solution to the problem is to subvert religious fiction from within. Indeed, the correspondent grants that the "circulating library" (95) is loaded with dangerously anti-Christian fiction that promotes "sophistry, baneful excitement, and the fascinations of adventure" (95). But even though the correspondent's language here echoes that of the earlier review, he sidesteps the reviewer's claims about active readers and grants all the agency to the novels themselves. This opens up a space for him to claim a homeopathic solution to the novel problem: religious novels, which despite "address[ing] themselves chiefly to the feelings," nevertheless ensure that "the passions and the imagination are won, or at least inclined to the right side; and this is no trifling matter in the case of a being who is oftener led by

---

8. As Kyle Roberts has demonstrated, the changes that Legh Richmond's *The Dairyman's Daughter* underwent show us how religious tracts responded to reader demand (esp. 245–51).

the impulses of the heart than by the reasonings of the head" (96). The function of religious fiction at the present time, in other words, is Wordsworthian in flavor: by playing upon the sentiments, the religious novelist can transform the reader's understanding of what religious feeling might be, at any rate, even if he or she cannot do much for theology. What the earlier reviewer had dismissed as the lower form of religious fiction, the "sentimental" novel, here becomes the only really possible way of making the form work. But significantly, this correspondent and the reviewer he interrogates have dovetailed on an important point. The reviewer worried that all novels act on the reader in the same way; the correspondent suggests that a religious novel can only be successful if it emulates all the strategies of its secular counterparts—and, thus, if it has the same effects, only for good instead of evil.

CONCLUSION

Elsewhere in this volume, Charles LaPorte reminds us that Victorian criticism frequently sought out the theological, the "prophetic," in works considered high literature. But literature that sought first and foremost to be religious at the most literal level did not enjoy the kind of cultural cachet that could be ascribed to the difficult poems of Robert Browning. But as Dominic Janes argues in the next chapter, it was impossible in practice to separate the worlds of religion and the marketplace: clergymen and other religious authors appropriated popular trends to attract audiences (or congregations), but then walked a tightrope when it came to calculating what sorts of pleasure might be spiritually useful, rather than spiritually deadening or misleading. The religious novel's success implied that even evangelical faith, the "religion of the heart," could be successfully codified, mechanized, and marketed. For many denominational and nondenominational reviewers, the form of the religious novel, which (depending on the reader) might be either too open to misreading *or* too given to controlling monologue, undermined its use value. Yet the religious novel was also always under threat from its own readers, inasmuch as they demanded entertainment from even the staunchest Christian authors and, when texts attempted to foreclose on alternative readings, managed to extract their pleasures at the expense of their educations. More optimistic observers felt that harnessing such readerly tendencies might be the best route for making peace with the genre. But all conceded that there was no escaping the pull of new evangelical markets. In 1851 George Borrow's quasi-novel *Lavengro* satirically summed up this state of affairs: the narrator offers his potential publisher several possibilities, ranging from a scholarly collection of "ancient songs of Denmark" (in the tradition of Walter Scott and Thomas Percy) to a "romance in the German style" (Gothic) (2:16, 2:17). Every imitative option is dismissed by the publisher as yet another example of a genre glutting the market. But evangelical fiction is different. "Sir," confides the publisher, "I could afford as much as ten pounds for a well-written tale in the style of the 'Dairyman's Daughter'; that is the kind of literature, sir, that sells at the present day!" (2:18–19). Even though the publisher dismisses evangelicals as "canting scoundrels" (2:19), he marks them out as the sole niche audience whose appetite for fiction has not yet been sated. Religious fiction is merely the newest fad to succeed the Gothic, and the evangelical desire for it is no different than the desire of readers looking for the newest thrill. In the literary marketplace, religious fiction is no more and no less a commodity than any other (empty) form.

WORKS CITED

A. A. "Observations on Novel-Reading." *The Christian Observer*, vol. 14, no. 164, Aug. 1815, pp. 512–17.

"An Address to Christians, on the Distribution of Religious Tracts." *The Publications of the Religious Tract Society*, vol. 1, 1801, pp. 1–16.

Anon. "Rev. of *Coelebs in Search of a Wife*." *The Monthly Review*, vol. 58, Feb. 1809, pp. 128–36.

Anon. "Rev. of *Hints toward Forming the Character of a Young Princess*." *Eclectic Review*, vol. 2, Jan. 1806, pp. 114–21.

Anon. "Rev. of *The Infidel Father*." *The Anti-Jacobin Review*, vol. 15, no. 59, May 1803, pp. 41–48.

Anon. "Rev. of *Influence*." *The New Monthly Magazine and Literary Journal*, vol. 4, no. 23, Nov. 1822, pp. 26–27.

Anon. "Rev. of *May You Like It!*" *The Christian Observer*, vol. 23, Oct. 1823, pp. 645–53.

Anon. "Rev. of *The Modern Martyr*." *The Edinburgh Literary Journal; or, Weekly Register of Criticism and Belles Lettres*, no. 20, 28 Mar. 1829, p. 273.

Anon. "Rev. of *The Story of Isabel*." *The Monthly Magazine*, vol. 2, no. 10, Oct. 1826, pp. 427–28.

Anon. "Rev. of *Thornton Abbey*." *Eclectic Review*, vol. 2, Dec. 1806, pp. 1029–34.

Anon. "Rev. of *Tremaine, or the Man of Refinement*." *The New Monthly Magazine and Literary Journal*, vol. 13, no. 52, 1825, pp. 321–34.

Altick, Richard D. *The English Common Reader: A Social History of the Mass Reading Public, 1800–1900*. 1957. U of Chicago P, 1967.

Atkins, Gareth. "'Idle Reading'?: Policing the Boundaries of the Nineteenth-Century Household." *Studies in Church History*, vol. 50, Jan. 2014, pp. 331–42.

Blair, Kirstie. *Form and Faith in Victorian Poetry and Religion*. Oxford UP, 2012.

Borrow, George. *Lavengro: The Scholar—The Gypsy—The Priest*. John Murray, 1851. 3 vols.

Branch, Lori. *Rituals of Spontaneity: Sentiment and Secularism from Free Prayer to Wordsworth*. Baylor UP, 2006.

Brown, Candy Gunther. *The Word in the World: Evangelical Writing, Publishing, and Reading in America, 1789–1880*. U of North Carolina P, 2004.

Demers, Patricia. *Heaven upon Earth: The Form of Moral and Religious Children's Literature to 1850*. U of Tennessee P, 1993.

Downs, Jack M. "David Masson, *Belles Lettres*, and a Victorian Theory of the Novel." *Victorian Literature and Culture*, vol. 43, no. 1, 2015, pp. 1–21.

Eliot, Simon. *Some Patterns and Trends in British Publishing 1800–1919*. Bibliographical Society, 1994.

Fischer, Benjamin L. "A Novel Resistance: Mission Narrative as the Anti-Novel in the Evangelical Assault on British Culture." *Studies in Church History*, vol. 48, Jan. 2012, pp. 232–45.

Gettelman, Debra. "'Those Who Idle over Novels': Victorian Critics and Post-Romantic Readers." *A Return to the Common Reader: Print Culture and the Novel, 1850–1900*, edited by Beth Palmer and Adelene Buckland, Ashgate, 2011, pp. 55–68.

Gilmartin, Kevin. *Writing against Revolution: Literary Conservatism in Britain, 1790–1832*. Cambridge UP, 2007.

Grenby, M. O. *The Child Reader 1700–1840*. Cambridge UP, 2011.

Killick, Tim. *British Short Fiction in the Early Nineteenth Century: The Rise of the Tale*. Ashgate, 2008.

Klancher, Jon. *The Making of English Reading Audiences, 1790–1832*. U of Wisconsin P, 1987.

Krueger, Christine L. *The Reader's Repentance: Women Preachers, Women Writers, and Nineteenth-Century Social Discourse*. U of Chicago P, 1992.

"Logophiloi" (Λογοφιλοι). "On the Lawfulness and Expediency of Religious Novels." *The Christian Observer*, vol. 24, Feb. 1823, pp. 94–96.

Macaulay, T. B. ["Candidus"]. "Observations on Novel-Reading." *The Christian Observer*, vol. 15, Dec. 1816, pp. 784–87.

[Macaulay, Zachary]. "Rev. of *Coelebs in Search of a Wife*." *The Christian Observer*, vol. 8, no. 2, Feb. 1809, pp. 109–21.

Mays, Kelly J. "The Disease of Reading and Victorian Periodicals." *Literature and the Marketplace: Nineteenth-Century Publishing and Reading Practices*, edited by John O. Jordan and Robert L. Patten, Cambridge UP, 1995, pp. 165–94.

[McGavin, William]. *A Reply to Smith's Dialogues on the Catholic and Protestant Rules of Faith; To Which Is Added, a Review of* Alton Park, a Popish Novel. John Reid, 1832.

Michals, Teresa. *Books for Children, Books for Adults: Age and the Novel from Defoe to James*. Cambridge UP, 2014.

More, Hannah. *Hints toward Forming the Character of a Young Princess*. T. Cadell and W. Davies, 1805. 2 vols.

Morgan, David. "Mediation or Mediatisation: The History of Media in the Study of Religion." *Culture and Religion*, vol. 12, no. 2, 2011, pp. 137–52.

Nelson, Claudia. "Adult Children's Literature in Victorian Britain." *The Nineteenth-Century Child in Consumer Culture*, edited by Dennis Denisoff, Ashgate, 2008, pp. 137–49.

Pearson, Jacqueline. *Women's Reading in Britain 1750–1835*. Cambridge UP, 1999.

Pickering, Samuel F. Jr. "Literature and Theology: The 'Christian Observer' and the Novel, 1802–1822." *Historical Magazine of the Protestant Episcopal Church*, vol. 43, no. 1, Mar. 1974, 29–43.

Roberts, Kyle. "Locating Popular Religion in the Religious Tract: The Roots and Routes of *The Dairyman's Daughter*." *Early American Studies*, vol. 4, no. 1, Spring 2006, pp. 233–70.

Rosman, Doreen. *Evangelicals and Culture*. 2nd ed., Pickwick Publications, 2011.

Scott, Patrick. "The Business of Belief: The Emergence of 'Religious' Publishing." *Sanctity and Secularity: The Church and the World*, edited by Derek Baker, Basil Blackwell, 1973, pp. 213–24.

Simeon, Charles. *Horae Homeleticae: Or Discourses (Principally in the Form of Skeletons) Now First Digested into One Continued Series, and Forming a Commentary upon Every Book of the Old and New Testament*. Holdsworth and Paul, 1833. 21 vols.

Smith, Sydney. "Hannah More." *The Works of the Rev. Sydney Smith*. Vol. 1, Longman, Orme, Brown, Green, and Longmans, 1839, pp. 202–10.

Stubenrauch, Joseph. "Silent Preachers in the Age of Ingenuity: Faith, Commerce, and Religious Tracts in Early Nineteenth-Century Britain." *Church History*, vol. 80, no. 3, 2011, pp. 547–74.

Sweet, Nanora. "The *New Monthly Magazine* and the Liberalism of the 1820s." *Prose Studies*, vol. 25, no. 1, 2002, pp. 147–62.

Targoff, Ramie. *Common Prayer: The Language of Public Devotion in Early Modern England*. U of Chicago P, 2001.

Thackeray, W. M. "Madame Sand and the New Apocalypse." *The Paris Sketch Book of Mr. M. A. Titmarsh; and the Memoirs of Mr. Charles J. Yellowplush*, Smith, Elder, 1869, pp. 200–223.

Wallbank, Adrian J. *Dialogue, Didacticism and the Genres of Dispute*. 2012. Routledge, 2015.

Warner, William. *Licensing Entertainment: The Elevation of Novel Reading in Britain, 1684–1750*. U of California P, 1998.

Yelle, Robert A. *The Language of Disenchantment: Protestant Literalism and Colonial Discourse in British India*. Oxford UP, 2013.

CHAPTER 10

Material Religion

C. H. Spurgeon and the "Battle of the Styles" in Victorian Church Architecture

DOMINIC JANES

ART AND ARCHITECTURE were central to disputes concerning the boundaries of the sacred and the profane in nineteenth-century Britain, as was the definition of religion and its relationship to the world, because of the nature of the divisions between Christian denominations concerning the status of what we now term the material culture of religion. A large number of Protestants claimed that "true religion" was a matter of the spirit and that spectacular visual displays of religiosity therefore were idolatrous. In a narrow sense, their critique applied to the worship of idols, but in a broad sense it encompassed the worship of or devotion to anything that intervened between the believer and God. The apprehension surrounding "idolatry," however, did not stem (and, in fact, even fed) an intense interest in understanding the medieval—and thus, implicitly, the Roman Catholic—Church as an inspiration for contemporary sanctity in early Victorian England, as a number of Catholicizing Anglicans began to use a much more complex form of ritual involving vestments, candles, and incense. Many evangelicals and Dissenters, unsurprisingly, opposed these innovations on the grounds that they represented the vanguard of Popery. Yet there was also a tradition of Protestant interest in medieval art and design—one which had led to the eighteenth-century rise of the Gothic—that associated Gothic styles with patriotic insular values (Friedman 185–351; Bradley; Aspin).[1] Therefore,

---

1. I wish to thank William Whyte for his advice on architectural history.

despite previously shunning Gothic Revival architecture due to its Roman Catholic associations, many Nonconformist denominations in the nineteenth century increasingly looked to medievalist styles for inspiration in the realms of both art and architecture (for instance, on art, see Richmond; Bury). By the end of the Victorian period Gothic Revival architecture was widely employed by Nonconformists.

This chapter examines Protestant opposition to Gothic architecture in ways that look beyond the trope of anti-Catholicism in order to uncover attempts not merely to displace Catholic and Catholicizing material culture but to dismiss Gothic architecture from the conceptual category of "true religion." My focus will be on the attitudes of Charles Haddon Spurgeon (1834–92), who was one of the most popular and influential preachers of the mid-Victorian period. While mainstream Protestantism held that sacred space was, above all, that of the biblical text, Spurgeon, intriguingly, openly admitted his interest in Catholic-style visual splendor even while he proselytized against it. In holding this position, he fell somewhere between Catholicizing support for and Protestant opposition to the use of Gothic Revival style in Nonconformist spaces. Champions of the Gothic Revival, on the one hand, argued that the architectural style could be read as a sacred text; they maintained that classical architecture, by contrast, was imbued with pagan meaning as a result of its origins in the ancient Greek world. On the other hand, Protestant opposition to the Gothic style rebutted such arguments, maintaining that such buildings could hardly be read as sources of moral symbolism. If they *could* be read as having moral meaning, no doubt this visual language was indelibly tainted by its association with the Catholic Middle Ages.

Spurgeon was one of the foremost Protestant advocates of the classical style for chapels in Victorian Britain and a critic of the use of Gothic styles. Nevertheless, he admitted in these attacks that he found the Gothic to be visually alluring. Moreover, while he did not wish to read architecture as a material counterpart to the Bible, he did make use of visual analogies—including references to buildings—when explaining Scripture. I argue that Spurgeon's failure unambiguously to uphold the conceptual boundary between human material production and the realm of the fully "religious" indicates that we need to think of such modes of production as constitutive components of lived "religion" in Victorian Britain, even in the case of apparently hardline Dissenters. In making this argument, I draw inspiration from scholars such as David Morgan, who has undermined notions of Protestants as lacking a distinctive visual and material culture (*Protestants and Pictures* 44; *Visual Piety* 184). Indeed, by examining figures such as Spurgeon we can see that nineteenth-century religion was as deeply embedded in the realm of the material as in that of the immaterial, and that this embedding led to considerable contestation and negotiation around the relationship between spirit and form.

Certainly, Victorian religion was thoroughly enmeshed in the burgeoning visual and material culture of its age. However, the material abundance of the nineteenth century led to some tension between the more ascetic, world-denying aspects of Christianity and those aspects that took a softer view of sensuous worldly pleasures. Mary Wilson Carpenter's chapter in this volume, for instance, highlights the material importance of the often handsomely illustrated "Family Bible" and the backlash against the supplementary material it included in order to make "pure" Scripture more comprehensible and enjoyable. In a related vein, Miriam Burstein draws attention elsewhere in this volume to the ambivalent status of the "religious novel." A similar tension informed nineteenth-century religious architecture. If nineteenth-century "religion" is to be defined and understood in all its contemporary richness, it needs to be read not only from literary but also from visual and material texts (such as church buildings that were sometimes intended to function as sermons in stone).

THE GOTHIC REVIVAL AND CLASSICISM

The most influential Gothic Revival architect of the first half of the nineteenth century was A. W. N. Pugin (1812–52), who was a zealous convert to Roman Catholicism. In a series of volumes including *Contrasts; or, a Parallel between the Noble Edifices of the Fourteenth and Fifteenth Centuries, and Similar Buildings of the Present Day* (1836) and *An Apology for the Revival of Christian Architecture in England* (1843), he set out the provocative and contentious opinion that Gothic architecture was essentially Catholic and possessed devotional significance even when employed in apparently secular contexts such as the building of railway arches. The true faith of Catholicism, he argued, was expressed by soaring steeples and in painstaking recreations (really reinterpretations) of medieval metalwork. By contrast, classical architecture was irredeemably "pagan," even when applied in the construction of churches. Scholars have extensively studied the ways that these ideas came to widely shared by Roman and Anglican Catholics.[2] But it has also long been clear that many Catholics failed to see any necessary connection between their adherence to Rome and the use of a particular decorative or architectural style (Pat-

---

2. There is a huge literature on this subject. See, for example, Hill; Janes, *Victorian Reformation* 3–50.

rick). The "battle of the styles" is particularly associated with the competition launched in 1855 for the design of the new Foreign Office in London. But the phrase was also used in a wider sense to refer to rivalry between advocates of the rival virtues of gothicism and classicism in terms not merely of their taste and utility but also of their morality and propriety (Porter; Mays 4–8). (For a wider discussion of style and styles in architecture, see Crook.)

Nonconformists such as Methodists, whose beliefs and practices placed them in relatively closer relation to the sacerdotal forms of Catholicism and Anglicanism, took to the Gothic style earlier than Presbyterians and Baptists. Notable evidence of this is provided by F. J. Jobson's articles in *The Watchman* that were collected and published as *Chapel and School Architecture, as Appropriate to the Buildings of Nonconformists, Particularly to those of Wesleyan Methodists* (1850). This book popularized the view, derived from Pugin, that Gothic was somehow a more fitting and more devotional style for religious buildings, one in tune with the national spirit of the times. However, Jobson distanced himself from Pugin's historicizing strictures on "correct" and "incorrect" Gothic styles and advocated for the importance of utility, simplicity, and directness of architectural expression (Jobson 11; Davies 11; Whyte 260). These developments were not unique to the United Kingdom. Pugin and his Anglican followers had also inspired many American Episcopalians. Moreover, Gothic came increasingly into use by a wide range of Protestant denominations in the US in the course of the nineteenth century. As Jeanne Halgren Kilde observes in *When Church Became Theatre: The Transformation of Evangelical Architecture and Worship in Nineteenth-Century America* (2002), the evangelical adoption of Gothic was not simply the result of new fashions in architecture. Instead it was a means of expressing the growing diversity of American religion, as well as an attempt to project forms of religiosity that possessed both a historicized sense of development over time and universal values (57–58, 76).

Similar ideas were to inspire James Cubitt (1836–1912), who designed the remarkable Congregationalist Union Chapel in Islington in London (1876–77) and who was perhaps the most influential architect of what came to be referred to as "dissenting gothic" (Binfield). In *Church Design for Congregations* (1870), Cubitt argued that there was indeed a venerable tradition of Christian Gothic architecture but that the key challenge was how to adapt ancient exempla to contemporary needs. The primary purpose of English medieval churches, for example, was to facilitate liturgical performances by the clergy rather than to help audiences listen to sermons. He also wrestled with the challenge of how to combine what was seen as the structural authenticity of Gothic (notably as expressed through supporting columns) with the need for everyone present to get a good view of the preacher. His belief that this represented a challenge rather than an insurmountable conundrum was expressed in the closing sentiments of his book: "Bygone periods do not come again. We cannot restore the old: we *may* transfuse what was good and permanent of it into the new. That age can never return: but art has other golden ages beyond, for those who press forward instead of going back" (Cubitt 105; emphasis in original). In this manner, the Gothic used by Dissenters came to be a "distinctive style in its own right," one that was notable for being open to diverse, international influences (Rosman 261).

It is important to stress that Cubitt not only hoped to set an agenda for a new Dissenting idiom; he also wished to distance himself from some of the eclectic and poorly conceived examples of Gothic Revivalism that had been built in the previous decades. In this latter goal, he was joined by the younger architect John Sulman (1849–1934). In a piece appearing in *Building News* in 1875, Sulman was quoted as expressing regret that Nonconformist Gothic had become "a byword and a reproach among men of taste and culture" (qtd. in "Congregationalists" 528). Where Pugin had once attempted to defend his Catholic Gothic from accusations of effeminate aestheticism by stressing its allegedly manly structural forms, the Dissenters found that the overuse of ironwork in their new Gothic-style buildings struck some as emasculating and feminine. In Sulman's words, these styles were the "millinery of architecture," which lacked "the flesh, blood and bones of good design" (528). Gothic or classical elements were being applied merely as elements of ornamentation.

This was the case with the largest Nonconformist preaching-house to have been built in the previous two decades: Charles Haddon Spurgeon's Metropolitan Tabernacle in Southwark in south London. Spurgeon began his preaching career at the age of seventeen when he accepted the pastorate of the Waterbeach Baptist Chapel in Cambridgeshire. News of his prodigious energy and abilities soon spread to London. There had been a Baptist Tabernacle Fellowship in the metropolis since the mid-seventeenth century. When Spurgeon joined them in 1854, the descendants of that community were worshipping at the New Park Street Baptist church, then the largest Baptist chapel in London. So powerful was Spurgeon's rhetoric that not only Baptists but also those of many other denominations, from all ranks of society, flocked to hear his oratory. In fact, his services were so successful that the chapel was enlarged in an attempt to accommodate all those who wished to hear him. It was this success that was both mocked and admired in "Catch 'Em Alive O" (circa 1855) (fig. 10.1). The title of this print referred to the contemporary slang for flypaper. The brightly colored creatures of society—including an attractive young lady in a fashionable purple dress—buzz about and adhere to his person.

"Battle of the Styles" in Victorian Church Architecture   195

FIGURE 10.1. "Catch 'Em Alive O" (Charles Haddon Spurgeon), after unknown artist, lithograph, circa 1855. © National Portrait Gallery, London.

It rapidly became clear that an entirely new building would be required. While this edifice—the future Metropolitan Tabernacle—was under construction, Spurgeon held services at the Music Hall in Royal Surrey Gardens and at an older center of evangelical preaching, Exeter Hall. The Tabernacle was dedicated on March 18, 1861, and Spurgeon continued to preach there until his last service on June 7, 1891 (Ellison 58). William Wilmer Pocock (1813–99) won the competition to design the Tabernacle, which had stipulated that schemes in the Gothic mode would not be successful (Ray 252). This was in consonance with Spurgeon's belief that as Greek was the language of the New Testament, so classical architecture was appropriate to a chapel (Wakeling, "'A Room'" 273

FIGURE 10.2. E. Johnson. "The Earliest Photograph of the Interior of the Metropolitan Tabernacle: Taken in 1861." Reproduced in Charles Ray, *The Life of Charles Haddon Spurgeon,* Passmore and Alabaster, 1903, p. 273.

n21). He emphasized this sentiment at the opening ceremony, saying, "There are two sacred languages in the world: there was the Hebrew of old; there is only one other sacred language, the Greek, which is very dear to every Christian heart. Every Baptist place should be Grecian, never Gothic" (qtd. in Carlile 155). One entered the Tabernacle via a vast classical portico, which led to a multigalleried interior supported by Corinthian columns executed in etiolated ironwork (fig. 10.2) (Wakeling, "Nonconformity" 58). Pugin's designs had strained toward the sublime through verticality, but, here, a sense of awe was instilled by the sheer scale of the edifice. Indeed, Spurgeon framed the success of the building not in terms of its aesthetics but in the language of utility and mass production. As he summarized his achievement,

> There is room for 6,000 persons without excessive crowding; and we have also a lecture-hall holding about 900, schoolroom for 1000 children, six

class-rooms, kitchen, lavatory, and retiring rooms below stairs. We have a ladies' room for working meetings, young men's class-room, and Secretary's room on the ground floor; three vestries, for pastor, deacons, and elders on the first floor, and three store-rooms on the second floor. The accommodation is all too little for the work to be carried on. (*The Metropolitan Tabernacle* 79–80)

The cost was £31,000, but, the prudent reader was reassured, this had been paid without recourse to a mortgage or other form of debt. The main auditorium was similar to the design by Horace Jones (famous later in life as the co-designer of Tower Bridge) for the aforementioned Music Hall, a floridly decorated iron structure that the *Illustrated London News* described as being "degenerate Italian, relieved by French taste" ("The New Music Hall" 91).

By this time, Spurgeon was not merely an important Baptist leader but a popular celebrity—robustly Protestant, disdainful of scholastic nuance, and hugely keen to engage with the modern urban world (Ellison 67). He belonged to a category of celebrity preachers, who performed in grand edifices and mingled not just with ordinary people but also with the rich and powerful. Thanks to generous donations and the sale of tracts, these men had access to abundant funding. It comes as no surprise that such preachers—and their buildings—were often attacked for their alleged excessive worldliness. Such slurs, of course, were not new in the 1860s. Indeed, twenty years earlier, the newly founded satirical journal *Punch* directed a consistent stream of mockery from journalists such as Douglas Jerrold towards Exeter Hall. The Hall, which occupied a prime site of the Strand in central London, had been opened in 1831 and had cost the considerable sum of £36,000. This money had paid for a large assembly room, which was extended in 1850 to seat 3,000 people. Around the assembly room was a complex of offices and lesser meeting rooms. Inside and out, the Hall was designed in the classical style, adorned in particular by a tall entrance flanked by Corinthian columns (Partington 3:725). Jerrold sneered,

> This building stands on the north side of the Strand, and is dedicated to piety and virtue. Its architecture and materials are, therefore, of corresponding holiness and worth. Staircases of highly-polished marble, with bannisters of cedar, curiously inlaid with gold, lead to the various magnificent chambers of this magnificent structure. In one place we see Sidonian tapestries and hangings of Tyre—in another the carvings and paintings of Egypt, with flaming carbuncles, and all the jewelled glories of the East. (203)

The preachers at the hall, Jerrold admitted, were soberly dressed. However, this only underscored their hypocrisy; their modest dress, no doubt, was intended to conceal their considerable affluence. These men, he railed, epitomized the "fireside philanthropist, the good and easy man, for whom life has been one long lounge on a velvet sofa" (203; see also White).

Spurgeon, like Pugin before him, pointed to the evidence of his extraordinarily busy working life as well as his modest family origins in defense against such accusations of worldliness and self-indulgence. It seems clear that the interior of the Tabernacle was plainer and more cheaply executed than that of Exeter Hall. Unfortunately, however, neither survive. The latter was demolished in 1907, and the former burned down in 1898, leaving only the portico intact. The replacement auditorium lasted until a bombing raid in 1941, after which it was rebuilt once more albeit on a reduced scale (Chadwick).

"THE AXE AT THE ROOT"

In a sermon preached at the Tabernacle on June 17, 1866, Spurgeon gave one of his most detailed discussions regarding his objections to the Gothic style. This sermon, "The Axe at the Root: A Testimony against Puseyite Idolatry," was inspired by John 4:23–24: "But the hour cometh, and now is, when the true worshippers shall worship the Father in spirit and in truth, for the Father seeketh such to worship him. God is a Spirit: and they that worship him must worship him in spirit and in truth." His core contention was that the followers of Anglican theologian E. B. Pusey, who were popularly referred to as "ritualists" or "Puseyites," were interposing items of Catholic material culture, such as stone altars, between God and His worshippers. By pandering to what he termed the "natural resort of the carnal mind, namely, to religious discourse upon points of outward observance," the Puseyites, in effect, encouraged the idolatrous worship of material objects (325).

Spurgeon drew from the history of Jewish and Christian forms of worship to make his arguments. He began by reminding his listeners of Christ's declaration that the time of the importance of the Temple in Jerusalem was at an end. Referring to this passage, he explained, "The carnal heart dreads the contact of spiritual truth, and finds a most convenient way of avoiding it by running to questions of holy places, holy times, and holy customs" ("Axe" 325). Jesus's dismissal of the Temple, in Spurgeon's reading, thus amounted to a sea-change in proper religious expression: "external" forms are "of no importance now, for the hour cometh, yea and now is, when the external is to be abolished and the *ritualistic* is to be put away, and a purer, simpler, and more spiritual worship, is to take its place" (325; emphasis mine). Following this, he presented what he termed "a brief outline of the history of worship." The first phase was that of primitive sacrifice, from which elaboration on the basis of "taste" was, in fact, the sign of man's fallen and degenerate nature:

> This simple form of worship seems to have been too high, too spiritual for fallen man at the first; at any rate the seed of the serpent could not endure it, for Cain at the very first commenced a schism; instead of bringing a sacrifice by blood he must needs bring a sacrifice of the fruits of the ground. Perhaps he was a man of taste, and desired to bring something that should look more decorous than a poor bleeding victim; he would lay those rich grapes, those ruddy fruits upon the altar; and those fair flowers that gemmed the bosom of earth, surely he might consecrate those. At any rate he was the first man who set up taste and self as the guide in religious worship, and God had no respect unto his sacrifice. The two stood by their altars; Abel by faith, exercising spiritual worship, offered a more acceptable sacrifice than Cain; Cain's offering was possibly even more fair to look upon but it was of his own invention; Abel was accepted, but Cain discarded. (328)

Thus innovations in worship on aesthetic grounds were to be despised, as these forms had led to Pagan worship and modern idolatry alike. However, Spurgeon was quick to explain that the subsequent form of Temple worship was categorically different, because it had been instituted by God:

> He saw that the children of Israel whom he loved were but a mob of slaves; their spirits had been broken by bitter bondage; like the poor African race of the present day, they seemed as a whole incapable of rising at once to mental dignity, and needed to pass through a generation or two before they could as a nation achieve manly self-government. So when he brought his people out of Egypt the Lord did not try them with an altogether spiritual form of worship; because of the hardness of their hearts among other reasons, though he was still to be worshipped as a spirit, yet he gave them certain outward signs by which they might be enabled to understand his character. (329)

In the passage, Spurgeon implies that material culture is sensuous and intensely alluring, particularly for those groups that he characterizes as lacking rational self-control, including nonwhite races, women, and children. Used sparingly, such material symbols could help these groups better apprehend God. If facilitated by priests in the Temple, then, this form of worship was "suitable . . . to the infancy of God's church" (329). But Spurgeon drove home that this dependency of "certain outward signs" was entirely different from "the symbology of that false Church," which he accused of "trying to raise up and revive the beggarly elements; there men bow before a cross; a piece of bread inside a box is reverenced and treated with worship; cast-off clouts and rotten rags, called relics, are the objects of adoration" (330).

Spurgeon was disgusted by such materialism, but he did not find it incomprehensible. He understood the strong appeal of visual and material forms, and he expressed frustration at the relatively limited appeal of language: "Oh the many times I have tried to preach spiritual worship here, and yet I am conscious that when I try at it I do not interest many of you, and some of you think, 'if he would only give us more metaphors, more anecdotes, and so on'; I say I will do that, for I believe we should speak by parable, but sometimes I do not know how to clothe these spiritual things without making you look at the clothing rather than the spirit" ("Axe" 332–33). This fascinating statement reveals a deep concern about semiotic confusion between symbols and their referents on the part of weak and suggestible humanity. God himself, argued Spurgeon, would be incapable of such confusion:

> What a child's toy must coloured glass be to God! I can sit and gaze upon a cathedral with all its magnificence of architecture, and think what a wonderful exhibition of human skill; but what must that be to God, who piles the heavens, who digs the foundation of the deep, who leads Arcturus with his sons? Why, it must be to him the veriest trifle, a mere heap of stones. I delight to hear the swell of organs, the harmony of sweet voices, the Gregorian chant, but what is this artistic sound to him more than sounding brass or a tinkling cymbal? As a sight, I admire the choristers and priests, and the whole show of a grand ceremonial; but do you believe that God is imposed upon by those frocks and gowns of white, and blue, and scarlet, and fine linen? It seems to me as if such a notion brings down God to the level of a silly woman who is fond of finery. (334)

Nevertheless, Spurgeon could not rid himself of the desire to look for the material evidences of grace, since "even God himself, great as he is, does not despise the [material] tear that drops from a repentant eye" ("Axe" 334). Indeed, a strong reform tradition of reading evidences of divine will in worldly forms seems to have influenced his thinking and writing. Thus, in an 1866 sermon in reference to Psalm 146:6, he built on Calvinist precedent by arguing that "the book of nature has three leaves, heaven, earth and sea" and averring that the world could be read as a "Natural Bible" ("Expositions of the Psalms" 323 n1; Willison). But Spurgeon did not limit himself to natural imagery in his teaching practice; notably, he also drew on the productions of industrial modernity. On February 26, 1871, he preached on the passage, "I lay my sins on Jesus, the spotless lamb of God," addressing "some of you, who are growing into young men and young women," who might recollect that he had, a few years back, brought in some colorful cloth that did not fade when washed. He used this cloth to illustrate the principle that only Jesus can get out every stain (Spurgeon and Harrald 3:92). This startling example (which he called an "illustration") of Christ's teaching depended on the discovery of the color-fast dye "mauveine," also known as analine purple, invented in 1856. No doubt he justified the use of this profane example because, initially, he had been addressing an audience of children. Moreover, Spurgeon's very fame was predicated on the mechanisms of industrial modernity, which spread news of his skills as an orator via mass-circulation newspapers and generated a seemingly insatiable desire to buy copies of his tracts that sold in the hundreds of thousands (Twyman 133). Despite often critiquing dependence on material signs and symbols in religion, Spurgeon depended on and actively made use of material culture to advance his spiritual teaching. As the designer of "Catch 'Em Alive O!" noticed, there was plenty of fashionable and attractive (and presumably profane) color in Spurgeon's life.

GOTHIC ALLUREMENTS

Spurgeon seems to have been peculiarly wary of styles such as the Puginesque Gothic that purported to mingle spiritual and material attributes. This was not because he was contemptuous of design but because he was so strongly aware of the fascinating quality of the visual realm and of worldly beauty.[3] He admitted, "As a matter of taste I have a great liking for noble architecture. Many an hour have I lingered in the ruins of some splendid abbey or our own majestic buildings still used for sacred worship. I have a great delight in a well-painted window" ("Axe" 335). Fascinatingly, he was less dismissive of Catholic than of Protestant Gothic:

> I cannot say that I like most Dissenting painted windows, because they look to me as if they were a sort of would be if you could. I cannot say I have any kind of liking for most of our Dissenting Gothic, for it seems to me such a paltry thing to build a front just like St. Paul's or Westminster Abbey, and then as if to cheat the Lord to make the back part shabby. I cannot say I care for that kind of thing. But a really splendid place of worship I admire,

---

3. Harvey on the visualization of religion in Welsh Nonconformism provides useful parallels.

as a matter of taste. I like an organ very well, as a matter of musical taste. But, my brethren, I feel that these are times when we must stand out even against allowable things, lest going one step we should go another. I do pray you therefore if you have any influence anywhere always use it in favour of simplicity. (335)

Part of the danger of the Gothic style, Spurgeon thus perceived, was that it was so appealing. His nervousness regarding the appeal of pretty outward forms found expression in the 1883 essay "How to Attract a Congregation." Advertising and promotion, he argued, were fine, but "puffery"—that is, inflated and spurious claims—was not. "Puffery," after all, was what ritualists did. Their forms of worship involved the creation of a pretty show aimed at attracting a congregation. In its "mix-up of things secular and sacred," this show was misleading and deleterious to genuine worship (420). The use of Gothic styles seemed to run a similar moral risk. As Ryan K. Smith notes in regard to nineteenth-century American Protestantism, market competition was a significant factor in the adoption of Gothic style by anti-Catholic congregations. Even as they used elements of Gothic style to attract more worshippers, they deployed anti-Catholic rhetoric to distinguish moderate Protestant practice in décor from that of allegedly excessive Romanism. The result was an "uplift of de-Romanized art" (Smith 155). A similar dynamic, perhaps, led Spurgeon to see the adoption of Gothic by Nonconformists as both an "utter abomination" ("How to Attract" 420) and an admission of promotional weakness.

For Spurgeon, religion was rightly established in the heart. However, this required the widest dissemination of the Truth, an enterprise based on commercial transaction and print technologies, and one that occupied him on a grand scale. In 1866—the same year that he preached his sermon on "The Axe at the Root"—he established a Colportage Association that sold tract literature door to door on commission. In 1892, the last year of his life, ninety-six "colporteurs" sold £153,784 3s 6d of merchandise via 11,822,637 visits to homes (the exactitude as well as the size of the recorded figures is telling in itself; Janes, "*The Wordless Book*" 31–32). It seems appropriate, then, that the postwar redevelopment of land around the Tabernacle included the construction of the London College of Printing (subsequently renamed the London College of Communication) in 1964 and, a year later, what was billed as Britain's first indoor shopping mall.

The "battle of the styles" was about more than Gothic versus classical detailing. It should not simply be studied as an episode in the history of taste; it should also be situated in relation to patterns of competition between Christian denominations in Victorian Britain. Attractive and fashionable styles acted as promotional tools and, therefore, when employed in churches and chapels, became implicated in competing claims to the possession of religious truth. In the case of Spurgeon, his exceptionally robust theological resistance to Gothic architecture was based on his fear that his congregation—not to mention, he himself—could be seduced away from Scripture by the beauty of Gothic, seeing in the architecture an equivalent to the sacred text. Buildings, he maintained, could provide material analogies to truths expressed in the Bible but were not fit to serve as exemplars of moral instruction in their own right. For Spurgeon, the fact that the New Testament was written in Greek implied that classical architecture was a safer resource for such object-based teaching than the Gothic style that had originated in the Roman Catholic Middle Ages. However, Spurgeon's views were not to predominate. Gothic came to be employed extensively as an architectural frame surrounding scripturally focused Protestant worship. As the influence of Pugin faded, Gothic architecture was no longer seen as pertaining solely to one particular Christian tradition, and the style soon ceased to be so clearly associated with Catholic doctrines that could serve as the gateway to idolatry.

WORKS CITED

Aspin, Philip. "'Our Ancient Architecture': Contesting Cathedrals in Late Georgian England." *Architectural History*, vol. 54, 2011, pp. 213–32.

Binfield, Clyde. "A Chapel and Its Architect: James Cubitt and Union Chapel, Islington, 1874–1889." *Studies in Church History*, vol. 28, 1992, pp. 417–47.

Bradley, Simon. "The Englishness of Gothic: Theories and Interpretations from William Gilpin to J. H. Parler." *Architectural History*, vol. 45, 2002, pp. 325–46.

Bury, Laurent. "Which Medievalism? The Case of Ford Madox Brown." *Cahiers victoriens et édouardiens*, vol. 73, Spring 2011, pp. 93–106.

Carlile, J. C. *C. H. Spurgeon: An Interpretative Biography*. London, Religious Tract Society and Kingsgate Press, 1933.

Chadwick, Rosemary. "Spurgeon, Charles Haddon (1834–1892)." *Oxford Dictionary of National Biography*, Oxford UP, 2004, http://www.oxforddnb.com/view/article/26187. Accessed 10 Dec. 2015.

"Congregationalists and Their Chapels." *Building News and Engineering Journal*, vol. 29, 12 Nov. 1875, p. 528.

Crook, J. Mordaunt. *The Dilemma of Style: Architectural Ideas from the Picturesque to the Post-Modern*. London, John Murray, 1987.

Cubitt, James. *Church Design for Congregations: Its Developments and Possibilities*. London, Smith, Elder, 1870.

Davies, Horton. *Worship and Theology in England. Vol. 4: From Newman to Martineau, 1850–1900*. Princeton UP, 1962.

Ellison, Robert H. *The Victorian Pulpit: Spoken and Written Sermons in Nineteenth-Century Britain*. Susquehanna UP, 1998.

Friedman, Terry. *The Eighteenth-Century Church in Britain*. Yale UP, 2011.

Harvey, John. *Image of the Invisible: The Visualization of Religion in the Welsh Nonconformist Tradition*. U of Wales P, 1999.

Hill, Rosemary. *God's Architect: Pugin and the Building of Romantic Britain*. Allen Lane, 2007.

Janes, Dominic. *Victorian Reformation: The Fight over Idolatry in the Church of England, 1840–1860*. Oxford UP, 2009.

———. "*The Wordless Book*: The Visual and Material Culture of Evangelism in Victorian Britain." *Material Religion*, vol. 12, no. 1, 2016, pp. 26–49.

Jerrold, Douglas ["Q"]. "Exeter Hall." *Punch*, vol. 2, 14 May 1842, p. 203.

Jobson, F. J. *Chapel and School Architecture, as Appropriate to the Buildings of Nonconformists, Particularly to those of Wesleyan Methodists*. London, Hamilton, Adams, 1850.

Kilde, Jeanne Halgren. *When Church Became Theatre: The Transformation of Evangelical Architecture and Worship in Nineteenth-Century America*. Oxford UP, 2002.

Mays, Kelly J. "How the Victorians Un-Invented Themselves: Architecture, the Battle of the Styles, and the History of the Term 'Victorian.'" *Journal of Victorian Culture*, vol. 19, no. 1, 2014, pp. 1–23.

Morgan, David. *Protestants and Pictures: Religion, Visual Culture and the Age of American Mass Production*. Oxford UP, 1999.

———. *Visual Piety: A History and Theory of Popular Religious Images*. U of California P, 1998.

"The New Music Hall, Royal Surrey Gardens." *Illustrated London News*, 26 July 1856, p. 91.

Partington, Charles F. *The British Cyclopedia of Literature, History, Geography, Law and Politics*. London, Orr and Smith, 1836. 3 vols.

Patrick, James. "Newman, Pugin and Gothic." *Victorian Studies*, vol. 24, no. 2, 1981, pp. 185–207.

Porter, Bernard. *The Battle of the Styles: Society, Culture and the Design of the New Foreign Office, 1855–1861*. Continuum, 2011.

Pugin, A. W. N. *An Apology for the Revival of Christian Architecture in England*. London, John Weale, 1843.

———. *Contrasts; or, a Parallel between the Noble Edifices of the Fourteenth and Fifteenth Centuries, and Similar Buildings of the Present Day*. 1836. London, Charles Dolman, 1841.

Ray, Charles. *The Life of Charles Haddon Spurgeon*. London, Passmore and Alabaster, 1903.

Richmond, Velma Bourgeois. "Ford Madox Brown's Protestant Medievalism: Chaucer and Wycliffe." *Christianity and Literature*, vol. 54, no. 3, 2005, pp. 363–96.

Rosman, Doreen. *The Evolution of the English Churches, 1500–2000*. Cambridge UP, 2003.

Smith, Ryan K. *Gothic Arches, Latin Crosses: Anti-Catholicism and American Church Designs in the Nineteenth Century*. U of North Carolina P, 2011.

Spurgeon, C. H. "The Axe at the Root: A Testimony against Puseyite Idolatry [sermon no. 695]." *Metropolitan Tabernacle Pulpit*, vol. 12, 1867, pp. 325–36.

———. "Expositions of the Psalms: Psalm XIX." *Sword and the Trowel*, vol. 2, 1866, pp. 323–31.

———. "How to Attract a Congregation." *Sword and the Trowel*, vol. 19, Aug. 1883, pp. 417–24.

———. *The Metropolitan Tabernacle: Its History and Work*. London, Passmore and Alabaster, 1876.

Spurgeon, S., and J. Harrald, editors. *C. H. Spurgeon's Autobiography: Compiled from His Diary, Letters, and Records*. London, Passmore and Alabaster, 1897–1900. 4 vols.

Twyman, Michael. "The Illustration Revolution." *The Cambridge History of the Book in Britain*, vol. 6: *1830–1914*, edited by David McKitterick, Cambridge UP, 2009, pp. 117–43.

Wakeling, Christopher. "Nonconformity and Victorian Architecture." *Dissent and the Gothic Revival*, edited by Bridget Cherry, Chapels Society Occasional Publication 3, London, Chapels Society, 2007, pp. 39–71.

———. "'A Room Nearly Semi-Circular': Aspects of the Theatre and the Church from Harrison to Pugin." *Architectural History*, vol. 44, 2001, pp. 265–74.

White, Bruce A. "Douglas Jerrold's 'Q' Papers in *Punch*." *Victorian Periodicals Review*, vol. 15, no. 4, 1982, pp. 131–37.

Whyte, William. "Sacred Space as Sacred Text: Church and Chapel Architecture in Victorian Britain." *Sacred Text, Sacred Space: Architectural, Spiritual and Literary Convergences in England and Wales*, edited by Joseph Sterrett and Peter Thomas, Brill, 2011, pp. 247–67.

Willison, John. *A Treatise Concerning the Sanctification of the Lord's Day*. Albany, New York, 1820.

CHAPTER 11

Wilde's Uses of Religion

MARK KNIGHT

THERE IS a long-standing difficulty for critics in knowing what to make of Wilde's interest in Christianity.[1] Although his writing makes repeated reference to Christian language, ideas, and practice, many scholars are unwilling to take the interest at face value, suspecting that something else must be going on beneath the religious veneer and preferring to mine these possibilities rather than heed Wilde's warning in the preface to *The Picture of Dorian Gray* (1891) that "those who go beneath the surface do so at their peril." The desire to get beneath the surface of Wilde's religion is not universal, and Patrick R. O'Malley is among those who recognize that "the depth model of interpretation ultimately cannot encompass the complexity of this novel, particularly in its final pages" (*Catholicism* 187). But suspicion about Wilde's religious interest remains widespread, and might be thought about in terms of a hermeneutic that several recent scholars have declared to be dominant within literary studies. Named variously as the hermeneutics of suspicion, depth reading, symptomatic reading, or critique, this hermeneutic has come under increasing scrutiny since the start of the twenty-first century.[2] Attempts to explore

---

[1]. In seeking to address the difficulty myself, I am grateful for the comments on this chapter offered by Jo Carruthers, Joshua King, Kimberly J. Stern, and Winter Jade Werner.

[2]. See, for example, Rita Felski's *Uses of Literature* (2008) and *The Limits of Critique* (2015), Bruno Latour's reservations about critique, Heather Love's exploration of descriptive reading, and Stephen Best and Sharon Marcus's essay on surface reading.

alternate ways of reading found a rallying point in the 2009 special issue of *Representations*, which saw Stephen Best and Sharon Marcus grouping these options under the heading of "surface reading," yet subsequent discussion suggests a lack of conviction among literary scholars regarding surface reading as a way forward. Although I share these doubts, exercising greater caution over our desire to go beneath or behind the material before us does seem a helpful starting point for thinking about the references to Christianity that we find in Wilde's writing. My argument in this chapter is that the determination to look for a secular reality behind Wilde's religious guises stems from a long-standing Protestant tradition, in which ritual is the subject of suspicion and true religion is thought about primarily in terms of internal assent to a particular set of beliefs. The influence of this Protestant mind-set can be seen in the reading of those who do not believe in the Christian faith as much as in the attitudes of Wilde's Protestant contemporaries. If Christian theology is at risk of losing its intellectual vitality after the Reformation, as its essential nature is located within narrower and narrower spheres that only retract as other explanatory modes emerge, there should be no surprise that Christian theology is a frequent casualty whenever our reading becomes overly dominated by suspicion. By way of response, this chapter explores a different possibility and entertains the notion that Wilde's writing might be read as liturgical.[3]

There are good reasons to be concerned about the various uses to which religion is put in the nineteenth century and in our subsequent reading of that era: the risks involved when mobilizing religion for political, social, or economic ends; the coercion that can be seen when we understand how religion functions as a disciplinary category; and the problems that result when religion configures personal identity in a destructive fashion. We might also worry about the focus on use distracting us from the religious tradition itself. This last concern can seem most pressing to those of us who see a particular religious tradition as integral to our academic or personal identity. If we are professionally invested in an academic subject—here, some aspect of religion in the nineteenth century—we are likely to be frustrated by casual and apparently uninformed references to that subject, and we will want to question clumsy uses of a vocabulary we think deserves greater nuance. And those of us who identify personally with a religious tradition may well feel unease

---

3. For a related project, focused on Wilde's early writings and theoretical debt to Roman Catholicism, see McQueen.

about the uses of religion diluting and/or distorting a faith that we hold dear and struggle to recognize in the manifestation before us.

While I am sympathetic to all these concerns, I wonder whether they stem from a peculiarly Protestant viewpoint, in which there is an underlying suspicion that all uses and all rituals distract us from a more basic and authentic spiritual truth. I am aware that this claim is more applicable to some parts of Protestantism than others, but what I have in mind is a tradition going back to the Reformation and most prominent in Puritanism and evangelicalism. It is a viewpoint that seeks to strip away anything superfluous in search of a more authentic expression of Christianity. The fear that all forms of mediation are potentially idolatrous is evident in Dominic Janes's account, in this volume, of the Protestant anxiety surrounding visual culture, and is part of an aesthetic that Jo Carruthers has described as Protestant simplicity, the form that claims to have no form. This Protestant distrust of form is predicated on an essential account of religious belief in which proper Christian theology is understood to reside within: in one's head or one's heart. On such a reading, genuine Christian theology is thought to be about an individual believing certain things about God with sufficient sincerity and personal conviction.[4] A similar view of theology can be traced in the work of many scholars who identify as secular but continue to be shaped by a Protestant tradition in which they do not believe. Like their religious counterparts, these secular critics see the trappings of religion as something that need to be unmasked. Whereas Protestants remain committed to the idea that faith exists in the hearts of authentic believers, thinkers who prefer to position themselves as secular are likely to be more skeptical about finding such a thing when they penetrate appearances. What they share with their religious counterparts, however, is the belief that if genuine theology exists at all, it would have to be found beneath the surface.

Given Wilde's considerable fascination with Roman Catholicism, it is unsurprising that those who think about religion from a Protestant mind-set struggle to know what to make of his attention to Christianity. The last two decades have seen a renewal of interest among scholars in Wilde's religion, yet there is still a reluctance to take Wilde's theology seriously as a discourse that might be worth exploring on its own terms or as something that bears relation to more orthodox accounts of the Christian faith. At the suspicious end of the critical spectrum, Richard Ellman's still influential biography repeatedly plays down the significance of Wilde's religious views, and Regenia Gagnier

---

4. Although there is typically a minimum of theological content to these Protestant beliefs, such as the conviction that Jesus is the Son of God and the Savior of the World, the emphasis is more likely to fall on the personal import of these beliefs than on their doctrinal nuance.

sees in Wilde's *De Profundis* "the great joke on a Christian society of making Jesus Christ his hero" (187), insisting that the description of Jesus we find there is deliberately "banal" (190).⁵ But there are problems at the other end of the critical spectrum, too. Commentators who set out to be more sympathetic and alert to religion, such as Jarlath Killeen, also encounter difficulties in knowing how to deal with Wilde's theology, even though they readily acknowledge that it is part of his thought. Killeen's recognition in *The Faiths of Oscar Wilde* (2005) and *The Fairy Tales of Oscar Wilde* (2007) that the language of religion is present in Wilde's writing is overtaken by an interpretative paradigm that finds more explanatory power in talk of Irish nationalism: for all his historical precision when talking about religion, and his awareness of how religion and politics often collide, Killeen struggles to register the theological significance of Wilde's work.

More productive is scholarship that focuses on queer theology, a mode of theological reflection that not only "answers to the queerness of God, who is not other than strange and at odds with our 'fallen' world," but also, as Gerard Loughlin goes on to explain, joins with queer theory in finding that "gay sexuality is not marginal to Christian thought and culture, but oddly central" (*Queer Theology* 8–9). I see the importance of thinking about the subversive uses of Christianity as we examine how, to quote Dominic Janes in *Visions of Queer Martyrdom from John Henry Newman to Derek Jarman* (2015), religion is "constitutive" for Wilde (136).⁶ But while one might reasonably insist that queer theology is recognizably theological because Christian belief should always be subversive and queer in its orientation, the corresponding reticence to tie such readings to anything that might be associated with the rest of the Christian tradition can prove limiting. There is a false binary at work when we insist too strongly on differentiating the radical thought of Wilde from the story of God that is told by various parts of the Christian church, and Loughlin's "Introduction" to *Queer Theology* (2007) charts a helpful middle course when he seeks to underline how his subject matter "reprises the tradition of

---

5. To give just one example, Ellman writes: "What he would say later of Dorian Gray was true of himself: 'It was rumoured of him that he was about to join the Roman Catholic communion; and certainly the Roman ritual had a great attraction for him . . . But he never fell into the error of arresting his intellectual development by any formal acceptance of creed or system, or of mistaking, for a house in which to live, an inn that is but suitable for the sojourn of a night'" (91).

6. See also Patrick O'Malley's essay "Religion," where he sees the references in *De Profundis* to "Catholicism and sexual transgression" as "surprisingly similar articulations of his [Wilde's] resistance to socially-prescribed norms" (178); and the chapter on Wilde in Ellis Hanson's *Decadence and Catholicism* (1997), where he notes "Wilde's theatrical mastery of Catholic rhetoric and Catholic gestures" and acknowledges how Wilde "appreciated the performative dimension of religion" (230).

the church in order to discover the queer interests that were always already at play in the Spirit's movement, in the lives and devotions of saints and sinners, theologians and ecclesiastics" (9).

I appreciate that the distance between Wilde's religion and the rest of the Christian tradition is encouraged by some of Wilde's own comments, such as the declaration in *De Profundis* (1897), arguably his most religious of texts, that "religion does not help me" (103). For Simon Critchley, writing in the *Faith of the Faithless* (2012), talk in *De Profundis* of the need for "an order for those who cannot believe" (*De Profundis* 103) inspires the idea that "those who cannot believe still require religious truth and a framework of ritual in which they can believe" (Critchley 3). Critchley continues: "At the core of Wilde's remark is the seemingly contradictory idea of the *faith of the faithless* and the *belief of unbelievers,* a faith which does not give up on the idea of truth, but transfigures its meaning" (3). Yet the repurposing of religious ritual in ways that divorce it from existing narratives of theological commitment, and/or the transfiguration of truth so that it is no longer embedded in a recognizably Christian tradition, does not, I argue, do justice to the religious rituals that permeate and sustain Wilde's writing.

For when Wilde tells us in *De Profundis* that "agnosticism should have its ritual" (103) too, his comments are more in line with theological orthodoxy than their initial provocation suggests. The history of the Church is as much the history of those who struggle to believe as it is of the saints celebrated for their beliefs. Aquinas's final fears that his theological writing was made up of straws, Peter's denial of Jesus, and the writer of Psalm 130 who cries to God "out of the depths," can be described as agnostic as much as expressions of faith.[7] Agnostics need rituals, not because they are distinct from the people of God, but because they are part of that people and dependent on a faith that is necessarily embedded in the rituals, practices, and grammar of faith. As the contemporary theologian Stanley Hauerwas put it in a commencement address for the Eastern Mennonite Seminary: "To speak well, to talk right, requires that our bodies be habituated by the language of the faith. To be so habituated requires constant repetition. Without repetition, and repetition is but another word for the worship of God, we are in danger of losing the grammar of the faith" (*Working with Words* 87). Rather than thinking of theology as something that is subsequently put to use in ritual, we would do better to

---

7. Acknowledging that the title *De Profundis,* with its allusion to Psalm 130, was chosen by Robert Ross, Wilde's literary executor, Andrew Tate still argues that "Wilde's epistle similarly identifies with the dispossessed and spiritual destitute and echoes the Psalmist's hope that redemption and forgiveness are possible" (591).

think of those rituals as theological acts, deliberate stories of repetition in which the narrative of the Christian story is told, remembered, and acted out.

Seeing Christian ritual as inherently theological rather than as a barrier to true religion opens up new possibilities for thinking about *De Profundis*. It enables us to see, for instance, the self-serving and accusatory nature of Wilde's talk of forgiveness as no less theological for its failures. Whatever the weaknesses in Wilde's own soul-searching, his text shows acute awareness of his shortcomings and seems alert to the idea that forgiveness is an act to be continually worked on rather than a state that can be achieved by the elect. At one point Wilde acknowledges the point in a manner reminiscent of the psalmists: "There is much more before me. I have hills far steeper to climb, valleys much darker to pass through" (103). Elsewhere in the letter, he writes, "And the end of it all is that I have got to forgive you. I must do so. I don't write this letter to put bitterness into your heart but to pluck it out of mine" (99). The reference here to plucking seems carefully chosen, perhaps conveying recognition of the difficulties accompanying forgiveness and possibly alluding to the dramatic language of the Gospels in which Jesus calls his followers to confront the sin in their own lives rather than rely on their observance of ethical norms (e.g., Matt. 5:29, 18:9; Mark 9:47). More important, though, is the way in which Wilde describes forgiveness as an act that one must perform repeatedly. The act of confession sometimes seems odd to Protestants such as myself who have grown up thinking that the giving and receiving of forgiveness are relatively straightforward internal decisions that do not need external forms of mediation. But the reason why the act came to take the form it does in the Roman Catholic Church is that the giving and receiving of forgiveness were deemed demanding and in need of mediation through regular rituals and imperfect practice. Advising Douglas on how his epistle should be read, Wilde writes, "There will be much that wounds your vanity to the quick. If it proves so, read the letter over and over again till it kills your vanity" (45). Spiritual transformation, suggests Wilde, requires repetition.

James K. A. Smith articulates a similar idea in the essay "Secular Liturgies and the Prospects for a 'Post-Secular' Sociology of Religion" when he tells us that "faith takes practice" (160). But how do we know that it is specifically *religious* faith that is being practiced? It is worth pausing to consider Smith's argument in the essay, for it raises a broader question about the way in which I am reading Wilde. For Smith the liturgical is central to the whole of life and can be seen in unlikely spheres as much as in those areas that are more commonly thought of as religious. Liturgies, he explains, are "rituals of ultimate concern" (167), forms that express and shape "our most fundamental motivations" (167). While Smith's work here and elsewhere is openly confessional in its theological orientation, the line of thought he advances in this essay owes much to the interpretative moves routinely undertaken by those sociologists of religion who define their object of study primarily in terms of function.[8] A functional understanding helps us to see the "religious" in all sorts of unlikely places, and in the context of my chapter here, it would accommodate a broadly spiritual reading of Wilde by allowing us to simply look for a functional equivalence between the rituals recorded in Wilde's writing and the liturgy practiced by the church. But this is not a move that I want to make, for an overly functional reading of religion renders theology a redundant discourse that can be explained more effectively through a sociological lens. Reading a letter may be functionally equivalent to certain types of religious practice, and we might grant such reading a broadly spiritual quality, but there seems little reason to keep talking about the specificities of Christian theology if we pursue this route.[9]

Religion can and should be thought about in terms of its repeated activities, but the function of these practices cannot be endlessly translated and still thought about as theological. There is something more particular to the Christian religion, something that marks a distinction, albeit blurred, between me reading any letter through an affective register and me suggesting that a particular letter is written with a theological goal in mind.[10] That distinction does not rest on inner conviction, nor does it depend on the fixed set of dogmas championed by fundamentalism. And it is not reliant on the vague talk of transcendence that we might associate with the work of Rudolph Otto. To see Wilde's reading as Christian, to describe it as liturgical, involves attending to the way that his practices are marked by the vocabulary and grammar

---

8. While the argument of Smith's essay emphasizes the proximity and overlap between the sacred and secular, elsewhere, particularly in *Desiring the Kingdom*, he draws greater attention to their difference, writing: "'Secular' liturgies are fundamentally formative, and implicit in them is a vision of the kingdom that needs to be discerned and evaluated. From the perspective of Christian faith, these secular liturgies will often constitute a *mis*-formation of our desires" (88).

9. Smith's argument is more theologically complex and less dependent on a functional account of religion than my engagement here might suggest, and there is a great deal in his extended work on cultural liturgies with which I agree. But I note the point of divergence to help me articulate what I do and do not mean when I talk about a theological reading of Wilde's practice.

10. In insisting on such a distinction, my argument is at odds with Walter Pater's claim in his essay on "Style" that the theological is merely one illustration of the spiritual (or, as he terms it, the soul). Pater writes: "By mind, the literary artist reaches us, through static and objective indications of design in his work, legible to all. By soul, he reaches us, somewhat capriciously perhaps, one and not another, through vagrant sympathy and a kind of immediate contact . . . The way in which theological interests sometimes avail themselves of language is perhaps the best illustration of the force I mean to indicate generally in literature, by the word *soul*" (25).

of the Christian faith, as it is told, retold, and practiced by the community of believers over time. Defining the Christian religion in this way has the added benefit of explaining why it is that so much of Wilde's faith is thought about textually; for while rituals are not solely textual, the rhythm of language and the language of faith is central to the theology of the church, which helps explain why Wilde and so many other writers see literature as an appropriate site for religious practice.

There is plenty of encouragement in Wilde's writing for reading him as a participant in the Christian story of faith, from the wealth of biblical allusion in "The Selfish Giant" to the extended-if-strange reflections on an episode from the New Testament in his play *Salome*. Wilde's fascination with the Gospels in particular was considerable, and his rereading of this material was evident over the course of his life. One of the encouragements for understanding this reading as religious ritual is the moment in *De Profundis* when he talks about his acquisition of a Greek New Testament and his morning habit of reading "a little of the Gospels, a dozen verses taken by chance anywhere . . . a delightful way of opening the day" (123). The thinking behind his method of reading is not explained. It could be wholly ironic, though there is little in *De Profundis* to support that view. Perhaps it is a nod to the reading practices of those parts of the church that have long read the Bible in a similarly unsystematic and open-ended way, or perhaps, as Wilde himself suggests, it is the sort of reading one does when they are trying to disrupt the familiarity that comes with knowing a text too well. We can only speculate on the reasons why Wilde read the Gospels in the way that he did, but his practice here is remarkably akin to the devotional routine that one typically associates with religious believers.

"Remarkably akin to the devotional routine" of "religious believers." In providing that caveat, I am struck by my persistent caution in this chapter about naming Wilde's rituals as Christian. It is hard to know whether the latest barrier to my doing so is the subversive quality of Wilde's writing or my own ongoing immersion in a literary community that finds it hard to avoid suspicion when it comes to reading religion. That suspicion is not always misplaced, of course, and the challenge for our reading of Wilde's rituals is to combine such insights with other modes of reading, including the hermeneutics of faith that Paul Ricoeur describes in *Freud and Philosophy: An Essay on Interpretation* (1965) as a necessary partner to the hermeneutic of suspicion. Caroline Levine's *Forms: Whole, Rhythm, Hierarchy, Network* (2015) offers a useful way forward when she encourages us to rethink the ways in which "repetitive temporal patterns impose constraints across social life" (49). Those patterns can "coerce and organize," as Michel Foucault and others have long taught us, but Levine insists that these temporal patterns also "have the potential to work with and against other forms to surprisingly transformative political effect" (52). One reason why rhythmic forms can lead us to such different ends is that they "depend on citations borrowed from the past," which break with "any single context" (64) and entail more heterogeneous models of thought. Levine's reading helps us see how the suspicions we might harbor about how rituals function in Wilde can be thought about alongside more constructive and liberating readings.

When Wilde performs religious rituals in his texts, he repeats the story of faith in another setting. But that story was never static in the first place, and Wilde is certainly not introducing the idea that stories, rituals, and performances constitute the Christian faith. As Joseph McQueen reminds us, "The creeds repeated at every liturgy are not expressions of deeply held belief; rather, they are forms that construct and inculcate belief" (878). Wilde's rituals take on new lines of thought, but the same could be said of established religious rituals too, which is why I disagree with Ellis Hanson's claim that "Wilde's most important strategy for making his own God was to rewrite or reinterpret the Bible" (235). Rather than thinking that the presence of religious rituals in Wilde's writing presents us with choice between conservative and radical readings—a commitment to a fixed body of traditional belief or the subversion of that belief—we might instead see how Wilde's participation in and reworking of religious ritual is continuous with the practice of a body of believers that have long retold the story of faith. Indeed, as Gerard Loughlin reminds us in *Telling God's Story* (1996), "The Church is the community that tells Christ's story by being itself the continuing story of Christ; embodying the story of Christ in the circumstances of its day" (84).

If we stop thinking that Wilde's frequent criticism of the church forces him outside that community, we are better able to understand how it is that Wilde so frequently chooses to think of himself as a worshipper. To describe Wilde as a worshipper seems odd, I realize, but one major contribution of those who work on queer theology has been to make us more aware of the fundamental strangeness of the Christian life. Wilde may be an odd worshipper, but that is the only sort of worshipper there is. I make this observation as a prelude to reflecting on his fascination with the biblical accounts of a woman (sometimes named as Mary) breaking the alabaster jar and anointing Jesus in an act of worship (Matt. 26:6–13; Mark 14:3–9; Luke 7:36–60; John 12:1–8). Wilde alludes to the episode in *De Profundis* when he recalls, "Mary Magdalen, when she sees Christ, breaks the rich vase of alabaster that one of her seven lovers had given her and spills the odorous spices over his tired, dusty feet, and for that one moment's sake sits for ever with Ruth and Beatrice in the tresses of the snow-white Rose of Paradise" (127). And he expounds on the same story with less artistic license but at greater length in "The Ballad of Reading Gaol" when he draws our attention to this anointing as a genuine act of worship. As those familiar with the Gospel accounts will know, the disciples and religious leaders in the various biblical accounts are disturbed by the erotic overtones of this act. But as the Gospel writers tell the story, the religious figures' emphasis on what falls short in the scene blinds them to the beauty of what takes place and the authentic worship expressed through this act of devotion. Here is Wilde's reworking of the biblical material:

> And every human heart that breaks,
>   In prison-cell or yard,
> Is as that broken box that gave
>   Its treasure to the Lord,
> And filled the unclean leper's house
>   With the scent of costliest nard. (607–12)

Against those who might want to see the scene as more sensual than theological and nothing more than a sign of Wilde's preference for the aesthetic over the religious, the biblical story insists that the act of worship is no less theological for its sensuality.

I am not suggesting that *De Profundis* and "The Ballad of Reading Gaol" are straightforward models of worship. Both texts twist and turn too much for that, though the same could probably be said of the Psalms, at least when they are read as a whole. But worship does seem to be present through these texts, as Wilde explores the self with reference to the person of Christ and finds theological truth in his fragmented explorations: "How else but through a broken heart / May Lord Christ enter in?" ("Ballad" 617–18). In Wilde's poem, the reorientation of the self to Christ proceeds through a complex set of shifting identifications. Initially, Wilde identifies with the soldier on death row and uses the refrain "each man kills the things he loves" (37) to position both prisoners as "outcast men" (170). The theological talk of love and the lost is picked up and complicated by Emily Walker Heady in her discussion of Wilde's ideas about conversion. She notes a shift from the speaker's identification with the soldier to "merely grieving for him" (147), with Wilde coming to write about the fearfulness of feeling guilt for "blood we had not spilt" ("Ballad" 270). For those who see Wilde's identification with the soldier on death row as a self-serving manipulation of another's story, it is worth remembering that the same stanza that speaks of a prison wall surrounding them both is the one that ends by talking of "Sin" (173) having "caught us in its snare" (174). In this moment, at least, the poem registers its self-serving agenda as part of the problem. Aware, perhaps, of the difficulties accompanying all efforts at identifying with another, the poem moves unevenly between seeing Wilde as one with the other prisoners and as a man set apart. And the deployment of images from the New Testament and its retellings—including the cock that crows, the blood and wine, the betrayal by a kiss, and direct references to Christ—serve to liken both the soldier and Wilde to Christ in still further variations on the act of identification.

Whereas Heady sees the poem's points of identification as a linear narrative of conversion, I think the narrative of "The Ballad of Reading Gaol" retains a greater degree of ambiguity. One reason is that if Jesus's suffering provides any sort of comfort for Wilde, then it follows that Wilde's identification with Christ through the poem becomes similarly imbued with a quasi-redemptive quality. Who, the reader might well ask, is being converted to what? Yet the narrative direction of the poem does not necessarily need to be determined for a religious reading to proceed, and the confusion caused by shifting acts of identification does not make the poem any less theological. While Christian worship ultimately has a center, the liturgical framework recognizes the to-and-fro involved when a community of people finds different ways of orientating themselves to the triune God. To see Wilde's text as an act of worship may restrict its interpretative possibilities at one level, but this does not require us to read the text in a linear manner, and, on another level, one might argue that any reading that insists on the infinite nature of God opens up as many interpretative doors as it closes.

There is another and perhaps more significant potential problem with my reading of Wilde. If the rituals of worship are directed towards reorientating the self to God, then how does this fit with the common view that Wilde sees the self as an endless series of masks? For Ruth Robbins, Wilde is an exemplar of those modern theories of subjectivity that seek to erase the "self" altogether. She explains, "Not only is modern life complex and relative, so too is the modern narrative that attempts to record it; and its complexity is borne out of Wilde's conviction that selfhood is not a deep structure, securely possessed as unique individuality by anyone" (125). I do not disagree with the specific claims here: subjectivity is mutable, it exceeds our ability to record it, and I am in sympathy with Wilde's efforts to overturn a long history of thinking about selfhood in terms of depth. Yet we still act as selves within the world, and Robbins's reading of Wilde continues the all-too-frequent attempt by literary critics to distance the self so that they—we—no longer have to confront the challenges of our own subjective existence in the world. "We," and I use that term with every intention of trying to admit its complexity, remain agents at some level, subjects who live in relation to and are constituted by our surroundings, and subjects who make choices about how we treat one another and respond to the God spoken about in Christian theology.

While "The Ballad of Reading Gaol" may not mark a radical departure from the focus on surface, mutability, and performance that we see elsewhere in Wilde's writing, the existential implications of coming to terms with our choices and experiences do seem to be apparent and are perhaps more explicit here than in some of Wilde's earlier work. And, significantly, these implications are articulated through a religious framework that runs counter to a theory of masks. When, for instance, the poem considers the Chaplain and tells us how he is "glad" (197) the "hangman's hands were near" (198), Wilde initially sees the comment as strange, insisting that a professional watcher "Must set a lock upon his lips, / And make his face a mask" (203–4). But Wilde then continues to view that mask as a barrier to human pity, suggesting that masking one's identity is not the ultimate goal of Wilde's theory of the self, and encouraging us to think through the theological implications of the shifting self that appears in "The Ballad of Reading Gaol." The shifting self is one with a capacity for development and, more importantly in the Christian tradition, relation to the life of God. If the concept of the mask retains any theological significance for Wilde, it has less to do with personal avoidance and an erasure of self, and more to do with how human beings are made in the image of an ineffable God—"Him who now doth hide his face" ("Rome Unvisited" 56)—that they are called upon to worship.

Other aspects of Wilde's thinking about the self are also more indebted to traditional theological practice than many critics have wanted to allow. Take, for example, Wilde's extended meditations in *De Profundis* on Christ as the ultimate artist, an idea that is commonly understood with reference to Romanticism and an aesthetic agenda that celebrates the autonomy of art. Without wanting to overturn such readings entirely, I would point out that the argument for Christ as an artist of the world that we inhabit relies on the doctrine of the Incarnation—a theological concept of long-standing importance to Wilde, who wrote to his friend William Ward in July 1876, "I wonder you don't see the beauty and necessity of the *incarnation* of God into man to help us to grasp at the skirts of the Infinite" (*Letters* 20)—and is closer to the eschatological vision of the Book of Revelation than to neo-Platonic talk of heaven as a place for disembodied souls. If we think of Christ as the one who transforms, rejuvenates, and completes God's work of creation, then we can better understand the distinction that Wilde makes between Christ and the Romantic artist in *De Profundis*: "To the artist, expression is the only mode under which he can conceive life at all. To him what is dumb is dead. But to Christ it was not so. With a width and wonder of imagination, that fills one almost with awe, he took the entire world of the inarticulate, the voiceless world of pain, as his kingdom, and made of himself its eternal mouthpiece" (120). Wilde's subsequent suggestion that "out of his own imagination entirely did Jesus of Nazareth create himself" (122) may idealize the autonomy of the artist in an aspirational sense, but it is also in tune with orthodox ideas of God's self-sufficiency in the act of creation and the limitations of trying to define God by way of the things that we know.

It would be misleading to play down the potential conflict between Wilde's radical aestheticism and the widespread insistence elsewhere in the Christian tradition that theology involves a different sort of relation between art and the world. But these tensions should not be understood as a straightforward binary between aestheticism and theology, and Wilde himself seems to look for common ground in *De Profundis* when he insists that "Christ's place indeed is with the poets" (115). When it comes to thinking about how the Self encounters Christ through the rituals of worship, Wilde's complex account is only properly at odds with the Christian faith if we confine theological ideas of personhood to a narrow tradition. Parts of Protestantism have promoted the model of depth that Wilde complains about, privileging an essential and eternal soul beneath outward appearances and presuming that the locus of that soul is a spiritual set of personal beliefs that exists prior to and apart from ritual, practice, and experience. But overturning this religious idea does not require a move away from Christianity: a theological understanding of the self surely begins with the story of a God who becomes incarnate in the person of Jesus, who lives in divine relation (Father, Son, and Spirit), and who invites humanity to participate in that triune life. Understood in this way, a theological view of the self is rooted in talk of an actual Messiah who wrestles with the suffering and brokenness of lived experience, not an ethereal Christ who exists timelessly in divine abstraction. Christian accounts of personhood are rooted in the God whose multidimensional story is recorded in the Scriptures, and the accounts take form as that story is remembered and retold by communities of faith.

Working with the resulting theological language—the language of experience, brokenness, story, personal relations, Christ's suffering, and so on—we are better able to return to "The Ballad of Reading Gaol" and see its Christological implications. We do not need to be put off by those aspects of the poem that seem to be at odds with received notions of what Christ is meant to be like, for, as Stanley Hauerwas has argued, there is a fundamental problem with Christologies that, in the interests of emphasizing "the cosmic and ontological Christ . . . make Jesus' life almost incidental to what is assumed to be a more profound theological point" ("Jesus" 117). Wilde's heavily human reading of Christ—with its considerable debt to Wilde's reading of Ernest Renan[11]—has its limitations, but these are no more theologically impoverished than the exclusively divine readings of Christ sometimes found in nineteenth-century evangelicalism. Moreover, there is nothing exceptional about the way in which Wilde's theology sometimes aims at revising the Christian tradition. Christian theology is a fluid and changing discourse, and revision is integral to its self-understanding and existence. Thus, when Wilde celebrates in *De Profundis* how Christ "swept . . . aside" the orthodoxy of religious leaders (127), he finds himself among a panoply of Christian writers who have seen their work in similar terms, as correctives to idolatrous ideas about the nature of God.

Graham Ward reminds us how, from its earliest appropriation by the early church, the term "theology was synonymous with doxology" (3). Recognition of this association has long been integral to the church's creation and use of liturgy, a form designed to help selves reflect on the temporal nature of their existence and understand that existence in relation to God. Given the rich tapestry of thought that liturgy makes available, it is unsurprising that Wilde found more freedom here than in the sermon form preferred by many Victorian Protestants. That freedom had its limits, but Wilde's enthusiasm for Roman Catholicism was not put off by this fact, and both "The Ballad of Reading Gaol" and *De Profundis* make more sense when they are seen as continuous with the life of the church rather than as a set of inauthentic rituals that are deliberately practiced outside the community of faith. The story of God is contested by those who read it, and there are major points of disagreement between Wilde and some of his religious contemporaries, particularly those belonging to the parts of Protestantism that sought to understand the Christian faith in more tightly defined ways. But there are enough moments of continuity and convergence for me to think that we might dare to speak of Wilde's uses of religious ritual as something that deserves to go by the name of Christian theology.

---

11. In an essay calling for scholars "to become more attuned to the range of meanings that came to be attached to the figure of Christ and were thus available for Wilde's use" (259), Arata "acknowledge[s] the enormous importance of Renan's *Vie de Jésus*, specifically for Wilde but also for the later nineteenth century as a whole" (261) and writes about Renan and Wilde at length.

WORKS CITED

Arata, Stephen. "Oscar Wilde and Jesus Christ." *Wilde Writings: Contextual Conditions*, edited by Joseph Bristow, U of Toronto P, 2003, pp. 254–72.

Best, Stephen, and Sharon Marcus. "Surface Reading: An Introduction." *Representations*, vol. 108, no. 1, 2009, pp. 1–21.

Carruthers, Jo. "The Aesthetics of Simplicity." *The Routledge Companion to Literature and Religion*, edited by Mark Knight, Routledge, 2016, pp. 165–66.

Critchley, Simon. *The Faith of the Faithless*. Verso, 2012.

Ellman, Richard. *Oscar Wilde*. Penguin, 1987.

Felski, Rita. *The Limits of Critique*. U of Chicago P, 2015.

———. *Uses of Literature*. Blackwell, 2008.

Fong, Bobby, and Karl Beckson, editors. *The Complete Works of Oscar Wilde*. Vol. 1: *Poems and Poems in Prose*. Oxford UP, 2000.

Gagnier, Regenia. *Idylls of the Marketplace: Oscar Wilde and the Victorian Public*. Stanford UP, 1986.

Hanson, Ellis. *Decadence and Catholicism*. Harvard UP, 1997.

Hauerwas, Stanley. "Jesus and the Social Embodiment of the Peaceable Kingdom." *The Hauerwas Reader*, edited by John Berman and Michael Cartwright, Duke UP, 2001, pp. 116–41.

———. *Working with Words*. Cascade Books, 2011.

Heady, Emily Walker. *Victorian Conversion Narratives and Reading Communities*. Ashgate, 2013.

Janes, Dominic. *Visions of Queer Martyrdom from John Henry Newman to Derek Jarman*. U of Chicago P, 2015.

Killeen, Jarlath. *The Fairy Tales of Oscar Wilde*. Ashgate, 2007.

———. *The Faiths of Oscar Wilde: Catholicism, Folklore and Ireland*. Palgrave Macmillan, 2005.

Latour, Bruno. "Why Has Critique Run Out of Steam? From Matters of Fact to Matters of Concern." *Critical Inquiry*, vol. 30, no. 2, 2004, pp. 225–48.

Levine, Caroline. *Forms: Whole, Rhythm, Hierarchy, Network*. Princeton UP, 2015.

Loughlin, Gerard. *Telling God's Story: Bible, Church and Narrative Theology*. Cambridge UP, 1996.

———, editor. *Queer Theology: Rethinking the Western Body*. Blackwell, 2007.

Love, Heather. "Close but Not Deep: Literary Ethics and the Descriptive Turn." *New Literary History*, vol. 41, no. 2, 2010, pp. 371–91.

McQueen, Joseph. "Oscar Wilde's Catholic Aesthetics in a Secular Age." *Studies in English Literature*, vol. 57, no. 4, 2017, pp. 865–86.

O'Malley, Patrick R. *Catholicism, Sexual Deviance and Victorian Gothic Culture*. Cambridge UP, 2006.

———. "Religion." *Palgrave Advances in Oscar Wilde Studies*, edited by Frederick Roden, Palgrave, 2004, pp. 167–88.

Otto, Rudolph. *The Idea of the Holy*. Translated by John W. Harvey, 2nd ed., Oxford UP, 1968.

Pater, Walter. *The Works of Walter Pater: Appreciations, with an Essay on Style*. Cambridge UP, 2011.

Ricoeur, Paul. *Freud and Philosophy: An Essay on Interpretation.* 1965. Translated by Denis Savage, Yale UP, 1970.

Robbins, Ruth. *Subjectivity.* Palgrave, 2005.

Smith, James K. A. *Desiring the Kingdom: Worship, Worldview, and Cultural Formation.* Baker Academic, 2009.

———. "Secular Liturgies and the Prospects for a 'Post-Secular' Sociology of Religion." *The Post-Secular in Question: Religion in Contemporary Society,* edited by Philip S. Gorski et al., New York UP, 2012, pp. 159–84.

Tate, Andrew. "Decadence." *The Blackwell Companion to the Bible in English Literature,* edited by Rebecca Lemon et al., Wiley-Blackwell, 2009, pp. 587–99.

Ward, Graham. *True Religion.* Blackwell, 2003.

Wilde, Oscar. "The Ballad of Reading Gaol." Fong and Beckson.

———. *De Profundis. De Profundis and Other Prison Writings,* edited by Colm Tóibín, Penguin, 2013.

———. *The Letters of Oscar Wilde.* Edited by Rupert Hart-Davis, Rupert Hart-Davis, 1962.

———. "Rome Unvisited." Fong and Beckson.

PART III

Religion and Poetics in Postsecular Literary Studies

CHAPTER 12

Reading Psalms in Nineteenth-Century England

The Contact Zone of Jewish–Christian Scriptural Relations

CYNTHIA SCHEINBERG

I. THE "GREAT INCONVENIENCE": JEWISH IDENTITY IN NINETEENTH-CENTURY CHRISTIAN PSALM CULTURE

> What lyric language can refuse to borrow its tone from, and therefore but faintly echo, the devotional Psalms of David, and of those who followed him? (Henry Hart Milman 440)

> How can we assume to ourselves all his Words in our personal or public addresses to God, when our condition of Life our Time, Place and Religion are so vastly different from that of David? (Isaac Watts x–xi)

The Psalms might be considered the first canon of poetry in both Jewish and Christian cultures. Their idealized literary status is evident across Jewish and Christian historical cultures, comprising a major part of Anglican and Nonconforming liturgies as well as being understood as the most revered body of poetry in English history. The passage above by Henry Hart Milman, from his *History of the Jews* (first published 1829), typifies the approach invoked by a wide range of literary critics and clerics, who saw the Psalms as a model for all lyric poetry.[1] However, along with their reverence for the Psalms as prayer and

---

1. *Lyric* as a term has a long and complex history; see Jackson and Jackson and Prins for more details. Jackson notes that the nineteenth-century critics sought to create a "transcen-

poetry, many Christian critics also grappled with the problem of the Psalms' particular Jewish origins in the Hebrew Bible (or Old Testament).[2] The challenge that the Jewish authorship of the Psalms posed to Christian culture was not a new issue, as the second passage above from the Reverent Isaac Watts's 1719 translation of the Psalms makes clear. In the preface to his edition, which he termed an "imitation" rather than a translation, Watts poses a key question about Christian identification with the Psalms, asking how Christian readers can "assume to ourselves" the Psalms of David, since they were written by a Jew living in a different time and place. Watts argued that for Christian readers, any reference to the Judaic ("things personal or peculiar to David and the Jews") in the Psalms risked highlighting the essential historical and religious differences between Jews and Christians, thus disrupting Christian readers' poetic and spiritual identification with the Psalms. As a response, Watts's unique translation of the Psalms purges the poems of any Jewish references; in Watt's words, this erasure of all Jewish markings "remove[s] this great Inconvenience" of the Psalms' Jewishness to allow for deeper Christian engagement (vi).

Watts's ambitious project of erasing the Jewishness from the Psalms challenged certain established conventions of Christian scriptural reading that long preceded the eighteenth century. For, throughout Christian history, a variety of interpretative approaches to Jewish texts were designed to render the Judaic legible within Christian epistemology. One such method, typology, maintains the religious authority of the Jewish scriptures, while nevertheless converting Judaic characters and symbols into "types"—figures or precursors to Christ, thus reading Jewish narratives, symbols, and images as foreshadows of Christian "truth." While Christian commentary can often maintain the historical (ancient) Jewishness of biblical texts, it often finds recognizing the contemporary and relevant Jewish meaning of Jewish scripture more challenging. Further, while various interpretative strategies like typology reconceptualize the meaning of Judaic references as figural rather than literal, typology can never fully account for the Jewish origins and authorship of those texts, beyond a dubious strategy of naming Jewish authors as potentially capable of naïve or unknowing Christian prophecy, or, as I discuss below, by recasting the problematic Jewish voice of the Psalms as a divine rather than human utterance.

---

dent" poetic genre while often collapsing various past definitions for lyric (831). When I refer to *lyric* in this chapter, I use it in this nineteenth-century sense of lyric as a category that indicates the heightened value of first-person-voice poetry.

2. I use the terms *Hebrew scriptures* and *Christian scriptures,* working to avoid the problematic anti-Judaic implications in "Old" and "New"; when I do refer to those latter terms in relation to Christian commentators, I put the terms in quotation marks.

What makes Watts's work radical, then, is that it implicitly points to the insufficiency of typology to manage the "inconvenien[t]" Judaic origins of the Psalms for Christian readers. Significantly, Watts's 1719 version of the Psalms went through twenty-nine editions, remaining very popular throughout the nineteenth century with readers across a variety of Christian denominations. However, by the mid-Victorian period, a plethora of other editions and commentaries of the Psalms challenged Watts's methodology, offering different ideas about how to manage the problem of the Psalms' Jewish origins. Exploring some of these editions and commentaries in what follows, I suggest that nineteenth-century Anglican explorations of the Psalter demonstrate an increasingly complicated relationship to the strategy of typology and its figuring of the Judaic as a strategy for containment.

Compounding the complexity of figuring the Judaic in nineteenth-century England was the re-establishment of the Anglo-Jewish community, which marked a new phenomenon of Jewish presence in English history. For, prior to 1780, the Anglo-Jewish community in England was only just re-establishing itself after close to four hundred years of the enforced expulsion of Jews. In Watts's 1719 moment, Jews had been readmitted in England for about thirty years, and were not yet a significant cultural, social, or political presence. By the turn of the nineteenth century, however, a fully viable and thriving Jewish community of over 30,000 was posing real challenges to questions of English national identity through intense debates in Parliament, English society, and the press about the removal of Jewish disability. These debates had been going on since the passage (1753) and subsequent repeal (1754) of the Jewish Naturalization Bill, which proposed removal of some civil disabilities by allowing certain categories of Jewish residents to be naturalized without the taking of the Sacrament. The issues of Anglo-Jewish identity were heightened by the repeal of the Test Act in 1828, which made the Jews the largest religious group in England still denied a set of civil rights. Suddenly, "the Jewish problem," as it was termed, was no longer just a question of figural identities and ancient scriptural representations; by 1800 Jews, living in growing communities and worshipping visibly in England, offered a politically alive, and potentially threatening, manifestation of Jewishness, in contrast to an earlier mythic/abstracted sense of Jewish people and practices.[3]

This chapter engages both nineteenth-century Anglican Psalm interpreters and the Anglo-Jews who spoke out, in a range of responses from vehement to conciliatory, about the Psalms' complex role in Judaism and Christianity

---

3. For more on nineteenth-century Anglo-Jewish history, see Endelman; Ragussis; Ruderman.

and their status as cultural icons of lyric poetry. I read this set of responses to the Psalms as not quite a dialogue, but rather as what critic Mary Louise Pratt has termed a "contact zone," which she defines as "a social spac[e] where cultures meet, clash and grapple with each other, often in highly asymmetrical relations of power" (34). Exploring the nineteenth-century discourses on the Psalms as a contact zone enables a complex vision of Jewish–Christian relations and their intersections with discourses of lyric poetry, while acknowledging those "highly asymmetrical relations of power" that existed between the two groups laying claim to this shared canon of poetry. I ultimately argue that these coexistent but divergent ideas about the Jewish authorship of the Psalms in the Victorian period necessarily entwine with emergent Romantic poetics and its assumptions about how readers might "identify" or sympathize with poetry by a poet of a different identity, culture, religion, or even historical moment.[4] Situating this Jewish–Christian discourse within larger theories of lyric poetry, I seek to connect two particularly urgent "questions" in nineteenth-century English culture: "the Jewish question" and the "what is poetry" question.

II. HEBREW POETICS AND POST-ROMANTIC LYRIC: THE CHALLENGES OF POETIC IDENTIFICATION

Our indebtedness to Hebrew poetry withdrawn, it would be impossible to form any adequate conception of what civilization would have been … (J. B. Selkirk [1878] 162)

There are innumerable moments in nineteenth-century English literary criticism when Psalms are invoked as the highest form of poetry, as the passage from Scottish critic J. B. Selkirk, above, suggests. Selkirk invokes the Psalms not only as central to the formation of civilization but also as a "rebuke" to other forms of contemporary devotional poetry for which he has few kind words. Selkirk's comments are representative of a wide body of critics who likewise see the Psalms as central to the very definition of poetic identity in a Christian culture, and who thus blur the distinctions between poetics and religion, a fusion that Charles LaPorte explores in more depth in the next chapter in this volume.

---

4. It is worth noting that most contemporary accounts of lyric exclude any reference to the Psalms as a source/model despite the importance of this idea in nineteenth-century criticism; see this exclusion in Jackson, Jackson and Prins, and Leighton. I address this issue of the later exclusion of the Psalms as lyric model in the larger project from which this chapter is taken.

Increased nineteenth-century interest in the religious and literary significance of the Psalms is manifest in a vast number of new editions published in the first half of the century. William Chamberlin's *Catalogue of English Bible Translations* notes over 180 editions of the Psalms published between 1800 and 1850; in that same period, just twenty versions of the Song of Solomon and fifteen of Isaiah were published, suggesting that there was what we might call an obsessive interest in the Psalms in the first half of the century. This interest was related to other movements and discourses in the nineteenth century that saw a renewed interest in biblical texts. In particular, new historicizing methods in the field of biblical studies, often termed "the Higher Criticism," put a spotlight on the ancient cultural origins of both Jewish and Christian scriptures, situating them in Near Eastern and specifically Jewish contexts, often challenging (not without controversy) prior constructions of scriptural history. Coinciding with the increasing visibility of a contemporary Anglo-Jewish community, the Higher Critics' re-establishment of "Jewish" contexts for both "Old" and "New" Testaments recast the historical Jewish contexts of texts central to Christian identity.[5]

At roughly the same historical moment, Romantic poetic theory emerged to reconstruct the terms on which lyric poetry should be categorized, read, and theorized, asking important new questions about the relationships between poets and readers. Romantic poets sought to elevate the role of the lyric poet in English culture, suggesting a prophetic ability to describe experiences that while necessarily personal could nevertheless resonate with a broad spectrum of readers as universally true. We can see Wordsworth grappling with this relationship between poet and reader and the construction of universal poetic truth at many moments in his "Preface to *Lyrical Ballads*." He writes:

> In spite of difference of soil and climate, of language and manners, of laws and customs: in spite of things silently gone out of mind, and things violently destroyed; the Poet binds together by passion and knowledge the vast empire of human society, as it is spread over the whole earth, and over all time.... Poetry is the first and last of all knowledge—it is as immortal as the heart of man. (Wordsworth 167)

Here the poet is not bound to a particular identity because his "passion and knowledge" dissolve the distinctions that might emerge from geographical, historical, or cultural differences, those "difference[s] of soil and climate, of language and manners, of laws and customs." Cast precisely as the literary

---

5. For more on the ways nineteenth-century Christian biblical criticism dealt with the Jewish problem, see Manuel and Sheehan, as well as Jeffrey Morrow on Renan in part I.

genre that can voice "immortal" truth not bound by identity or history, lyric poetry becomes fully idealized in Romantic and post-Romantic poetics, central to the development of civilization precisely because it can bridge the gap between differently located individuals and their particular identities. Likewise, as Joshua King reminded me, this particular element of Romantic poetic theory circles back to the work of the Higher Criticism, which also insisted on the human dimension of scriptural texts that nevertheless claimed spiritual authority far beyond their historical moment.

Yet, as I demonstrate in what follows, it was increasingly difficult for Christian clerics and critics to extend to a *Jewish* poet that capacity for universal lyric utterance, that is, utterance that can transcend time, place, and, in this case, religious and ethnic identity in order to speak specifically to Christians. Many other critics and historians before me have drawn links between Higher Criticism and the primarily Anglican Romantic poets;[6] in this chapter, I show how issues of Jewish identity trouble such nineteenth-century biblical and lyric poetics, particularly their assumptions about connections formed between poets and readers by the act of reading lyric poetry. (See Michael Hurley, in this part of the volume, who also calls for renewed scrutiny of nineteenth-century biblical and lyric poetics, suggesting that the impact of biblical scholarship is still insufficiently appreciated in studies of nineteenth-century verse craft and metrics.)

III. "THE MERE DEVOTIONS OF AN EXTINCT RELIGION": FIGURAL AND "REAL" JEWS IN NINETEENTH-CHRISTIAN PSALM CRITICISM

> Unquestionably it is mistaken theology, which would debar Christian nations and statesmen from the instruction afforded by the Jewish Scriptures, under a notion, that the circumstances of that people were altogether peculiar and unique, and therefore irrelevant to every other case. (Keble 129)

In 1833 John Keble preached these words in his famous "National Apostasy" sermon in Oxford. Most read this sermon as a specific response to the Roman Catholic Relief Act of 1829 and the 1828 repeal of the Test Act, which by changing the required oath for government positions to "on the true faith of a Christian" from a specifically Anglican oath, had resulted in Dissenter and Catholic emancipation. Because the repeal of the Test Act did not relieve the restrictions on Jews of England, Jewish emancipation emerged as the next obvious

---

6. See especially Balfour; Hepworth; LaPorte, *Victorian Poets*; Sheehan; Legaspi.

question related to English political and religious diversity. In the passage above, Keble echoes Watts's language of the "peculiar and unique" Jews of the Bible, but countering Watts, he terms it "mistaken theology" to question contemporary Christian identification with Jewish scriptures. Keble's approach to connecting the historical contexts of Jewish scripture and his contemporary moment is a common rhetorical strategy in the nineteenth century; it also speaks to Wordsworth's claim that a poet can in fact bridge those historical or cultural differences. Turning now to other texts of Keble's as well as to those of other Anglican critic-clerics, I explore how this Anglican commitment to the poetics of identification across (religious) difference often falters when confronting the Jewishness of the Psalms.

Though Keble is probably best known for his original series of poems, *The Christian Year* (1827), the single most popular volume of poetry published in the century, in 1839 he published a singularly less popular book of poems, his new translation of the Psalms.[7] Keble's translation took almost the exact opposite approach from Watts's eighteenth-century edition by insisting on maintaining "the tenor of the Hebrew Verity"—that is, a very literal translation of the Hebrew as the most correct form of approaching the Psalms. Keble defends his approach in his preface, explaining how this commitment to literal translation honors the notion that the Psalms are divinely rather than human authored, noting that his edition seeks

> to observe the rule, which He who spake by the Prophets has (if it may be said) appointed for Himself in all His communications to mankind; to disclose, rather than exhibit, His dealings and His will . . . Considering the Psalms especially as divine Poems, this surely is a quality which we should expect to find in them: a certain combination of reserve with openness being of the very essence of poetry: and the Psalms being apparently ordained to leaven the poetry of the whole world, as the history of the Old Testament to be "the Sun of all other histories." (xi)

Here, Keble solves the problem of Davidic (Jewish) authorship, by replacing David's authorship with a larger divine intelligence, "He who spake by the prophets." In addition, Keble's commitment to the Tractarian theory of "reserve" frames scriptural texts as withholding their true meaning from readers not sufficiently enlightened by Christian truth. With the theory of reserve, Keble can dispense with the problem of any simultaneous contemporary Jewish meaning of the Psalms, as, for him, their Jewish context is merely a veil

---

7. For a detailed reading of the impact of *The Christian Year,* see King, *Imagined Spiritual Communities,* chapter 4. See Churton for a somewhat negative review of Keble's translation of the Psalms.

that withholds the true Christian meaning from those not ready to receive it; for Keble, the Psalms model this particular role for biblical poetry, thus "leaven[ing] the poetry of the whole world."

As his collaborator in the development of Tractarian poetics, John Henry Newman shared many of Keble's theories about the scripture and poetics. Yet when Newman turns directly to the problem of the Psalms' Jewish origins in his 1840 sermon "Condition of the Members of the Christian Empire," his engagement with the Psalms reveals some important differences from Keble's approach. Newman begins by noting that "the inspired words of the Prophets of Israel have been in the mouth of the children of grace" for centuries and throughout the world. This formulation echoes Keble's vision of a divine intelligence that animates the Psalms, though it maintains a vague connection to the Psalms' Jewish origins through reference to the "Prophets of Israel." Then, however, Newman goes on to confront the Psalms' Jewishness directly:

> Some free-thinkers have said, what is the book to us, relating, as it does, the history and expressing the feelings of a people who lived two or three thousand years ago? I grant it: if the book of Psalms be but a Jewish book, it is not a Christian book; but the question on which all turns is, whether the Psalms are the mere devotions of an extinct religion or no. (289)

Newman's rephrasing of the "freethinker's" question seems to focus specifically on the ancientness of the Jewish authorship as that which makes the Psalms potentially irrelevant for contemporary Christians. Newman, like Watts, raises the issue of Christian identification when he asks "what is this book to us," given its source from the Psalmist who wrote "two or three thousand years ago?" But Newman presses beyond this issue of historical distance, focusing on the status of Judaism itself when he asks "the question on which all turns": namely, whether the Psalms are "the mere devotions of an extinct religion or no."

Colleagues in this collection have suggested a variety of interpretations of this cryptic phrase, noting that perhaps it refers simply to the idea that the Psalms emerged from an "extinct" context of Israelite Temple rituals that might be considered "extinct" even in contemporary Judaism.[8] However, in asking whether the Psalms "are the mere devotions of an extinct religion," Newman could suggest not only the dangers inherent in allowing the Psalms to remain "Jewish" but also the potential danger of recognizing the contemporary existence of Jews practicing Judaism. Thus, the passage highlights the importance, for Newman, of claiming the Psalms' relevance on exclusively

---

8. Charles LaPorte and Joshua King were very helpful in interpreting this passage.

Christian terms, a claim that necessarily erases the fact that contemporary Anglo-Jews continued to interpret and integrate the Psalms into their present-day Jewish liturgy in ways quite differently—as I chart below—than Newman and his Christian colleagues would understand or support. Ultimately, then, we find an astonishing formulation of Jewish erasure in England in 1840 given the very alive presence of Jews and Judaism, and the energy around the Jewish question at this time.

What does it mean for a major English cleric to talk about Jews and Judaism in these terms, the same year that Isaac Goldsmid was knighted by Queen Victoria, and Lord Shaftesbury proposed a paper to the Foreign Secretary (Palmerston) arguing that supporting a Jewish return to Palestine was in the best interests of English foreign policy? Newman's remarkable approach is (at best) based on blurring and obfuscating the relationship of living Judaism to its ancient roots, and (at worst) a remarkable resistance to the very obvious living status of Judaism in his own day. Not surprisingly, Newman goes on to conclude that the Psalms are not "really" Jewish, and to revalidate the typological method in order to confirm the Psalms as fully Christian, somewhat ironically interpreting this Psalm as prophetically depicting the plight of the embattled Anglican Church in 1840 and the challenges being posed (by non-Anglicans) to its hegemonic status in English culture. His sermon thus demonstrates the integral relationship between *both* Jewish problems: the problem that is explicitly that posed by the Jewish origins of the biblical Psalms and the problem of contemporary Jews in England and the status of their civil rights.

In the same year Newman delivered that sermon, Coleridge's *Confessions of an Inquiring Spirit* (1840) was published posthumously. It was likely written between 1820 and 1824, as it was originally conceived as a preface to *Aids to Reflection*, published in that year.[9] Framed as a series of letters on much broader theological questions, *Confessions* also takes up the problem of the Psalms' Jewish origins, but Coleridge diverges from the Tractarians by insisting on the poetic importance of conceptualizing the Psalmist as a real man rather than simply an instrument of a divine author. Directly challenging the doctrine of the divine dictation of the Psalms, Coleridge asks: "Why should I not believe the Scriptures throughout [were] dictated, in word and thought, by an infallible Intelligence?" His answer is that "the Doctrine in question petrifies at once the whole body of Holy Writ" because it denies that there is a human living breathing body behind the scriptural voice, and he goes on to elaborate on the importance of this point:

---

9. H. J. Jackson and J. R. de J. Jackson discuss the probable dates of composition in their edition of "Confessions of an Inquiring Spirit" in Coleridge's *Shorter Works and Fragments* for the *Collected Works of Samuel Taylor Coleridge*.

This breathing organism, this glorious panharmonicon, which I had seen stand on its feet as a man, and with a man's voice given to it, the Doctrine in question turns at once into a colossal Memnon's head, a hollow passage for a voice, a voice that mocks the voices of many men, and speaks in their names, and yet is but one voice, and the same;—and no man uttered it, and never in a human heart was it conceived. (Coleridge, *Confessions* 51–52)

What troubles Coleridge about this theory of divine intelligence animating scriptural poetry is that such a doctrine removes human agency from that poetic production.[10] Here, Coleridge offers his clear commitments to the Romantic poetics he helped to conceive, a poetic that idealizes the process of "a [real] man speaking to men" as a key component of the ideal lyric process, and in so doing, also seems to commit to recognizing the essential human, and thus Jewish, identity of the Psalmist.

Re-establishing the material body behind the biblical voice as a crucial aspect of poetic identification, Coleridge concludes this section with a specific mention of the Psalmist as a Jew. He describes the distinctly physical relationship of lyric identification—where "every several nerve of emotion, passion, thought, that thrids the flesh-and-blood of our common humanity, responded to the touch," and argues that if he could (wrongly) believe the doctrine of divine dictation, "—that this sweet Psalmist of Israel was himself as mere an instrument as his harp, an automaton poet, mourner, and supplicant;—all is gone,—all sympathy, at least, and all example" (Coleridge, *Confessions* 54–55). For true lyric poetic "sympathy," or identification, with the Psalms, Coleridge describes a distinctly physical relationship of "submission" that a reader makes to the implicitly Jewish body of "sweet Psalmist of Israel."

However, another of Coleridge's texts about reading the Psalms written roughly at the same time counters this idea of "submitting" one's poetic identification to a Jewish body. Importantly, we know that Coleridge had significant relationships with Jews of his own day, specifically Hyman Hurwitz, with whom he corresponded between 1818 and 1830.[11] Coleridge recommended Hurwitz for the professorship of Hebrew at University College, and it was Hurwitz himself who tutored Coleridge in Hebrew so that he could read the Psalms in the original language. Yet, it is specifically Hurwitz as reader, rather

---

10. Joshua King pointed out that while challenging the notion of divine *dictation*, Coleridge was not in conflict with the issue of divine *influence* over scriptural texts. For a more detailed exploration of Coleridge's ideas about the problem of attributing divine authorship to the Bible, see Joshua King's larger analysis of Coleridge's critique of the "bibliolatrous doctrine of infallibility" ("Coleridge's Late Confessions").

11. For more on Hurwitz and his role as poet, see Weisman.

than tutor, who reappears in Coleridge's *Literary Remains,* on the section from "Notes on the Book of Common Prayer," in reference to Psalm 126; Coleridge addresses Hurwitz directly as he likens reading the Psalm to the experience of seeing a "transparency" (a window decoration) that works by having a lamp illuminate its pictures from within the house so that the pictures are visible from without.

> As a transparency on some night of public rejoicing, seen by common day, with the lamps from within removed—even such would the Psalms be to me uninterpreted by the Gospel. O honored Mr. Hurwitz! Could I but make you feel what grandeur, what magnificence, what an everlasting significance and import Christianity gives to every fact of your national history—to every page of your sacred records! ("Notes on the Book of Common Prayer" 28)

In this figure, Christian belief becomes the inner light that is "removed" from the transparency, rendering it less beautiful and meaningful when only seen "by common day." The "lamps from within" thus become Christian orientation, which ultimately illuminates the true value of the Psalms for Coleridge. It is light that is apparently absent when the Psalms are read by Jews themselves, like Hurwitz.

Putting these two interactions between Coleridge and the Psalms together, it seems that Coleridge's idealization of the Psalms depends on a lyric relationship with the human/Jewish Psalmist and the light of the Gospel. And though he relies on a Jewish man (Hurwitz) to teach him to read the Psalms, Hurwitz is ultimately cast in the role quite common in the New Testament as a bad (Jewish) reader of scripture, who does not really understand the grandeur and significance of his Jewish texts because he lacks a Christian orientation.[12] Despite Coleridge's unique articulation of the varied aspects of Jewishness that play into his relationship with the Psalms, his contradictory representations of the Psalms' Jewish identity reflect a pattern in Anglican Psalm criticism at this moment—made possible, I argue, by the interactions between Romantic notions of poetic sympathy and identification, and a coincident revival of the Anglo-Jewish community.

A similar pattern emerges in Henry Hart Milman's monumental *History of the Jews,* first published in 1829, and later revised and republished in 1863 and 1867. In a late chapter on contemporary Jewish history, Milman reiterates that distinct flavor of Christian Psalm reverence that idealizes the Psalms as

---

12. For more on nineteenth-century Christian representations of "bad" Jewish readers, see Scheinberg, "Beloved Ideas Made Flesh."

the highest form of lyric poetry: "what lyric language can refuse to borrow its tone from, and therefore but faintly echo, the devotional Psalms of David, and of those who followed him?" (440). Attributing the power of all "lyric language" that "follow[s]" to David's Psalms, Milman situates the Jewish poet as the primary source for lyric poetry. Yet, in what follows this statement, Milman uses the superiority of the (ancient) Psalms to condemn (contemporary) Jewish poetry: "I may sum up in one word—to be poets, in Europe and in our days, the Jews must cease to be Jews; whether retaining their creed or not, they must abandon their language" (449). Milman's odd formulation of "Jews must cease to be Jews" emerges out of a larger discussion of contemporary Jewish European poets who attempt to write in Hebrew; Milman expands on this idea when he goes on to explain that the Christian convert Heinrich Heine offers the best example of "what Jewish poets can become, if they will, I would that I could in his case say, Christianize (though I believe that Heine's last hours were far different from his earlier ones), at all events fully and entirely Europeanize themselves" (449). Though revered by Anglo-Jews of his time for his generous reading of Jewish history that recognized the legacies of oppression faced by the Jews, Milman does not escape from the pattern I have been revealing in Christian Psalm theory: when Anglican commentators idealize the Psalms as lyric poetry, they end up simultaneously invoking and discrediting contemporary Jewish spiritual or poetic agency, often reverting to a conversionist rhetoric of erasing Jewishness.

IV. ANGLO-JEWISH RESPONSES: PSALM CRITICISM AS "AUTOETHNOGRAPHY"

> Christians, who have written on Jewish affairs, frequently describe customs and opinions as if they solely related to the former state of the Hebrews.... Their code, their creed, and themselves as a people, are now existing as they always existed. With the Israelite everything is ancient, but nothing is obsolete. (Disraeli 3, 7)

In his 1833 *The Genius of Judaism*, Isaac Disraeli directly challenges many of the aforementioned Christian strategies of invoking and discrediting contemporary Jewishness in relation to biblical poetics. Though often critical of the contemporary relevance of orthodox practice, Disraeli articulates a clear connection between biblical Jewishness and contemporary Jews. In the passage above, Disraeli does not treat the issue of poets per se, but his work exemplifies a central strategy of Jewish writers in this period: to reclaim, and refute the Christian methods for reading, Jewish scripture.

Disraeli's approach offers a lens through which to understand other Jewish responses to the Psalms that simultaneously confront and refute hegemonic Christian readings of the Psalms as well. In this sense, nineteenth-century Anglo-Jewish writing on the Psalms can be read as "autoethnographic texts" which Pratt suggests are key features of contact zones: they are "text[s] in which people undertake to describe themselves in ways that engage with the representations others have made of them[—] . . . representations that the so-defined others construct in response to or in dialog with" the dominant cultural mode (Pratt 35). In particular, Pratt describes autoethnographic texts as "involv[ing] a selective collaboration with and appropriation of idioms of the metropolis or the conqueror" rather than texts that simply refute or erase those idioms (35). Pratt's model allows for an understanding of the Christian appropriation of Jewish scriptures as a kind of "conquering" of Jewish culture and scripture to which Jewish writers throughout the ages have responded, both to counter the often-anti-Judaic hegemonic diasporic cultures in which they lived and to bolster Jewish identification in their own often assimilationist communities. In what follows, I chart some specific Anglo-Jewish responses to the Psalms and Christian Psalm criticism.

Selig Newman (1788–1871) was a German-born rabbi serving the Jewish community in Plymouth and teaching Hebrew at Oxford to Christians, though he was barred from a formal professorship as a Jew. His most famous work seems to have been published after his departure for New York, where he published *The Challenge Accepted: A Dialogue Between A Jew And A Christian: The Former Answering A Challenge Thrown Out By The Latter, Respecting The Accomplishment Of The Prophecies Predictive Of The Advent Of Jesus* (1850). Strikingly, the argument Selig Newman makes in 1850, specifically about Psalm 110, echoes many of the ideas of a precursor, Solomon Bennett, who published *The Constancy Of Israel: An Unprejudiced Illustration of Some Of The Most Important Texts Of The Bible: Or A Polemical, Critical, And Theological Reply To A Public Letter, By Lord Crawford, Addressed To The Hebrew Nation* (1809). Both Newman's and Bennett's analyses of Psalm 110 deny that the Psalm refers prophetically to the advent of Jesus Christ, using a variety of interpretive and rhetorical arguments to make their case.

Bennett's reading of this Psalm 110 focuses specifically on Christian commentators' faulty translations of Hebrew as the basis of their readings. He notes: "I will only say in general, that they have corrupted and altered nouns, verbs, tenses, and syntax, and accordingly changed the proper meaning. I will then only present the original Hebrew text with a literal translation, the contrast will then appear very striking, and the text will defend my explanation against those of contrary opinion" (Bennett 62). Likewise, Selig Newman turns to what Keble referred to as the "veracity of the Hebrew," while nevertheless coming to a very different conclusion about the Psalm's meaning than Keble did. As we might imagine Hurwitz did in his role as Coleridge's tutor, these Jewish Hebrew scholars assert a particular kind of authority with the originary language of the Bible as part of their refutation of Christian co-optation of the Psalms' meaning. Establishing their superior grasp of Hebrew, they correct certain historical misconceptions about the Psalms, often calling on Talmudic sources to bolster their historical authority. Bennett challenges the notion of both Davidic or prophetic authorship of the Psalms: "It is observable, that the Psalms were not all composed by David himself, many of them were written by different Levitical Poets; as Asaph, Hyman, Jeduthun, &c. They consist of prayers, hymns, prosody, &c. alluding to various circumstances of public or private facts" (62). Arguing that the Psalms were authored by various Jews and represent specific historical or religious aspects of ancient Jewish life, Bennett highlights the human production behind the poems as a way to deny any prophetic claims to Jesus. This strategy also creates a distance between the notion of the Psalms as a model for universalized or immortal lyric poetry, focusing instead on their (Jewish) historical specificity. Selig Newman similarly uses the Jewish voice in his literary dialogue to challenge the Christian voice's idea that the Psalms prophesize about Jesus. He also has the Jewish voice challenge the idea that David authored all the Psalms:

> No one could be astonished more than David himself, could you tell him in what sense you apply the said Psalm to him. His answer would surely be, "My friend, this Psalm is neither my composition, nor is it a prophecy at all. Besides, you do me too much honor; you know that I never was a Prophet, and on all occasions, whether in favor or out of favor with God, he only spoke to me through one of the Prophets, Samuel, Nathan, or Gad." (S. Newman 28)

Recreating David's voice to refute the possibility of his own prophetic utterance, Selig Newman uses this point that David did not author the Psalms to challenge the Christian voice, which assumes the poet to be David, and therefore argues that if David calls his offspring "My Lord" he must be making reference to Jesus. The Jewish voice offers a different reading, in which the reference to "My Lord" is not spoken by David but addresses David; thus, the voice of the Psalms cannot be referring to any future lineage of David's that might lead to Jesus. Bennett and Newman situate the Psalms in specific historical and cultural Jewish contexts that, for them, are neither transcendent, universally Christian nor even particularly literary.

Grace Aguilar was perhaps the most renowned Jewish writer of the day, but when we compare her ideas on the Psalms with those of the Jewish men of her day, it becomes clear that as a woman, she cannot adopt these same strategies of linguistic and historical scholarly expertise, a subject Richa Dwor treats in part II of this volume in her discussion of the historical and cultural challenges that Anglo-Jewish women writers faced in this period. Aguilar's work asserts Jewish ownership of Jewish texts, but she diverges from her Jewish male counterparts through her reverence for Romantic poetics.[13] As a starting place, Aguilar stands firm in her insistence that the "Old Testament" is a Jewish book. In Aguilar's *The Jewish Faith* (1846), a volume of fictional letters in the voice of an older Jewish woman to a younger Jewish girl considering Christian conversion, the narrator asserts: "We must remember the Old Testament is ours. That of the glorious truths it reveals, and the precepts it bestows, no one can deprive us, unless we disregard them ourselves, and, by indifference and neglect, permit others to think we have neither right nor interest in them" (359). Having made this claim, Aguilar goes on to recast and reconstruct the issues around Jewish identity, lyric poetry, and Christian interpretation to create her own complex response to the contact zone of the Psalms in nineteenth-century England.

In *The Jewish Faith,* Aguilar maintains the notion of Davidic authorship of the Psalms, interrogating the role of David as man, a poet, or prophet. Aguilar writes:

> It has been objected, that David was neither a law-giver, nor a prophet, but merely a man like ourselves; and his words and experiences, therefore, are of no more weight than those of any other man. But the fallacy of this opinion is proved, not only from the thousand and thousand years, during which those Psalms have been acknowledged as inspired prayer and praise; but because there never has arisen any other man to write the same, or sacred poems in any way resembling them. (142–43)

---

13. Aguilar makes many complex connections to Romantic poetics in her writing that other critics have examined in depth. See Dwor, *Jewish Feeling*; Galchinsky; Page; Scheinberg, "Judaism."

Countering the approach of Selig Newman and Solomon Bennett, Aguilar upholds a notion of Davidic authorship, focusing on David as a [Jewish] "man" whose poetry has never been replicated as it has maintained its meaning over thousands of years. Thus, unlike her Jewish male counterparts, Aguilar retains the Romantic language of the "inspired" special man/poet to describe the Psalms, and like the Anglican critics, upholds the Psalms as idealized and unique poetic models.

Yet, while upholding a Coleridgean notion of David as the great human poet of the Psalms, Aguilar diverges from Romantic poetics when interpreting the Psalms in nineteenth-century England. In a posthumously published work, *Sabbath Thoughts and Sacred Communings* (1853), Aguilar directly challenges the sermon of an Anglican minister ("Mr. Anderson"), who reads Psalm 22 as a prophecy about Jesus Christ—a convention in Christian readings. Psalm 22 includes the famous lines—"My God, my God, why hast thou forsaken me?" (Ps. 22:1, Matt. 27:46, AV)—uttered by Jesus on the cross in the Gospels of Matthew and Mark, and it describes the mocking oppressors, "dogs," "lions," and "wild oxen" who torment the speaker, details Mr. Anderson reads as evidence that the Psalms refers to Christ's suffering on the cross. In her response, Aguilar "endeavor[s] to meet Mr. Anderson's arguments with others, that would render the same Psalm equally prophetic of my faith" and notes:

> And though Mr. Anderson laid much stress on these words being exactly descriptive of the mode of punishment inflicted upon Christ, they cannot appear as anything to me, but as figurative of the tortures inflicted on us by the barbarous nations amongst whom we have been scattered, when indeed our hands and feet were pierced, for we were tortured to give up our faith, or to disclose our hidden treasures. (5)

Aguilar upholds the notion of the Psalms' lyric value across historical periods and reclaims the Jewish convention of reading the Psalms as prophetic of later Jewish, rather than Christian history. Her reference to the forced "disclos[ure of] our hidden treasures" as a marker of Jewish oppression in the Diaspora seems a particularly apt figure to describe the Christian appropriation of Jewish scriptural poetry. Aguilar renews her interpretive authority to claim those treasures in her conclusion to the essay: "had I never heard Mr. Anderson preach on this beautiful Psalm, I might have read and read again, and never thought it prophetic; but hearing how he took it to support his faith, it led me to examine and think, for somewhat wherewith to defend my belief." Aguilar, unlike Selig Newman and Bennett, has no problem adapting Christian methodologies for reading Psalms, even as she comes to very different, specifically Jewish conclusions about their meaning.

V. CONCLUSIONS

> What are the consequences of recognizing that conversion is at once the master trope of a powerful genre (comedy) and the master institution of a powerful culture (Christianity)? (Ragussis 78)

> Determining the boundary between "Judaism" and "Christianity" became a critical concern for all of Christian aesthetics, and ... as a result, Judaism became a critical term that could threaten all "Christian" art. (Nirenberg 389)

In *Figures of Conversion: "The Jewish Question" and English National Identity* (1995), Michael Ragussis posed the idea that the genre of comedy itself embodies an explicitly Christian structure through its emphasis on conversion of personal identity. My thinking in this chapter owes an obvious debt to Ragussis's powerful claims about the relationships between generic and theological structures, claims that historian David Nirenberg broadens in his theory of how the presence of the Judaic in Christian culture necessarily threatens Christian aesthetics. This sense of the dangerous Judaic, I have argued, was eminently present in nineteenth-century England and contributed to the complex contortions that Christian commentators made to maintain the religious and artistic relevance of the Psalms for Christian culture, while finding ways to reject, co-opt or convert the specificity of the Psalms' Jewish origins. As Anglo-Jewish commentators sought to reclaim their scriptural poetry for specifically Jewish purposes, their responses both challenged and embodied this sense of the "dangerous" Judaic impulse as they rebutted and recreated assumptions about scripture, poetry, and Jewishness in nineteenth-century English Christian culture.

This chapter has sought to represent the "contact zone" of nineteenth-century English religious and literary cultures, focusing on how the biblical Psalms galvanize a set of intersecting discourses—scriptural criticism, lyric poetry, and Jewish/Judaic identity—that converge in this moment. The question on which all turns, to return to John Henry Newman's formulation, is not whether the Psalms can be both Christian and Jewish poetry, for history has already deemed they must be both. Rather, this chapter has explored how the very possibility of that shared interpretative legacy affects theories of lyric (Christian) universality being developed in nineteenth-century England that continue to exert a powerful influence over theories of literary value.

If the genre of lyric poetry is understood as successful through its capacity to generate universal truth across a potentially diverse set of readers, as Romantic lyric theory argues, then the capacity of the Psalms to maintain both specifically Christian and Judaic truth simultaneously might at first glance seem to represent the triumph of the Psalms as lyric models. But for Christian commentators, the maintenance of Jewish meaning represents an ironic failure of lyric to realize Christian universalist claims, whereas for Jewish commentators, the capacity of the Psalms to generate Christian truth always threatens Jewish identity. Thus, the problem of the Psalms' Jewish origins is not only a manifestation of the anti-Judaic aesthetics that mark so much of Christian culture; the "Jewish problem" of the Psalms ultimately becomes a larger problem of lyric identification. For the "success" of the Psalms in these nineteenth-century Christian contexts comes at the moment they can erase the particularity of their (Jewish) source to speak to a supposed "universal" Christian identity. Yet in a Jewish context, the Psalms represent only that particular Jewish moment and articulation of Jewish identity; if they make claims to a poetic truth other than that of their historical sources, Jewish commentators insist in a variety of ways that the truth remains specifically Jewish.

This reading of the Psalms is, of course, possible because of the many ways in which nineteenth-century England blurred the lines between religion and poetry, as Charles La Porte and J. Barton Scott also explore in their chapters of this volume. Yet beyond a notion of blurred discursive boundaries, I have tried to suggest here how the very understanding of the genre of lyric poetry in the nineteenth century depended upon a particular Christian assumption about the possibility of a "universal" poetry, that ultimately assumes a Christian perspective. It is the presence of the unconverted and particular Jew who insistently ruptures that religious and generic premise; thus, at the moment of a resurgence in actual Jewish presence in England, the problem of the lyric in the shared poetic canon of the Psalms becomes more urgent.[14]

Ultimately, I suggest, along with Ragussis, that genre has never been a neutral or purely formal category. In the case of the Psalms, their idealized status as lyric poetry, coupled with their Jewish origins, creates a particularly rich contact zone that connects the discourses of both biblical (textual) and contemporary Jewish–Christian relations. Unraveling these connections highlights the problem inherent in the politics of (Christian) lyric itself: how do readers from different historical or religious or gendered identities find shared truth claims in texts that emanate from particular and other historical, religious, and cultural origins? Posing this question highlights how the problem of Jewish difference, and its complicated religious historical and textual relationship to Christian identity, has posed particular challenges for English

---

14. Weisman offers another exploration of Anglo-Jewish engagement with the genre of elegy in relation to Jewish–Christian relations.

literary history and critical method.[15] Acknowledging the *literary* implications of the rise of the Anglo-Jewish community, we can better recognize how integrally linked the dynamics of nineteenth-century Jewish–Christian relations were to English literary history. With this acknowledgment, we are perhaps better able to understand how the modern construction of the secular literary *canon* in English has never been a completely secular process, just as the term suggests.

WORKS CITED

Aguilar, Grace. *The Jewish Faith: Its Spiritual Consolation, Moral Guidance, and Immortal Hope, with a Brief Notice of the Reasons for Many of Its Ordinances and Prohibitions.* 1846. Philadelphia, L. Johnson, 1864.

———. *Sabbath Thoughts and Sacred Communings.* London, Groombridge and Sons, 1853.

Balfour, Ian. *The Rhetoric of Romantic Prophecy.* Stanford UP, 2002.

Bennett, Solomon. *The Constancy of Israel. An Unprejudiced Illustration of Some of the Most Important Texts of the Bible; Or a Polemical, Critical and Theological Reply to a Public Letter, by Lord Crawford, Addressed to the Hebrew Nation.* London, W. H. Wyatt, Pickett Street, Temple Bar, 1809.

Chamberlin, William J. *Catalogue of English Bible Translations: A Classified Bibliography of Versions and Editions including Books, Parts, and Old and New Testament Apocrypha and Apocryphal Books.* Greenwood, 1991.

Churton, Edward. *The Book of Psalms in English Verse: And in Measures Suited for Sacred Music.* Oxford, J. H. Parker, 1854.

Coleridge, Samuel Taylor. *Confessions of an Inquiring Spirit and Some Miscellaneous Pieces.* London, W. Pickering, 1840.

———. *Shorter Works and Fragments.* Vol. 2, edited by H. J. Jackson and J. R. de J. Jackson, Princeton UP, 1995.

Coleridge, Samuel Taylor, William G. T. Shedd, Henry Nelson Coleridge, Sara Coleridge Coleridge, and James Marsh. "Literary Remains: Notes on the Book of Common Prayer." *The Complete Works of Samuel Taylor Coleridge: With an Introductory Essay upon His Philosophical and Theological Opinions.* Vol. 5, New York, Harper & Bros., 1884, pp. 21–28.

Disraeli, Isaac. *The Genius of Judaism.* London, E. Moxon, 1833.

Dwor, Richa. *Jewish Feeling: Difference and Affect in Nineteenth-Century Jewish Women's Writing.* Bloomsbury Publishing, 2017.

Endelman, Todd M. *The Jews of Georgian England: 1714–1830: Tradition and Change in a Liberal Society.* U of Michigan, 1999.

---

15. Many essays in Sheila Spector's volume *Romanticism/Judaica: A Convergence of Cultures* explore new methodologies for integrating Anglo-Jewish literature into English literary-critical traditions. See especially Scrivener. See also J. Barton Scott in this volume for his cogent analysis of the protestant [sic] bias in the study of religion, which I would argue (and Scott implies) necessarily affects the history of literary criticism as well—a conclusion also suggested by Mark Knight in this volume.

Galchinsky, Michael. *The Origin of the Modern Jewish Woman Writer: Romance and Reform in Victorian England*. Wayne State U, 1996.

Hepworth, Brian. *Robert Lowth*. Twayne, 1978.

Jackson, Virginia. "Lyric." *The Princeton Encyclopedia of Poetry and Poetics*. 4th ed., edited by Roland Green et al., Princeton UP, 2012, pp. 826-34.

Jackson, Virginia, and Yopie Prins. "General Introduction." *The Lyric Theory Reader: A Critical Anthology*, edited by Virginia Jackson and Yopie Prins, Johns Hopkins UP, 2014, pp. 1-8.

Keble, John. "National Apostasy" (1833). *Sermons, Academical and Occasional*. 2nd ed., Oxford, John Henry Parker, 1848.

———. *The Psalter or Psalms of David*. 2nd ed., Oxford and London: James Parker and Co., 1839.

King, Joshua. "Coleridge's Late Confessions: Personification, Convention, and Free Agency." *Romanticism and Victorianism on the Net*, vol. 62, October 2012, http://ravonjournal.org

———. *Imagined Spiritual Communities in Britain's Age of Print*. The Ohio State UP, 2015.

LaPorte, Charles. *Victorian Poets and the Changing Bible*. U of Virginia P, 2011.

Legaspi, Michael C. *The Death of Scripture and the Rise of Biblical Studies*. Oxford UP, 2010.

Leighton, Angela. "Lyric and the Lyrical." *The Cambridge History of Victorian Literature*, edited by Kate Flint, Cambridge UP, 2012, pp. 151-71.

Lowth, Robert, G. Gregory, and C. E. Stowe. *Lectures on the Sacred Poetry of the Hebrews*. Boston, Crocker & Brewster, 1829.

Manuel, Frank E. *The Broken Staff: Judaism through Christian Eyes*. Harvard UP, 1992.

Milman, Henry Hart. *The History of the Jews: From the Earliest Period down to Modern Times*. 3rd ed., vol. 3, London, J. Murray, 1863.

Newman, John Henry. "Condition of the Members of the Christian Empire." *Sermons Bearing on Subjects of the Day*, London, Printed for J. G. F. & J. Rivington, 1843, pp. 288-309.

Newman, Selig. *The Challenge Accepted; A Dialogue between a Jew and a Christian: The Former Answering a Challenge Thrown Out by the Latter, Respecting the Accomplishment of the Prophecies Predictive of the Advent of Jesus*. New York, Isaacs and Solomon, 1850.

Nirenberg, David, "The Judaism of Christian Art." *Judaism and Christian Art: Aesthetic Anxieties from the Catacombs to Colonialism*, edited by Herbert L. Kessler and David Nirenberg, U of Pennsylvania P, 2011, pp. 387-428.

Page, Judith W. "Grace Aguilar's Victorian Romanticism." Spector 85-98.

Pratt, Mary Louise. "Arts of the Contact Zone." *Profession*, 1991, pp. 33-40.

Ragussis, Michael. *Figures of Conversion: "The Jewish Question" and English National Identity*. Duke UP, 1995.

Ruderman, David B. *Jewish Enlightenment in an English Key: Anglo-Jewry's Construction of Modern Jewish Thought*. Princeton UP, 2000.

Scheinberg, Cynthia. "'The Beloved Ideas Made Flesh': *Daniel Deronda* and Jewish Poetics." *ELH*, vol. 77, no. 3, 2010, pp. 813-39.

———. "'Judaism Rightly Reverenced': Grace Aguilar's Theological Poetics." *Women's Poetry and Religion in Victorian England Jewish Identity and Christian Culture*. Cambridge UP, 2009, pp. 146-89.

Scrivener, Michael. "Rethinking Margin and Center in Anglo-Jewish Literature." Spector 157-68.

Selkirk, J. B. "The Correlation of the Religious and Poetical Instincts." *Ethics and Aesthetics of Modern Poetry.* London, Smith, Elder, 1878, pp. 155–200.

Sheehan, Jonathan. *The Enlightenment Bible: Translation, Scholarship, Culture.* Princeton UP, 2005.

Spector, Sheila A. *Romanticism/Judaica: A Convergence of Cultures.* Ashgate, 2011.

Watts, Isaac. *The Psalms of David, Imitated in the Language of the New Testament and Applied to the Christian State and Worship.* 1719. London, printed by J. Barker, 1784.

Weisman, Karen. "Mourning, Translation, Pastoral: Hyman Hurwitz and Literary Authority." Spector, pp. 45–55.

Wordsworth, William. *The Prose Works of William Wordsworth.* Vol. 1, edited by W. J. B. Owen and Jane Worthington Smyser, Oxford UP, 1974.

CHAPTER 13

Postsecular English Studies and Romantic Cults of Authorship

CHARLES LAPORTE

ENGLISH DEPARTMENTS have never fully escaped the religious cultures that prevailed at the time of their emergence in the nineteenth century. The pervasiveness of religion during this era makes it perverse to take up any one example, but we could do worse than "The Study of Poetry" (1880), in which Matthew Arnold famously contrasts the deteriorating fortunes of Christianity with the rosy future of poetics, assuring his readers that the growth of latter will make up for the loss of the former:

> The future of poetry is immense, because in poetry, where it is worthy of its high destinies, our race, as time goes on, will find an ever surer and surer stay. There is not a creed which is not shaken, not an accredited dogma which is not shown to be questionable, not a received tradition which does not threaten to dissolve.... But for poetry the idea is everything; the rest is a world of illusion, of divine illusion. Poetry attaches its emotion to the idea; the idea is the fact. The strongest part of our religion to-day is its unconscious poetry. (Ward xvii)

Scholars often invoke Arnold in histories of literary professionalization and of European secularization alike, so this quotation offers a convenient place to start. Prior to "The Study of Poetry," Arnold had spent a decade championing the implications of the Higher Criticism and (though it does not necessarily follow) doing battle with old-time religion in studies like *Literature and Dogma* (1873) and *God and the Bible* (1875). Yet it will be clear from the above that Arnold concerns himself with the transformation of Jewish and Christian impulses, rather than their eradication (King 99; McKelvy 1–2).

In short, Arnold dismisses the dogmatic and supernatural aspects of religion while promoting poetic inspiration as the best and strongest part of religion's legacy. If his theology smacks of secularism, his secularism remains theological. I do not mean by this merely that Arnold was mistaken in his suggestion that traditional religion might soon disappear from the world during his lifetime (it didn't), nor that his stance on poetry here and throughout remains richly sermonic (it does). I mean that his very ideas about secularity rely upon a discourse borrowed from theology: of destiny (or "destinies"), of the divine, of that "surer stay" upon which we may rest our souls. (Several chapters in this volume speak to an association of religion and poetry ubiquitous in nineteenth-century culture: Michael Ledger-Lomas on Queen Victoria's devotional attitudes to Tennyson, Richa Dwor on Grace Aguilar's lyric conflation of genius and religion, Mark Knight on Wilde's "Ballad of Reading Gaol," Cynthia Scheinberg on the interreligious complexities of Victorian criticism of the Psalms, Michael Hurley and Peter Otto on the poetics of Gerard Manley Hopkins and William Blake.) Many scholars now urge that something similar might be claimed of all secularism: it remains forever imbricated with religious culture because it is oppositional in nature rather than a supposedly neutral space of freedom (Asad; Pecora, *Secularization and Cultural Criticism*; Taylor, *Secular Age*; Warner, VanAntwerpen, and Calhoun). If such scholars are right, then secularization must remain a movement "without end," as Vincent Pecora puts it in a monograph of that title (*Secularization without End*). And even should we hesitate to make claims about the future of secularization, still the past of literary studies, at least in the West, demonstrates just what Pecora describes: a field whose agonistic relationship with its own religious history tends to disguise the unifying threads that underlie and hold together that complex legacy.

The first part of this chapter addresses how secular literary criticism, which often represents itself as a break from the religious past, actually tends to perpetuate devotional attitudes to literature endemic to Victorian literary criticism, or what William McKelvy calls "the English Cult of Literature." In the chapter's second part, I revisit amateur literary criticism of the fin de siècle to consider what this prehistory suggests about the university English departments that come to supersede it, or what we might learn by revisiting a quaintly and unabashedly religious prehistory of the field. In doing so, I hope to explore the question not merely of whether literary studies can ever be fully secularized, but also of whether this is a reasonable desire. My third section brings the first two parts together. There remains a significant sense in which we in literary studies have never been secular, to repurpose a well-known phrase of Bruno Latour's. Nonetheless, if we can agree that academic literary study has been, upon balance, a good thing—and I hope that most scholars can do so—then its theological underpinnings may not be the problem that we keep imagining them to be. The rich and insightful legacy of literary studies, that is, may be said to justify itself.

I. SECULAR SCRIPTURES

First, a brief history of the academic profession. When English departments as we now know them first arose in the Victorian fin de siècle, they made it their business to professionalize the study of English and divorce it from casual reading, belle-lettrism, and amateur literary societies. Literary scholars made reading into an art and a science quite literally by placing their departments in colleges of arts and sciences. And as the field matured, first early- and then mid-twentieth-century critics distanced themselves from their forebears, whom they tended to portray as unsystematic, idiosyncratic, and given to religious enthusiasm. Casual reading still endured, of course, and belle-lettrism flourished both beyond and within the gates of the academy, but it also became reduced to a subplot of the academic story, and fashionable critics tended to dismiss its flowers as mere weeds. Each generation offered newer, ever more "scientific" sets of hermeneutics. This should be obvious to anyone who has studied the New Critics in an American context, or of F. R. Leavis and the *Scrutiny* crowd in a British context, or the Russian Formalists in a European one: collectively, the folks who gave English departments close reading.

The emergence of newer literary sciences (or "sciences") nonetheless always served to create its own cultic attitudes. The New Critics redeemed and renewed Arnold's cult of literature despite themselves; Cleanth Brooks and W. K. Wimsatt decried "Arnoldian prophecy" much as critics of the later twentieth-century would decry their methods (Arac 117; Guillory 186–96). Leavis's ostensibly secular stance was irresistible to many of a religious cast of mind; "He is what our mothers would have called CHAPEL," snorted Maurice Bowra (Hilliard 75).[1] And when such midcentury critics made way for new

---

1. Bowra's remark identifies Leavis with Dissenting traditions, but Christopher Hilliard reminds us of Leavis's High Church and Catholic followers, as well (82–85).

avant-garde critical movements like deconstruction and new historicism, the same issues recurred all over again.

Take the case of Northrop Frye, an ordained minister in the United Church of Canada, who would respond to the New Criticism in 1957 by insisting that "everyone who has seriously studied literature knows that the mental process involved is as coherent and progressive as the study of science" (*Anatomy* 10–11). Frye's claim, by no means self-evident, is typical of an epoch that regularly aspired to boost the status of literary studies by hitching them to an unrelated field. (In such moments, it is tempting to apply to Frye his own description of James G. Frazer, "who thought he was a scientist because he had read so much anthropology"; Frye, *Great Code* 35.) But Frye's "scientific" approach is also an ongoing hermeneutic investigation into what he will come to call in a later book *The Secular Scripture* (1976). Harold Bloom then smirks at Frye for becoming a canonizer in the vein of Arnold but turns about to spend the rest of his long career promoting kabbalistic, gnostic, and "bardolatrous" approaches to literature (Bloom, *Kabbalah and Criticism*; *Shakespeare*). And so with other postwar theorists. Paul de Man chastises Frank Kermode for hinting that "the teaching of literature, in the university, should be a substitution for or a complement to the teaching of religion" (Quoted in Knight, 155). But Robert Scholes can later accuse de Man and the Yale deconstructionists of a "still more desperate and constricted attempt to keep the transcendental aura of literature alive" (*Rise and Fall* 28). Scholes repudiates de Man and Bloom as de Man and Bloom repudiated Kermode and Frye. John Guillory repudiates the New Critics as the New Critics repudiated Arnold and the Victorian Browning Societies. Clearly, this whole process is endlessly repeatable, for each generation of literary high priests and hierophants can be pooh-poohed by the high priests and hierophants of the next generation.

The openly acknowledged theological dimension that we see reflected in the generation of Arnold thus spends the entire twentieth century behind a sort of moving wall; it reappears only as each new generation of scholars deprecates the metaphysical recidivism of its predecessor, which has somehow gone back to doing theology again—or never left off. The most prestigious elements of the twentieth-century English professorate amount to what Scholes calls in *The Rise and Fall of Literature* (1998) "a clergy without a dogma, teaching sacred texts without a God" (27). (And the overwhelming maleness of the priestly line traced above may be no coincidence.) Scholes himself urges that we take the extreme step of excising the term "literature" from our vocabularies in order to exorcise our cultic ghosts. Wonderfully, though, in an instance of just the sort of recidivism that I wish to outline, his follow-up book, *English after the Fall* (2011), not only revisits the objectionable term *literature* but actually recommends that the field of English must be renewed through the teaching of "sacred texts" (53–88). Sooner or later, such iconoclasm always manifests its kinship to holy zeal.

It is a real curiosity of literary studies, indeed, that the field so regularly denounces its own most basic premises. Consider the classic essay "The Death of the Author" (1967), in which Roland Barthes opines that to approach the œuvre of a given author *as such* is already to indulge in a sort of theological, implicitly Judeo-Christian, activity.

> We know now that a text consists not of a line of words, releasing a single "theological" meaning (the "message" of the Author-God), but of a multi-dimensional space, in which are married and contested several writings, none of which is original. (52–53)

Or take a far more recent twenty-first-century call for distant reading, in which the Marxist critic Franco Moretti condemns close reading *as such*:

> The trouble with close reading (in all of its incarnations, from the new criticism to deconstruction) is that it necessarily depends on an extremely small canon. . . . [Y]ou invest so much in individual texts *only* if you think that very few of them really matter. Otherwise, it doesn't make sense. And if you want to look beyond the canon . . . close reading will not do it. . . . At bottom, it's a theological exercise—very solemn treatment of very few texts taken very seriously. (57)

Both Barthes and Moretti seek to demystify literature. Neither says a lot about what makes a reading "theological" because both invoke it as a term of opprobrium. For them, it goes without saying that theology is very bad indeed, and that to call something theological ought to put it beyond the pale. But observe how that which a Victorian like Arnold would call "inspiration" here becomes so awfully threatening that we are called upon to throw out the most fundamental parts of our literary criticism in our attempts to supersede it: we must first deny that literary works have authors (Barthes) and then drop minute investigations into what a text actually says (Moretti). These suggestions are akin to Scholes's idea that we must abandon the very idea of literature lest we find ourselves seduced into some kind of theological backsliding. I link them in part because Barthes's essay is already fifty years old, whereas Moretti's essay is relatively recent. But it is only a matter of time before someone denounces Moretti in his turn as performing some kind of covert theology.[2]

---

2. UPDATE: Since this chapter has been in press, Moretti has indeed been identified (though not denounced) as a theologian *malgré lui* in Matthew Wickman's fine *PMLA* article "Theology Still?"

We have seen this game play out before. When twenty-first-century authors caution us against theologizing in our criticism, they go through the motions of a predictable routine.

Nothing that I have claimed to this point is especially controversial. To the contrary, one might fault me for rehearsing an old song and dance.[3] Yet my point pertains to this fact: precisely to the *routine* nature of the song and dance, with its aspirational (but never fully realized) secularity. Twentieth-century literary criticism grew up in the shadow of its own unacknowledged God, and twenty-first-century critics who offer to help take us out of that shadow repeat a weary rhetorical appeal. But what if devotional attitudes can be imagined to present a perfectly appropriate human approach to literature? Indeed, what if we return to them inescapably because, in the end, they possess some (if merely psychological) validity or what philosophers in the pragmatic tradition of William James call usefulness? To take seriously Barthes, Scholes, and Moretti, we ought to grant that by their own logic, the overwhelming majority of modern literary study today remains intractably theological, concerned as it is with authors and with the meaning of artistic expressions.

What happens if we hesitate to devalue the scholarly field in so cavalier a fashion? Let us consider whether literary study might be a sadly impoverished endeavor if we collectively banned from its purview the concepts of authorship, literature, and close reading. Let us consider the possibility that Barthes, Scholes, and Moretti might be perfectly correct in their analyses but wrong in their value judgments about them. Maybe theological thinking is a *sine qua non* for certain very basic kinds of human understanding; maybe "atheism is by no means as easy as it looks," as Terry Eagleton has recently argued (viii). (This is to say nothing of my fellow contributors' point that religion remains a required context for historical literatures.) Maybe literary study is on some level intractably theological but not less valuable for that. Maybe it brings out the best parts of theology and redeems its most compelling elements in a fuller and richer legacy than Arnold himself could have imagined. Such possibilities take us back in intriguing ways to the attitudes of our Victorian predecessors, who suddenly merit a serious reconsideration.

II. THE VICTORIAN POET AS PROPHET

Amateur literary criticism from the Victorian era, like its professional academic counterpart (and successor), develops in part through a struggle

---

3. For an alternative, though compatible, account of this history, see Branch, "Rituals of our Re-Secularization."

with religious ways of thinking that it associates with rules and fixity, hence Arnold's pointed contrast between "literature" and "dogma." Victorian criticism privileges devotional reading, however, instead of suspending it. It neither uses theology as a term of opprobrium nor takes its presence as a sign that things have gone awry. Arnold sometimes seems to conceive of his own criticism as an escape from theology as such, but so too did contemporaries whose religiously inflected criticism became a byword for future generations of critics. Consider the following passage from Dorothea Beale's 1882 paper for the London Browning Society, "The Religious Teaching of Browning":

> Browning seems to me a prophet whom God has given to our storm-tost age, a pilot who has learnt by long experience the hidden rocks and sandbanks on which the vessel of faith may be wrecked, now that the old anchor chains are burst asunder. An infallible Church, an infallible Book, an infallible Pope, all these have failed us—failed us that, rejecting the stones of the desert, we may learn that man doth not live by bread alone, but by the word of God. (Browning Society [London] 326)

I do not have space here to get into the ins and outs of Beale's position on what makes something prophetic; suffice it to point out that for her "the word of God" includes the poetry of Robert Browning, whom she identifies as "a prophet." Many Victorians took Browning for a kind of prophet, indeed—as they did Elizabeth Barrett Browning and Lord Tennyson (LaPorte; Peterson). More importantly for us, however, Beale's position mirrors that of Arnold in the same historical moment. Whether or not Beale knew of Arnold's essay, she precisely reproduces what Michael Kaufmann calls the "Arnoldian replacement theory": Christian dogma is in shambles, but poetry offers us a limitless supply of new prophets and new scriptures (Kaufmann 621). Indeed, we could swap out whole phrases from Arnold and replace them with Beale, or vice versa, and few scholars would be the wiser. For both writers capitalize upon the Romantic cult of literary genius, which had reached a fevered pitch in the mid-nineteenth century: a notion that great literary artists are "celestial genius[es]" who "descend among men" with heaven-borne messages, as Goethe puts it in *Wilhelm Meister's Apprenticeship* (307; see Scheinberg's analysis, in the preceding chapter, of how this Romantic notion of the poet shaped nineteenth-century debates about the Psalms and their Jewishness).

From our vantage, Beale's views may seem overheated, but they were widely shared at the Browning Society meetings. As the biblical critic Brooke Foss Westcott proclaimed to the Cambridge Browning Society in that same year of 1882,

All life, all nature, is . . . the legitimate field of the poet, as prophet[.] There is an infinite, an eternal, meaning in all, and it is his office to make this intelligible to his students. . . . No modern poet has more boldly claimed the fullness of his heritage of life than Browning. He has dared to look on the darkest and meanest forms of action and passion, from which we commonly and rightly turn our eyes, and he has brought back for us from this universal survey a conviction of hope. . . . He has laid bare what there is in man of sordid, selfish, impure, corrupt, brutish, and he proclaims in spite of every disappointment and every wound, that he still finds a spiritual power in him, answering to a spiritual power without him, which restores assurance as to the destiny of creation. (223–24)

Like Beale's, Westcott's words will appear hyperbolic to twenty-first-century eyes, unless those eyes have just come from something like Barrett Browning's letters. But Victorian literary societies regularly preach the religious value of secular poetry in this way. The creation and rededication of shrines to secular authors in and after this period offers further testimony to its appeal; Shakespeare's Birthplace in Stratford, the Folger Shakespeare Library in Washington, Casa Guidi in Florence, the Armstrong Browning Library in Texas (with its marvelous stained-glass depictions of the Brownings' poetry), and even Somersby Rectory in Lincoln stand as literary monuments to this lingering Victorian impulse to memorialize what Westcott calls "the poet, as prophet." Barthes and Moretti belittle this cultic tendency, of course, with its arch-Romantic view of genius, but their professional careers capitalize upon it as well (as did the whole line of critical hierophants with whom I began). This circumstance must complicate our own retrospective orthodoxies about Victorian literary societies, which link amateur literary scholarship with unstudied theology.

William S. Peterson, who has written the only full study of the Victorian London Browning Society, reports that "in the end, the ladies and their clerical counterparts produced an atmosphere of such cloying religiosity that many writers and scholars abandoned the Browning Society, which then strangled on its own theological preoccupations" (52–53). Peterson, writing in 1969, charts a sharp divide between "writers and scholars" on the one hand and "the ladies and their clerical counterparts" on the other. He sets aside theology with a knowing smirk as unintellectual and feminine. But his taxonomies now seem badly dated. Consider how he invites us to roll our eyes at a Dorothea Beale or a B. F. Westcott for inadvertently strangling their literary society in the folds of their religious sentiment. Never mind that the nineteenth century was the first time in history that it became widely recognized that "the ladies" *were* often "the writers" and were sometimes also the scholars. Never mind that a relative majority of the scholars in Victorian Britain were clerics. Never mind that Beale was a solid and respectable critic, and Westcott one of the most significant biblical scholars that England has ever produced, a renowned editor of the Greek Christian scriptures and author of over twenty monographs. (Few humanities scholars, now or then, would dare to compare their *vitae* to Westcott's.) For Peterson, as for Barthes and Moretti, the term *theological* is a sneer that delegitimizes them as "writers and scholars." Nonetheless, as I have tried to emphasize, Peterson's sneer may be endlessly recycled: his own book remains intractably theological by the logic of either Barthes (a single-author study) or Moretti (a "very solemn treatment of very few texts taken very seriously"). The question is what happens if literary critics take theology seriously as a significant element of our work—one that has always reappeared, despite repeated efforts to squash it—and stop using it as a shorthand for failure.

Let us, then, turn to a Browningite whom even Peterson can admire as a "writer" and a "scholar": the great philologist and critic F. J. Furnivall, co-founder of the London Browning Society, early editor of the *Oxford English Dictionary*, and a pugnacious agnostic who worked hard to put down the openly theological yearnings of his fellow Browningites and to cultivate a secular literary criticism. (In one inadvertently comic episode, Furnivall quarreled with the atheist poet James Thomson for Thomson's praise of Browning's religious perspective.) One of Furnivall's own contributions to the Society papers is an 1887 reading of Browning's "O Lyric Love," which he introduces as an escape from theology:

> Several of my colleagues and friends in the Society have at divers times said to me, "What *can* be done to get away from the perpetually recurring discussions of Browning's theology? The subject turns up at almost every meeting; and the same old things are said every time.... Won't somebody write on Browning's art or his metre, collect his first rymes, or examine his grammar?" I have always defended folk's right to discuss Browning's theology as shown in his works; that is fair game; and thought and talk are free. Still, the mention of Grammar toucht me... I have therefore tired my hand at one of our poet's gnarly pieces, a lyric which it seems profanation to dissect like a dead body, so full of life and love is it. But Syntax is the Bond of Sentences, like Law is of Communities. Poems should be rightly constructed. They can't be lucid unless they are. Poets, as well as other writers, are bound to lessen by all possible means the friction of the vehicle by which they convey their thoughts into their readers' minds. (Browning Society [London], 165–66)

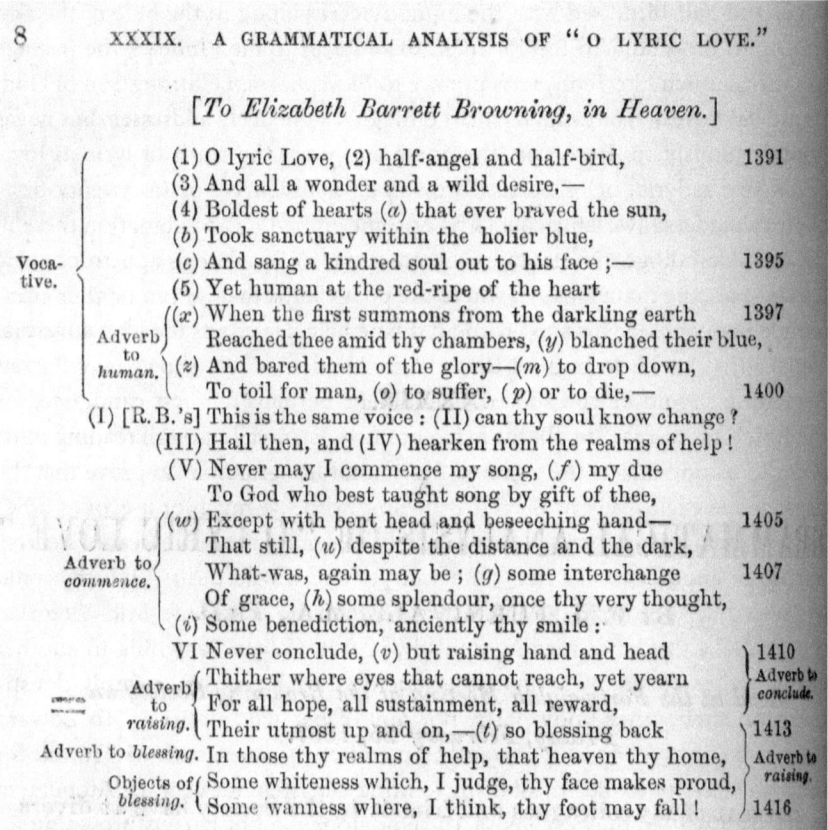

FIGURE 13.1. Furnivall's diagram of Browning's "O Lyric Love."

Furnivall deliberately and explicitly proffers his reading as an alternative to theological approaches to Browning. Moreover, to Furnivall's mind, the grammar of Browning's poem clearly establishes the earthly nature of the love being celebrated, and thus defeats the religious readings that other scholars had presumed to give it. Furnivall diagrams the lines as seen in fig. 13.1. "O Lyric Love" is Browning's invocation to the muse at the conclusion of the first book of his epic masterpiece, *The Ring and the Book* (1868). Furnivall, as we see, understands the lyric as an address to the poet's late wife: "*To Elizabeth Barrett Browning, in Heaven.*" But this subtitle appears nowhere in Browning (Furnivall appends it), and it implies a great deal more clarity than the poem's actual context provides. Most immediately, this passage forms the culmination of *The Ring and the Book*'s famously tortuous introduction to Browning's historiography. The lyric addresses the spirit of love; this much is plain. Yet the person incarnating that divine love remains ambiguous and variously rendered: "half-angel and half-bird," red with the human heart's blood in the blue of the sky, willing to descend, "To toil for man, to suffer or to die." Indeed, the passage functions much like Tennyson's preface to *In Memoriam* ("Strong Son of God, immortal Love"), from which Christ emerges as the likely addressee, but never unambiguously so. Here, too, the poem addresses the spirit of lyric as love, or of love as lyric, or of Barrett Browning, or of Christ, or (as twenty-first-century readers invariably conclude) of some ambiguous combination thereof.

Furnivall diligently diagrams the grammar of Browning's apostrophe. He teases apart the main clauses, where the poet claims that he can neither commence nor conclude his song without divine help. He charts the long adverbial clauses that attach to both of these ideas. He definitively shows why Barrett Browning should be considered a candidate, perhaps the best candidate, for the lyric's addressee. But all this being granted, Furnivall's overall reading must seem to us quixotic in the extreme. He cannot use grammar to prove that the passage fits exclusively to Barrett Browning while so much of it evokes other possibilities. It is one thing to call Barrett Browning the "[b]oldest of hearts," but quite another to call her "all a wonder and a wild desire," which would seem to describe love in the abstract rather than the poet's wife. Mid-Victorian mores make this latter reading unlikely, in fact. (When Browning in another poem writes of his own "lips once sanctified by Hers," he certainly doesn't mention their other body parts, nor any of her wild desires ["To Edward Fitzgerald" 972].) More importantly, several of the lines, such as "To toil for man, to suffer or to die," must bring to mind Christian ideas of the Atonement more plainly than they do any sacrifice or atonement of Barrett Browning's.

Curiously, for so prominent a literary scholar, Furnivall mistrusts ambiguity. He aims here to affix his preferred reading to grammar and definitively to rule out alternative readings. Far from celebrating ambiguity and paradox as literary critics have done reflexively since the New Criticism, Furnivall wants to solve the poem like a puzzle, to show that it has but one meaning when it is "rightly constructed." (This drive could be something of a mania with Furnivall; he would later boast that his Chaucer Society had found "the key" to Chaucer's career in the chronology of the minor lyric "The Complaint unto Pity.") Why does Furnivall strain his evidence so far? Here, it is partly to resist the interpretation offered by Victorian critics like the Scottish theologian George McCrie, who disliked the Victorian cults of Browning and Tennyson, and who took this particular passage as an apostrophe to Christ. McCrie, indeed, adopts a diametrically opposed view to Furnivall's:

> If anything could serve to show how preposterous is the obscurity in which he [Browning] involves himself occasionally, it is to find that intelligent

readers should have supposed that these lines addressed to the Saviour (as we understand them) were an Invocation to Mrs. Browning! (87)

Browning's "gnarly" style, treated by Furnivall as a treasure mine, becomes in McCrie's hands an impenetrable fog. The marks of his inspiration become proofs of his unintelligibility. Furnivall badly resented such insinuations: "This feeble and pretentious religionist," he writes in riposte, "understands Browning's glorious Invocation to his wife; 'O Lyric Love . . .' in the *Ring and the Book*, to apply to Christ!" (*Bibliography* 101).

It remains unclear whether, to Furnivall's mind, McCrie's feebleness and pretentiousness owe to his religion or vice versa, but, apparently, they go together. That being said, it seems significant that Furnivall singles out for reprimand a scholar who refuses to find anything sacred and sublime in Browning. McCrie holds in contempt the obscurity that Browning Society scholars revered: "A feeling has universally obtained that these poets have been broaching novel religious tenets," writes McCrie, "but owing to the obscurity, especially of Browning's style, few seem to know exactly what they are" (xi). Furnivall seeks to prove McCrie wrong: to show exactly "what they are." McCrie's iconoclasm, then, his scorn of the cult of Browning from the vantage of Christian orthodoxy, directly evokes Furnivall's scorn of McCrie's Christian orthodoxy from the vantage of the cult of Browning. Iconoclasm and devotion here perform the usual pas de deux, outlined in this chapter's first section.

Surely, at all events, there is something risible about Furnivall's attempting to secularize his own Browning Society with Browning's appeal "To God, who best taught song by gift of" Love. His truculent skepticism never extends to poetry. Speaking to a roomful of mostly religious Browning enthusiasts, Furnivall shares the idea that it might be a desecration to take apart the syntax of this "lyric which it seems profanation to dissect like a dead body, so full of life and love is it." He seems genuinely to worry about making these sacred verses profane. If he were not perfectly explicit about trying to offer alternatives to theological readings of Browning, one would suspect him of trying to promote such readings. One suspects him anyway. Perhaps Furnivall worked at cross-purposes with himself, simply, for his form of religious iconoclasm was always also a form of worship. And maybe this explains why Furnivall failed to win many fellow Browning Society members to his secularist interpretation, as his postscript to the published essay frankly acknowledges.

My own point is that the theologically inflected Victorian poetics of critics like Dorothea Beale or a B. F. Westcott deserve our respect as much as the iconoclastic (but also theologically inflected, as it turns out) criticism of ardent secularists like Furnivall. Peterson's imagined gulf between them seems motivated more by ideology than by evidence. Moreover, in either case, the theology might be the very thing that now merits our interest.

III. CONCLUSION: ON MORE GENEROUS FORMS OF CRITIQUE

I do not mean to present myself here as the last of a long line of literary scholars who unmask the covert theologies of the unmaskers who have come before them. Such unmasking amounts to an endless game. Instead, I have tried to indicate how academic poetry studies offers a terrific example of what Pecora calls secularization without end. Victorian criticism remains a far cry from ours. But today we see a burgeoning of interest in "post-suspicion" hermeneutics that may help us to understand it: a revival of Paul Ricoeur's call for a hermeneutics of sympathy in Eve Sedgwick's call for affective, "reparative" reading and Rita Felski's and Elizabeth Anker's questions about the limits of critique, as well as various kinds of affective reading and new formalisms (Ricoeur 213–38; Sedgwick 123–51; Felski; Anker and Felski). Such movements dovetail meaningfully with the religious turn in twenty-first-century literary criticism and may even speak to Lori Branch's radical view that humanities scholarship "ought to own up to the religiousness of all intellectual endeavor" (*Rituals of Spontaneity* 221). Ricoeur's works bear witness to his form of Protestantism, Sedgwick ends *Touching Feeling* (2003) with a personal celebration of Buddhism, and Felski finds most promise for a "post-suspicion" hermeneutics in the Catholic philosopher Latour (who shares Arnold's and Beale's view that "art is too mysterious, too spiritual, too haunted . . . too perverse as well to accompany religion for long in its meanderings"; Latour 105). Twenty-first-century literary criticism is everywhere looking for more generous forms of critique.

I wish to ask what happens when we take a page out of Dorothea Beale's book and acknowledge that a thread of theology might always remain at the core of literary criticism, yet—or, rather, as I would urge, *and*—still grant that literary criticism remains a good thing. What happens when we seize this postsecular moment to remind ourselves that this dialectic between skepticism and theological recidivism has, after all, produced in the field of literary studies an astonishingly rich and often dazzling testament to the beauty and power of art? The history of literary studies shows us the endless creativity of a dance between iconoclasm and reverence. (A dance that also animates nineteenth-century poets' own criticism, as Michael Hurley emphasizes in the next chapter.) In this respect, as in so many others, Victorian thinkers may be just what the philosopher Charles Taylor calls them: "our Victorian contemporaries" (*Sources of the Self* 393). So what happens when we stop thinking about religion as a box from which English studies needs to be rescued, and start thinking about it as a kind of blueprint?

Twenty-first-century English departments may have a duty both to reinvent our visions and to revivify the kind of zeal that created them in the first instance, as Mark Edmundson urges throughout his 2004 *Why Read?* Over a century of professional criticism testifies (often despite itself) to Beale's and Westcott's idea that literary texts can be inspired. Most of this criticism remains secular in intent, for certain, but intent must remain beside the point. A beautiful text might deserve our reverence even if we only arrive at reverence in oblique and roundabout ways. The nineteenth-century philosopher Josiah Royce, a pragmatist and friend of William James, insisted in the Boston Browning Society in 1896 that the power available in Browning's poetry was not doctrinal in nature, but that it amounted to the same thing. "What matters the name of the tale," he asked, "so long as it arouses afresh the thought to which the doctrine of the incarnation bears witness, the thought that, if ever we pierce through the world of Power to the heart of it, to that which is beyond Power, we find, as the Over-God, Love?" (Boston Browning Society 31). One need not share Royce's theological convictions to take an interest in his eagerness to apply them to Browning. Marx's mentor, Ludwig Feuerbach, would depict such love as a human aspiration rather than the divine reality that Royce imagines. But such a distinction may be irrelevant, since it seems that we get a form of theology either way.[4] For us the relevant fact must rather be that far more has been written in recent decades on literature as a mask for power than on literature as a mask for love. And yet the life of our criticism has depended upon some kind of love, after all, all along.

WORKS CITED

Anker, Elizabeth, and Rita Felski, editors. *Critique and Postcritique*. Duke UP, 2017.

Arac, Jonathan. *Critical Genealogies*. Columbia UP, 1987.

Asad, Talal. *Formations of the Secular: Christianity, Islam, Modernity*. Stanford UP, 2007.

Barthes, Roland. *The Rustle of Language*. Translated by Richard Howard, U of California P, 1986.

Bloom, Harold. *Kabbalah and Criticism*. Continuum, 1999.

———. *Shakespeare: The Invention of the Human*. Riverhead Books, 1998.

---

4. Dominic Erdozain's contribution to this volume might be read alongside Paul Ricoeur's argument that Marxism is at heart "an event . . . of western theology" (215).

Boston Browning Society. *The Boston Browning Society Papers, Selected to Represent the Work of the Society from 1886–1897.* New York, Macmillan Co, 1897.

Branch, Lori. *Rituals of Spontaneity: Sentiment and Secularism from Free Prayer to Wordsworth.* Baylor UP, 2006.

———. "The Rituals of Our Re-Secularization: Literature between Faith and Knowledge." *Religion and Literature*, vol. 26, nos. 2–3, 2014, pp. 9–33.

Browning, Robert. *The Poems: Volume Two.* Edited by John Pettigrew and Thomas J. Collins, Yale UP, 1981.

Browning Society (London). *The Browning Society's Papers.* London, Browning Society, 1881.

Eagleton, Terry. *Culture and the Death of God.* Yale UP, 2014.

Edmundson, Mark. *Why Read?* 1st US ed., Bloomsbury, 2004.

Felski, Rita. *The Limits of Critique.* U of Chicago P, 2015.

Frye, Northrop. *Anatomy of Criticism.* Princeton UP, 1957.

———. *The Great Code: The Bible and Literature.* Harcourt Brace Jovanovich, 1982.

Furnivall, Fredereck J., editor. *A Bibliography of Robert Browning, from 1833 to 1881.* Publisht [sic] for the Browning Society by N. Trübner & Co., London, 1881.

von Goethe, Johann Wolfgang. *Wilhelm Meister's Apprenticeship.* Translated by Thomas Carlyle, Edinburgh, Oliver & Boyd, 1824.

Guillory, John. "The Ideology of Canon-Formation: T. S. Eliot and Cleanth Brooks." *Critical Inquiry*, vol. 10, no. 1, 1983, pp. 173–98.

Hilliard, Christopher. *English as a Vocation: The "Scrutiny" Movement.* Oxford UP, 2012.

Kaufmann, Michael W. "The Religious, the Secular, and Literary Studies: Rethinking the Secularization Narrative in Histories of the Profession." *New Literary History*, vol. 38, no. 4, 2007, pp. 607–28.

King, Joshua. *Imagined Spiritual Communities in Britain's Age of Print.* The Ohio State UP, 2015.

Knight, Christopher J. *Uncommon Readers: Denis Donoghue, Frank Kermode, George Steiner and the Tradition of the Common Reader.* U of Toronto P, 2003.

LaPorte, Charles. *Victorian Poets and the Changing Bible.* U of Virginia P, 2011.

Latour, Bruno. *Rejoicing: Or the Torments of Religious Speech.* Translated by Julie Rose, Polity, 2013.

McCrie, George. *The Religion of Our Literature: Essays upon Thomas Carlyle, Robert Browning, Alfred Tennyson, Etc.* London, Hodder and Stoughton, 1875.

McKelvy, William R. *The English Cult of Literature: Devoted Readers, 1774–1880.* U of Virginia P, 2007.

Moretti, Franco. "Conjectures on World Literature." *New Left Review*, vol. 1, 2000, pp. 54–68.

Pecora, Vincent P. *Secularization and Cultural Criticism: Religion, Nation, & Modernity.* U of Chicago P, 2006.

———. *Secularization without End: Beckett, Mann, Coetzee.* U of Notre Dame P, 2015.

Peterson, William S. *Interrogating the Oracle; a History of the London Browning Society.* Ohio UP, 1969.

Ricoeur, Paul. *The Philosophy of Paul Ricoeur: An Anthology of His Work.* Edited by Charles E. Reagan and David Stewart, Beacon Press, 1978.

Scholes, Robert. *English after the Fall: From Literature to Textuality.* U of Iowa P, 2011.

———. *The Rise and Fall of English: Reconstructing English as a Discipline*. Yale UP, 1998.

Sedgwick, Eve Kosofsky. *Touching Feeling: Affect, Pedagogy, Performativity*. Duke UP, 2003.

Taylor, Charles. *A Secular Age*. Harvard UP, 2007.

———. *Sources of the Self: The Making of the Modern Identity*. Harvard UP, 1989.

Ward, Thomas Humphry. *The English Poets*. Vol. 1, London, Macmillan, 1880.

Warner, Michael, Jonathan VanAntwerpen, and Craig J. Calhoun, editors. *Varieties of Secularism in a Secular Age*. Harvard UP, 2010.

Westcott, B. F. *Thoughts on Revelation and Life: Being Selections from the Writings of Brooke Foss Westcott*. Edited by Stephen Phillips, London, Macmillan and Co., 1891.

Wickman, Matthew. "Theology Still?" *PMLA*, vol. 132, no. 3, May 2017, pp. 674–80.

CHAPTER 14

Theologies of Inspiration
William Blake and Gerard Manley Hopkins

MICHAEL D. HURLEY

HOPKINS HARDLY EVER mentions Blake; across the extraordinarily rich literary correspondence that has come down to us, he only ever refers to him twice, and fleetingly—four sentences in total.[1] Yet these scant references tell a powerful story. The first occurs as a seemingly throwaway remark, when he is remonstrating with his old friend Canon Dixon for failing to admire Wordsworth's "Intimations of Immortality." Hopkins's apologia is moving and instructive in itself, but his testimony gestures beyond that single poem (which he calls "one of the dozen or of the half dozen finest odes of the world"), to suggest an entire theological poetics in which Blake is equivocally implicated. Here is Hopkins's central claim:

> There have been in all history a few, a very few men, whom common repute, even where it did not trust them, has treated as having had something happen to them that does not happen to other men, as having *seen something*, whatever that really was. Plato is the most famous of these. Or to put it as it seems to me I must somewhere have written to you or to somebody, human nature in these men saw something, got a shock; wavers in opinion, looking

---

1. Hopkins was not especially prolific by the standards of some men of letters in his lifetime (only 443 of his letters are extant); yet his missives are crammed with brilliant literary opinion, theory, and insight. See Hurley, "Passion and Playfulness in the Letters of G. M. Hopkins."

back, whether there was anything in it or no; but is in a tremble ever since. Now what Wordsworthians mean is, what would seem to be the growing mind of the English speaking world and may perhaps come to be that of the world at large/ is that in Wordsworth when he wrote that ode human nature got another of those shocks, and the tremble from it is spreading. This opinion I do strongly share; I am, ever since I knew the ode, in that tremble. You know what happened to crazy Blake, himself a most poetically electrical subject both active and passive, at his first hearing: when the reader came to "The pansy at my feet" he fell into a hysterical excitement. Now commonsense forbid we should take on like these unstrung hysterical creatures: still it was a proof of the power of the shock.[2]

Rousing stuff, yet Hopkins is no "crazy Blake." Though the poem makes Hopkins "tremble" still, there is, he makes clear, intellectual sobriety to his swooning; earlier in the letter, he anticipates and refuses the suspicion that his claims might be "extravagant" (*Collected* 2:821). Whereas Blake is "unstrung" and "hysterical," Hopkins authenticates his reaction by highlighting Wordsworth's general shortcomings as "an imperfect artist," the "matter" of whose poems "varied in importance," "as he varied in insight." It is only in this particular instance, we are to understand, where Wordsworth's "matter" is of the "highest" "interest and importance," and where "his insight was at its very deepest": "hence . . . the extreme value of the poem" (2:822).

Hopkins's claims in this passage might be interpreted in different ways, but the dominant critical impulse among contemporary scholars of literature is to try to read past the passage's words; or rather, to try to read past our own twenty-first-century assumptions about its words, so that we might instead read for the historical assumptions that motivated and shaped Hopkins's language in the first place. In that spirit, perhaps the most inviting line of inquiry might be to explore his arresting and repeated use of "electrical" imagery of "shock." Jason R. Rudy's study of how poets in this period were imaginatively informed by developments in the electrical and physiological sciences offers a compelling case for how Hopkins especially employs the figure of electricity "for the work he imagines poetic form—and stress in particular—to accomplish" (129). The valency of "shock" might be further elaborated via the work of Jill L. Matus, who has shown how Victorian writers "use terms like 'flash,' 'pulse' and above all 'shock' to describe modes of cognition, especially modes of epiphany" (136). Rudy does not refer to this particular passage from Hop-

---

2. *Collected Works of Gerard Manley Hopkins*, vol. 2, ed. R. K. R. Thornton and Catherine Phillips, p. 821. Cited hereafter as "*Collected*" with volume and page numbers.

kins in his book, and Matus does not mention Hopkins at all in her study (which focuses on fiction rather than verse), but it is hard to imagine a more vivid exemplification of Rudy's general thesis, or of Matus's account of "electrical" epiphany in particular, than Hopkins here figures for Wordsworth's verse. Such a line of inquiry connects also, it might be noted, with the kind of claims that readers have been making for some time about how Wordsworth is (as M. H. Abrams once suggested, unwittingly echoing Hopkins's lexicon) "preeminently a poet of the revelatory and luminous Moment, of the gentle shock of mild surprise" (387).

Before going any further down this track, however, promising though it may be, it is worth reflecting on the general enterprise of historicizing literary subjects in this way. As a critical practice, historical poetics has taken sundry forms over the last couple of decades, and at its best it has enormously enriched our understanding of reading and writing practices that might otherwise be obscured to us today. Yet there have been losses as well as gains; notably, in the way that critics have simplified questions of verse style and of religion, both of which are typically treated—if they are treated at all—with a reductive kind of abstraction.

Studies especially attentive to prosody investigate the purported associations of different meters, in speculating the reason that a poet or school of poetry might choose one metrical form over another, or the way in which metrical choices might have been felt and understood by contemporary readers. But scholarship of this sort, though valuable on its own terms, inevitably dwells less rigorously on the particular realization of meter by rhythm in particular verse instances, and on what that might then imply for the writer's intentions or, more subtly, the writer's quality of thinking and feeling with and through verse. (And the same applies to matters of, say, rhyme or stanza, in which the general scheme invites general comment, whereas little attention is paid to its sui generis instantiation.) Relatedly, modern literary criticism—which Charles LaPorte, in this part of the volume, characterizes as one long and unsuccessful attempt to rid itself of theological preoccupations—is often indifferent to religious faith in poetry, if not openly skeptical or actually hostile towards it: tending to reinterpret expressions of devotion or desire as sublimations of other, darker needs.[3] Even where religion is taken seriously in poetry, critics typically read for theme and content, at the level of paraphrase. How and why the nonfungible particularities of verse craft might inform and

---

3. See Hurley, *Faith in Poetry*, introduction. While the trend of indifference towards and reductive reinterpretation of religious faith in poetry remains dominant in literary criticism, the number of notable exceptions does appear to be growing (as suggested by the exemplary critical works cited within this chapter, this part of the volume, and the collection as a whole).

interplay with the particularities of religious belief remains largely neglected. While Hopkins is surely a ready subject for the dominant mode of literary-critical historicism, his observations on Wordsworth and Blake quoted above might also provoke us to think differently about the nature of religious poetry across the century that these poets span: by inviting us to consider how poetry that claims to be animated by transcendent insight might be appraised not merely for its explicit, verbal expressions of such faith but also for its implicit warrant of inspiration that is tendered through its prosodical punctilio.

Returning, then, to the quotation with which this chapter began, it is well to observe that although Hopkins vaunts Wordsworth's vision on this occasion, he really did harbor serious reservations about him, finding fault even with some of his most celebrated verses: "beautiful as they are," he once sniffed, Wordsworth's sonnets "have an odious goodiness and neckcloth about them which half throttles their beauty" (*Collected* 1:267). While still an undergraduate, Hopkins confronted the question of what makes "poetry proper" (1:67), and his answer is direct and uncompromising, and persists throughout his later life and career: "inspiration." Without inspiration, even the most accomplished versifiers misfire; they might achieve local moments of interest by lapsing into self-plagiarism, and the outcome might be passable—but it is no more than what Hopkins calls "Parnassian." Such poetry, for all its charms, ultimately "palls." Tennyson and a number of worthies are indicted in this way; but in elaborating his argument, Hopkins's devastating verdict is that, of all the poets one might adduce, "no author palls so much as Wordsworth" (1:69).

When Hopkins comes, here, to write of Wordsworth having *seen something*, and as having created a poem that might "shock" its readers into a comparable vision, he is not therefore indulging a general affection for a pet poet: he is identifying an exceptional rather than a characteristic success, according to his own severe criterion for what counts as "poetry proper."[4] "In a fine piece of inspiration every beauty takes you as it were by surprise," Hopkins averred, "not of course that you did not think the writer could be so great," but rather that "every fresh beauty could not in any way be predicted or accounted for by what one has already read." Whereas with Parnassian poetry one might conceive oneself writing it if one were the poet, works of inspiration refuse that conceit. Do not say, then, that if you were Shakespeare you could imagine yourself writing *Hamlet*, because, Hopkins insists, "that is just what I think

---

4. Hopkins's claim complements Wordsworth's own estimation of his gift: "That poets, even as prophets, each with each / Connected in a mighty scheme of truth / Have each for his peculiar dower a sense / By which he is enabled to perceive / Something unseen before" (*The Prelude* [1805], 12:301–5).

what you can *not* conceive" (*Collected* 1:69). Seeing something, surprise, shock: what poets experience in the act of composition is also what poetry proper might in turn elicit, in the act of reading. But how exactly is inspiration thus channeled from poet to reader?

Perhaps Hopkins responded so powerfully to Wordsworth's ode simply because it engaged a sentiment that was already painfully familiar. Where Wordsworth writes of how "The earth, and every common sight" had seemed to him "Apparelled in celestial light, / The glory and the freshness of a dream" (*Poetical Works* 4–5), but that in later life "there hath past away a glory from the earth" (18), Hopkins records that in his youth "crimson and pure blues seemed to me spiritual and heavenly sights fit to draw tears once," but that in later life (he is writing this in December 1880, around the same age when Wordsworth wrote his ode), he could only "just see" what he once saw, and could "hardly dwell on it and should not care to do so" (*Collected* 1:413). The experience of these poets is intriguingly similar, but it is instructive also to note exactly how Hopkins explains the disenchantment that comes with adulthood: "because the mind after a certain number of shocks or stimuli, as the physiologists would say, is spent and flags" (1:412). Too many shocks cease, after a while, to seem shocking.

At least as far as poetry goes, however, Wordsworth's ode is itself a prime proof for Hopkins that benumbed readers—however spent and flagging—might yet be precipitated into fresh stimulations, through the singularity of inspired composition hard-won through the discipline of verse craft. So it is that Hopkins's reflexive account of his trembling gives way to an objective attempt to explain *how* the poem revitalizes that subjectivity, according to Wordsworth's artisanal achievement:

> His powers rose, I hold, with the subject: the execution is so fine. The rhymes are so musically interlaced, the rhythms so happily succeed (surely it is a magical change "O joy that in our embers"), the diction throughout is so charged and steeped in beauty and yearning (what a stroke "The moon doth with delight"!). (*Collected* 2:822)

Hopkins breaks off at this point to acknowledge that he is still only describing an aesthetic object, and that this does not itself necessarily excite an aesthetic experience: "It is not a bit of good my going on," he concedes, "if, which is to me so strange in you and disconcerting, you do not feel anything of this" (2:822). But Hopkins also knows that the ability of language to express more than abstract ideation only arises, if it ever does, from the resources of its style. A great number of literary critics and indeed theologians have intuited and advanced this contention before and after his—from Samuel Johnson to Jacques Maritain—but a recent study by Rowan Williams invites special notice here, for the reason that, without reference to Hopkins, it happens to fall in with his same terms of inspired execution: how words might be "persuaded to say more than they initially seem to mean" by the application of "carefully calculated shocks" (146, 148). Taking Hopkins's and Williams's cue, the "shock" of Wordsworth's ode, its inspired "surprise," is to be glossed not simply as a matter of what Wordsworth saw, but also as a matter of the careful way he refined that vision into verse: his powers rose *with* his subject, which he was inspired not only to see but also to express.

Hopkins's whimsical finale in his letter to Dixon imagines that "St. George and St. Thomas of Canterbury wore roses in heaven for England's sake on the day when that ode, not without their intercession, was penned" (*Collected* 2:822). Hopkins was fiercely *partis pris* when it came to discussing his nation and his religion, and he occasionally conflated his ambitions for the two ("A great work by an Englishman is like a great battle won by England"; 2:813, 785–86). But this picturesque image of boutonnière-sporting saints is neither straight-faced nationalism nor mere silliness. Readers familiar with Hopkins's letters will recognize his interleaving style, where he pursues the most serious subject, and most earnestly, with wry playfulness.[5] The vignette is comic, for sure, but it is also sincere. He really does think the poem is a triumph for England, and especially for the souls of England. And he really does believe that the poem gave a salutary jolt to human nature, for being the product of divine intercession, in both conception and execution.

Nonetheless, Hopkins's playfulness around the theme of inspiration helpfully reminds us that the word and concept did not have a stable or single sense in the period. It moves between secular and divine associations, referring at some points to "inspired vision or passion," and at others, to "divinely given"; and this occurs even within the writings of individual poets. Indeed, Hopkins's very last words in his letter to Dixon veer towards the classical sense of afflatus: "May the Muses bring you to a better mind. May God Almighty, and this without reserve" (*Collected* 2:822). But Hopkins is not really shifting his ground from Christian to classical inspiration here, any more than when he elsewhere taps the pagan tradition of the genius loci; when he calls Wales his "mother of Muses," say, or "England [. . .] wife / To my creating thought" (2:804).[6] In such cases, Hopkins writes with the tacit understanding of his audience in mind. Complaining to Robert Bridges of trying to compose with-

---

5. See Hurley, "Passion and Playfulness in the Letters of G. M. Hopkins."
6. *Poems of Gerard Manley Hopkins*, edited by Gardner and MacKenzie, p. 101. Cited hereafter as *P.*

out Minerva's blessing, for instance (*"graviter invita Minerva"*), he is only ever alluding to the classical tradition rather than actually invoking its divinities; and should there be any doubt, he retracks within the same sentence, via a semicolon: "rather I am afraid it may be Almighty God who is unwilling" (1:437).

There is, then, an Augustinian generosity in Hopkins's attitude towards inspiration, which figures transcendent insight as available outside of the consciously Christian tradition (Plato had *seen something* too), even as he is keen to clarify that such insight is most truly realized through the revelation of the Christian God Almighty. The continuity Hopkins imagines here is common to many Christian poets before him, but it was by no means inevitable within the context of nineteenth-century authorship. On the one hand, a secular skepticism that ripens through the period impatiently derides inspiration as superstition and argues instead for the sole agency of the artist. This new grudge against inspiration might be seen as a negative expression of a positive desire to elevate the person of the poet, as Paul Valéry indicated by his truck with the "naïve notion" that imagines poetic production either as "a result of pure chance" or as "a kind of supernatural communication"; both hypotheses, Valéry complains, "reduce the poet to a wretchedly passive role" (212). For William Morris, self-conscious both as an atheist and an artisan, "the talk of inspiration is sheer nonsense, there is no such thing. It is a mere matter of craftsmanship" (Mackail 186). On the other hand, both the Platonic and the biblical traditions present poet-prophets as ventriloquizing what they have not themselves conceived or fashioned into language, and which they may well not fully understand. Both these traditions are at odds with the emergent poetics of individual creativity, recalling instead a premodern conception of authorship as a public and collective act rather than a private, confessional one (Burke 1–12).

The picture is actually even more complicated. There is indeed a tug-of-war between inspiration and poetic craftsmanship across the century, but it expresses itself in diverse and sometimes unexpected ways that cannot be neatly explained by a secularization narrative, whereby those who reject God reject inspiration. Percy Bysshe Shelley, an avowed atheist, is the author of one of the most stirring contemporary accounts of inspiration (*A Defence of Poetry*), as an extension of his Romantic idealization of the poet as *vates*; and at the other end of the century, Algernon Charles Swinburne, another atheist-provocateur, would likewise devote much imaginative energy to advocating the Muse (Zonana 39–50). Yet it remains meaningful to notice the strain of secularity that increasingly informs nineteenth-century accounts of writing (and indeed the period's accounts of inspiration itself) and to generalize about the tension that intensifies over time, between claims for verse as inspired and claims for the agency of the individual poet. In *The Theory of Inspiration*, Timothy Clark has well documented this tension as a "crisis of subjectivity," of the sort that Edgar Allan Poe memorably confronts in his essay on "The Philosophy of Composition," published at the very tipping point of the century (1846), which descants on the deceitfulness whereby "most writers—poets in especial—prefer having it understood that they compose by a species of fine frenzy—an ecstatic intuition—and would positively shudder at letting the public take a peep behind the scenes" (Poe 481).

If Poe is the prototypical inspiration-deflating writer, Charles Lamb exemplifies the rudely disillusioned reader, "staggered" as he was to discover the manuscript of *Lycidas* "interlined, corrected as if their words were mortal, alterable, displaceable at pleasure!"; "as if inspiration were made up of parts, and these fluctuating, successive, indifferent!" (365 n). The tussle staged in these accounts presents the relationship between inspiration and verse craft as a zero-sum game. To demote the former is to promote the latter, and vice versa. Hopkins, however, exemplifies how the benison of divine inspiration might be reconciled with the individual responsibility of the artist's striving to be true to that gift: not according to some division of labor between God and man, but as a model of commensurability. This is the last poem Hopkins ever wrote, dated 22 April 1889, just seven weeks before he died:

To R. B.
The fine delight that fathers thought; the strong
Spur, live and lancing like the blowpipe flame,
Breathes once and, quenchèd faster than it came,
Leaves yet the mind a mother of immortal song.
Nine months she then, nay years, nine years she long
Within her wears, bears, cares and moulds the same:
The widow of an insight lost she lives, with aim
Now known and hand at work now never wrong.
Sweet fire the sire of muse, my soul needs this;
I want the one rapture of an inspiration.
O then if in my lagging lines you miss
The roll, the rise, the carol, the creation,
My winter world, that scarcely breathes that bliss
Now, yields you, with some sighs, our explanation. (P 108)

Dedicated to Bridges, with whom Hopkins had shared more of his verse theory and practice than anyone else, there is a curious sense in which this poem, written while Hopkins was already fatally ill, reads like his *Summa*. Formally, it epitomizes his investment in (to use Hopkins's own words) the "abrupt" and "stressy" life of the innovative meter he called "sprung rhythm." Thematically, it explores the extent to which, for Hopkins, verse must be invested with not only inspirational ardor but also exacting craftsmanship. What is most telling, though, what reveals most about Hopkins's double vision of poetry's need for both divine gift and cultivated skill, is the way that these formal and thematic concerns mutually animate each other.

"Fine delight" is thus not merely described but dramatized in the opening line, through its "fine execution," as fricatives and dentals clarify and enliven through their crisp concatenation ("*fi*ne *d*eligh*t* tha*t f*athers though*t*")—before that filigree precision gives way to a newly muscular movement that erupts across the line break: "strong / Spur." It is a perfectly Hopkinsian moment, making the most not only of the words' complementary sounds and rhythms but also of their contrasts; in this case, heightening the alliterative clatter of his stressed monosyllables by splicing them across the line end in an effect that modern prosodists identify as *rejet* (but which Hopkins probably learned from Milton). The percussive potency of "Spur" is not flatly described as "strong," then: its strength is realized through its stress ("Stress is," in Hopkins's definition, "the making a thing more, or making markedly, what it already is; it is the bringing out its nature"; *Collected* 2:629). As the sentence continues, liquid chimes run through "*l*ive and *l*ancing *l*ike the b*l*owpipe flame," which, together with other consonantal echoings, lend the first four lines such winning, performative vitality.

But the vitality of these first four lines is not purely prosodical; their sounds and rhythms have a lexical reference, and indeed a theological one. Hopkins is writing of the energizing moment of inspiration that enables "immortal song." His progenitive metaphors are suggestive, drawing as he does on both fathering (line 1) and mothering (line 4), not least for the poignant contrast they present with those moments in his letters and notebooks where he confesses to feeling uninspired, on which occasions he figures himself as unable to give birth to poetry, or even to exhibit the creative potency to take up his pen. We need only go so far as his retreat notes written just a few months before "To R. B." to find his anguished complaints of living "without spur," which he glosses with the devastating sentence: "All my undertakings miscarry: I am like a straining eunuch" (*Sermons* 262).[7]

---

7. *Sermons and Devotional Writings of Gerard Manley Hopkins,* ed. Christopher Devlin S. J., p. 262. Cited hereafter as "*Sermons*" with page numbers.

When Hopkins was first grappling with his ideas on inspiration, his account was almost bathetically prosaic, glossed as a state of "mental acuteness" enabled by a physical condition of wellbeing (he notes factors such as "the length of time after a meal"; *Collected* 1:67–8). By the time he matured into the poetry for which he is now celebrated, he had developed a subtler account of inspiration as divine gift, which, in his poetry, finds explicit articulation in "The Blessed Virgin compared to the Air we Breathe" ("This air, which, by life's law, / My lung must draw and draw / Now but to breathe its praise"; *P* 94).[8] Emphatic elaborations of the same occur in his sermons as well: "even the sigh or aspiration itself is in answer to an inspiration of God's spirit and is followed by the continuance and expiration of that same breath which lifts it . . . to do or be what God wishes his creature to do or be" (*Sermons* 156). Man is said to receive inspiration, in the fullest sense, as a form of grace, which is God's own "finger touching the very vein of personality." Hopkins goes on to suggest that man can do so little to "respond" to this gift ("by no play whatever, by bare acknowledgement only"), and that he can summon no more than "the counter stress which God alone can feel": "the spiration in answer to his inspiration" (*Sermons* 158).

It would take another chapter to tease out the distinct but overlapping ways in which Hopkins is imagining inspiration here. His conception of prevenient grace and the grace to cooperate in man's salvation is not identical with his understanding of how poems might be conceived and composed, but such differences as might be delineated tend to the same end when viewed in the context of Hopkins's cardinal conviction that man's duty is to praise God ("This then was why he [man] was made, to give God glory and to mean to give it"; *Sermons* 239). With this praise-imperative in mind, where Hopkins's poetic creations are designed to celebrate the created world and the God who created it, we may reread them for how their forms and themes speak back and to and through each other. In the case of "To R. B.," the presence of God exalted in the octave is then found wanting (in both senses) in the sestet; and "Breathes" from the third line (linked to "immortal song") finds its dark pendent in the symbolically "winter world" of barrenness in which he "scarcely breathes that bliss," redeeming the possibility of raptured inspiration of which the poem records the lack, even as that record itself becomes the "immortal song" of poetry proper that it desires.

---

8. Breathing provides the air required to utter praise—but more profoundly, Hopkins figures the physical inspiration of literal breathing in conjunction with its spiritual counterpart (receiving grace, mediated from God through Mary and the physical world, including air), such that Hopkins also depends on what he praises in the sense of giving back the gift he receives (including, the poem suggests, in the "inspired" act of poetic composition itself).

Importantly, Hopkins's anxious concern for inspiration as divine inspiration is not self-standing; it is compounded by the sense of his own responsibility as craftsman. On the heels of the vaulting vision of "immortal song" comes, "Nine months she then, nay years, nine years," which moves the governing metaphor from pregnancy's natural term to the Horatian notion in *Ars Poetica* that a poem should—to allow second thoughts and revisions—be kept for nine years before publication. The "live and lancing . . . blowpipe flame" is thus checked by the cooler processes of lucubration. "Now this is the artist's most essential quality," he advised Dixon: "masterly execution" (*Collected* 2:792). That means choosing words with sufficient "point and propriety," making images "brilliant" (1:265, 482), and the prosody "highly wrought" (2:544, 748, 919). As he once wryly intimated to Bridges: "Only remark, as you say that there is no conceivable licence I shd. not be able to justify, that with all my licences, or rather laws, I am stricter than you and I might say than anybody I know" (2:280). Hopkins throws waspish emphasis on the corrected statement. What might look to be licenses in his poetry are actually higher laws that bind him with unprecedented stringency.

While some licenses are established as law through convention,[9] others can be compensated for within the individual form itself, which is why he asserts that "apparent licences are counterbalanced, and more" by his "strictness" (*Collected* 1:281).[10] But Hopkins goes further: "In fact all English verse, except Milton's, almost, offends me as "licentious." Remember this" (1:281). It is a provoking boast—and not only for its teacherly caution not to forget, and so not to repeat the libel. Whereas Hopkins previously demanded that his poetics be reappraised by way of inversion—aesthetic licenses must in fact be read as aesthetic laws—here he switches the ground from aesthetics to moral theology, as license becomes associated with "licentiousness." Tugging at this law-license-licentious thread reveals a great deal about the conjunction of poetics and metaphysics for Hopkins, which I have elsewhere sought to draw out.[11] The argument of this chapter is tilted rather differently, however: towards a comparative sense of the play between these categories in the period, for which Hopkins's second and only other extant reference

---

9. Of certain rhymes, for instance, he writes of "the ordinary licence of rhyming s's proper or sharp to s's flat or z's, th proper to th = dh and so on" (*Collected* ii:594).

10. He identifies "outriding feet" as a license but distinguishes his usage from similar effects in late Shakespeare, where they are employed as mere "licence," "whereas" Hopkins's are "calculated effects" (*Collected* 1:318). But he also concedes: "Some of my rhymes I regret" (2:576); run-over rhymes were "experimental, perhaps a mistake" (2:747).

11. This chapter extends my separate accounts of Blake and Hopkins from my study of *Faith in Poetry*, to consider, by comparative evaluation, the extent to which these poets converge in their conceptions of poetic inspiration.

to Blake is further suggestive. Like the first reference, it occurs in a letter to Dixon, though this one appears some eleven years later, in mid-December 1887:

> I have Blake's poems by me. Some of them much remind me of yours. The best are of an exquisite freshness and lyrical inspiration, but there is mingled with the good work a great deal of rubbish, want of sense, and some touches of ribaldry and wickedness. (*Collected Works* 2:910)

Characteristically, Hopkins separates the "best" from the "rubbish" with clean strokes of his pen; his estimation admits no fussing in the middle ground. The former category, the "best" poems, are marked by "freshness" and "inspiration": to be inspired is to produce something "fresh," something that has been newly seen, something surprising—shocking. Yet Hopkins also believed that what's fresh must not be too fresh, or it might end up like "rubbish." Craft is a necessary check and refinement. Norman H. MacKenzie closes his insightful gloss of "To R. B." by regretting that the circumstances of Hopkins's death "prevented a poem which has many beautiful phrases in it from being subjected to the maturing agencies of time and critical discussion" (it was sent to Bridges "a bare week after it was written"; *Reader's* 209, 207). But MacKenzie underestimates how delicate the balance was for Hopkins between writing and overwriting. Maturation by mediation easily becomes meddling, and damages the "freshness" that was, for Hopkins, inspiration's primary recommendation. Poetry's beauties are, Hopkins thought, all the more valuable for being delicate, liable to perish. While execution is required to refine inspiration into poetry, too much of it mitigates "the freshness" he "wanted and which indeed the subject demands" (*Collected* 2:552).

For a poet as obsessive and precise as Hopkins—his drafts are a thicket of carets and corrections—overengineering was an ever-present risk. Of "The Sea and the Skylark," he confessed to Bridges: "There is, you see, plenty meant; but the saying of it smells, I fear, of the lamp" (*Collected* 2:552). Ripeness needs to be cultivated but can easily become overripe; virtue quickly curdles into vice. He called "Tom's Garland" "a very pregnant sonnet and in point of execution very highly wrought. Too much so, I am afraid" (2:919). Hopkins is keenly alive, as well he might be, to "the danger and difficulty of making more than verbal alterations in works composed long ago and of a bygone mood not being to be recovered" (2:610–11). The valorization of freshness has a theological as well as thematic place in Hopkins's several poems on innocence and vitality, from the Edenic afterglow he finds in "Spring" to the "fresh thoughts" of the uncorrupted child in "Spring and Fall," to "the dearest freshness deep down things" in "God's Grandeur." Figuring inspiration as progenitive refuses the notion of poetry as mere "making" (*poiesis*).

But does "crazy Blake" strive for a comparable mediation between writerly modes, or does he care only for that "strong / Spur," without being appropriately tempered by craft and time? A reader could be forgiven for doubting the deliberation of a poet whose verses run from the roughshod balladic ditties that populate his earlier collections, to the long-lined, metrically equivocal prophecies associated with his later writings. *Europe a Prophecy* was, Northrop Frye thought, Blake's "greatest achievement," written in "a kind of 'free verse' recitativo in which the septenarius is mixed with lyrical meters" (185). Here is the briefest sample from that poem, plucked almost at random:[12]

> The shrill winds wake!
> Till all the sons of Urizen look out and envy Los:
> Seize all the spirits of life and bind
> Their warbling joys to our loud strings
> Bind all the nourishing sweets of earth
> To give us bliss, that we may drink the sparkling wine of Los!
> And let us laugh at war,
> Despising toil and care,
> Because the days and nights of joy, in lucky hours renew.

Confronted with lines that are so rhythmically various and open to different renderings, Frye's "kind of" prosodical classification is, no doubt, as analytically precise as one can confidently get; and that will hardly reassure the reader who is keen to admire the surety of the poet's art. Hopkins's own account of Blake does not in any case attempt to parse his poems, but notes instead his sense of the poet himself as "hysterical," and as "a most poetically electrical subject" whose very person offends "commonsense." Blake apparently abets this verdict of irrationality, insofar as he styles himself a superconductor for the supernatural, in which he contributes nothing to the poetry that flows through him. One of his long prophetic poems was written, he claimed, "from immediate Dictation," "without Premeditation & even against my Will." He further suggested that it happened instantly ("the Time it has taken in writing was thus rendered Non Existent") and that his "immense Poem . . . which seems to be the Labour of a long Life" was in fact "all produced without Labour or Study" (*E* 728–29). No will, no study, no labor: crazy

---

12. *Complete Poetry and Prose,* edited by Erdman, p. 62. Cited hereafter as *E,* with page numbers; where appropriate, plate and line numbers are also given.

indeed. Yet Blake balked at the accusation that he was merely raving. The "aspersion of Madness" was, Blake countered, "Cast on the Inspired" by "the tame high finishers of paltry Blots, / Indefinite, or paltry rhymes, or paltry harmonies" (plates 41.8–10; *E* 142). His defense is subtle but essential: while he, like Hopkins, thought inspiration to be the prerequisite for poetry proper, Blake wished (as Hopkins also wished) simultaneously to insist on disciplined expression:

> I have heard many People say Give me the Ideas. It is no matter what Words you put them into & others say Give me the Design it is no matter for the Execution. These People know <Enough of Artifice but> Nothing Of Art. Ideas cannot be Given but in their minutely Appropriate Words nor Can a Design be made without its minutely Appropriate Execution[.] (*E* 576)

Blake's rail against the demystification and naturalization of inspiration as a labor "earned and learned in time" must thus be read, as Sarah Haggarty has shown, alongside his countervailing conviction that it was "pernicious to sacrifice the artist's mental and mechanical activity to some abstract, exterior donor" (112). As a self-styled "prophet," Blake puts a heavy accent on originality: it is the "crooked roads" that are, he thought, the "roads of Genius" (plate 9.66; *E* 38). But here he can again sound a lot like Hopkins, who confessed that the effect of studying masterpieces was to make him admire but wish to do otherwise—"So it must be on every original artist to some degree" (*Collected* 2:963).

What's radical in the self-conscious individualism of both poets is, by these rationalizations, also radically paradoxical, insofar as what made them so stylistically outlandish was the conviction that their apparent licenses actually expressed laws that ran deeper than the conventional orthodoxies. It was, Blake claimed, the "determinate and bounding form" that distinguished great artists of all ages, who are likewise to be thought of as prophets, not for some speculative gift in fortune-telling ("Prophets in the modern sense of the word have never existed"; *E* 550, 617) but as oppositional voices in the Old Testament tradition; that is, as visionaries of divine truth.

For Hopkins as for Blake, then, the claim to divinely inspired vision was necessarily and intimately caught up with a claim to inspired execution. An investment in "form" and "law," as against license, is never merely aesthetic: it is theologically charged, as it is also double-edged. Clear bounding lines are the precondition for creativity (what Blake called the "hard and wirey line of rectitude"), but pre-existing forms and laws may also oppress the imagination, and only facilitate "lame imitators" (*E* 550). Both poets recur to the imperative that laws are necessary, but that lawbreaking is too, when sanctioned by a higher insight, as (Blake was fond of saying) Christ consistently showed through his life's example. That might look like they are investing in transgression, but the opposite is in fact the case. Theologically and aesthetically, they are committed to a faithful engagement with the truth expressed through the quiddity of what Blake called "minute particulars" (*Jerusalem* alone contains eleven iterations of this phrase), and what Hopkins (following Duns Scotus) referred to as *haeccitas*, and which he otherwise sought to capture through his coinages of "inscape" and "instress."

Hopkins is self-aware enough to know that his investment in particularity was a major source of difficulty in his writing, and that his poetry consequently erred "on the side of oddness": "Now it is the virtue of design, pattern, or inscape to be distinctive and it is the vice of distinctiveness to become queer. This vice I cannot have escaped" (*Collected* 1:334). Where Hopkins regretted the "strangeness" in his verse style that might prevent his "creating thought" from serving in "the campaign to win England back to the faith, or increase the fame of her literature,"[13] Blake seemed happier to align himself with the figure of the "just man" who "rages in the wilds" (plate 2.19; *E* 33). Idiosyncrasy was his sanction. He urged not merely artistic dignity but divine legitimacy for his wildness, which recalled the unheeded biblical prophets, as "The Voice of one crying in the Wilderness" (*E* 1). Some readers and critics have also explained and excused Blake's opacity by aligning him with the mystics. But to follow this reasoning too far is misleading, given that Blake was himself at such pains to stress the concrete clarity of his vision, not only as he saw it but also as he articulated it: "A Spirit and a Vision are not, as the modern philosophy supposes, a cloudy vapour or a nothing: they are organised and minutely articulated beyond all that the mortal and perishing nature can produce" (*E* 541). It might be added that Blake's choice to write in poetry at all was fired by the example of Milton, who had shown its capacity as a mode of expression to affect the national character by altering its religious vision (Ryan 154). Blake's commitment to poetry clearly extended beyond the mere expression of his vision, to an ambition to provoke that vision in his readers: to awaken a "cleansed" perception of the "infinite" (plate 14; *E* 39).

Still, it remains a question of some nicety how Blake or Hopkins effected such a provocation in poetry. When it comes to evaluating their respective verse styles, it is no exaggeration to suggest that these two poets have incited more contrariety and confusion than any others in the whole of the nineteenth

---

13. This is MacKenzie's gloss on Hopkins's confessional poem "To seem the stranger" (*P* 445–47).

century. In their lifetimes, they were both consistently accused of falling into metrical error and heterodoxy, and the same charge marks their reception even up to the present day. This chapter does not presume to offer yet another attempt to explain the formal discipline (or lack thereof) in their writings, but aims instead to evince a convergence between these poets that was not adequately appreciated by Hopkins, and has not attracted much commentary from subsequent readers and critics, either. In particular, by thinking about inspired vision and inspired execution as mutual concomitants, it becomes possible to think further about the extent to which contemporary criticism of the Bible—which, for both Hopkins and Blake, offered the ultimate exemplifying case for divinely inspired poetry—provided a warrant as well as a model for their poetic ambitions.

It has been many decades now since scholars showed how nineteenth-century studies of biblical Hebrew poetry were informed by divine notions of inspiration and enlisted "the full authority of the Holy Spirit for the new ideas of organic form" (Prickett 113). While such arguments have been well developed by scholars, there is still much to learn from about the influence of biblical scholarship in this period, as Cynthia Scheinberg, also in this part of the volume, valuably demonstrates, by elucidating contested intersections between Jewish identity, Romantic lyric theory, and biblical criticism in Christian and Anglo-Jewish commentary on the Psalms. But the gap in scholarship is even more marked when it comes to poetics, where critics interested in verse craft continue to overlook, or at least underestimate, the extent to which poets were profoundly influenced by biblical verse, and contemporary theories of biblical verse, and inevitably approach their metrics either according to prior literary precedents, or else through the abstractions of subsequent verse theories (such as generative prosody). Those literary-critical approaches that dominate modern scholarship may be necessary ways of evaluating the poets of the nineteenth century, but they are not in themselves sufficient: a truer account of the period's poets, and of such poets as Blake and Hopkins in particular, who pursue their writings with such paradigm-breaking individualism, requires also an appreciation of the influence that biblical scholars such as Robert Lowth and Thomas Howes had on their poetic endeavors. It would be significant step to recognize that it was Blake (rather than Wordsworth, say, or Coleridge) who first, most fully, and most explicitly drew on Lowth and Howes when rationalizing his poetics, by developing and exercising the law or license granted by "organic form" as a kind of inspired style.[14] And the

---

14. Engell, for instance, lays groundwork for this in his chapter on Lowth in *The Committed Word*.

same applies to Hopkins, who, in the second half of the nineteenth century, looked to the principle of parallelism in poetry as articulated by Lowth, which he developed more deliberately and innovatively than the other virtuoso stylists of his era (such as Tennyson or Swinburne).

What's "shocking" in the poetries of both Blake and Hopkins, then, might be better understood when viewed not only within the English canon of literature to which they responded, but also within the distinctive, rhetorical mode of the Old Testament. Historical poetics offers valuable methods and models for coming to terms with what poets find shocking in the verse they read and seek to write, by attending to the lexicon of their shock, insofar as it might insinuate its vitality by analogy with electrical science, or anything else for that matter. But additionally, and more potently, the ambition and poetical capacity to shock was, for Blake and Hopkins (among many other religious poets of the period), excited by a consciously biblical mode. That includes the prophetic verse of the Old Testament, but it extends also to the Jesus's own pedagogical praxis in the New Testament, which was itself—as Williams reminds us (149)—deliberately designed to rattle settled assumptions, by "carefully calculated shocks," through such parables as The Unjust Steward or the Unjust Judge.

When it comes to accounting for their religious convictions and ambitions, Blake and Hopkins continue to provide work for scholars to do (a task to which Peter Otto, in this volume, impressively contributes),[15] as these poets also present the starkest challenge to critics who take an interest in poetic form. Among verse theorists, no other poets from the nineteenth century—one is tempted to say no other poets in any century—have generated so much head-scratching, because their prosodical repertoires not only resist taxonomy by poetic precedent, they fret at the very limits of metricality itself. And yet the biggest lingering challenge facing metrists is not one that can in the end be met by counting syllables, weighing stresses, and adjudicating on verse junctures. To make fullest sense of their respective verse practices and religious visions requires not merely an account of their poetics and metaphysics, but a corollary understanding of how these modes might shape each other in their minutest particulars, and in ways that are radically commensurate.

---

15. In the next chapter, Peter Otto proposes a different theo-poetics for Blake than is offered here, teasing between accounts of his apparent heresy and orthodoxy; in Hopkins studies, see Martin Dubois's brilliant revisionary account.

WORKS CITED

Abrams, M. H. *Natural Supernaturalism: Tradition and Revolution in Romantic Literature.* 1971. Norton, 1973.

Burke, Seán, editor. *Authorship: From Plato to Postmodernism: A Reader.* Edinburgh UP, 1995.

Clark, Timothy. *The Theory of Inspiration: Composition as a Crisis of Subjectivity in Romantic and Post-Romantic Writing.* Manchester UP, 1997.

Devlin, Christopher S. J., editor. *The Sermons and Devotional Writings of Gerard Manley Hopkins.* Oxford UP, 1959.

Dubois, Martin. *Gerard Manley Hopkins and the Poetry of Religious Experience.* Cambridge UP, 2017.

Erdman, David V., editor. *The Complete Poetry and Prose of William Blake.* Newly revised ed., commentary by Harold Bloom, Anchor-Doubleday, 1988.

Engell, James. *The Committed Word: Literature and Public Values.* Pennsylvania State UP, 1999.

Frye, Northrop. *Fearful Symmetry.* 1947. Princeton UP, 1990.

Gardner, W. H., and N. H. MacKenzie, editors. *The Poems of Gerard Manley Hopkins.* 4th ed., Oxford UP, 1967.

Haggarty, Sarah. *Blake's Gifts: Poetry and the Politics of Exchange.* Cambridge UP, 2010.

Hurley, Michael D. *Faith in Poetry: Verse Style as a Mode of Religious Belief.* Bloomsbury, 2017.

——. "Passion and Playfulness in the Letters of G. M. Hopkins." *Letter Writing among Poets: From William Wordsworth to Elizabeth Bishop,* edited by Jonathan Ellis, Edinburgh UP, 2015, pp. 141–54.

Lamb, Charles. "Oxford in the Vacation." *London Magazine,* vol. 2, no. 10, Oct. 1820, p. 365.

Mackail, J. W. *The Life of William Morris.* London, Longmans, Green, & Co., 1899. 2 vols.

MacKenzie, Norman H. *A Reader's Guide to Gerard Manley Hopkins.* Thames and Hudson, 1981.

——, editor. *The Poetical Works of Gerard Manley Hopkins.* Clarendon, 1990.

Matus, Jill L. *Shock, Memory and the Unconscious in Victorian Fiction.* Cambridge UP, 2009.

Poe, Edgar Allan. *The Fall of the House of Usher and Other Writings.* Edited by David Galloway, Penguin, 1968.

Prickett, Stephen. *Words and the Word: Language, Poetics and Biblical Interpretation.* Cambridge UP, 1986.

Rudy, Jason R. *Electric Meters: Victorian Physiological Poetics.* Ohio UP, 2009.

Ryan, Robert. "Blake and Religion." *The Cambridge Companion to William Blake,* edited by Morris Eaves, Cambridge UP, 2003, pp. 150–68.

Thornton, R. K. R., and Catherine Phillips, editors. *The Collected Works of Gerard Manley Hopkins: Correspondence.* Vols. 1 and 2, Oxford UP, 2013.

Valéry, Paul. "Remarks on Poetry." *The Art of Poetry,* translated by Denise Folliot, Princeton UP, 1985.

Williams, Rowan. *The Edge of Words: God and the Habits of Language.* Bloomsbury, 2014.

Wordsworth, William. "Ode, Intimations of Immortality from Recollections of Early Childhood." *The Poetical Works of William Wordsworth.* 2nd ed., edited by Helen Darbishire and Ernest De

Selincourt, vol. 4, Oxford UP, 1958. *Oxford Scholarly Editions Online,* 21 May 2015. Accessed 25 May 2018.

———. *The Prelude 1799, 1805, 1850.* Edited by Jonathan Wordsworth et al., W. W. Norton and Co., 1979.

Zonana, Joyce. "Swinburne's Sappho: The Muse as Sister-Goddess." *Victorian Poetry,* vol. 28, no. 1, 1990, pp. 39–50.

CHAPTER 15

William Blake, the Secularization of Religious Categories, and the History of Imagination

PETER OTTO

ALTHOUGH NEGLECTED for much of the nineteenth and early twentieth centuries, Blake is now commonly regarded as one of the six canonical Romantic poets, a key figure in the history of art, a perceptive observer of his own times, and an important literary and artistic influence on the modern and contemporary. Perhaps still more remarkably, given that his major works were once upon a time dismissed as crazy, Blake is now more commonly placed in debate with or seen as anticipating the work of philosophical luminaries such as Isaac Newton (Ault), G. W. F. Hegel (Punter), Søren Kierkegaard (Clark; Rovira), Friedrich Nietzsche (Birenbaum), Sigmund Freud (George), and, most recently, Gilles Deleuze (Colebrook). In this context, the most recent shift in the intellectual landscape of Blake studies is significant because it allows us to see Blake's work, and its legacy in the present, with new eyes. More particularly, it pushes us to think again about the relation between terms, crucial to Blake studies *and* modern cultures, that we normally keep insulated from or at war with each other: religion, the secular, heresy, and the imagination.

The recent "shift" to which I am referring began in 1999, when Keri Davies announced that Blake's mother's maiden name was Wright and that her first marriage, on 14 December 1746, was to Thomas Armitage, not Thomas Harmitage or Hermitage as had been previously suggested ("William Blake's

Mother").[1] This set the scene for Marsha Keith Schuchard's discovery, two years later, that the pair had been closely involved with the Moravian Society in London's Fetter Lane, which had been formed in 1738—so closely involved that in 1750 they were admitted to the Congregation of the Lamb, the Society's inner circle (Davies and Schuchard 39–41; Schuchard, *Why Mrs. Blake Cried* 13). Just as remarkably, it is possible that Blake's paternal grandparents, and the parents of his "later business partner, James Parker," were in 1743 members of the Fetter Lane Society, when the Congregation of the Lamb was formed from the Society's members (Davies and Schuchard 38). All this changed, in important ways, the picture that until then had been drawn of Blake's life, family, friends, and work.

The Moravian Church or Unitas Fratrum ("Unity of the Brethren") are a Protestant sect that traces its lineage to the fifteenth-century Hussite movement in Bohemia and Moravia (Fogleman 4–5), more than sixty years before the Reformation was begun in 1517 by Martin Luther (1483–1546). During the Counter-Reformation (1545–1648), the "Brethren" were persecuted, forced into hiding, and dispersed across Northern Europe. This might have been the end of their story, but in 1727 a group of Moravian refugees, who had gathered at Herrnhut in Upper Lusatia, experienced a powerful collective sense of "rebirth" and "renewal." Energized by this experience and led by Count Nicolaus Ludwig von Zinzendorf (1700–1760), they developed an innovative spirituality and radical religion of the heart, which valued faith, community, emotion and, particularly during the "Sifting Time" (1743–53), sexuality and the body as well.[2]

The discovery that Blake's mother had been involved with this movement dispatched the widely held view, almost a truism in Blake studies, that Blake's parents were Nonconformists or Radical Dissenters—Baptists, perhaps (Bentley, *Blake Records* 7–8), or, according to E. P. Thompson, Muggletonians (120–21)—whose beliefs set them apart from the Church of England. In 1743 the Congregation of the Lamb represented itself "as a Society within the Church of England in union with the Moravian Brethren" (Reichel 300). Seven years later, the Moravians were recognized, in the preamble to an Act of Parliament, as "an antient Protestant Episcopal Church" (Great Britain 636; see Podmore 229–66), which made them "a sister church to the Church of England" (Ankarsjö 38). Just as importantly, the Moravians were evangelical

---

1. Margoliouth (380–81) notes that "Harmitage is probably a phonetic spelling of Hermitage . . . Much less probable," he continues, is that "the name is a mistake for Armitage." Thompson (120–21) decides firmly on Hermitage.

2. For a history of the Moravian Church, see Crews; and for accounts of their history in Britain, see Podmore and Stead.

and ecumenical rather than proselytizing, and therefore "encouraged those who joined [them] not to sever their tie with whatever denomination they had been born into" (Davies and Schuchard 38). All this doesn't necessarily mean, of course, that Blake himself was less radical than has often been assumed.

In the story of a person's life, mothers are always important. But in Blake's case, Davies's and Schuchard's discoveries had an added cachet because so little is known about his early years. As they remark, "Bentley's *Blake Records* spreads the known information about Blake's life over 418 pages. But the years 1757 to 1800, half of his life, occupy just the first 61 pages" (37).³ The name of his mother, Catherine Wright-Armitage-Blake, brought in its wake the discovery of the names of his maternal grandparents (Gervase and Mary) and their children, (Richard, Katharin, Robert, John, Elizabeth, a second Elizabeth, Catherine, and Benjamin—two of whom died young), and also the name of the place where his mother had been brought up, "the little Nottinghamshire village of Walkeringham, some twenty-four miles from Cudworth, Yorkshire, where her first husband, Thomas Armitage, was born in 1722" (Davies and Schuchard 41). Further, it introduced the tantalizing prospect that Catherine's Moravian faith held the key to Blake's early and perhaps also his late religious beliefs; and this swept Davies's and Schuchard's discoveries into the midst of a still-unresolved debate, one arguably at the center of current scholarship on Blake.

In *The Theology of William Blake* (1948), J. G. Davies begins by noting that "Blake, perhaps more than any other writer, was essentially a religious poet." Many would agree. But even if one belongs to that camp, what kind of religion or even spirituality (an equally slippery term) are we talking about? In Davies's account, Blake's "critics are of little help in this respect, for few of them agree among themselves, and a collation of their estimate of his beliefs is bewildering in the extreme" (1): "in the opinion of some, he was a Gnostic; others return a verdict of pantheism. A more cautious group dismisses him as 'unorthodox.' While . . . some critics affirm that he was after all a Christian, whose Christianity was 'orthodox in its main outlines'" (2).

In the years since then, the range of possibilities has increased rather than diminished. Blake appears variously as "more 'orthodox' than the orthodox" (Jesse 122; see also Ryan 43–79), Methodist (Farrell; Jesse), Behmenist (Aubre), mystic (Damrosch 47–51), Neoplatonist (Harper; Raine), Christian Kabbalist (Spector), "enthusiast of enthusiasts" (Beer 95; see also Bentley, *The Stranger*, 7–11), Gnostic (Nuttall; Sorenson), antinomian (Mee; Thompson); a Christian

---

3. Davies and Schuchard are referring to the first edition of *Blake Records* (1969). In the second edition (2001), the first half of Blake's life occupies 85 of 560 pages. Parenthetical references to the *Blake Records* refer to the second edition, cited hereafter as *BR*.

influenced by "Swedenborgian, Kabbalistic, Tantric, Hermetic and Moravian" thought (Schuchard, *Why Mrs. Blake Cried* 336); Christian atheist (Altizer), post-Christian (Potkay 172), no Christian at all (Bloom 411), and more than a little mad (Youngquist).

This wealth of interpretations might seem only to reflect a literary-critical establishment intent on multiplying differences. And yet even those who knew Blake well couldn't agree whether he was orthodox (Frederick Tatham [*BR* 685]); enthusiast (William Hayley [*BR* 94]), or saint *and* heretic (John Linnell [*BR* 430]). John Thomas Smith admits that, during the last forty years of his life, Blake didn't "attend any place of Divine worship"; but he then quickly adds that Blake was not "in any degree irreligious" (*BR* 606–7). After speaking with Blake, Henry Crabb Robinson found it "hard to fix Blake's station between Christianity Platonism & Spinozism." On another occasion, he is uncertain whether to call Blake "Artist or Genius—or Mystic—or Madman" (*BR* 420); and, on a third, he is surprised to hear "the doctrine of the Gnostics repeated with sufficient consistency to silence one so unlearned as myself" (*BR* 422, 701). Others, like Robert Southey, who met Blake in 1811, saw things more straightforwardly: he was a "madman" (*BR* 530–31).

For those of us adrift on this ocean of possibilities, Davies's and Schuchard's discoveries looked, at first glance, like dry land.[4] As the former announced, Blake could now "be linked (if tangentially) to at least two ... definable religious movements" ("Lost Moravian History" 1317). In other words, Blake's brief involvement with the Swedenborgian New Church, when he was in his early thirties, could be coupled with a childhood influenced, at least in part, by Moravian culture and sensibility. Rather than bare rocks, the words "Swedenborgian" and "Moravian" now named an island, in relation to which Blake's early life could be placed.

For the purposes of this argument, the main features of this island can be brought into view through the following observations. First, although he left the Fetter Lane Society in 1740, the founder of Methodism, John Wesley (1703–91), along with Charles Wesley (1707–88) and George Whitefield (1740–70), was among its earliest members. This suggested that the genealogy of Blake's religious thought could therefore be traced back to a Society that has been called "the main seed-bed from which the English Evangelical Revival would spring" (Podmore 39).

Next, Catherine and Thomas Armitage joined the Congregation of the Lamb during the Sifting Time, when Moravian valorization of emotion over

---

4. Davies and Schuchard write that "for Blake scholars, the discovery of the Armitage and Blake documents in the Moravian Archives at Muswell Hill opens up a new frontier in Blake studies" (42).

reason, and of faith over works, "combined with the belief that the union with Christ could be experienced during sexual intercourse," led to the "antinomianism" most provocatively expressed in the belief that this union "could be experienced not only during marital intercourse but during extramarital sex as well" (Peucker 2). Remarkably, Blake's own mother could now be construed as a possible source for his character Oothoon's celebration of free love in *Visions of the Daughters of Albion* (1793).

And third, in 1744–45 and 1748–49 the visionary Emanuel Swedenborg (1688–1772) was a regular visitor to Fetter Lane (Schuchard, *Why Mrs Blake Cried* 60, and *Emanuel Swedenborg* 440–44). Owing to the interest in Kabbalism and visionary sex that he shared with Zinzendorf and his son, Christian Renatus (1727–52), elements of Blake's work that previously had seemed discordant (Swedenborgianism, Moravianism, Kabbalah, "free love," "visionary sex") could now be seen as part of an ongoing conversation in a historical cultural environment. As Schuchard writes, "by recovering the previously lost Swedenborgian-Moravian-Jewish-Yogic history, we can shed new light on William Blake's development into a visionary artist, antinomian theosopher, and difficult husband" (*Why Mrs Blake Cried* 60).

These prehistories of Blake's thought are richly suggestive; and yet, by touching on matters of his mother's religion during her first marriage, which predate not just William's birth but the marriage of his parents, they raise the question of just how *tangentially*, to use Davies's word, was Blake linked to Moravianism and Swedenborgianism?

Blake was probably introduced to Swedenborgian thought in the mid-1780s and, towards the end of the decade, he and his wife Catherine attended the First General Conference of the New Church, where they signed the letter setting out why a New Church had to be established (Rix 48). And yet in *The Marriage of Heaven and Hell*, which Blake first printed the following year, Swedenborg is dismissed as "the Angel" who, after Christ's resurrection, was left "sitting at the tomb," and "his writings" are disparaged as "the linen clothes folded up" (plate 3, *E* 34).[5] But rather than simply leaving Swedenborg behind, Blake takes from him key elements of his language, iconography, and psychology which he then deploys to new ends. Rejection here goes hand in hand with re-visioning.

If emotion were an indicator of lasting commitment, we could be confident that Moravian preoccupations played a key role in Blake's childhood. "I am a pore crature full of wants," Catherine Armitage writes in the letter

---

5. All quotations of Blake's poetry and prose are taken from *The Complete Poetry and Prose*, ed. Erdman. Parenthetical references to this volume give plate, line (when relevant), and (preceded by *E*) page number.

requesting that she be admitted to the inner circle of the community at Fetter Lane, "but . . . thanks be to him last friday at the love feast Our Savour was pleased to make me Suck his wounds and hug the Cross more then Ever and I trust will more and more till my fraile nature can hould no more" (Davies and Schuchard 40). Despite the depth of feeling evident here, Catherine left the Fetter Lane congregation after the death in 1751 of her first husband, not much more than twelve months after she was admitted to its inner circle, and there is little evidence to suggest that in later years she, or her second husband, James Blake, whom she married in 1752, were closely involved with the Moravians. And although Moravian thought and iconography undoubtedly left their mark on Blake's work, the most unequivocal of these marks, found on page 46 of *The Four Zoas,* offers a scathing critique of Moravian sexual-religious ideology (Otto, *Blake's Critique of Transcendence* 147–49).

Catherine Armitage's admission to the Moravian "Congregation of the Lamb" informs Ankarsjö's confidence that we can now speak of Blake—the child as well as the adult—as a Moravian (Ankarsjö 8); her exit from the same community seems to underwrite Rix's confidence that, whatever we decide about his childhood, if we begin with his writing "there is no substantial evidence to connect him directly with specific Moravian ideas" (Rix 22); and an earlier phase of the Fetter Lane Society seems to underwrite Farrell's and Jesse's confidence that Methodism is the context in which Blake's work can most accurately be placed. The truth probably lies somewhere beyond these three points. As Keri Davies argues, I think correctly, "Moravianism and Swedenborgianism [and we can add Methodism as well] . . . *marked* Blake" and "left their recoverable traces on his work"—but he adds that whether Blake "reacted against his religious background [or fell] in with it" is an open question ("Lost Moravian History" 1315). This last remark brings us full circle, to a Blake that is and is not a Moravian, is and is not a Swedenborgian, is and is not a Methodist, and, for that matter, is and is not a Christian. But perhaps this string of equivocations (and the either/or logic that governs their relation to each other) indicates that we are asking the wrong question.

The studies we have been discussing attempt to recover the immediate contexts within which Blake was working and, when they turn to Blake's work, to coordinate Moravian/Swedenborgian/Methodist and Blakean motifs so that the former can act as a key to the latter. They are not primarily interested in the poet's rereading of these contexts. This is ironic given that Blake's relation to systems of belief, of whatever kind, is more strongly informed by an impulse to rearticulate by moving away from (rather than to reform so that he can then draw near to) their central tenets. This chapter therefore reverses their emphases, first by focusing on Blake's rereading of his sources. Second, by focusing on a topic arguably at the core of Blake's work, the Incarnation, it discusses Blake's relation to Swedenborgianism and Zinzendorf's Moravianism in a wider context and, in so doing, it begins to explain his simultaneous *attraction to* and *disgust at* the Christian religion, in its Moravian and Swedenborgian, as well as its more conventional, forms. Through revising these religious systems, Blake articulates his understanding of imagination in a way that troubles fixed oppositions between the secular, the religious, and the heretical. As I propose in the following pages, he does this by suggesting, rather provocatively, that the ability of imagination to veer from the given, and the association of this capacity with the deepest (most divine) impulses of life, associates the heretical, perhaps even the secular at certain moments of history, with the active spiritual life that (in Blake's view) religion struggles to find. (Scheinberg, Hurley, and LaPorte, all in this part of the volume, also challenge tidy divisions between the "secular" and the "religious" in evaluations of nineteenth-century poetry and poetics, though Hurley and I diverge productively in our accounts of Blake's theo-poetics.)

My argument moves through three phases, which I call revolution, critique, and heresy. The first focuses on the last plate of Blake's *There Is No Natural Religion*, the earliest of Blake's illuminated books, which was etched in 1788; the second discusses the eleventh of Blake's watercolor illustrations to Job, which were drawn in 1805, when Blake, after putting *The Four Zoas* (1797–1804) to one side, had begun work on *Milton a Poem* (1804–11); and the third turns to the concluding plate of *The Gates of Paradise* (1793), which was added to this book of emblems in 1820.

REVOLUTION

There Is No Natural Religion comprises two sequences of emblematic designs and aphoristic propositions ("series a" and "series b"), each of which develops an argument that contradicts the other. The first begins with the claim, echoing the thought of John Locke, that "Man cannot naturally Perceive. but through his natural or bodily organs," which puts us on the path to the conclusion that "The desires & perceptions of man untaught by any thing but organs of sense, must be limited to objects of sense" (*E* 2). The second, dismissing the premise that introduces the first and the conclusion drawn from it, begins with the assertion that "Mans perceptions are not bounded by organs of perception"; and this sets in motion a train of thought that leads to the conclusion, which is also a discovery, that "If it were not for the Poetic or Prophetic character. the Philosophic & Experimental would soon be at the ratio of all things & stand still, unable to do other than repeat the same dull round over again" (*E* 3). "Poetic" here means "creative, formative, productive" (*OED*), while "Prophetic" can be glossed as critique, judgment, and prediction.[6] Their collocation suggests the modern discovery that the "'lack of reality' of reality," engineered by the prophetic, is indivisible from the "invention of other realities" (Lyotard 77), the work of the poetic.

This entangling of religious, Enlightenment, and Romantic impulses becomes still more surprising when we turn to the "Application," which invites readers/viewers to draw a parallel between, on the one hand, the finite and the infinite (the human and the divine) and, on the other hand, the closed and the open (the respective subjects of series a and b): "He who sees the Infinite in all things sees God" (*E* 3) This parallel is then supplemented by a second, discussed below, which invites readers/viewers to draw a correspondence between the Poetic/Prophetic character and the Incarnation: the former, now identified with the latter, introduces the infinite into the finite, the open into what had been simply closed, producing an "In- / -finite world" (*E* 3) in which, as Blake writes two years later in *The Marriage of Heaven and Hell*, "God only Acts & Is, in existing beings or Men" (plate 16, *E* 40).

Blake elaborates this second parallel, between the Poetic/Prophetic character and the Incarnation, on plate b12 (fig. 15.1), the concluding plate of *There Is No Natural Religion*. This plate is divided into three locales: the upper two-thirds of the design, which is filled with text that seems to be floating in an empty sky; the space immediately beneath the text, where a naked man, with rays of light radiating from his head, is lying on a bed of light; and the "darkness visible" (Milton, *Paradise Lost* 1:63) beneath him, which seems to be rising up from the bottom of the page in order to hold him aloft (an effect that is heightened in copies b and c).

These disparate locales are fairly obvious evocations of Heaven, Earth, and Hell, with the second midway between the light of the first and the darkness of the third. But it is possible to be more precise than that. Rather than conventional Christian cosmologies, where each of these realms is placed at a vast distance from the others, the arrangement on this plate recalls the Swedenborgian universe, where Hell's "infernal mansions" lie immediately below "every mountain, hill, rock, plain, and valley" of Heaven, and Earth lies in the cramped zone (on the line) between these realms, where it is marked by both (Swedenborg, *Heaven and Hell* par. 588).

---

6. In the margins of his copy of Watson's *An Apology for the Bible* (1797), Blake writes that "Every honest man is a Prophet he utters his opinion both of private & public matters / Thus / If you go on So / the result is So / He never says such a thing shall happen let you do what you will" (*E* 617).

The Secularization of Religious Categories

FIGURE 15.1. William Blake, *There Is No Natural Religion*, plate b12 (6.1 x 4.6 cm), copy B, composed 1788, printed ca. 1794, Yale Center for British Art, Paul Mellon Collection. In the public domain and provided through the Center's online collection catalog according to its open access policy.

The rays of light shining from the head of the man who occupies the intermediate locale identify him as Jesus, the incarnated word, and this in turn identifies this cosmic scene as the moment of Incarnation. As the text announces in summary fashion:

Therefore
God becomes as
we are, that we
may be as he
    is
(plate b12; *E* 3)

In *The Doctrine of the New Jerusalem,* Swedenborg writes that, during the Incarnation, "the Lord assumed in the World a Humanity *conceived* of Jehovah, . . . which humanity was born of the Virgin Mary." He therefore had "both a Divinity and Humanity: a Divinity from his Godhead that was from Eternity, and a Humanity from the Virgin Mary born in Time" (par. 59). This inserts the divine into the temporal but nevertheless leaves the border between these realms intact. Swedenborg adds to the passage quoted above, apparently to ensure that the distinction between Divinity and Humanity is maintained, that "Jesus put off the latter Humanity [in the crucifixion], and put on or assumed a Divine Humanity, which is what is meant in the Word by the Son of God" (par. 59).

In Moravian theology, Incarnation is a still more dramatic event because, rather than "a Divinity [emanating] from his Godhead," Jesus is also the Father, "the Creator of the universe." As proof of this claim, Zinzendorf cites "the first chapter of the Gospel of John," which, he argues, "clearly paints Jesus as the preexistent *logos* who is the creative force in the universe" (Atwood 80–81). This enables him to emphasize, in much more material terms than Swedenborg, the humanity of Christ, which in turn underwrites his rejection of "the long Christian tradition of contempt for the body, particularly the sexual organs" (Atwood 88).

Notwithstanding these differences, both agree that the Incarnation invites us to follow Christ by casting off our earthly humanity in order to assume a divine humanity—not by canceling our bodily desires but by sublimating them. For Swedenborg, the process is initiated by the mind, which, by opening itself to influx from Heaven (troped as a sexual/electrical fluid), shapes life into forms congruent with the divine.[7] For Zinzendorf, a similar metamorphosis is effected by the emotions: by focusing attention on the death and suffering rather than the birth or resurrection of Jesus, we are re-formed by His "spilled blood," which is "the conduit of the Holy Spirit and the means of re-creating the entire world . . . [and restoring] all things to their original purity" (Atwood 101).[8]

Blake's design echoes both of these accounts of Incarnation, but it does so in order to veer from them. First, Jesus is identified here with the poetic/prophetic character. This draws Blake apart from Swedenborg, for whom God the Father is the only legitimate making or shaping power, and seems at first to bring him close to Zinzendorf, for whom, as I have mentioned, Jesus is the Creator (the Son and the Father are one)—but Zinzendorf, of course, doesn't

---

7. I describe this process in "Organizing the Passions."
8. According to Zinzendorf, Christ's "blood of reconciliation is the *proprium quarti modi* [essential principle] of the entire holy creature, of the entire blessed universe" (qtd. in Atwood 101).

identify Jesus the Creator with the poetic/prophetic, which rests on human faculties found in everyone. His reticence is understandable, given that this step implies another, which is summarized by Blake's claim that Christ "*is the only God . . .* And so am I and so are you" (*BR* 421).

Second, and following from this secularization of the divine, Blake's design implies that during the Incarnation Heaven is emptied of much of its power. The vertical line formed by the words "**becomes**," "**are**," "**be**," and "**is**" quietly enacts, as we read, what the text describes, namely the descent of the divine—now troped as the poetic/prophetic, which is presented in this book as isomorphic with life itself. This recalls Zinzendorf's conviction, reminiscent of the *Patripassism* heresy, that God suffered on the cross and, more radically, that "'God himself is dead, He has died on the cross" (Zinzendorf, qtd. in Atwood 80). But, of course, rather than the crucifixion, Blake's design is focused on the birth/resurrection of Jesus. And rather than looking up to Heaven or down to Hell, Jesus/God therefore looks out to the reader, from within time, as if urging us to take part in the revolution he has begun, which will shift power from those on high to the humanity beneath them.

Next, once the transcendent Heaven has been emptied of its power, the endless struggle between Heaven and Hell can take a different form. Indeed, one of the striking features of this design is that the human divine emerges at the boundary between, and therefore we can say in the interactions between, up and down, sky and Earth, Heaven and Hell—and men and women as well, if one notices that the reclining figure has large breasts and long hair. This last point echoes Moravian representations of Jesus as androgynous (Fogleman 5), but here the birth of this figure is coincident with his resurrection, and both occur in time. More broadly, to adopt terms used by Blake in *The Marriage of Heaven and Hell*, Heaven and Hell are contraries, which are both necessary for human life, rather than opposites determined to put each other out of business. Blake, it can be argued, is here already beginning to reimagine Swedenborg's cosmology as a psychology and sociology.

And finally, the New Jerusalem is transferred from the end of time to the present, where the poetic/prophetic opens a new world that will sweep away the old. The former, although still seen against the backdrop of the latter, can be glimpsed in the rising sun/son, the bed of light on which the divine humanity is lying, and the human landscape that appears to be taking shape—which is arguably the result of the friction between a Heaven, an Earth, and a Hell no longer bound to a higher authority or to prescribed relations with each other.

There Is No Natural Religion, we can say in partial summary of this phase of my argument, concludes in this design with revolution—an attempt to turn

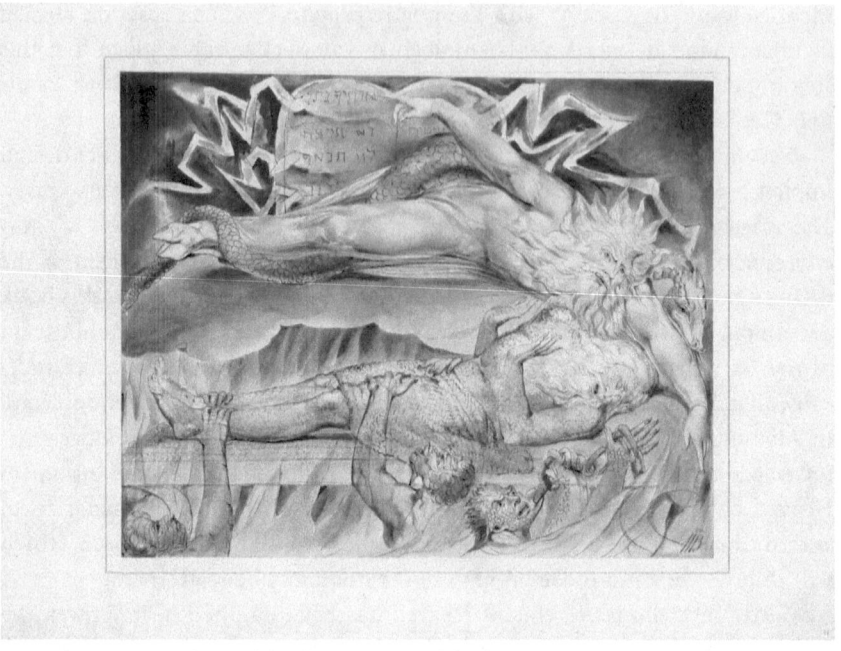

FIGURE 15.2. William Blake, "Job's Evil Dreams" (23.4 x 28 cm), Number eleven of the twenty-one original drawings executed for Thomas Butts, ca. 1805–10, illustrating the Book of Job. Used with permission from the Pierpont Morgan Library, New York.

the wheel of time full circle—and in so doing to bring us back to the primitive essence of religion in the poetic/prophetic, which is Jesus in each person. This remnant of the transcendent in the temporal guarantees that the force exerted by "things as they are" is not insurmountable—it is for Blake, one might say, the subject of liberation. But this means that for the status quo, Jesus is Satan—a figure who breaks all of the commandments because he acts "from impulse: not from rules" (23–24; E 43).

And yet, beginning with *The Book of Thel,* published only one year after *There Is No Natural Religion,* Blake becomes more pessimistic about the forces that bind us to the world in which we are born. In this phase of his career, the imagination is personified as Los (loss)—an inverted Sol or dark sun—who is in league with gods, priests, and kings. Blake therefore returns with renewed intensity to religion, and to Swedenborg and Zinzendorf, in order to map its dynamics. In broad terms, revolutionary return and the glad tidings it brings is followed (rather than preceded) in Blake's oeuvre by the grim news offered by critique. The intensity of this critical return to religion and the complexity of its products can be glimpsed if we turn briefly to the eleventh of Blake's watercolor illustrations to the Book of Job, "Job's Evil Dreams," which stands at the center of the series (fig. 15.2).

CRITIQUE

In the biblical story, Job is introduced as a "perfect and upright" man, who "feared God, and eschewed evil" (1:1)—but virtue is here the catalyst for disaster rather than the foundation for reward. Amazed by Job's obedience, God draws him to Satan's attention, who is much less impressed. If you withdraw your largesse, he argues, then Job will "curse thee to thy face" (1:11); and he asks for permission to put God's upright man to the test. When this is granted, in rapid succession Job loses his possessions, his servants, sons, and daughters, and his health—but nevertheless remains steadfast in his virtue.

This ought to be the end of the test. And indeed, in the last chapter of the book, what Job has lost is returned with interest. But this occurs only when he accepts that God's reasons are beyond his comprehension, judges *himself* (rather than the order of the universe) to be abhorrent, and "repent[s] in dust and ashes" (42:6). It is hardly surprising, therefore, that the Book of Job is sometimes read as a work of ideology, which attempts to justify what can't be justified, namely the suffering of the innocent (Larrimore 4).[9]

While closely following the course of this narrative, Blake's illustrations recontextualize it, most overtly at the beginning, end, and center of the sequence ("Job and His Family," "Job and His Family Restored to Prosperity," and "Job's Evil Dreams" [fig. 15.2]). In the first, Job and his wife are seated, with open books on their laps, in the midst of their family, on the edge of a vast world that extends from the line of sheep in front of them to the spires and tents, hills and mountains, and rising moon and setting sun behind them. As the words inscribed on the sun confirm, they are praying to "Our Father which art in Heavn"—a realm conjured by the musical instruments hidden in the branches immediately above Job and his wife (the silent music of the spheres).

In the last illustration, this scene is reversed: the world created by God the Father is now eclipsed by Job, his wife, and their family, who have replaced their books with scrolls, taken the musical instruments down from the tree, and stood up to play them. It is now the moon that is setting, the sun that is rising, and the day that is beginning to dawn. In this emergent world, as the words inscribed on the sun underline, prayer to a transcendent God has become praise for a God who, as the now heavenly-earthly music suggests, "only Acts & Is, in existing beings or Men" (plate 16; *E* 40).

Midway between these opposites, "Job's Evil Dreams" (fig. 15.2) maps the dynamics of the world in which the story of Job unfolds, where the active

---

9. The Book of Job is more complex and its interpretations much more varied than my summary of its plot allows. With regard to these matters, Larrimore, Lamb, and Sanders are helpful guides.

forces of life have been put to sleep and, consequently, are at the mercy of an inhuman world. It is at the same both a terrifying warning, designed to draw Job back to the beginning of the narrative, and a riddle, which if solved will take him forward, to the book's conclusion. In this second guise, the design develops a profound critique of Moravian and Swedenborgian, as well as more orthodox, attempts to turn the senses from temporal to eternal things.

In "Job's Evil Dreams," as in *There Is No Natural Religion*, Heaven, Earth, and Hell occupy respectively the upper, middle, and lower third of the design, with the second drawing the line that divides upper from lower regions. The first of these realms proceeds from God, who is represented, first, by the stone tablets of the Law that hang in the air just below the center of the upper-boundary of the design; next, by the bolts of lightning that pierce the sky; third, by the Heavenly Man, who in Swedenborgian iconography is a figure for both God and Heaven; and, fourth, by the *spiritual sun*, represented by the head of the Heavenly Man, which, as Swedenborg claims it ought, hangs permanently in the east, at an angle of forty-five degrees to the horizon (*True Christian Religion*, par. 29).

The downward pressure of this immense spiritual realm is matched by the upward force exerted by Hell, whose demons reach up from a sea of fire to grasp Job's legs and loins. And together these antagonistic locales define Earth—the narrow space within which Job (who functions also as a synecdoche for Earth) has been confined. In contrast to the concluding plate of *There Is No Natural Religion*, where life emerges in the open-ended interactions between Heaven, Earth, and Hell (which, for Blake, signify reason, imagination, and energy), the Earth here becomes the locale where humanity must choose between God and Satan, Heaven and Hell—a choice eloquently presented by the Heavenly Man's outstretched arms and pointing fingers.

The body of the serpent coiling around the body of the Heavenly Man makes the situation in which Job finds himself much more complicated than I have suggested. The former emerges three times from behind the latter, each time increasing in size—first from behind the sole and over the heel of his left foot, a portion of the body associated by Swedenborg with "the grossest of natural things" (*The Spiritual Diary*, par. 3453), which is here marked by a cloven hoof; then from between his legs, where it doubles as a giant phallus; and then, finally, to the right of the Heavenly Man's head, where the serpent waits ready to strike.

Heaven is here driven by sublimated sexual energy, which it turns against the body from which it has been drawn. And, with the serpent and cloven hoof now in mind, when one looks again at the devils they seem to be trying

FIGURE 15.3. William Blake, *For the Sexes: The Gates of Paradise,* plate 19 (9.5 x 6.3 cm), copy D, ca. 1825 (PML 63936). Used with permission from the Pierpont Morgan Library, New York.

to protect Job's body from the monstrous being above him. Reading from the left to the right: the first and second are protecting his feet and loins respectively, while the third is getting ready to throw a chain around the head of the serpent.

But Job seems unaware of these details and, moreover, whether he turns to Heaven or Hell, his decision will intensify the wars of religion that are tearing him apart. Just as significantly, at this point in the narrative, the drama in which he is involved is so compelling that he seems unable to take the only other course open to him, namely to wake up. This third possibility becomes still more obvious to the viewer, although just as hidden from the dreamer, in the concluding plate of *The Gates of Paradise.*

HERESY

For Children: The Gates of Paradise (1793) offers a profoundly pessimistic view of the stages of life, as a sequence of births/resurrections from confined to larger worlds, in which we are imprisoned all over again. In the course of this book, the hopes of revolutionary second birth are eclipsed by catastrophe (plates 6–10); the glad tidings of religious "second birth" take us to the grave (11–16); and this end brings us back to the beginning of the story, where vegetative life is drawn once more from the grave (1–5). The title of this book is therefore cruelly ironic: in each of life's stages, the Gates of Paradise remain locked. What we had thought were Gates transport us only to the misery evoked by the last line, an echo of Job 17:14, through which we can hear Job's voice:

> (plate 11) My days are past, my purposes are broken off, even the thoughts of my heart . . . (14) I have said to corruption, Thou art my father: to the worm, Thou are my mother, and my sister. (15) And where is now my hope? as for my hope, who shall see it? (plates 11, 14–15; *E* 32–33)

This seems conclusive. And yet, in 1820, when Blake reissued *The Gates of Paradise*, he addressed it to the Sexes rather than Children and added a prologue, two plates of verse, entitled "The Keys of the Gates," and an epilogue addressed "To The Accuser who is The God of This World" (fig. 15.3). But rather than using these keys to pass through the Gates, for the purposes of this chapter we can confine our attention to the plate that brings the volume to a close.

Like plate b12 from *There Is No Natural Religion*, plate 19 of *For the Sexes: The Gates of Paradise* is divided between text in the upper half of the plate and an image in the lower half. At the bottom of both designs a man lies naked on his back, although in the later design this is not a moment of Incarnation or emergence. Rather than appearing at the point of intersection between up and down, sky and earth, Heaven and Hell, and so on, the man here lies within a world that predates him, on a slab of rock, in an empty landscape.

As the staff beside him suggests, this is the Lost Traveller mentioned in the last line of text on this plate, exhausted by his journey, who now lies fast asleep. Filling the space between his body and the text high above him is his "Dream under the Hill," with the Dream represented as a bat-winged demon, who has turned his back to the viewer; stretched his arms and wings out wide; and swung his outstretched left leg back from the hip, and lower right leg back from the knee, until the heels of both feet are at roughly the same height as his buttocks. This awkward pose makes it appear that the demon is floating in the air; and yet, contradicting this impression, the shin of his left leg presses down hard on the upturned left side of the Traveller's chest, while the toes of his right foot touch the man near his genitals, suggesting that the one provides the foundation and the other the upward pressure that keep the demon/nightmare aloft.

Steven Blankaart writes in *The Physical Dictionary* (1702), echoing Robert Burton's popular *Anatomy of Melancholy* (1621), that "*Incubus*, [or] the Night-Mare, is a depraved Imagination, whereby People asleep fancie that their Wind-pipe is oppressed by some superincumbent Body, that their Breath is stop'd" (qtd. in Rivière 152). In this case, however, the "superincumbent Body" pressing down on the Traveller's chest is "The God of this world," as well as the world for which He is the ground, which is conjured by the sun, ten stars, and crescent moon emblazoned on (or seen through) his wings. Further, it is not just the imagination that is holding this heavy weight aloft. "The white sole of the demon's right foot doubles as the Traveller's almost-erect penis, suggesting the sublimated sexual energy that drives 'This World' and animates its God" (Otto, *Multiplying Worlds* 126).[10] And the heel of the demon's left foot points towards the dreamer's head, the seat of reason, suggesting that "This World" is a product not just of co-opted imagination and sublimated energy but of reason as well. The point is underlined, on the one hand, by the heavy line that joins the demon's left ankle and the dreamer's head (Norvig 110) and, on the other hand, by the line that runs from the demon's right foot, along the middle of his back, up to the top of his head.

While the Traveller is asleep, this god and his world seem real; but if he were to awake we would in effect be returned to the moment of emergence depicted on the concluding plate of *There Is No Natural Religion*—but with at least three differences. First, the poetic/prophetic character, laboring inside the Traveller's body, can here be identified as Los, Blake's personation of the poetic-prophetic faculty, who has here, with the aid of sublimated desire and religious/secular reason,[11] helped build this nightmare world. Second, waking is pictured here not as the creation of a world (that would be insufficient to break from the dynamic depicted) but as a resurrection from a solitary to a

---

10. See also Hilton, *Literal Imagination* (166) and "Some Sexual Connotations" (169).

11. Religious and secular reason are normally opposed to each other; but in Blake's oeuvre they appear as different expressions of the same impulse, viz. the urge (driven by fear and anxiety) to confine life within the given. They are therefore represented by the same figure—Urizen ("your reason" or the "horizon" drawn around life by the powerful)—who appears variously as god, king, priest, empiricist, natural philosopher (scientist), and so on. This identification brings religious reason into the heart of the secular.

shared world. And third, the locale and meaning of the Incarnation shifts—rather than the creator of worlds, Jesus—who, again, for Blake is identified with the imagination—is the creative power able to open our worlds to the complexity that lies outside them. This is why Jesus the imagination is characterized in Blake's oeuvre as an iconoclast and breaker of limits, who "breaking through the Central Zones of Death & Hell / Opens Eternity in Time & Space; triumphant in Mercy" (*Jerusalem* plate 76: 21–22; *E* 231).

In Blake's later works, these twin aspects of imagination can't be divided from each other. Instead, imagination is understood as a bivalent process: it is an iconoclastic power that strives to open apparent reality to the complexity that eludes it and, at the same time, a creative power that draws and then draws again the line between order and complexity, the visible and the invisible, the given and the possible, and the religious and the secular as well.

If we accept Niklas Luhmann's claim that religion is an attempt to mediate between what we do and what we don't understand, and to find a semantics adequate to this disjunction, then prophecy is one of its most powerful tools: it reduces the tension between the known and the unknown by placing historical events in relation to a transcendental authority. But if the temporal world is an open-ended field composed of multiple interacting forces and there is no transcendental reality to which it can be referred—as Blake's rereading of Swedenborg and Zinzendorf proposes—then what becomes important "is not the potential for security" provided by prophecy, but rather "a potential for insecurity." And "not dependence" on a transcendental reality or God "but rather freedom: the place of capriciousness that cannot find a home" (Luhmann 43). This "freedom" is closely aligned with the ability of the poetic/prophetic to veer from the given, through the bivalent process I have sketched above.

In Blake's oeuvre, the prophet is accordingly displaced by the poet-prophet; the eternal world by the temporary forms of art; and the soul by the imagination (now defined as an open-ended potential rather than fixed essence). Rather than revealing the ideal (the eternal reality) to which the actual must conform, art becomes "the space of the emergence of the new, the unthought, the unrealized" (Grosz 77), and its imagined worlds the locus of attempts to supplement, compete with, or transform the actual world. At the conclusion of these metamorphoses it is possible to say, anticipating Nietzsche and Deleuze (although with very different emphases), that "'we the artists' = 'we the seekers after knowledge or truth' = 'we the inventors of new possibilities of life'" (Deleuze 103).

Where revolution attempts to recover the primitive essence of things, and critique rails against the veil that hides this essence, the poetic/prophetic, understood as the ability both to open apparent reality to a complexity that exceeds it *and* to veer from the given, might be described as the original heresy—a heresy that brings religious sensibilities into the heart of the modern secular world. Heresy in this sense is perhaps best evocated by the twin claims that Swedenborg "has written all the old falsehoods" because "He conversed with Angels who are all religious, & conversed not with Devils who all hate religion, for he was incapable thro' his conceited notions" (*Marriage of Heaven and Hell* plates 22–23; *E* 43) and, still more forcefully, that "he who is out of the Church & opposes it is no less an Agent of Religion than he who is in it. to be an Error & to be Cast out is a part of Gods design" (*Vision of the Last Judgment* plate 84; *E* 562).

Statements such as these imply that the boundary between the religious and the secular, the orthodox and the heretical, can be revised, in part because, in both of these pairs, each term is implicated in the fate of the other. But in so doing they raise a more fundamental question, which is the chief preoccupation of Blake's late thought, namely:

> How to transform the hierarchical unity of orthodoxy and heresy such that they regain equal right within a new thought, putting an end to the violent acts of orthodoxy, without any longer claiming to make of heresy a new principle of absolute rebellion which risks simply reversing the historical state of things and maintaining the religious exploitation of man under another form? (Laruelle 28)

In Blake's time this "new thought" was, and in our own time arguably is, the most unsettling heresy and the most important to affirm.

WORKS CITED

Altizer, Thomas J. J. *The New Apocalypse: The Radical Christian Vision of William Blake*. Michigan State UP, 1967.

Ankarsjö, Magnus. *William Blake and Religion: A New Critical View*. McFarland & Co., 2009.

Atwood, Craig D. *Community of the Cross: Moravian Piety in Colonial Bethlehem*. Pennsylvania State UP, 2004.

Aubre, Bryan. *Watchmen of Eternity: Blake's Debt to Jacob Boehme*. UP of America, 1986.

Ault, Donald D. *Visionary Physics: Blake's Response to Newton*. U of Chicago P, 1974.

Beer, John. *Blake's Humanism*. Manchester UP, 1968.

Bentley, G. E., Jr. *Blake Records*. Yale UP, 1969.

———. *Blake Records*. 2nd ed., Yale UP, 2001.

———. *The Stranger from Paradise: A Biography of William Blake*. Yale UP, 2001.

Birenbaum, Harvey. *Between Blake and Nietzsche*. Bucknell UP, 1992.

Blake, William. *The Complete Poetry and Prose of William Blake*. Newly rev. ed., edited by David V. Erdman, commentary by Harold Bloom, Anchor-Doubleday, 1988.

Bloom, Harold. *Blake's Apocalypse: A Study in Poetic Argument*. Gollancz, 1963.

Burton, Robert. *The Anatomy of Melancholy vvhat it is. VVith all the Kindes, Causes, Symptoms, Prognostickes, and seuerall Cures of it*. Oxford, 1621.

Clark, Lorraine. *Blake, Kierkegaard, and the Spectre of Dialectic*. Cambridge UP, 1991.

Colebrook, Claire. *Blake, Deleuzian Aesthetics and the Digital*. Continuum, 2012.

Crews, Daniel C. *Faith, Love, Hope: A History of the Unitas Fratrum*. Moravian Archives, 2008.

Damrosch, Leopold. *Symbol and Truth in Blake's Myth*. Princeton UP, 1980.

Davies, J. G. *The Theology of William Blake*. Clarendon P, 1948.

Davies, Keri. "The Lost Moravian History of William Blake's Family: Snapshots from the Archive." *Literature Compass*, vol. 3, no. 6, 2006, pp. 1297–1319.

———. "William Blake's Mother: A New Identification." *Blake: An Illustrated Quarterly*, vol. 33, no. 2, Fall 1999, pp. 36–50.

Davies, Keri, and Marsha Keith Schuchard. "Recovering the Lost Moravian History of William Blake's Family." *Blake: An Illustrated Quarterly*, vol. 38, no.1, Summer 2004, pp. 36–43.

Deleuze, Gilles. *Nietzsche and Philosophy*. Translated by Hugh Tomlinson, Columbia UP, 2006.

Farrell, Michael. *Blake and the Methodists*. Palgrave Macmillan, 2014.

Fogleman, Aaron Spencer. *Jesus Is Female: Moravians and the Challenge of Radical Religion in Early America*. U of Pennsylvania P, 2007.

George, Diana Hume. *Blake and Freud*. Cornell UP, 1980.

Great Britain. *An Act for encouraging the people known by the name of Unitas Fratrum or United Brethren, to settle in His Majesty's colonies in America*. London, 1749.

Grosz, Elizabeth A. *Architecture from the Outside: Essays on Virtual and Real Space*. MIT Press, 2001.

Harper, George Mills. *The Neoplatonism of William Blake*. U of North Carolina P, 1961.

Hilton, Nelson. *Literal Imagination: Blake's Vision of Words*. U of California P, 1983.

———. "Some Sexual Connotations." *Blake: An Illustrated Quarterly*, vol. 16, no. 3, Winter 1982/1983, pp. 166–71.

Jesse, Jennifer. *William Blake's Religious Vision: There's a Methodism in His Madness*. Lexington Books, 2013.

Lamb, Jonathan. *The Rhetoric of Suffering: Reading the Book of Job in the Eighteenth Century*. Oxford UP, 1995.

Larrimore, Mark. *The Book of Job: A Biography*. Princeton UP, 2013.

Laruelle, François. *Future Christ: A Lesson in Heresy*. Translated by Anthony Paul Smith, Continuum, 2010.

Luhmann, Niklas. *Observations on Modernity*. Translated by William Whobrey, Stanford UP, 1998.

Lyotard, Jean-François. "Answering the Question: What Is Postmodernism?" *The Postmodern Condition: A Report on Knowledge*, translated by Régis Durand. 1984. U of Minnesota P, 1997, pp. 71–82.

Margoliouth, H. M. "The Marriage of Blake's Parents." *Notes and Queries*, no. 192, 6 Sept. 1947, pp. 380–81.

Mee, Jon. *Dangerous Enthusiasm: William Blake and the Culture of Radicalism in the 1790s*. Clarendon P, 1992.

Milton, John. *The Poems of John Milton*. Edited by John Carey and Alastair Fowler, Longmans, Green and Co., 1968.

Norvig, Gerda S. *Dark Figures in the Desired Country: Blake's Illustrations to* The Pilgrim's Progress. U of California P, 1993.

Nuttall, Anthony David. *The Alternative Trinity: Gnostic Heresy in Marlowe, Milton, and Blake*. Clarendon Press, 1998.

Otto, Peter. *Blake's Critique of Transcendence*. Oxford UP, 2000.

———. *Multiplying Worlds: Romanticism, Modernity, and the Emergence of Virtual Reality*. Oxford UP, 2011.

———. "Organizing the Passions: Minds, Bodies, Machines, and the Sexes in Blake and Swedenborg." *European Romantic Review*, vol. 26, no. 3, 2015, pp. 367–77.

Peucker, Paul. *A Time of Sifting: Mystical Marriage and the Crisis of Moravian Piety in the Eighteenth Century*. Pennsylvania State UP, 2015.

"poetic, adj. and n." *OED Online*, Oxford UP, Mar. 2018, Accessed 27 May 2018.

Podmore, Colin. *The Moravian Church in England, 1728–1760*. Clarendon Press, 1998.

Potkay, Adam. *The Story of Joy: From the Bible to Late Romanticism*. Cambridge UP, 2007.

Punter, David. *Blake, Hegel and Dialectic*. Rodopi, 1982.

Raine, Kathleen. *Blake and Tradition*. The A. W. Mellon Lectures in the Fine Arts. Routledge & Kegan Paul, 1969.

Reichel, W. C. *A Register of Members of the Moravian Church, . . . Transcribed from a MS in the Handwriting of the Rev. Abraham Reincke*. Nazareth, 1873.

Rivière, Janine. *Dreams in Early Modern England: "Visions of the Night."* Routledge, 2017.

Rix, Robert. *William Blake and the Cultures of Radical Christianity*. Ashgate, 2007.

Rovira, James. *Blake and Kierkegaard: Creation and Anxiety*. Continuum, 2010.

Ryan, Robert M. *The Romantic Reformation: Religious Politics in English Literature, 1789–1824*. Cambridge UP, 1997.

Sanders, Paul S., editor. *Twentieth Century Interpretations of the Book of Job*. Prentice-Hall, 1968.

Schuchard, Marsha Keith. *Emanuel Swedenborg, Secret Agent on Earth and in Heaven*. Brill, 2012.

———. *Why Mrs. Blake Cried: William Blake and the Sexual Basis of Spiritual Vision*. Century, 2006.

Sorenson, Peter J. *William Blake's Recreation of Gnostic Myth: Resolving the Apparent Incongruities*. Edwin Mellen Press, 1995.

Spector, Sheila A. *Wonders Divine: The Development of Blake's Kabbalistic Myth*. Bucknell UP, 2001.

Stead, Geoffrey. *The Exotic Plant: A History of the Moravian Church in Britain, 1742–2000*. Epworth Press, 2003.

Swedenborg, Emanuel. *The Doctrine of the New Jerusalem Concerning the Lord*. London, 1784.

———. *The Spiritual Diary*. Translated by Alfred Acton, Swedenborg Society, 1977.

———. *A Treatise concerning Heaven and Hell, and of the Wonderful Things therein, as Heard and Seen.* 2nd ed., translated by William Cookworthy and Thomas Hartley, London, 1784.

———. *True Christian Religion; Containing the Universal Theology of the New Church.* London, 1781. 2 vols.

Thompson, E. P. *Witness Against the Beast: William Blake and the Moral Law.* Cambridge UP, 1993.

Youngquist, Paul. *Madness and Blake's Myth.* Pennsylvania State UP, 1989.

CONTRIBUTORS

(Listed in Order of Appearance)

JOSHUA KING is Associate Professor of English at Baylor University and Margarett Root Brown Chair in Robert Browning and Victorian Studies at Baylor's Armstrong Browning Library. He is author of *Imagined Spiritual Communities in Britain's Age of Print* (The Ohio State UP, 2015) and has published numerous articles on Romantic and Victorian poetry, religion, and print culture. He is at work on a new book, tentatively titled *The Body of Christ, the Body of the Earth*, which recovers formative relationships between poetics, Christology, and emergent ecological awareness in Victorian literature and culture.

WINTER JADE WERNER is Assistant Professor of English at Wheaton College in Massachusetts. Her essays have appeared in *Nineteenth-Century Literature, Dickens Studies Annual, Nineteenth-Century Contexts,* and *Victorians Institute Journal,* and she is currently working on her first monograph (forthcoming from The Ohio State UP), *Missionary Cosmopolitanism in the British Nineteenth Century: Literary Experiments in Global Thought.*

JEFFREY L. MORROW is Associate Professor of Theology at Immaculate Conception Seminary School of Theology at Seton Hall University. He is the author of *Three Skeptics and the Bible* (Pickwick, 2016), *Theology, Politics, and Exegesis* (Pickwick, 2017), and *Alfred Loisy and Modern Biblical Studies* (Catholic U of America P, 2018).

J. BARTON SCOTT is Assistant Professor of Historical Studies and the Study of Religion at the University of Toronto. He is the author of *Spiritual Despots: Modern Hinduism and the Genealogies of Self-Rule* (U of Chicago P, 2016) and the co-editor of *Imagining the Public in Modern South Asia* (Routledge, 2016).

MIKE SANDERS is Senior Lecturer in Nineteenth-Century Writing at the University of Manchester. He is the author of *The Poetry of Chartism: Aesthetics, Politics, History* (Cambridge UP, 2009), as well as a number of other articles about Chartist cultural production. His current research project explores the role of religion within the Chartist movement. Mike prefers crooked roads.

DAVID NASH is Professor of History at Oxford Brookes University. He has written and published on the history of the secular movement and on blasphemy in Britain and the wider world for over thirty years. He has also published on the history of secularization and has advised governments and NGOs in Britain, Ireland, Australia, and the European Commission about issues around modern blasphemy laws and their repeal.

DOMINIC ERDOZAIN is a Research Fellow at King's College London and a visiting scholar at Emory University. He is the author of *The Soul of Doubt: The Religious Roots of Unbelief from Luther to Marx* (Oxford UP, 2015) and *The Problem of Pleasure: Sport, Recreation and the Crisis of Victorian Religion* (Boydell Press, 2010). He is currently writing a religious history of the gun in America.

MARY WILSON CARPENTER is Professor Emerita of Queen's University in Kingston, Ontario. She is the author of *George Eliot and the Landscape of Time: Narrative Form and Protestant Apocalyptic History* (U of North Carolina P, 1986), *Imperial Bibles, Domestic Bodies: Women, Sexuality, and Religion in the Victorian Market* (Ohio UP, 2003), and *Health, Medicine and Society in Victorian England* (Praeger, 2010). She is currently writing a book on Margaret Mathewson, a Wesleyan Methodist from Shetland who wrote a "Sketch" about being operated on by Joseph Lister in 1877 for tuberculosis of the shoulder joint.

MICHAEL LEDGER-LOMAS is a Lecturer in the History of Christianity in Britain at King's College London. He is currently completing a monograph on Queen Victoria's religion.

RICHA DWOR is an Instructor in the English Department at Douglas College. Her monograph, *Jewish Feeling: Difference and Affect in Nineteenth-Century Jewish Women's Writing* (Bloomsbury Academic, 2015) reads Grace Aguilar and Amy Levy alongside George Eliot and Henry James. She is the editor of the anthology *Religious Feeling*, forthcoming in the Routledge series *Nineteenth-Century Literature, Religion and Society*.

MIRIAM ELIZABETH BURSTEIN is Professor of English at the College at Brockport, State University of New York. She is author of *Narrating Women's History in Britain, 1770–1902* (Ashgate, 2004) and *Victorian Reformations: Historical Fiction and Religious Controversy, 1820–1900* (U of Notre Dame P, 2013), and editor of Mary Augusta Ward's *Robert Elsmere* (2nd ed., Victorian Secrets, 2018). She is currently working on a new history of the religious novel in nineteenth-century Britain.

DOMINIC JANES is a cultural historian who studies texts and visual images related to Britain in its local and international contexts since the eighteenth century. Within this sphere he focuses on the histories of gender, sexuality, and religion. His most recent books are *Picturing the Closet* (Oxford UP, 2015), *Visions of Queer Martyrdom* (U of Chicago P, 2015), and *Oscar Wilde Prefigured* (U of Chicago P, 2016). He has been the recipient of a number of research awards including fellowships from the UK Arts and Humanities Research Council and the British Academy.

MARK KNIGHT is Senior Lecturer in the Department of English Literature and Creative Writing at Lancaster University. His books include *Chesterton and Evil* (Fordham UP, 2004), *Nineteenth-Century Religion and Literature: An Introduction* (with Emma Mason, Oxford UP, 2006), *An Introduction to Religion and Literature* (Continuum, 2009), and *Good Words: Evangelicalism and the Victorian Novel* (The Ohio State UP, 2019). He is also editor of *The Routledge Companion to Literature and Religion* (2016) and co-editor of the Bloomsbury series *New Directions in Religion and Literature*.

CYNTHIA SCHEINBERG is Professor of English Literature and the Dean of the Feinstein School of Humanities, Arts and Education at Roger Williams University in Bristol, Rhode Island; prior to this position, she was a Professor of English and served in various administrative roles at Mills College in Oakland, California. Her scholarship focuses on intersections between Victorian literature, religious discourse, women writers, and Jewish studies and includes her book, *Women's Poetry and Religion in Victorian England: Jewish Identity and Christian Culture* (Cambridge UP, 2002) as well as a many journal articles, book chapters, and reviews. She has received awards and fellowships from the National Endowment for the Humanities, the Carnegie Foundation for the Advancement of Teaching, the Harvard Divinity School, the Oxford Centre for Hebrew and Jewish Studies, and the Woodrow Wilson / Mellon Fellowship Foundation.

CHARLES LAPORTE is Associate Professor of English at the University of Washington. He works on poetry and on the intersection of religion and literature, and his *Victorian Poets and the Changing Bible* (U of Virginia P, 2011) was awarded the Sonya Rudikoff Prize for a best first book in Victorian studies. He has recently edited a pair of issues of the journal *Nineteenth-Century Literature* on the topic of New Religious Movements and Secularization.

MICHAEL D. HURLEY teaches English at the University of Cambridge, where he is a Fellow of St Catharine's College. His books include *Faith in Poetry: Verse Style as a Mode of Religious Belief* (Bloomsbury, 2017), *G. K. Chesterton* (Northcote House, 2012) and, with Michael O'Neil, *Poetic Form: An Introduction* (Cambridge UP, 2012). He is editor of the new Penguin Classics edition of *The Complete Father Brown Stories,* and co-editor, with Marcus Waithe, of *Thinking Through Style: Non-Fiction Prose of the Long Nineteenth Century* (Oxford UP, 2018).

PETER OTTO is Professor of Literature and Director of the Research Unit in Enlightenment, Romanticism, and Contemporary Culture at the University of Melbourne. His recent publications include *Multiplying Worlds: Romanticism, Modernity and the Emergence of Virtual Reality* (Oxford UP, 2011) and *21st Century Oxford Authors: William Blake* (forthcoming, Oxford UP, 2019). He is completing a book on *Blake and the History of Imagination.*

INDEX

A. A., 177

Abrams, M. H., 264

Adam Bede (Eliot), 135, 149

affect: definitions of, 156n3, 159, 159n7; institution, tension with, 57–62; Jewish feeling and, 156, 159, 168; midrash and, 159–60; Mozoomdar's commonwealth of affection, 54, 57–61; Sen's affective bonds, 55–56; Spinoza's *affectus* and *affectio*, 159–60, 168; spirit and, 60; theological goal vs. affective register, 212. *See also* Jewish women's writing and affect

aggadic midrash, 157–60, 163n12

agnosticism and ritual, 210

Aguilar, Grace: about, 162–63; *Days of Bruce*, 149; "Dialogue Stanzas," 167–68; "The Importance of Religion to Genius," 163–66, 167; *The Jewish Faith*, 239–40; King James Bible and, 130–31; *Sabbath Thoughts and Sacred Communings*, 240; *The Women of Israel*, 166–67

Alastor (Shelley), 165–66

Albert, Prince, 140, 142, 145–49

Alec Forbes of Howglen (Macdonald), 150

Alice, Princess, 148

Alpha Course, 93

Alton Park (Anon.), 184

Anderson, Benedict, 184

Andover-Harvard Theological Library. *See* Family Bibles

Anglicanism (Church of England): Gothic architecture and, 190, 193; liturgy and, 176; Methodism and, 193; Moravians and, 282; Psalms and, 227, 231–36, 240; Public Worship Regulation Act (1874), 140; Puseyites (ritualists), 198; Victoria and, 140, 143–46

Ankarsjö, Magnus, 286

Anker, Elizabeth, 258

antinomianism, 285

Anti-Persecution Union, 90

Apology for the Bible, An (Watson), 288n6

Arabian Nights, 175

Arata, Stephen, 219n11

Aravamudan, Srinivas, 54

architecture, neoclassical: Exeter Hall, London, 197–98; Greek language and, 195; Metropolitan Tabernacle, London, 194–98, 196 fig. 10.2; as pagan, 192

architecture, neogothic. *See* Gothic architecture and the battle of styles

Armitage, Thomas, 281–85

Arnold, Matthew, 246–52, 258; "The Study of Poetry," 246–47

Arnold, Thomas, 145–46

Arnoldian replacement theory, 252

Arnstein, Walter, 82, 139–40

Ars Poetica (Horatio), 272

Aryanism, 30–31

Asad, Talal, 27, 28–29

Asia, affect linked to, 57–58

atheism: Bradlaugh and, 82; Eagleton on, 251; Holyoake and, 90; Marx and, 104; Marx-

· 307 ·

ism and, 66; Monaco and, 39; Morris and, 268; New Atheists, 94; Pasternak on, 99; Shelley and, 268; Swinburne and, 268; Thomson and, 254. *See also* eliminationists vs. substitutionists; secularism

Augustine, 74, 78

authorship, Davidic, 226, 231–32, 236, 238–40

authorship, Romantic cults of. *See* literary criticism and Romantic cults of authorship

autoethnographic texts, 237

Avenir de l'Angleterre, L' (Montalembert), 146

Bagehot, Walter, 58

Baker, Pacificus, 144–45

Ball, John, 66, 70

"Ballad of Reading Gaol, The" (Wilde), 215–19

Barrett Browning, Elizabeth, 252–56

Barthes, Roland, 250, 251, 253–54

Beal, Timothy, 117

Beale, Dorothea, 252–54, 257, 258, 259

Beesley, Edward Spencer, 83

Bennett, Solomon, 237–39

Bentham, Jeremy, 100–101

Berger, Peter, 84, 90, 92

Berlant, Lauren, 61–62

Best, Stephen, 207

Bible: architecture and, 191, 203; Coleridge and, 234; divine inspiration or dictation of, 233–34, 269, 272, 277; Douay-Rheims translation, 129; Engels on, 110; fulfillment theology and, 55; Jewish women and the King James Bible, 163; Keble's translation of Psalms, 231; King James translation (Authorized Version), 115, 120–21, 130; Loisy on, 26, 31–34; Marx and, 104, 105, 107; new editions of, 128n12; Stephens's use of biblical analogy, 69–70; teaching as maternal function, 131; Victorian reading culture and, 141–42; Wilde and, 213–15. *See also* Family Bibles; Hebrew Bible; New Testament; Psalm reading as Jewish-Christian contact zone

Bible societies, 117

biblical criticism: Catholic modernist controversy and, 32; Hopkins, Blake, and, 277; Leo XIII's *Providentissimus Deus*, 33–34; Loisy and, 33; scholarly privileging of Christianity, 5–6

Black, William: *Madcap Violet*, 151

Blair, Kirstie, 176

Blake, Catherine Wright Armitage, 281–86

Blake, James, 286

Blake, William: Aguilar and, 165; antinomianism and, 285; biblical scholarship, influence of, 277–78; *The Book of Thel*, 292; *For Children: The Gates of Paradise*, 296; *Europe a Prophecy*, 274; family and Moravian/Swedenborgian/Methodist connections, 281–87; *The Four Zoas*, 286; Heaven, Earth, and Hell cosmology, 288, 291, 294–95; Hopkins on, 262, 272–73, 274; Hopkins's inspiration and craft compared to, 274–77; on imagination, 297–99; *Jerusalem*, 276; "Job's Evil Dreams," 292 fig. 15.2, 293–95; *The Marriage of Heaven and Hell*, 285, 288, 291, 299; mysticism and, 276; poetic/prophetic character, 287–88, 291–92, 297–99; *For the Sexes: The Gates of Paradise*, 295 fig. 15.3, 296–99; *There Is No Natural Religion*, 287–92, 289 fig. 15.1; "The Tyger," 165

Blankaart, Steven, 297

Bloom, Harold, 249

Bodin, Jean, 28

Bonhoeffer, Dietrich, 74n10, 93

Boobbyer, Philip, 102

Book of Thel, The (Blake), 292

Borrow, George: *Lavengro*, 188–89

Bose, Rajnarain, 52

Bourdaloue, Louis, 147

Bowra, Maurice, 248

Bradlaugh, Charles, 82, 83, 85, 88, 89, 97

Brahmo Samaj: background, 51; comparative religion and global Brahmoism, 50–53; eclecticism and, 53–55; impact of, 50; juxtapolitical space and, 61–62; Mozoomdar's commonwealth of affection, 54, 57–61; Sen's New Dispensation and affective bonds, 55–56

Branch, Lori, 4, 258

Bridges, Robert, 267–68, 269, 272, 273

British Library, 116n3, 118n7, 123

Brooks, Cleanth, 248

Brown, John, 118, 125, 135, 140

Brown, Wendy, 50, 111

Browning, Robert, 188, 252–56, 259; "O Lyric Love," 254–56, 255 fig. 13.1

Browning Societies, 50, 249, 252–54, 257, 259

Brunton, Emily, 182

INDEX 309

Buddhism, 27, 31, 258
Budick, Sanford, 160
Bunting, Jabez, 68
Burns, Robert, 165
Burton, Robert, 297
Butler, Rachel, 149

Cambridge Companion to Literature and Religion, The, 10–11
Capital (Marx), 102
Caputo, John, 8
Carlile, Richard, 82–83, 89
Carlyle, Thomas, 109
Carpenter, Mary Wilson, 19, 123
Carruthers, Jo, 208
Casanova, José, 14
Cassell's Illustrated Family Bible, 129
Catholic Church. *See* Roman Catholic Church
Cavanaugh, William T., 28–30
Challenge Accepted, The (Newman), 237–38
Chalmers, Thomas, 72–74
Chamberlin, William, 229
Chartist movement, 67–68, 74–79, 109
Chaucer, Geoffrey, 256
Cheap Repository Tracts, 173, 183
Chesterton, G. K., 111
Cheyette, Bryan, 157
Chidester, David, 46–47
Christ. *See* Jesus Christ
Christianity: de-Semitization, over-Hellenization, and Aryanization of, 30–31; Hinduism judged against standard of, 53; Marx's critique of, 106–10. *See also* ritual; Roman Catholicism
Christian Observer, 174, 181–85
Christian's Mistake (Craik), 150
Christian's New and Compleat Family Bible, The, 122
church and state in France, 38–41
church authority, 29–30
Church of England. *See* Anglicanism
civic associations, Hindu. *See* Brahmo Samaj
Clark, Timothy, 269
close reading, 248, 250
Coelebs in Search of a Wife (More), 173–74, 178, 181–82

Colburn, Henry, 179
Coleridge, Samuel Taylor: comparative religion and, 49; *Confessions of an Inquiring Spirit*, 233–34; "Notes on the Book of Common Prayer," 235
colonialism, 30–31, 46–47, 53
Colportage Association, 202
Columbian exposition, 59, 62
commonwealth of affection, 54, 57–61
communal nature of religion, 36–37
Communist League, 108
Communist Manifesto (Marx and Engels), 100, 102–4, 108, 111
communitarianism, 72–73, 89
comparative religion: "Eastern" religions and Christian standard, 53; literary precedent for, 49; Müller's Science of Religion and, 46; Sen's affective community and, 56; transnational history of, 47; Victorian, and alliance with empire, 46–47
Compleat History of the Old and New Testament, The (Rayner), 121, 124
Comtean Positivism, 89
"Condition of the Members of the Christian Empire" (Newman), 232–33
confession, 211
Confessions of an Inquiring Spirit (Coleridge), 233–34
conflict model of secularism, 82–85
Congregation of the Lamb (Moravian), 282
conscience, 101–2, 110
Constancy Of Israel, The (Bennett), 237–38
Constitutional History of England, The (Hallam), 146
Cornwallis, Mary, 144
cosmopolitanism, 53–61
craft, poetic. *See* poetic inspiration and craft
Craik, Dinah Mulock: *Christian's Mistake*, 150; *Fifty Golden Years*, 151–52; *A Noble Life*, 150; *The Unkind Word*, 150–51; Victoria and, 149–52
Craven, Madame Augustine (Pauline de la Ferronays), 151
Critchley, Simon, 210
Critique of Hegel's Philosophy (Marx), 104
Cubitt, James, 193–94
Cunningham, John W.: *World without Souls*, 174, 181–82
Cuppit, Don subsidiarity and, 93

Dairyman's Daughter, The (Richmond), 185n8, 187
Davidic authorship, 226, 231–32, 236, 238–40
Davies, J. G., 283
Davies, Keri, 281–86
Davys, George, 143–44, 145
Days of Bruce (Aguilar), 149
"Death of the Author, The" (Barthes), 250
"Definition of Religion, The" (Loisy), 36–37
Deleuze, Gilles, 281, 298
de Man, Paul, 249
Demers, Patricia, 182
De Profundis (Wilde), 209–11, 209n6, 210n7, 213–15
Desani, G. V., 54
"Dialogue Stanzas" (Aguilar), 167–68
Diggers, 70, 70n5
disenchantment, 3, 91, 111
Disraeli, Isaac, 236–37
Dissenters, 176, 193–94, 201, 230
Dixon, Canon, 262, 267, 272
Doctor Zhivago (Pasternak), 99–102
Donne, John: "Holy Sonnet 14," 165
Downs, Jack, 181
Duncan, Kathryn, 11n5
Duns Scotus, 276
During, Simon, 100–101
Dutt, Akkoy Kumar, 52
duty to gods vs. state, 28–29
Dwor, Richa, 130–31, 149

Eadie, John, 127–28
Eagleton, Terry, 251
"Eastern" religions, 53
eclecticism, 53–55, 85–86, 89
Eclectic Review, 174, 177
Economic and Philosophic Manuscripts (Marx), 102
Edinburgh Literary Journal, 181
Edinburgh Review, 173
Edmundson, Mark, 259
education, church role in, 38–40
electrical "shock," imagery of, 263–64, 278
eliminationists vs. substitutionists, 81–84
Eliot, George: *Adam Bede*, 135, 149; *The Mill on the Floss*, 126

Eliot, Simon, 178n4
Ellis, George Henry, 127
Ellman, Richard, 208, 209n5
Ely, Jane, 149
encyclicals, papal, 33–34
Engels, Friedrich: Christian political economy and, 110n2; *Communist Manifesto* (Marx and Engels), 100, 102–4, 108, 111; ethical sensitivity of, 67; *German Ideology* (Marx and Engels), 102–3; "Outlines of a Critique of Political Economy," 108–9; prophetic idiom and, 108–10; religious foundations and, 101–4
English Secularism (Holyoake), 86
Enlightenment: Blake and, 288; East vs. West and, 31; Hinduism and, 54; Marx and, 104, 105; Owen and, 82
Erdozain, Dominic, 141
eschatology, 78, 105, 108, 111, 217
"Essence of Money, The" (Hess), 108–9
Esther, Book of, 133–34, 157–59, 166–67
Ethicist/Positivists, 83
Eucharist, Victoria's readings on, 144–45, 147
Eucharistica (Wilberforce), 147
Eugénie of Montijo, 140
Europe a Prophecy (Blake), 274
evangelical novels. *See* novels, religious
evolutionary paradigm, 53
Exeter Hall, London, 195, 197–98
"Expostulation and Reply" (Wordsworth), 168

Family Bibles: in 20th and 21st centuries, 135–36; as business, 120–21; *Cassell's Illustrated Family Bible*, 129; *The Christian's New and Compleat Family Bible*, 122; collections of, 117, 118–20, 118n7; *Columbian Family and Pulpit Bible*, 123; *The Compleat History of the Old and New Testament* (Rayner), 121, 124; digital versions of, 120n10; features of, 115–16; as genre, 115; grand and golden age of, 128–29; *The Holy Bible, containing the Pentateuch, the Hagiographa . . .* (Gollancz), 129–30; *The Holy Bible containing the Old and New Testaments* (Scott), 131–32, 132 fig. 6.4; *The Illustrated Family Bible with Explanatory, Critical and Devotional Commentary*, 133 fig. 6.5; for Jewish families, 118, 129–31; King James translation (AV) and, 115, 120–21, 130; *National Illustrated Family Bible* (Eadie), 127–28; Noah's Ark engraving (Kirchner), 121, 123–24, 124 fig. 6.3; *The Pronouncing Edition of the Holy Bible*, 133–34, 135 fig. 6.6; *Royal Bible* (Howard), 122; *The Self-Interpreting Bible* (Brown), 118, 121 fig. 6.2, 125–27, 128; as "trash" or "treasure," 116–18; truths, lies, promises, and knowledge as commodity, 121–24; women, changing image of, 131–34; for working class, 118, 125–28

Farrar, Frederic William, 149
Farrell, Michael, 286
Feil, Ernst, 28
Felch, Susan M., 10–11
Felski, Rita, 258
Ferronays, Pauline de la (Madame Augustine Craven), 151
Fetter Lane Society, 282, 284–86
Feuerbach, Ludwig, 104, 259
Fifty Golden Years (Craik), 151–52
Figures of Conversion (Ragussis), 241
Filby, Eliza, 50
Fischer, Benjamin L., 174
Fish, Stanley, 1n1, 20
Foote, George William, 83
For Children: The Gates of Paradise (Blake), 296
forgiveness, Wilde on, 211
formalism, 160, 176, 181
For the Sexes: The Gates of Paradise (Blake), 295 fig. 15.3, 296–99
Foucault, Michel, 213
Fourier, Charles, 105
Four Zoas, The (Blake), 286
France, secularization of education in, 38–40
Frazer, James G., 249
Fromm, Erich, 105
Frye, Northrop, 249, 274
fulfillment theology, 55, 59–60
Furnivall, F. J., 254–57

Gagnier, Regenia, 208–9
Galchinsky, Michael, 160, 162
Gandhi, Leela, 54n2
Genius of Judaism, The (Disraeli), 236–37
German Ideology (Marx and Engels), 102–3

Gettelman, Debra, 181
Gilmartin, Kevin, 173
Gladstone, William Ewart, 142
"God's Grandeur" (Hopkins), 274
Goethe, Johann Wolfgang von, 252
Goldsmid, Isaac, 233
Gollancz, H., 129–30
Gothic architecture and the battle of styles: allurement and danger of visual appeal, 201–3; Cubitt and dissenting Gothic, 193–94, 201; Metropolitan Tabernacle, London, and, 194–98, 196 fig. 10.2; Nonconformists and, 192–93; overview, 190–92; poor examples of, 194; Pugin, Catholicism, and, 192–93; Puseyites, 198; Spurgeon's "The Axe at the Root" sermon on, 198–201
Gould, F. J., 83
Grand National Consolidated Trades Union, 89
Greek language, 195, 203
Greenspoon, Leonard J., 130
Guillory, John, 249
Guru English, 54

Hafiz, 58
Haggarty, Sarah, 275
halakhic midrash, 157
Hallam, Albert, 146
Hallam, Arthur, 148
Hallam, Henry, 146
Hanson, Abram, 67
Hanson, Ellis, 209n6, 214
Harnack, Adolf von, 36–37
Harrison, J. F. C., 88–89
Hartman, Geoffrey, 160
Hatcher, Brian, 54
Hauerwas, Stanley, 210, 218
Heady, Emily Walker, 215–16
heart, universal, 60–61
Heaven, Earth, and Hell cosmology in Blake, 288, 291, 294–95
Hebrew Bible ("Old Testament"): Aguilar and, 166, 239; Blake and, 275; English translations, availability of, 130; Higher Criticism, Jewish context, and, 229; Jewish origins, grappling with, 226; midrash, 157–60, 163n12, 167, 168; poetical capacity to shock, 278; prefiguration and, 55;

Stephens and, 105. *See also* Bible; Psalm reading as Jewish-Christian contact zone
Hegelianism, 60, 61
Heine, Heinrich, 236
Hell. *See* Heaven, Earth, and Hell cosmology in Blake
Henry, Matthew, 127–28
hermeneutics of suspicion, 2–3, 7, 206–9, 213
Hess, Jonathan, 157
Hess, Moses, 108–9
Higher Criticism, 229, 230, 246–47
Hill, Harvey, 39–40
Hilton, Boyd, 66, 67, 72–73, 110n2
Hinduism, 50, 53. *See also* Brahmo Samaj
Hints toward Forming the Character of a Young Princess (More), 174–75
History of the Jews (Milman), 235–36
Hobbes, Thomas, 28
Hofland, Barbara, 182
Holy Bible, containing the Pentateuch, the Hagiographa . . . , The (Gollancz), 129–30
Holy Bible containing the Old and New Testaments, The (Scott), 131–32, 132 fig. 6.4
Holyoake, George Jacob: eliminationists vs. substitutionists and conflict model of secularism, 81–84; *English Secularism*, 86; modern debate about the secular and, 91–96; *Principles of Secularism*, 84–85; provincial secularism and impact of, 87–88; reassessing, within Victorian religion, 88–91; Secularism, original conception of, 82, 101n1; secularism as conflict resolution, 84–86; Taylor and, 91, 95–96
"Holy Sonnet 14" (Donne), 165
Hooker, Richard, 176
Hopkins, Gerard Manley: biblical scholarship, influence of, 277–78; on Blake, 262, 272–73, 274; Blake's inspiration and craft compared to, 274–77; as craftsman, 272–74; "God's Grandeur," 274; on inspiration, 267–71; letter on Wordsworth's "Intimations of Immorality," 262–67; "The Sea and the Skylark," 273; "Spring," 273; "Spring and Fall," 273; "Tom's Garland," 273; "To R. B.," 269–71, 273
Horatio, 272
Howard, Leonard, 122
Howes, Thomas, 277

Howitt, William, 49
Howsam, Leslie, 117
"How to Attract a Congregation" (Spurgeon), 202
Hurwitz, Hyman, 234–35, 238

idolatry, 176, 190, 198–99, 203, 208
Illustrated Family Bible with Explanatory, Critical and Devotional Commentary, The, 133 fig. 6.5
imagination in Blake, 297–99
"Importance of Religion to Genius, The" (Aguilar), 163–66, 167
Incarnation, in Blake, 288–91
Incubus, 297
individualism, 36, 88, 275, 277
"Individualist Theory of Religion, The" (Loisy), 36
Influence (Anon.), 179
Ingersoll, Robert, 83
In Memoriam (Tennyson), 148, 151, 256
inner light, 49, 110, 235
inspiration, divine, 233–34, 269, 272, 277
inspiration, poetic. *See* poetic inspiration and craft
"Intimations of Immorality" (Wordsworth), 262–67
inward experience, religion as. *See* private belief and inward experience

Jackson, Virginia, 236n1
Jager, Colin, 4n3
James, William, 49, 251
Jane Eyre (Brontë), 115
Janes, Dominic, 209
Janz, Denis, 101
Jerrold, Douglas, 197–98
Jerusalem (Blake), 276
Jesus Christ: Blake on, 276, 290–92, 298; Brahmoism and, 60; Browning and, 256; Leicester Secular Society bust of, 87; Marx and, 107–8; Moravian sexual-religious theology on, 285; in Pasternak's *Doctor Zhivago*, 99–100; prefiguration and, 55, 226; Psalms and, 237–39, 240; Spurgeon on, 198, 201; Stephens on arrest in the garden, 76–77; Whately on, 145; Wilde on, 209, 211, 214–19

Jewish Naturalization Bill (1753), 227
Jewish women's writing and affect: affect and Jewish feeling, 156, 159, 168; Aguilar, 162–68; exclusion, opportunity, and tradition of flexibility, 160–62; gender and, 155–56; Midrash and, 157–60, 168; Moss sisters, 155–56; period before Jewish emancipation, 157
Jews: "dangerous" Judaic impulse, 241; Family Bibles for, 118, 129–31; formalism and, 176; reestablishment of Anglo-Jewish community, 227; Universities Tests Act and, 157n4. *See also* Psalm reading as Jewish-Christian contact zone
"Job's Evil Dreams" (Blake), 292 fig. 15.2, 293–95
Jobson, F. J., 193
Johnson, Samuel, 266–67
Jones, Andrew, 27
Jones, Horace, 197
justification, Stephens on, 73–74, 78, 105
just social order, Stephens on, 70–73 juxtapolitical space and, 61–62

Kant, Emmanuel, 101
Karim, Abdul, 140
Kaufmann, Michael, 252
Keble, John, 230–32, 238
Kilde, Jeanne Halgren, 193
Killeen, Jarlath, 209
King, Joshua, 234n10
Kingdom of Christ, The (Whately), 145–46
Kingsley, Charles, 140
Kircher, Athanasius, 123–24
Klancher, Jon, 179
Knight, Mark, 18
knowledge economy, 123
Krueger, Christine L., 173
Kuhn, William, 143

Labor Exchanges, 89
labor history: Chartist movement, 67–68, 74–79; Marx on, 107–8; National Holiday (general strike), 78–79; religion, theology, and working-class movement, 65–67. *See also* Stephens, Joseph Rayner
Lamb, Charles, 269

Lamentabili sane exitu decree, 34
Laruelle, François, 299
Latchmore, W. H., 148–49
Latour, Bruno, 248, 258
Lavengro (Borrow), 188–89
laws, British: Jewish Naturalization Bill (1753), 227; New Poor Law (1834), 68, 69, 71, 110; Public Worship Regulation Act (1874), 140; Roman Catholic Relief Act (1829), 230; Test Act repeal (1828), 227, 230; Universities Tests Act (1871), 157n4
Leavis, F. R., 248
Leeser, Isaac, 164n14
Lehzen, Baroness Louise, 143, 144–45
Leicester Secular Society, 87–88
Leo XIII, Pope, 33–34, 39
Levine, Caroline, 213–14
liberation theology, 69–70
"licentiousness," 272
literacy, mass, 141
literary criticism and Romantic cults of authorship: amateur criticism and the Victorian poet as prophet, 251–58; Arnold and, 246–52; post-suspicion hermeneutics and, 258; theological dimensions of secular literary studies, 248–51
liturgy. *See* ritual and liturgy
Locke, John, 101, 287
Λογοφιλοι ("Logophiloi"), 185
Loisy, Alfred: "The Definition of Religion," 36–37; excommunication of, 34; "The Individualist Theory of Religion," 36; life and scholarship of, 31–34; significance of, 25, 38–41; use of religion in writings of, 34–38
London College of Printing, 202
Loughlin, Gerard, 209–10, 214
Lowth, Robert, 277–78
Luhmann, Niklas, 298
Lumen Gentium (Second Vatican Council), 27
Lyall, Edna, 149
Lycidas (Milton), 269
lyric poetry: 19th-century meaning of, 225n1; Psalms and, 225, 228–30, 234–36, 240, 241–42; Romantic poetic theory and, 229–30

Macaulay, T. B., 177–78
Macaulay, Zachary, 174
Macdonald, George, 149–50; *Alec Forbes of Howglen*, 150; *Sir Gibbie*, 150
MacKenzie, Norman H., 273
Macleod, Norman, 148
Madcap Violet (Black), 151
Malthusianism, 69, 71, 72, 89
Manual of the Rudiments of Theology, A (Smith), 144
Marcus (pseud.), 69, 71
Marcus, Sharon, 207
Margaret Maitland (Oliphant), 150
Margoliouth, H. M., 282n1
Maritain, Jacques, 266–67
markets and religious novels, 178–86
Marriage of Heaven and Hell, The (Blake), 285, 288, 291, 299
Marx, Karl: *Capital*, 102; *Communist Manifesto* (Marx and Engels), 100, 102–4, 108, 111; *Critique of Hegel's Philosophy*, 104; *Economic and Philosophic Manuscripts*, 102; ethical sensitivity of, 67; *German Ideology* (Marx and Engels), 102–3; history of ideas, denial of, 103–4; McKeon and, 1–2; prophetic idiom and, 108–11; religious foundations and religious method of, 100–108; Stephens and, 105–6
Marxism: atheist assumption, 66; conscience and paradox of secularism in, 101–2, 110; history, denial of, 103–4; invention of the secular, notion of, 104, 110–11; moralism and economic determinism, 102–3; Pasternak's *Doctor Zhivago* and, 99–102; prophetic idiom in, 108–11; religious method underlying, 104–5; as religious reform, 105–8; Soviet ideology, tensions with, 102
Mason, Emma, 11
Masson, David, 181
Massumi, Brian, 159
Masuzawa, Tomoko, 30–31
material culture. *See* Gothic architecture and the battle of styles
Mathewson, Andrew Dishington, 129
Matus, Jill L., 263–64
Mays, Kelly J., 184n7
May You Like It! (Anon.), 181–85
McCrie, George, 256–57

McDannell, Colleen, 131, 135
McGavin, William, 184
McGrath, Alister, 74
McKeon, Michael, 1–2
McLaren, Scott, 117
McQueen, Joseph, 214
medieval period, secular as sacred in, 27
Melbourne, William Lamb, 2nd Viscount, 146, 149
Methodism: Blake and, 286; Moravians and, 284; Nonconformism and, 193; Primitive Methodists, 71; religious novels and, 173; working-class movement and, 65, 67. *See also* Stephens, Joseph Rayner
Metropolitan Tabernacle, London, 194–98, 196 fig. 10.2
midrash, 157–60, 163n12, 167, 168
Milbank, John, 26–27
Mill, J. S., 49
Miller, Julia, 126
Millites, 87–88
Mill on the Floss, The (Eliot), 126
Milman, Henry Hart: *History of the Jews*, 235–36
Milton, John, 272, 276
modernist controversy, Catholic, 32–34
modern Western understanding of religion: contemporary understanding as universal abstract phenomenon, 27–28; as generic category in Loisy, 34–37; state authority and private religion, 28–31; as system of beliefs in private sphere, 26
monasticism, 28
Montagu, Lily, 157n5
Montalembert, Charles de, 146
Montefiore, Charlotte, 163n12
Monthly Magazine, 181
Moravian Church (Unitas Fratrum), 282–86
More, Hannah: *Coelebs in Search of a Wife*, 173–74, 178, 181–82; *Hints toward Forming the Character of a Young Princess*, 174–75
Moretti, Franco, 250–51, 253–54
Morgan, David, 191
Morgan, Victoria, 11
Morris, William, 268
Moss, Celia (later Levetus), 155–56
Moss, Marion (later Hartog), 155–56

Mozoomdar, Protap Chunder, 51, 56–62
Müller, F. Max, 31, 46, 49, 51–52, 56, 57
Müntzer, Thomas, 66
Murray, Andrew, 126
museological representation, 59
mysticism, 49, 50, 276
myth, Loisy on, 35

Napoleon, 38
narratives, religious, 91, 92–93
National Illustrated Family Bible (Eadie), 127–28
National Secular Society, 88
"natural religion," 52
neoliberalism, 50
New Criticism, 248–49, 256
New Dispensation, 51, 52, 55–56
Newman, John Henry, 57, 241; "Condition of the Members of the Christian Empire," 232–33
Newman, Selig, 237–39
New Monthly Magazine, 179, 181, 185
New Poor Law (1834), 68, 69, 71, 110
New Testament: classical architecture and, 195, 203; Higher Criticism, Jewish context, and, 229; Loisy on, 37; Marx and, 106; new editions of, 128n12; poetical capacity to shock, 278; Stephens on, 76, 79; Whately and, 145–46; Wilde and, 213, 216. *See also* Bible
Nietzsche, Friedrich, 281, 298
Nirenberg, David, 241
Noah's Ark engraving (Kirchner), 121, 123–24, 124 fig. 6.3
Noble Life, A (Craik), 150
Nonconformists: Blake's parents and, 282; Gothic architecture and, 191, 193–94, 202; Holyoake and, 85; Spurgeon's Metropolitan Tabernacle, London, 194–98, 196 fig. 10.2; Universities Tests Act and, 157n4
Nongbri, Brent, 30
"Notes on the Book of Common Prayer" (Coleridge), 235
novels, religious: Catholic ritual and formalism, anxieties about, 176; effect, problem of, 181–82; market, genre, and commodity, 178–86; not considered novels, 174–75; Protestantism transformation and, 176–78; sectarianism and partisanship, anxieties about, 172–74; Thackeray's critique, 171–72

Oakeshott, Michael, 100
Occident, The, 164
Old Testament. *See* Hebrew Bible
Oliphant, Margaret, 149–51; *Margaret Maitland,* 150
"O Lyric Love" (Browning), 254–56, 255 fig. 13.1
O'Malley, Patrick R., 206, 209n6
Opie, John, 131–32, 132 fig. 6.4
Orientalism, 56, 57–58
Otto, Rudolph, 212
"Outlines of a Critique of Political Economy" (Engels), 108–9
Owen, Robert, 82, 88–90
Owenism, 85

Packer, George, 50
parliamentary representation, 59
particularisms, in postcolonial theory, 53n2
Pascendi dominici gregis encyclical, 34
Pasternak, Boris, 99–102, 110
Pater, Walter, 212n10
Pecora, Vincent, 247, 258
Peterson, William S., 253–54, 257–58
Phillips, Elizabeth, 78
"Philosophy of Composition, The" (Poe), 269
Pickering, Samuel, 174
Picture of Dorian Gray, The (Wilde), 206, 209n5
Pius X, Pope St., 25, 34, 40
Plato, 268
pluralism, religious, 52, 59
Pocock, William Wilmer, 195
Poe, Edgar Allan: "The Philosophy of Composition," 269
poetic inspiration and craft: biblical scholarship, influence of, 277–78; Blake compared to Hopkins, 274–77; Hopkins as craftsman, 272–74; Hopkins letter on Wordsworth's "Intimations of Immorality" and, 262–67; Hopkins on Blake, 262, 272–73, 274; Hopkins on inspiration, 267–71; reader expectations, 269
poetic/prophetic character in Blake, 287–88, 291–92, 297–99

poetics: comparative religion and Romantic poets, 49; historicizing of literary subjects and reductive abstraction, 264; inspiration, mystical and poetic, 49; metrical studies, 264; Romantic poetic theory, 229–30. *See also* lyric poetry; Psalm reading as Jewish-Christian contact zone; specific poets

political economy, 72–74, 109–10, 110n2

Political Pulpit series (Stephens), 70–79

political theory, 28–31

Portier, William, 32

positivism, 83, 89

postcolonial theory, 53n2

postsecular studies, 4

post-suspicion hermeneutics, 258

Pratt, Mary Louise, 228

prefiguration, 55

Price, Leah, 116–17

Primitive Methodists, 71

Principles of Secularism (Holyoake), 84–85

private belief and inward experience, religion as: early modern state authority and, 28–31; Loisy on, 36–37; protestant bias, 7, 48–50, 207, 208

Pronouncing Edition of the Holy Bible, The, 133–34, 135 fig. 6.6

protestant bias, 7, 48–50, 207, 208

Protestantism. *See specific movements and topics*

providence, general vs. special, 73

Providentissimus Deus encyclical, 33–34

provincial Secularism, 87–88

Psalm reading as Jewish-Christian contact zone: Anglo-Jewish responses and auto-ethnography, 236–40; Christian identification and, 226, 232–33; editions of Psalms, 229; figural and "real" Jews and erasure of Jewishness, 226–27, 230–36; Hebrew poetics and post-Romantic lyric, 228–30; Jewish identity in Christian Psalm culture, 225–28; the "Jewish Problem" and, 227, 242; typology strategy, 226–27

public realm, religion in, 30

Public Worship Regulation Act (1874), 140

Pugin, A. W. N., 192–93, 196, 201, 203

Purim, 166n15, 167–68

Pusey, Edward B., 52, 198

"Queen Esther," 133–34, 134 fig. 6.6

queer theology, 209–10, 214

quietism, 85, 90

Radcliffe, Ann, 180

Radway, Janice, 50

Ragussis, Michael, 241, 242

Ranters, 70–71

Rationalist Society, 82

Rayner, W., 121–22

reading practices, 161, 213. *See also* Family Bibles; Victoria, reading habits of

Reading the Abrahamic Faiths (Mason), 11

reason: in Blake, 294, 297; Holyoake's "life according to reason," 86; modernist controversy and faith vs., 32; Moravians and emotion vs., 284–85

Récit d'une Soeur, Le (Ferronays), 151

Rectenwald, Michael, 83, 92

re-enchantment narratives, 93–96

Reinventing Christianity (Woodhead), 12

Religio (Feil), 28

Religion and Literature, 8

religion as category and term: apparent simplicity of, 1–2; contemporary understanding as universal abstract phenomenon, 27–28; juxtapolitical space and, 62; Loisy's modern and premodern uses of, 34–38; protestant bias, 7, 48–50, 207, 208; state authority and private religion, 28–31; as system of beliefs in private sphere, 26; turn to, in humanities scholarship, 3–4, 8; as Western construction, 4; World's Parliament of Religions and, 58–59

Religion in the Age of Reason (Duncan), 11n5

"Religious Teaching of Browning, The" (Beale), 252

Religious Tract Society, 178, 183–84

Renan, Ernest, 31, 36, 39, 219, 219n11

retributive theology, 110n2

rhythm, 270

Richmond, Legh: *The Dairyman's Daughter*, 185n8, 187

Richmond, Wilfrid, 71n6

Ricoeur, Paul, 110, 213, 258

ritual and liturgy: Loisy on, 36, 37; Puseyite, 198; religious novels and anxieties about, 176; as theology, in Wilde, 211–13, 219; Wilde on agnosticism and, 210

Rix, Robert, 286
Robbins, Ruth, 216
Roberts, Kyle, 185n8
Robertson, Frederick William, 149
Robinson, Henry Crabb, 284
Robinson, John, 93
Roman Catholic Church: authority of, 29–30; Gothic architecture and, 190–91, 192–93; Loisy and church role in education, 38–40; Second Vatican Council, 27; wars of religion, complexity of, 29–30
Roman Catholicism: confession in, 211; modernist controversy, 32–34; secular as sacred in, 27; Thomism, 39; Universities Tests Act and, 157n4; university secularization and Catholic theology, 39; Wilde and, 208, 209n5, 219
Roman Catholic Relief Act (1829), 230
Romance of Jewish History, The (Moss and Moss), 155
Romantic poets and comparative religion, 49. *See also* Blake, William; Coleridge, Samuel Taylor; poetics; Psalm reading as Jewish-Christian contact zone; Wordsworth, William
Rose, Jonathan, 123, 142–43
Rosman, Doreen, 185
Routledge Companion to Literature and Religion, The, 10, 18
Roy, Rammohun, 52–53, 55, 57
Royal Bible (Howard), 122
Royce, Josiah, 259
Royle, Edward, 82
Rudy, Jason R., 263–64
Rushdie, Salman, 54
Rushton, Ben, 67

Sabatier, Louis Auguste, 36–37
Sabbath Thoughts and Sacred Communings (Aguilar), 240
sacred and secular, relationship between, 26–27, 100–101. *See also* religion as category and term; secularism; secularization
sacred-canopy thesis, 90, 92
"Sacrifice of Jepthah's Daughter, The" (Opie), 131–32, 132 fig. 6.4
Salome (Wilde), 213
Samuels, Maurice, 157
Satchel, John: *Thornton Abbey*, 173

Schama, Simon, 159
Scheffer, Ary, 132
Scheinberg, Cynthia, 19, 162–63
Scholes, Robert+, 249, 251
schools. *See* education
Schuchard, Marsha Keith, 282–86
"science of religion," 35, 46, 51–52
"scientific" approach to literary studies, 248–49
Scott, J. Barton, 19
Scott, Thomas, 127–28, 131
Scott, Walter, 145
scriptural model of religion, 49
"Sea and the Skylark, The" (Hopkins), 273
Seal, Brajendranath, 53
Second Vatican Council, 27
secularism: conflict model of, 82–85; eliminationists vs. substitutionists, 81–84; Holyoake as originator of concept, 82; Marx and paradox of, 101–2; provincial Secularism, 87–88; secular as sacred in medieval period, 27. *See also* Holyoake, George Jacob
secularization: 1960s numbers-game approach, 90–91; disenchantment and, 91; of education in France, 38–40; enduring religious narratives and, 90–91; re-enchantment narratives and, 93–96; religious culture, pluralism, and, 141; sacred-canopy thesis, 90, 92; "without end," 247. *See also* literary criticism and Romantic cults of authorship
secularization narratives: entrenched in literary studies, 8–9; Holyoake and anticipation of, 90, 92; inspiration and, 268; Marxism and, 101; turn to religion and, 3–4, 8
Sedgwick, Eve, 258
Self-Interpreting Bible, The (Brown), 118, 121 fig. 6.2, 125–27, 128
"Selfish Giant, The" (Wilde), 213
Selkirk, J. B., 228
Semitizing and de-Semitizing, 30–31
Sen, Keshub Chunder, 51–52, 55–57, 59–60
sentimentalism, Brahmo, 58–59, 62
separation of church and state in France, 38–41
sexual-religious theology, Moravian, 285, 286
Shaping Belief (Morgan and Williams), 11

Shelley, Percy Bysshe: Aguilar and, 165–66; *Alastor*, 165–66; inspiration and, 268
Sherwood, Mary Martha, 182
Shouse, Eric, 156n3
Simeon, Charles, 168, 176
Simon, Maurice, 158
Sir Gibbie (Macdonald), 150
Smith, Adam, 109
Smith, James K. A., 211–12, 212nn8–9
Smith, John Bainbridge, 144
Smith, John Thomas, 284
Smith, Ryan K., 202
Smith, Sydney, 173
socialism, 66, 88, 105, 109
Sola, Abraham de, 163n12
Solzhenitsyn, Aleksandr, 102
Southey, Robert, 284
Soviet ideology, 102
Sperber, Jonathan, 102, 109
spirit, doctrines of, 59–60
Spirit of God, The (Mozoomdar), 57
Spivak, Gayatri, 59n3
"Spring" (Hopkins), 273
"Spring and Fall" (Hopkins), 273
Spurgeon, Charles H.: on allurement and danger of visual appeal, 201–2; attitude toward Gothic Revival style, 191–92; "How to Attract a Congregation" (essay), 202; Metropolitan Tabernacle and, 194–98, 196 fig. 10.2; "The Axe at the Root" sermon, 198–201
Stanley, Arthur Penrhyn, 148, 149
St. Clair, William, 120, 125
Stedman Jones, Gareth, 102–3, 108
Stephens, Joseph Rayner: ambiguity or uncertainty in, 77–79; background, 68; biblical analogy, use of, 69–70; on justification, 73–74; on just social order, 70–73; Marx and, 105–6; *Political Pulpit* series, 70–79; on resistance and "God's insurrection," 74–79
Stirner, Max, 103–4
Story, R. H., 150
Story of Isabel, The (Anon.), 180
Stowe, Harriet Beecher, 57, 146
"Study of Poetry, The" (Arnold), 246–47
Styler, Rebecca, 161
subjectivity theories and Wilde, 216–18

subsidiarity, 93
substitutionists vs. eliminationists, 81–84
Sullivan, Winnifred Fallers, 49
Sumner, John Bird, 144
suspicion, hermeneutics of, 2–3, 7, 206–9, 213
Swedenborg, Emanuel, 285, 290–92, 294, 298, 299
Swedenborgianism, 284–86
Swinburne, Algernon Charles, 268
sympathy as affective bonds, 55–56, 60

Tales of Jewish History (Moss and Moss), 155
Tate, Andrew, 210n7
Taylor, Charles, 14, 91, 95–96, 111, 259
Taylor, Jane, 182
Ten Commandments, 72
Tennyson, Alfred, Lord: *In Memoriam*, 148, 151, 256
Test Act repeal (1828), 227, 230
Thackeray, W. M., 171–72
The Jewish Faith (Aguilar), 239–40
There Is No Natural Religion (Blake), 287–92, 289 fig. 15.1
Thomas Aquinas, St., 38, 39
Thompson, E. P., 67, 282
Thomson, James, 254
Thornton, William, 67
Thornton Abbey (Satchel), 173
Tillich, Paul, 93
"Tom's Garland" (Hopkins), 273
"To R. B." (Hopkins), 269–71, 273
Tremaine, or the Man of Refinement (Ward), 179
Tulloch, John, 149
"Tyger, The" (Blake), 165

Unitarianism, Christian, 52, 57
universal heart, 60–61
universalism, 53–56, 53n2
universal religion, 61
Universities Tests Act (1871), 157n4
Unkind Word, The (Craik), 150–51
utopianism: Brahmoism and, 55–56, 61–62; Owenism, 85, 88–89; Rationalist Society and, 82

Valéry, Paul, 268

Valman, Nadia, 157
Victoria, reading habits of: ascension to the throne and, 145; changes in Victorian religious culture and, 140–41; fiction and Scottish novels, 149–52; grief and, 147–49; liberal Anglican authors, 145–46; liberal politics and philanthropy, 146–47; overview of Victoria's faith, 139–40; reading culture and, 141–43; sacramental, 144–45, 147; in youth, 143–45
Viswanathan, Gauri, 50
vitalism, 60
Vivekananda, Swami, 57

Wallbank, Adrian J., 174n3
Ward, Graham, 219
Ward, Robert Plumer: *Tremaine, or the Man of Refinement*, 179
wars of religion (16th–17th centuries), 29–30
Watson, Nicholas, 8
Watson, Richard, 288n6
Watts, Isaac, 226–27, 231, 236
Weisman, Karen, 168
Weitling, William, 105
Welby, Justin, 94
Wellesley, Gerald, 148
Wells, H. G., 142, 143
Wesley, Charles, 284
Wesley, John, 284
Westcott, Brooke Foss, 252–54, 257, 259
Westphal, Merold, 111
Whately, Richard, 145–46
Whitefield, George, 284
Whyte-Melville, George, 149
Wickman, Matthew, 250n2
Widowed Queen, The (Latchmore), 148–49
Wiener, Joel, 82

Wilberforce, Samuel, 147
Wilde, Oscar: "The Ballad of Reading Gaol," 215–19; Catholicism and, 208, 209n5, 219; Christianity, interest in, 206; Christology of, 217–19; comments on religion by, 210; *De Profundis*, 209–11, 209n6, 210n7, 213–15; on forgiveness, 211; hermeneutics of suspicion, Protestant mindset, and, 206–9, 213; Levine's rhythmic forms and, 213–14; *The Picture of Dorian Gray*, 206, 209n5; queer theology and, 209–10, 214; reading practices of, 213; ritual as theological and, 211–13, 219; *Salome*, 213; "The Selfish Giant," 213; theory and theology of self, 216–18; worship and, 214–16
Williams, Clare, 11
Williams, Rowan, 266–67, 278
Wimsatt, W. K., 248
Winstanley, Gerard, 70n5
Women of Israel, The (Aguilar), 166–67
Woodhead, Linda, 12
Wordsworth, William, 183, 231; comparative religion and, 49; "Expostulation and Reply," 168; "Intimations of Immortality," Hopkins on, 262–67; Mozoomadar and, 61; "Preface to *Lyrical Ballads*," 229
working class, 65–68, 118
world religions as category, 30–31, 58–59
World's Parliament of Religions, 57–62
"World's Religious Debt to Asia, The" (Mozoomadar), 57–58
World without Souls (Cunningham), 174, 181–82

Zastoupil, Lynn, 52
Zinzendorf, Nicolaus Ludwig von, 282, 285, 290–92, 298
Zuckerman Collection of Family Bibles, 119–20, 123, 125

LITERATURE, RELIGION, AND POSTSECULAR STUDIES
Lori Branch, Series Editor

Literature, Religion, and Postsecular Studies publishes scholarship on the influence of religion on literature and of literature on religion from the sixteenth century onward. Books in the series include studies of religious rhetoric or allegory; of the secularization of religion, ritual, and religious life; and of the emerging identity of postsecular studies and literary criticism.

Constructing Nineteenth-Century Religion: Literary, Historical, and Religious Studies in Dialogue
    EDITED BY JOSHUA KING AND WINTER JADE WERNER

Good Words: Evangelicalism and the Victorian Novel
    MARK KNIGHT

Enlightened Individualism: Buddhism and Hinduism in American Literature from the Beats to the Present
    KYLE GARTON-GUNDLING

A Theology of Sense: John Updike, Embodiment, and Late Twentieth-Century American Literature
    SCOTT DILL

Walker Percy, Fyodor Dostoevsky, and the Search for Influence
    JESSICA HOOTEN WILSON

The Religion of Empire: Political Theology in Blake's Prophetic Symbolism
    G. A. ROSSO

Clashing Convictions: Science and Religion in American Fiction
    ALBERT H. TRICOMI

Female Piety and the Invention of American Puritanism
    BRYCE TRAISTER

Secular Scriptures: Modern Theological Poetics in the Wake of Dante
    WILLIAM FRANKE

Imagined Spiritual Communities in Britain's Age of Print
    JOSHUA KING

Conspicuous Bodies: Provincial Belief and the Making of Joyce and Rushdie
    JEAN KANE

Victorian Sacrifice: Ethics and Economics in Mid-Century Novels
    ILANA M. BLUMBERG

Lake Methodism: Polite Literature and Popular Religion in England, 1780–1830
    JASPER CRAGWALL

Hard Sayings: The Rhetoric of Christian Orthodoxy in Late Modern Fiction
    THOMAS F. HADDOX

Preaching and the Rise of the American Novel
    DAWN COLEMAN

Victorian Women Writers, Radical Grandmothers, and the Gendering of God
  GAIL TURLEY HOUSTON

Apocalypse South: Judgment, Cataclysm, and Resistance in the Regional Imaginary
  ANTHONY DYER HOEFER

www.ingramcontent.com/pod-product-compliance
Lightning Source LLC
Chambersburg PA
CBHW020637230426
43665CB00008B/211